HAUNTED

Malevolent Ghosts, Night Terrors,
and Threatening Phantoms

ABOUT THE AUTHORS

Award-winning writer Brad Steiger is the author of over 2,000 articles and more than 180 titles with inspirational and paranormal themes, including *Real Aliens, Space Beings, and Creatures from Other Worlds; Real Encounters, Different Dimensions, and Otherworldy Beings; Real Ghosts, Restless Spirits, and Haunted Houses;* and *Conspiracies and Secret Societies.* Brad is a veteran of broadcast news magazines such as *The Nightly News,* as well as a regular radio guest on shows ranging from Rob McConnell's *X-Zone* to *Coast to Coast* with George Noory. He passed away in early 2018.

Sherry Hansen Steiger is an expert on health and healing, spirituality, and the unexplained. She has authored or coauthored more than forty books, including the inspirational *Real Miracles, Divine Intervention, and Feats of Survival* and the best-selling "Miracles" series, including *Dog Miracles, Animal Miracles,* and *Christmas Miracles* (winner of the 2002 Storytelling Award).

HAUNTED

Malevolent Ghosts, Night Terrors, and Threatening Phantoms

Brad Steiger and Sherry Hansen Steiger

VISIBLE
INK
PRESS

Detroit

OTHER VISIBLE INK PRESS BOOKS BY BRAD STEIGER

Conspiracies and Secret Societies: The Complete Dossier, Second Edition
with Sherry Hansen Steiger
ISBN: 978-1-57859-368-2

Real Aliens, Space Beings, and Creatures from Other Worlds
with Sherry Hansen Steiger
ISBN: 978-1-57859-333-0

Real Encounters, Different Dimensions and Otherworldy Beings
with Sherry Hansen Steiger
ISBN: 978-1-57859-455-9

Real Ghosts, Restless Spirits, and Haunted Places, Second Edition
ISBN: 978-1-57859-401-6

Real Miracles, Divine Intervention, and Feats of Incredible Survival
with Sherry Hansen Steiger
ISBN: 978-1-57859-214-2

Real Monsters, Gruesome Critters, and Beasts from the Darkside
ISBN: 978-1-57859-220-3

Real Vampires, Night Stalkers, and Creatures from the Darkside
ISBN: 978-1-57859-255-5

Real Visitors, Voices from Beyond, and Parallel Dimensions
with Sherry Hansen Steiger
ISBN: 978-1-57859-541-9

Real Zombies, the Living Dead, and Creatures of the Apocalypse
ISBN: 978-1-57859-296-8

The Werewolf Book: The Encyclopedia of Shape-Shifting Beings, Second Edition
ISBN: 978-1-57859-367-5

The Zombie Book: The Encyclopedia of the Living Dead
with Nick Redfern
ISBN: 978-1-57859-504-4

"REAL NIGHTMARES" E-BOOKS BY BRAD STEIGER

Book 1: *True and Truly Scary Unexplained Phenomenon*

Book 2: *The Unexplained Phenomena and Tales of the Unknown*

Book 3: *Things That Go Bump in the Night*

Book 4: *Things That Prowl and Growl in the Night*

Book 5: *Fiends That Want Your Blood*

Book 6: *Unexpected Visitors and Unwanted Guests*

Book 7: *Dark and Deadly Demons*

Book 8: *Phantoms, Apparitions, and Ghosts*

Book 9: *Alien Strangers and Foreign Worlds*

Book 10: *Ghastly and Grisly Spooks*

Book 11: *Secret Schemes and Conspiring Cabals*

Book 12: *Freaks, Fiends and Evil Spirits*

ALSO FROM VISIBLE INK PRESS

Alien Mysteries, Conspiracies and Cover-Ups
by Kevin D Randle
ISBN: 978-1-57859-418-4

Ancient Gods: Lost Histories, Hidden Truths, and the Conspiracy of Silence
by Jim Willis
ISBN: 978-1-57859-614-0

The Bigfoot Book: The Encyclopedia of Sasquatch, Yeti, and Cryptid Primates
by Nick Redfern
ISBN: 978-1-57859-561-7

Control: MKUltra, Chemtrails, and the Conspiracy to Suppress the Masses
by Nick Redfern
ISBN: 978-1-57859-638-6

Demons, the Devil, and Fallen Angels
by Marie D Jones and Larry Flaxman
ISBN: 978-1-57859-613-3

The Dream Interpretation Dictionary: Symbols, Signs and Meanings
by J.M. DeBord
ISBN: 978-1-57859-637-9

The Government UFO Files: The Conspiracy of Cover-Up
by Kevin D Randle
ISBN: 978-1-57859-477-1

Hidden Realms, Lost Civilizations, and Beings from Other Worlds
by Jerome Clark
ISBN: 978-1-57859-175-6

The Horror Show Guide: The Ultimate Frightfest of Movies
by Mike Mayo
ISBN: 978-1-57859-420-7

The Illuminati: The Secret Society That Hijacked the World
by Jim Marrs
ISBN: 978-1-57859-619-5

The Monster Book: Creatures, Beasts, and Fiends of Nature
by Nick Redfern
ISBN: 978-1-57859-575-4

The New World Order Book
by Nick Redfern
ISBN: 978-1-57859-615-7

The Sci-Fi Movie Guide: The Universe of Film from Alien to Zardoz
by Chris Barsanti
ISBN: 978-1-57859-503-7

Secret History: Conspiracies from Ancient Aliens to the New World Order
by Nick Redfern
ISBN: 978-1-57859-479-5

Secret Societies: The Complete Guide to Histories, Rites, and Rituals
by Nick Redfern
ISBN: 978-1-57859-483-2

Supernatural Gods: Spiritual Mysteries, Psychic Experiences, and Scientific Truths
by Jim Willis
ISBN: 978-1-57859-660-7

The UFO Dossier: 100 Years of Government Secrets, Conspiracies, and Cover-Ups
by Kevin D Randle
ISBN: 978-1-57859-564-8

Unexplained! Strange Sightings, Incredible Occurrences, and Puzzling Physical Phenomena, Third Edition
by Jerome Clark
ISBN: 978-1-57859-344-6

The Vampire Book: The Encyclopedia of the Undead, Third Edition
by J. Gordon Melton, Ph.D.
ISBN: 978-1-57859-281-4

PLEASE VISIT US AT VISIBLEINKPRESS.COM

HAUNTED
Malevolent Ghosts, Night Terrors,
and Threatening Phantoms

Visible Ink Press®
43311 Joy Rd., #414
Canton, MI 48187-2075
Visible Ink Press is a registered trademark of Visible Ink Press LLC.

Most Visible Ink Press books are available at special quantity discounts when purchased in bulk by corporations, organizations, or groups. Customized printings, special imprints, messages, and excerpts can be produced to meet your needs. For more information, contact Special Markets Director, Visible Ink Press, www.visibleink press.com, or 734-667-3211.

Managing Editor: Kevin S. Hile
Art Director: Mary Claire Krzewinski
Typesetting: Marco Divita
Proofreaders: Larry Baker and Kevin S. Hile
Indexer: Shoshana Hurwitz
Cover images: image of Ararat Lunatic Asylum by Eldraque77 (Wikicommons); all other images, Shutterstock.

Names: Steiger, Brad, author.
Title: Haunted : malevolent ghosts, night terrors, and threatening phantoms / Brad Steiger.
Description: first edition. | Detroit, MI : Visible Ink Press, 2018. | Includes bibliographical references and index. | Identifiers: LCCN 2018019834 (print) | LCCN 2018032201 (ebook) | ISBN 9781578596829 (ebook) | ISBN 9781578596201 (pbk. : alk. paper)
Subjects: LCSH: Ghosts. | Apparitions.
Classification: LCC BF1461 (ebook) | LCC BF1461 .S8325 2018 (print) | DDC 133.1—dc23
LC record available at https://lccn.loc.gov/2018019834

10 9 8 7 6 5 4 3 2 1

Printed in the United States of America.

CONTENTS

ACKNOWLEDGMENTS

Over the past fifty years, I have had the privilege of meeting a number of paranormal researchers who are as devoted to exploring the Unknown and the various dimensions of Time and Space as I. I was honored when the following pioneers of the paraphysical contributed their thoughts and insights to this book:

Paul Dale Roberts and his wife, Deanna, Brian Allen, Theo Paijmans, Paul and Ben Eno, Richard Senate, Dr. Jack Hiller, Jerome Clark, Dr. C. Norman Shealy, Willam Kern, Paul Bartholomew, Robert A. Goerman, Rita Gallagher, Nick Redfern, Dr. P.M.H. Atwater, Jeff Belanger, Jim Harold, Brent Raynes, Wanda Sue Parrott, Joseph P. Warren, Stephen Wagner, Mark Lienweber, Timothy Green Beckley, Anita Stapleton, David J. Pitkin, Scott Corrales, Barry Conrad, Barry Taft, James Neff, and Clarisa Bernhardt.

A special thank you to Bill Oliver and Ricardo Pustanio for their magnificent artwork capturing the "haunted" vibration for this book, and to Dan Wolfman for his photos.

I wish also to express my gratitude to my publisher, Roger Jänecke for his unfailing support for this and previous works, to my editor Kevin Hile for his professional skills and courtesy, and to my agent Agnes Birnbaum for decades of skillful guidance. And most of all to my ever-supportive wife, Sherry, my strength and my Muse.

—Brad Steiger

Photo Sources

Bibliothèque Nationale de France: p. 276.
BsOu10e01 (Wikicommons): p. 32.
Jason Chang: p. 250.
Chester Beatty Library: p. 165.
Arístides Herrera Cuntti: p. 50.
John Duncan: p. 146.
G. W. Edmondson: p. 303.
Paul and Ben Eno: p. 336.
Federation of Spiritual Churches and
    Associations: p. 287.
Bernard Gagnon: p. 247.
Paul Hermans: p. 242.
Thomson Jay Hudson: p. 281.
Père Igor: p. 209.
Drew Jacksich: p. 262.
Roy Kerwood: p. 137.
Philippa Lehar: p. 19.
Library of Congress: p. 314.
Life Magazine: p. 187.
Los Angeles (Wikicommons): p. 86.
Magicpiano (Wikicommons): p. 25.
Rodolpho Hugo Mikulasch: p. 283.
Larry D. Moore: p. 68.
New York Sunday News: p. 197.
Bill Oliver: pp. 6, 44, 144, 333, 339.

Ortsmuseum Zollikon: p. 218.
Ricardo Pustanio: p. 229.
Nick Redfern: p. 305.
Philippe Semeria: p. 320.
Shutterstock: pp. 1 (and inset), 8, 12, 13,
    15, 22, 27, 30, 35, 37, 55, 57, 62, 63,
    70, 75, 78, 81, 88, 93, 95, 98, 101,
    104, 112, 114, 116, 119, 122, 124,
    128, 130, 133, 138, 139, 148, 151,
    154, 160, 167, 170, 173, 175, 177,
    180, 184, 190, 192, 194, 203, 205,
    215, 216, 224, 227, 235, 240, 249,
    254, 257, 260, 263, 327.
Smallbones (Wikicommons): p. 245.
Brad and Sherry Steiger: pp. 10, 16, 73,
    107, 163, 212, 251, 269, 270, 273,
    335, 338.
Thomson200 (Wikicommons): p. 41.
Warner Bros.: p. 200.
S. W. White: p. 47.
Dan Wolfman: pp. 307, 310.
Zereshk (Wikicommons): p. 331.
Public domain: pp. 28, 45, 220, 232, 279,
    285, 292, 295, 298, 301, 308, 317,
    318.

INTRODUCTION

It will come as no surprise to those readers, fans, and followers of Brad's works and writings that although his first published articles were of the paranormal in 1956, his very first major book in 1965 was entitled *Monsters, Maidens and Mayhem: A Pictorial History of Hollywood Film Monsters*, and his next big work was *Strange Guests*, which is about poltergeist phenomena—and that was in 1966!

Bizarre as it might seem in sending email to friends, fellow researchers, and associates, offering them the opportunity to share stories or accounts for this book, *Haunted: Malevolent Ghosts, Night Terrors, and Threatening Phantoms*, he announced that this was to be his final book. These words struck a note that brought a wave of responses of disbelief, followed promptly by pleas to "never say never" to which he acquiesced and vowed to take a little break, at least, from writing.

So now, in 2018, we come full circle. Whether or not he *knew* this truly was to be his very last book (on a soul level perhaps), he worked diligently and tirelessly, sharing the many hair-raising, goose-bumply stories with you, the readers.

Throughout his industrious career, he always cited how he, as "this little farm boy from Bode, Iowa, was blessed to fulfill his dream to be a writer." Raised in a mystical, magical Shangri-la-type surrounding in Humboldt County, Iowa, he published close to 180 works. Writing was truly his life, and although we have five fabulous, creative, and industrious children and ten grandchildren, he/we considered every book to be like one of our children. Although they require a different kind of nurturing, each authored work is truly a creation.

Brad went into "the Great Mystery," as he liked to call it, on May 6, 2018. I, too, am blessed, and I treasure each and every second that we shared 24/7. As we traveled the world, exploring, researching, lecturing, and conducting seminars, then writing about them in our many books, we were rarely ever apart. Going on forty years as husband/wife/best friend/partner/co-author, I find it hard to believe he does not still walk this plane. But free of earthly bonds, he perhaps now explores the many "Mysteries of Time and Space" and "Other Dimensions."

I know many of you grew up reading Brad's books since you were teenagers … and some of you are authors now, as well; so, it no doubt will also seem strange to you that he is gone or, at least, temporarily out of sight. One big family are we, traversing the known and unknown as we learn and grow in the rapid unfolding of new scientific discoveries that help us make sense or our life journey. The "Force," the "Great Mystery," is in us, around us, and *is* us.

The fact that Brad was known as "The Grandfather of All Things Paranormal" is *not* a mystery. He quite literally (no pun intended) spent his entire life with ghosts! He grew up in a haunted house, experienced the presence of ghosts, investigated, researched, and wrote about ghosts.

The very farm accident that almost took his life at age eleven, during which he had a near-death experience that proved to him that life survives death, catapulted him into a career of writing about ghosts.

The opening chapter of *Haunted*, "50,000 Years of Ghostly Encounters," is not about us researching for that long—although we'd often joke sometimes it seemed like we are that old—but instead refers to how the first chapter dovetails with the last chapter in the book in which Brian Allen postulates, "What is a ghost, really?"

Ghosts are many things to many people, but what they are, most importantly, is a reminder that there is something more to our existence than the day-to-day, material world.

As our friend and associate William Kern wonders, are ghosts from parallel universes? Or as Robert Goerman, also our friend and associate, suggests, the presence of a ghost implies that the astral essence of a human being survives physical death.

This book, full of hair-raising, spooky stories, true accounts of shared paranormal experiences—spirits, ghostly apparitions, and energies of all sorts and kinds from benevolent to malevolent—just may offer some kind of evidence or substantiation that life does continue.

There are those energies that seem to exist on many different levels of the unknown, maybe even at the same time!

These can be scientifically explained by Einstein's quantum entanglement theory, which basically describes paired particles that demonstrate a mysterious form of *instant* communication regardless of how far apart they are. Einstein called this "spooky action at a distance."

Dr. William Tiller, professor emeritus of materials science and engineering at Stanford University, told us that he believes there may be universes *beyond* our universe that are made up of more subtle kinds of matter, so there is no end to the reach of our being. He postulates that humanity might be experiencing a "biological transformation" to another sensory system.

We may be on the edge of some breakthrough discoveries through the efforts of other mainstream scientists as well. Dr. Dean Radin, Ph.D., of the University of Nevada—Las Vegas's Cognitive Research Division and post senior scientist of the Institute of Noetic Sciences (IONS) says that groups such as CRD are conducting respectable experiments and producing statistically significant results. Brian Josephson of the distinguished Cambridge University in England states that evidence for the paranormal and other subtle phenomena is accumulating, although the task of explaining them presents an interesting challenge.

That being said, our interest in writing this book is not to prove or disprove anything but to share the many stories that have been sent to both of us personally. We believe we must take care to think about the unthinkable, because when things become unthinkable, thinking *stops* and action becomes mindless. The universe is vast, deep, and profound, much more complex than any scientific "certainty." The late Thomas Berry, C.P., Ph.D., a Catholic priest, cultural historian, and ecotheologian, is famous for proposing the idea that a deep understanding of the history and function of the evolving universe is a necessary inspiration and guide for our own effective functioning as individuals and as a species. He expressed it like this: "The universe cannot be seen as a collection of objects but as a community of subjects."

And we say that YOU are a part of this vast, deep, and profound community, too. Explore its wonders. Contemplate its mysteries!

Brad's last words in this, his last book, say it for him: "Certainly in varying degrees of individual reality, that is what a ghost is—our individual messenger from that great beyond sent to prove that our struggle for hope and immortality is not in vain."

Brad's immortality will certainly remain and live on in all of his 180+ books, hundreds, if not thousands, of his articles, and his many appearances in radio, television, or print interviews, as well as in many hearts of his friends and family ... *forever.*

Perhaps that is the crux of this book. It is our hope that is what it will offer you—HOPE!

—Respectfully, Sherry Hansen Steiger,
fellow experiencer, investigator,
researcher, soul mate, and co-author

50,000 Years
of Ghostly Encounters

On October 24, 2015, the *New York Times* carried an article by Andrew Higgins with the intriguing title "Norway Has a New Passion: Ghost Hunting." Higgins observed, "Ghosts, or at least a belief in them, have been around for centuries but they have now found a particularly strong following in highly secular modern countries like Norway, places that are otherwise in the vanguard of what was once seen as Europe's inexorable, science-led march away from superstition and religion."

And speaking of religion, Higgins comments, the churches in Norway are virtually empty, and a belief in God is in "steady decline," while "belief in, or at least fascination with, ghosts and spirits is surging." A Methodist preacher commented that "God is out but spirits and ghosts are filling the vacuum." Even Norway's royal family, which is required by law to belong to the Evangelical Lutheran Church, has, according to Higgins's reporting, "flirted with ghosts, with a princess coaching people on how to reach out to spirits."

WHEN THE GHOST WALKED THROUGH HIM, HE FELT A SENSATION OF COLD

Damon B. says that while he was stationed in Landstuhl, Germany, from 1998 to 2003 he did not have to be coached by a Norwegian princess on how to reach out to spirits. While he was in Germany those five years, he repeatedly saw the ghost of a middle-aged man with a reddish-brown beard, who was dressed in blue overalls in the temporary building where he was working. Whenever Damon tried to speak to him, the man would walk away through the only door in the building. At times, he would walk away just to the side of Damon … or through him.

"When he would go through me," Damon said, "I would feel an incredible cold sensation throughout my body that would not subside for hours."

On those occasions when Damon would try to make the spirit talk to him, he would make a mess of the office, scattering papers and documents everywhere. Damon said that he took to calling the recalcitrant ghost "Mr. Blue."

When Damon left the Army, he took a job in Nashville, doubting that he would ever encounter another restless spirit, especially not Mr. Blue.

"I was wrong," Damon said in his report. "He appeared to me—perhaps not as strong or as vital—but twice during the year I lived there."

Damon moved again, this time to the Washington, D.C., area, where Mr. Blue has appeared to him approximately eight times, "but he is losing the clarity that I saw in him in Germany. However, there is no question that he is the same entity."

Nearly Everyone in Her Family Has a Ghost Story to Tell

When we asked Helen of Oxfordshire, England, if she believed in ghosts, she answered frankly, indicating a lifetime of spirit interaction: "Most of my family has one or more ghost stories to tell," she said. "My uncle's life was saved by a warning that his mother was given by his deceased aunt. My father spent a night at a haunted RAF airfield and experienced things that he still cannot explain forty years later. My mother and grandmother worked in a hospital where a ghostly grey lady protected the patients. My brother laughed at my belief in nature spirits until we walked in a Welsh wood, and he saw them all around just at the same time that I did. The day after my great-grandmother's death, she sat beside me on the bus as I came home from work."

Helen also told us that she had communication with benevolent spirit beings, especially with her ancestors. The spirit of her great-grandmother accompanies her on every paranormal investigation Helen undertakes.

Only once did she encounter a disruptive spirit being. "He was clearly malevolent, so I prayed and he fled."

His Little Grandson Recognized "the Man"

In the home that I purchased in 1977 in Riverhead, I felt the presence of a spirit as soon we moved in, and so we gave him a name. A few years later, one of my daughters called on the spirit to speak to us. He told us to look in the attic for proof. We pulled up some floorboards in the crawl space, and there were three large sheets of paper. One was a drawing of the house, another was a painting, and the third was a charcoal drawing of a man with a high, starched collar, dark hair and mustache, and dark suit. We hung up the drawing of the man to help it unroll. The next day, my not-quite-three-year-old grandson, Christopher, pointed to it and said, "The Man!" Before that, he used to pass the kitchen on the way into the living room and would turn toward the kitchen and say, "Hi, Man," so we knew he recognized the spirit.

Brazil's President Says Official Residence Has "Bad Energy"

As in the case of Norway's Royal Family, those who believe they have encountered ghosts may include presidents and governors as well as monarchs. In the case of Brazil's President Michel Temer, he was not at all pleased with his official residence in the capital, Brasilia. He wanted to move out because of the "bad energy … even ghosts."

In early March 2017, President Temer, 76, and his 33-year-old wife, Marcela, a former beauty queen, moved out of his official residence, a sprawling home that boasts a huge swimming pool, a chapel, cinema, and heliport in the capital, Brasilia, and to the smaller Jaburu Palace because of "bad energy" and the presence of ghosts.

"I felt something strange there. I wasn't able to sleep right from the first night. The energy wasn't good," Temer told *Veja*, a news weekly. "Marcela felt the same thing. Only Michelzinho [their seven-year-old son], who went running from one end to the other, liked it. We even started to wonder: could there be ghosts? Marcela called in a priest to drive out any evil spirits in the residence, without success."

New York's Governor Cuomo Says Eerie Noises in the Mansion Keep Him Awake

New York's governor's mansion is believed by many to be haunted, including by former and current governors.

Governor Andrew Cuomo says eerie noises are keeping him awake when he's upstate. "So, it's me alone, when I'm in the house because my family is in Westchester … and there are stories that this house is haunted," Cuomo told the *New York Post* (May 5, 2017). "Now, I don't believe in ghosts, and I'm a big, tough Italian guy, but I'll tell you, it gets creepy in that house, and there are a lot of noises that go on and you are very alone."

Former governor David Paterson told the *Post* that the 161-year-old Italianate mansion is haunted and that there is a ghost. He related that one night when he was governor he was in a second-floor bedroom when he heard a sound like a vase smashing. He searched two floors of the building but never found the source of the mysterious noise. The next day, house staff told him he had a run-in with the home's oldest resident.

Paterson said that a staff member "came to me and said, 'Governor, nobody wanted to say this to you, but it's the ghost.' One employee is afraid to clean one of the rooms because she thinks the ghost is in the room." Members

New York governor Andrew Cuomo (inset) has confessed to hearing noises from a "friendly ghost" in the governor's mansion (pictured) when he is there alone without his family.

of the staff believe that it is the spirit of a groundskeeper who served the mansion's original owners before the state bought the building in 1877.

"Governor Cuomo should be relieved," the former governor said. "It's a friendly ghost, like Casper."

WHEN DID WE START SEEING GHOSTS?

We cannot state dogmatically when the earliest members of our species (*Homo sapiens*, c. 30,000 B.C.E.) first began seeing ghosts, but we do know that they conducted burial rituals of a nature that would qualify them as believers in an afterlife. The evidence is undisputed that they buried their dead with care and consideration and included food, weapons, and various personal belongings with the body. Even the earlier Neanderthal species (c. 100,000 B.C.E.) placed food, stone implements, and decorative shells and bones in the graves with the deceased, which they often covered with a red pigment. Because of the placement of such funerary objects in the graves, it seems that even these prehistoric people believed that death was not the end and that there was some part of the deceased that still required nourishment, clothing, and protection in order to journey safely in another kind of existence beyond the grave. There seems little question that the graphic paintings found in the European caves of the Paleolithic Age (c. 50,000 B.C.E.) clearly indicate that early humans sought by supernatural means to placate the spirits of the animals they killed for food, to dispel the restless spirits of the humans they had slain in territorial disputes, and to bring peace to the spirits of their deceased tribal kin.

A recently uncovered Neanderthal burial site in Spain (c. 50,000 B.C.E.) has provided evidence that these ancient hominids believed in an afterlife and were capable of complex symbolic thought, all possibly before early *Homo sapiens* demonstrated these abilities. Although the earliest undisputed human burial dates back 130,000 years, experts say that it's not clear if it shows evidence of a larger, symbolic belief in some sort of afterlife or larger spiritual existence. For that, the earliest unarguable evidence in humans only goes back roughly 30,000 years, although there are possible indications of it going back at least 50,000 years. The positioning of the Neanderthal remains recently discovered in Spain may indicate some larger spiritual significance and reveal that it wasn't humans who first believed in an afterlife but rather our extinct cousins.

> A recently uncovered Neanderthal burial site in Spain (c. 50,000 B.C.E.) has provided evidence that these ancient hominids believed in an afterlife....

In his October 2014 article "Ghosts in the Ancient World" (*Ancient History Encyclopedia*), Joshua J. Mark writes that "to the people of the ancient world, there was no doubt that the soul of a human being survived bodily death.... [C]ulturally, they were brought up with the understanding that the dead lived on in another form that still required some kind of sustenance, in an afterlife that was largely dictated by several factors: the kind of life they had lived on earth, how their remains were disposed of at their death, and/or how they were remembered by the living. The details of the afterlife in different cultures varied, many seemed to believe that such a realm existed, that it was governed by immutable laws, and that the souls of the dead would remain there unless given license by the gods to return to the land of the living for some specific reason."

Mark stresses that the "appearance of ghosts of the departed, even those of loved ones, was rarely considered a welcome experience. The dead were supposed to remain in their own land and were not expected to cross back over to the world of the living. When such an event did occur, it was a sure sign that something was terribly wrong, and those who experienced a spiritual encounter were expected to take care of the problem in order for the ghost to return to its proper place. This understanding was so prevalent that ghost stories can be found, with very similar themes, in the ancient cultures of Mesopotamia, Egypt, Greece, Rome, China, and India as well as regions of Mesoamerica and the

Celtic lands of Ireland and Scotland. Ghosts are also depicted in the Bible in much the same way as they were in earlier Roman works."

RECENT POLLS INDICATE BELIEF IN GHOSTS IS ON THE RISE

If we average the numbers from recent polls conducted from 2005 to 2013 by *60 Minutes, Vanity Fair*, CBS, and *Huffington Post*, we discover that around 48 percent believe in ghosts or that the dead can return in certain situations. A Pew Research Center Survey found that 18 percent claim to have seen a ghost and that 29 percent believe that they had some kind of spiritual contact with a ghost.

In 2011 *LiveScience* released its poll's results that 71 percent of the population has had a paranormal experience. Belief in spirits and ghosts is held by 34 percent; 56 percent of that number are convinced that ghosts are spirits of the dead. Thirty-seven percent of the population believe that ghosts can haunt houses.

In his 1994 analysis of a national sociological survey, Jeffrey S. Levin, an associate professor at Eastern Virginia Medical School, found that two-thirds of

Surveys show that nearly half of Americans believe that ghosts or other spiritual beings that were once living humans can return to our plain of existence.

Haunted: Malevolent Ghosts, Night Terrors, and Threatening Phantoms

Americans claimed to have at least one mystical experience. Of that remarkably high number of experiencers, 39.9 percent said that they had an encounter with a ghost or had achieved contact with the spirit of a deceased person.

In an article on July 21, 2017, for the *Sunday Review of the New York Times* ("Don't Believe in God? Try UFOs"), Clay Routledge discusses evidence that "suggests that the religious mind persists even when we lose faith in traditional religious beliefs and institutions. Consider that roughly 30 percent of Americans report they have felt in contact with someone who has died. Nearly 20 percent believe they have been in the presence of a ghost. About one-third of Americans believe that ghosts exist and can interact with and harm humans; around two-thirds hold supernatural or paranormal beliefs of some kind, including beliefs in reincarnation, spiritual energy and psychic powers."

According to Routledge, such numbers are much higher than they were in previous decades, when more people reported being highly religious. Interestingly, he also presents data that states that "people who do not frequently attend church are twice as likely to believe in ghosts as those who are regular churchgoers. The less religious people are, the more likely they are to endorse empirically unsupported ideas about U.F.O's."

According to our own *Steiger Questionnaire of Mystical, Paranormal and UFO Experiences*, a survey process that we began in 1967 and have since distributed to over 30,000 men and women, 48.9 percent are convinced that they have seen a ghost; 43 percent have perceived the spirit of a departed loved one; and 63 percent state that they have encountered spirit entities in haunted places.

HOW DOES A REAL GHOST PERFORM?

How does a real ghost perform? Although there may be a single source for all ethereal and ghostly manifestations, in many accounts of paranormal appearances, the ghost acts more like an animated memory pattern than an entity of independent intelligence. It is as if some as yet unknown or undetermined energy has impressed an incident or happening upon a certain environment, and the pattern, like a brief strip of film being fed into a projector whenever the proper conditions are fulfilled, keeps "remembering" the same scenario night after night—or whenever the film is activated.

In our research, now spanning over sixty years, we have found the largest number of haunted houses are due to what we term "spirit residue." In these cases, a powerful human emotion—fear, jealously, hate, pain—has been somehow impressed into the environment of the house or place. It is our contention that the sounds and sights of the haunting may be perceived by the psyche of the sensitive as if they were images on a strip of motion picture that keeps being fed through a projector again and again. The percipients of these kinds of hauntings cannot interact with the ghosts any more than one can speak with the images on a motion picture or television screen and have the prefilmed images of the actors respond.

THE PHANTOM CAR

A good example of a residual haunting was experienced by a friend of ours from Illinois. When he and his family lived on their farm, they would, from time to time, hear an automobile coming down the lane, pull up in front of the house, then disappear. Recently, our friend brought us up to date on what he had come to call "the phantom car."

"The couple who bought our houses out in the country lost them to the bank a few years after buying them," he began. "After that, the son of the father-and-son team, who farms our ground for us, ended up buying them. I was happy about that as they are friends of the family. They allowed one of their hired men to live in the home place, and he was interested in buying the house. He had plans of putting a porch on three sides of the house instead of the single porch it has on the north side now. He had plans for some slight remodeling inside also. I stopped in one day when he was there and he was showing me around the old place and explaining what he had in his mind for the house. They were slight but sort of neat improvements.

"I'm not sure what happened," our friend continued, "but he was let go by the farmers a couple of years later and he moved into a town several miles away. I ran into him a few days ago; he said that he really missed living out in my old house. I agreed that it is nice out there.

They thought they saw a car come up the lane with its lights on, but when they investigated the car disappeared!

Haunted: Malevolent Ghosts, Night Terrors, and Threatening Phantoms

"Then he looked sort of shy and he said, 'You probably won't believe this, but several times while my girlfriend and I were living there, we saw a car that wasn't there. What I mean is, right before dark we would see it drive up the lane with its lights on, but when we would open the door to see who had come, there was nothing out there!'

"I said that he had seen the phantom car! Then I told him of my experiences with it all the years I was growing up there and then again when my wife and I moved back for several years as adults. He was happy that someone else had seen it, too, and that it wasn't in their minds. I told him we had the house full of people a few times when it happened and they all saw it too. So, no, he wasn't alone.

"He then asked me if I had any other experiences while living there, and I told him there had been a few. He asked me if one of them was someone humming in the bedroom in the upstairs southwest corner. I said, yes, that was one of them. They, too, had heard it, and he had gotten up and turned on the light only to have the sound continue humming. He did the same thing we had done. He walked over to where it sounded like it was coming from and then it would switch to the other side of the room. I told him that is exactly what we had experienced a few times. He said that he thought the car and the humming both were sort of fun, and he didn't feel threatened by it at all but it creeped his girlfriend out a little bit.

"I thought it was interesting that these things continue even though nobody from our family is living there now."

EXPANDING OUR DEFINITION OF A "REAL GHOST"

For many years we held somewhat stubbornly to the hypothesis that the vast majority of ghost sightings were individuals encountering bits of psychic residue. We strictly separated evidence of survival of the spirit after death from accounts of ghosts. However, as our on-site investigations increased in number, we encountered spirit manifestations that clearly seemed to be the result of identifiable intelligences that wished to communicate messages from the Other Side to loved ones or to interested parties. Other haunting phenomena appeared to be caused by earthbound spirits of deceased humans that were unable to detach themselves from the people, places, and things of the physical world and had not progressed to the light of a higher dimension.

THE OLD LADY GHOST LIKED TO CREEP UP BEHIND WILLIAM

Our friend William Kern is an artist, a writer, and an editor. He has written such books as Rampa: World of Illusions, Giants on the Earth: Amazing Suppressed Archaeological Discoveries, and several co-authored with Timothy Green Beckley, such as Cryptid Creatures from Dark Domains.

Author and artist William Kern believes that ghosts are entities from a parallel universe that we are sometimes able to see and hear.

I'm not certain I can define a ghost, although I have been vexed by a spirit of some kind for a number of years, and particularly about thirty years ago. This "ghost," which I call "Marie," is an elderly lady who died in the house in which we live. She would creep around and slam the doors or push objects from shelves onto the floor.

Occasionally, she would creep up behind me and say something that just scared the heck out of me. I was sitting at my computer one day several years ago, and she stole silently up behind me and asked, "What do you think you are doing?"

This question was not something in my mind but an audible question in English at a distance of about two feet from my right ear. I was so stunned, so surprised by the sound, that I left my computer and went in another room where I remained for nearly two hours, hoping she would give up and go away.

Marie doesn't speak any more, but she does creep about, slamming doors and sliding utensils off the counters and onto the floor. I can see her at times from the corner of my eye, but when I look, she is not really there. Or she makes herself "unseen."

I think ghosts are entities from a parallel universe that is right next to this one. They slip in and out from time to time just to let us know they are still here and that we, the so-called "living," are occupying space that was once allotted to them. Some ghosts may resent that and become violent or destructive; others just want to vex.

I am absolutely convinced that the human consciousness survives after "death" of the physical body. Why anyone would elect to return to this world is completely beyond my understanding.

THE GHOSTS OF SANDY'S RESTAURANT IN VENTURA, CALIFORNIA—AN INVESTIGATION BY RENOWNED PSYCHIC RICHARD SENATE

Sandy's is best known for its steak and seafood, but the regular customers believe this restaurant is haunted by at least two ghosts. The manager states that he has never seen anything, but he does admit that customers tell of odd happenings. Some say that they have seen a dark shadow following them into the place; still others say they hear things in the back room—like silverware moving about with an odd tinkling sound. Several years ago, a woman witnessed a glass levitate and fly across the room smashing against the wall.

There is a persistent cold in the back room of the place that is apparent even on a hot day. Could this cold spot be evidence of a ghost?

The stories that reached me were so dramatic that I felt I needed to conduct an on-site investigation. I drove out to the very modern-looking cinder block restaurant on the corner of Saviers and Bard Streets. It was deceptively ordinary looking.

When I pulled in, I started to get the impression that the stories were just so much folklore or perhaps the product of liquid spirits and nothing supernatural. But when I stepped into the place, the hair on the back of my neck shivered. It was a feeling I had felt many times when I entered a haunted site. As I was drawn into the building I felt something cold and invisible pass by me. Yes, I was convinced the stories were true—this place was haunted.

I met with George, the bartender, who confirmed what the patrons had seen. Some said they even saw a dark shadow-like form come through the bar area. The waitress, Lillian, said that a coffee pot had flown across the room and that strange crashing sounds were heard. The bartender confirmed her story and said some time back four people sitting at the bar felt something touch them; they turned and looked, but there was nothing there. He went on to say that the odd events seem to take place late at night after nine.

The restaurant was built perhaps forty years ago and was successfully managed by a friendly couple. When ill health forced them to sell, the present owners purchased the establishment. The original owners passed away, and it has been from the time of their deaths that there have been reports of ghosts wandering Sandy's Restaurant. Some speculate that the phantoms are the spirits of the former owners, checking back at the place they worked so hard to establish. Whatever the reason, my visit did confirm that the former owners could find little fault with the steak the present proprietors serve at the place or with the quality of the service. Perhaps that is the cause of the ghostly activity. So many people had so many good times at the restaurant that they return even as spirits.

The bar area and the front lobby seemed to me to be haunted. There was also a strange feeling in the last booth. If you go there, order the steak, and keep an eye on the bar for moving shadows. And keep a tight grip on the water glass—just to be sure it doesn't fly off by itself!

THE GHOST WHO FOLLOWED HIM TO CLASS

Ghosts can manifest anywhere and everywhere. However, sometimes only a few individuals may have the requisite sensitivity to see the visitors

The adult student John saw in the classroom could not be seen by the other students in the room. When confronted, the being disappeared, slamming the door and startling the class.

even though they may appear in the midst of a group of people—even in a college classroom.

John works in mental health rehabilitation, and he stresses that he personally has no episodes of schizophrenia or any other mental illness. His explanation for his interaction with ghosts is that "interdimensional beings have business with me or else I am just sensitive to them."

In the 1980s, John went back to college. Sometimes, in various classrooms, there would be "a perfectly normal-looking adult student sitting in the desk behind him." It took a number of odd looks and negative comments from the students around him for John to realize that none of the other people—or the professor—could see the individual.

"On one occasion," John said, "I confronted this being while I was alone in the hallway with him, and I asked him just what the hell he was. Why was he sometimes visible, other times invisible. He gave me some real slippery 'in your face' sophistry. When we returned to the classroom, he still seemed in a snit, and after a few minutes he once again became invisible and he told me that he was leaving. Everyone in the classroom was startled when the large heavy door opened and slammed shut. The professor, whose back had been turned to the class as he wrote on the blackboard, made some joke about 'the world being filled with critics' and that he hoped the student might transfer to another class."

John theorizes that the invisible student must have moved on to some higher halls of paranormal academia for he only recalls one other visitation. "He appeared one afternoon as I walked to my car after class and told me that such-and-such a bookstore had a book that would answer all my questions about our weird time together. Then he disappeared without telling me the title of the book."

A REAL GHOST MADE ANITA A BELIEVER IN LIFE AFTER DEATH

Anita Stapleton sent us her very convincing story of a real ghost who appeared to her: "Is life after death only a matter of religious beliefs? Is it just wishful thinking? Comfort for the bereaved? Or has it ever been proved?

"These questions pass, at one time or another, through the minds of most people. There have been many stories about visions and apparitions, ver-

Haunted: Malevolent Ghosts, Night Terrors, and Threatening Phantoms

bal and written messages from 'beyond.' Are they genuine, or were they caused by imagination, hallucination, self-hypnosis, mental telepathy, or any other form of brainpower?

"As a person with an inquisitive mind, I have reflected upon these questions many times, until one day I received an answer most unexpectedly.

"The day had been a normal one for me in my home in Labrador, Queensland, Australia. I had gone about my daily chores, watched television in the evening, and finally went to bed, while my husband was still watching the late movie on TV.

"The bedroom was not dark, because the bright light of a full moon fell through the window. I had just laid down, ready to go to sleep, when I suddenly noticed that I was not on my own. Right in front of the wardrobe, and looking directly at me—*Good God, what was this?*—was a middle-aged man dressed like a Catholic priest.

"I rubbed my eyes and pinched my arms to make sure I was fully awake. Yes, I most certainly was. Was I having hallucinations?

"The priest was still standing there, looking at me. He was rather a frail man with hollow cheeks. His face showed traces of a hard life and illness. If he had any hair at all, it was covered by his hat.

"He looked so real, not like a ghost. I was not a bit scared, because he radiated vibrations of utter peace and tranquility. There was nothing to fear.

"I decided to talk to him, keeping my voice as low as possible. 'Hello, Father,' I said. 'God bless you.'

"'And God bless you, my child,' came the priest's prompt reply. He was well-spoken, his voice soft. His English accent was not hard to distinguish.

"After giving me a few personal messages and stressing the point that there is survival after death, he told me who he was. He was Frederick William Faber, and he had lived in England from 1814 to 1863.

"When I remarked that at the time of his passing he was only forty-nine years old, he confirmed this and added that he had died of a kidney disease. After quietly talking about religious matters for a few more minutes, he bade me farewell and disappeared.

The priest seemed very real and appeared rather frail but kind. He delivered several personal messages to Anita.

"My mind was boggled. As late as it was, it was impossible to think of sleep. I wrote down my unearthly visitor's name and other details. Then I told my husband what had happened.

"Naturally, his first reaction was disbelief and the assertion that I had been asleep and dreaming. Of course, I knew I had been fully awake.

"The whole thing, however, seemed so incredible that doubts came into my mind. The name Faber seemed a bit unusual for an Englishman. Being German, I know quite a few Germans by that name. I recalled a friend, Hildegard Faber, who had gone to school with me. Was this some trickery by my subconscious mind?

"The incident troubled me for days. How could I ever find out the truth?

"Then my husband reminded me of Somerset House in London, where a record of every person born and deceased in Britain is kept. However, he did not know how far back these records went. Father Faber, if indeed he had existed, had been dead for over one hundred years.

"Should I write to Somerset House? I hesitated. I did not want to make a fool of myself in case the whole thing was just a hallucination.

"A few days later, however, I took the plunge and wrote to Somerset House, requesting a search. I was sent a form to fill out, giving details of the required person, and was asked to include a small search fee. This I did immediately.

"Now I waited for a reply from Somerset House. This suspense drama would soon reach its climax. Either I would be told: 'Sorry, there is no record of this person' or ... I did not dare finish this sentence.

"Two weeks later an airmail letter from London arrived. The sender was Somerset House.

"My hands were shaky. I trembled like a leaf. I was barely able to open the letter. Then I almost fainted.

"The letter contained a certified copy of a death certificate. It stated that Frederick William Faber's death had occurred on September 26, 1863, and that he had been forty-nine at the time of his death and had been a doctor of divinity, in Brompton, County of Middlesex. The cause of death was stated as kidney disease. In other words, the official document in my hands confirmed what the apparition had told me.

"If this is not a genuine case of a visit from beyond the grave, what is it? An authority like Somerset House would not send a fictitious document halfway around the world to back up someone's fantasy or hallucination. To the best of my knowledge, Father Faber had not been a well-known personality, so books would not have been written about him which I might have read and forgotten about. Nobody alive today is old enough to remember him.

"While it is true that I have been in England, I did not visit any cemeteries there, which rules out the possibility that I may have seen his name on a tombstone. I am absolutely positive that I had never before heard of Father Faber. As much as I rack my brain, I cannot find a logical explanation, but I now know for sure that there is life after death. To me it has been proved beyond the shadow of a doubt."

POLTERGEISTS, THE NASTY, THROWING GHOSTS

Violent, disruptive hauntings are said to be caused by poltergeists—raucous entities that toss objects about the room. In the view of many psychical researchers, such phenomena are born not in the machinations of a ghost or spirit entity but rather in the psyche of a living being who is undergoing some kind of stress, psychic upheaval, or severe and dramatic psychological adjustment. Such an individual (most often an adolescent) expresses unconscious aggression toward others through dramatic manifestations of psychokinetic power (mind over matter), such as the overturning of furniture and the propelling of objects through the room. In some cases we have investigated, poltergeist phenomena have interacted with the haunting manifestations that already existed in the home, thereby producing intensely negative and disruptive energy.

We used to be as dogmatically opposed to the concept of demonic possession as any modern investigator is supposed to be. Many years of research and encounters with entities that are unabashedly evil have convinced us that homes in which murders or other violent physical deeds have been committed may become repositories for nonphysical leeches of the soul that we prefer to call "spirit parasites." These beings are hideous and grotesque in appearance, often manifesting as reptilian-like entities. When humans make themselves physically and spiritually vulnerable through drug and alcohol abuse, promiscuous sex, and other excesses of the physical body, they may not be aware of spirit parasites in their presence that are capable of possessing and manipulating them.

These beings are more nonphysical than they are physical. Indeed, they may be

Poltergeists are annoying spirits known for their mischievous behavior such as moving furniture and throwing objects around the house.

Paul Dale Roberts, founder of Halo Paranormal Investigations.

paraphysical interlopers from other dimensions. They are "in-between" beings, posing from time to time as ordinary humans, disguising the fact that they are really phantoms, creatures that have materialized from some haunted dominion unknown to us. In some of the more frightening cases, they may be fallen angels that aim to deceive, lie, and enslave. Theoretical physicists now speak freely about parallel universes; perhaps from time to time these entities intrude into our world from a universe that may almost be a mirror image of our own. Or perhaps, as the ancient philosophers suggested long ago, the appearance of spirits is evidence that we are part of a larger community of intelligences, a complex hierarchy of powers and principalities, a universe of interrelated species, both physical and nonphysical.

SHADOW PEOPLE

Our friend and colleague Paul Dale Roberts, founder of Halo Paranormal Investigations, reminded us of a rather new category of ghosts that has become increasingly experienced by percipients—the Shadow People:

This is a type of haunting activity that has no real explanation. They are different from ghosts. They are usually shapeless dark masses. Mostly seen with your peripheral vision. They are known to do things that are different from ghosts. They can move between walls, they have no human features, they wear no clothes (except for the hat man/hooded figure shadow creatures). People who encounter them have a feeling of dread. Clairvoyants that encounter Shadow People say they do not feel they are human and consider them nonhuman.

Shadow People have no discernible mouths, noses, or facial expressions. Some are seen as child-sized dark humanoids. Some people say they seem to be made up of dark smoke or dark steam. At times when they move, they appear to be moving on an invisible track from one place to another, such as a toy train on a small-scale railroad track. They have been seen to hop or what appears to be a strange dance. They are known to stare at the floor.

Two common types of Shadow People are the "hat man," which looks like he or she is wearing a 1930s fedora hat, and the "hooded figure," which looks like the shadow person has a hood over his or her head. The hood and hat stand out as clothing, but otherwise, they are not wearing any clothing at all. There are also reports of shadow animals, such as a shadow in the form of a cat, with no discernible mouth, nose, or eyes.

THE SHADOW MAN WHO WALKED HOSPITAL HALLWAYS

Kelly was a twenty-eight-year-old nurse when she first saw the shadow of a man walking in the hallway of the hospital. At first she tried very hard to figure out some logical, physical reason for the shadow to appear when no such man was present. She always saw the dark shadow full-figured, never in profile. She tried to determine if somehow it was her own shadow in a trick of light, but when the image moved down the hallway and she remained standing still, she had to rule out that attempt at a rational explanation.

She had recently made a major move in her life away from family and friends, so she conceded that her mind was in a state of confusion as to whether or not she had done the right thing. Perhaps the Shadow Person was a sign that she had somehow complicated the lives of her children and herself by making such a dramatic turn in her life.

When we asked about her feelings immediately after she first sighted the Shadow Being, Kelly answered, "Shock ... doubt ... but strangely after all the weird feelings, an acceptance that such occurrences were 'cool.' I had believed that there were such things as ghosts, but I never wanted to experience them personally."

In retrospect, Kelly said that she assessed the experience as having a positive effect on her life: "If you would have told me before I saw the Shadow Man that I was going to experience such an encounter, I would have freaked out and said that I wouldn't be able to handle it. But as it has turned out, the experience hasn't been so bad. He comes around once in awhile, and I leave him alone. In a way, his presence just confirms the reality of things that I have believed could be real."

THE OLD WOMAN IN THE GOWN WHO GRABS CHILDREN

Beth, an elementary school teacher, described frightening encounters with a spirit that seemingly turned its visibility off and on.

"I teach at an elementary school in the inner city of Milwaukee," she writes. "Last May, I was going to lead a group of children to the lavatories in the basement. One little girl refused to budge, telling me that they regularly see an old woman in a white gown who tries to grab them."

Beth later found out that the building had been a hospital during the Great Depression years.

Beth told us that the children she teaches are the "hard-headed ghetto kids, who have survival skills that far, far surpass anyone that I have ever met. They use their paranormal skills to get through the day—or even to walk outside. Their abilities are accepted in their community. I am one of the few white teachers who takes their awareness of the paranormal seriously."

THE LARGEST NUMBER OF GHOSTS ARE PEOPLE WHO FOUND IT HARD TO LET GO

Our friend and fellow ghost writer and researcher, David J. Pitkin, author of such important books as *New England Ghosts* and *New York State Ghosts*, took delight in blending history and spirituality. In one of his letters to us, David explained: "I've been trying to build a personal understanding of just what the heck ghosts are, and I've had to work on a mix of religion or spirituality as well as my own objective experiences."

Pitkin believed that ghosts really aren't that mysterious and that emotions were a part of most hauntings. "It's hard to let go of people, places, and things," David said. "The hugest number of ghosts are people who are finding it hard to let go. I'm ready to say now that everybody, as part of their passing-over experience, is going to be a ghost. It's kind of like an exit interview."

David J. Pitkin gave his own "exit interview" on February 14, 2013.

GHOSTS, ACCORDING TO THE HOLZERS

The energetic and popular Jeff Belanger is the author of over a dozen books on the paranormal, including the best sellers The World's Most Haunted Places, Weird Massachusetts, and Our Haunted Lives. He's the founder of Ghostvillage.com, the Web's most popular paranormal destination according to Google, and a noted speaker and media personality.

In the February 2, 2005, issue of *Ghostvillage*, Belanger interviewed Hans Holzer regarding his long career as a paranormal researcher:

We talked about the difference between a ghost or a spirit—how a ghost is a residual entity, like a psychic imprint left in an area that some people can pick up, whereas a spirit is intelligent and interactive. Holzer also mentioned a third category I hadn't heard about before: the "stay behinds."

"Stay behinds are relatively common," he said. "Somebody dies, and then they're really surprised that all of a sudden they're not dead. They're alive like they were. They don't understand it because they weren't prepared for it. So they go back to what they knew most—their chair, their room, and they just sit there.

Next, they want to let people know that they're still 'alive.' So they'll do little things like moving things, appear to relatives, pushing objects, poltergeist phenomena, and so on."

Preparation for the afterlife is something to which most world religions devote their very existence. Holzer believes all religions have some of it correct in that they believe in a supreme power—a belief Holzer also holds. He considers himself an Evangelical Protestant and used to attend St. Bartholomew in Manhattan twice a year—on Christmas and Easter.

Shortly after Holzer's passing in 2009, Belanger interviewed the charming and accomplished Alexandra Holzer:

Q: Your father, Hans Holzer, the original Ghost Hunter, believed that ghosts don't know they are dead. Do you share this point of view?

Alexandra: Yes, I do. The term "ghost" means to be either "stuck" or in a state of confusion at times. Of course, this is all dependent on the poor soul's demise, but case in point, they do not realize they have left

Paranormal investigator and author Jeff Belanger (pictured) interviewed Hans Holzer about the nature of ghosts.

their bodies. In many cases, this perpetuates a Grade A haunting in which the person that is no longer lingers about—and again here, dependent on why.

For example, if one dies suddenly and tragically in a car accident, he very well could be wandering aimlessly around the crash site for a long period of time, confused and unaware that he is deceased. Other times—now I say this because, again, it is subjective based on a belief system—some believe angel guides come to help try and cross the ghost over.

In other instances, the newly deceased person can separate themselves from the accident scene and visit someone close to say goodbye and then cross. That case would make them a spirit, hence the term "free spirit," and has gone to the next level in their new life through the veil. Some folks are confused while others are stubborn and refuse to leave the premises.

Like art, a ghost's position can be subjective as in life, and how they choose to live at times. Stubborn in life can also be stubborn in death. I should know, my father *still* nags me from beyond!

Entities that Haunt Forests, Fields, and Streams

THE MINING GHOST TOWN OF JEROME, ARIZONA

As Sherry and I drove up Highway 89A from the Verde Valley and first saw the houses of Jerome, Arizona, stacked on the hillside before us, we felt as though we were about to enter a time warp and be transported back to an earlier time.

In 1876, Al Sieber, Civil War hero General George Crook's famous guide and chief of scouts in the campaigns against the Apache, filed the first claim to the copper ore that existed in a mountainside 2,000 feet above Arizona's picturesque Verde Valley. As wise in the ways of metallurgy as he was in the ways of the Apache, Sieber recognized the potential value of the ore in the rugged mountain terrain. As fate would have it, Sieber never made a cent out of his discovery, but he told Angus McKinnon and M. A. Ruffner about the area, and they began the work that would eventually lead to the excavation of 800 billion dollars' worth of copper from the mountainside. The city was named for a New York City financier who never even visited the area. In 1882, Eugene Murray Jerome invested some badly needed capital in the mining claims with the proviso that the camp be named after him.

For seventy-seven years, miners worked the claims, carving out an amazing eighty-seven miles of tunnels under the town. And in those years of brutish toil, there were a lot of accidents and deaths on the job, especially related to lung problems. Add to the equation deaths as a result of the flu epidemic of 1917, and you have a powerful potential for the kind of psychic residue that creates the ghostly echoes of the past.

At its peak in the 1920s, Jerome had a population of 15,000. When Phelps Dodge Corporation shut down the mines in 1953, the population dropped to

Jerome, Arizona, has a reputation for being a haunted area. The Jerome Grande Hotel (the large building toward the back of this photo) was once the United Verde Hospital and asylum that served the mining community. Today, it is, of course, haunted, along with other buildings in the town.

around 120. Today, the once grand old city is occupied by folks who maintain an artists' colony, operate art galleries, run antique shops, host colorful restaurants, and staff a number of museums that preserve former glories of the mining days. The population hovers around 450 people—and a whole lot of ghosts.

We soon learned that many accounts of ghosts centered around the United Verde Hospital that sits high on Cleopatra Hill. The hospital had been used to treat miners from 1927 to 1951. Some of the local artists liked to paint in the old building, making good use of the light from its many windows. But in order to do so, they had to learn to ignore the ghostly manifestations that occurred around them as they worked on their canvases.

"If you want to work here," one of the artists told us, "you just have to get used to the ghostly energy that's all over the place. You make your peace with the spirits. They won't hurt you. They're just people, after all."

Another told of being in the hospital one night after dark and having heard the sounds of coughing, labored breathing, as well as cries and moans of pain. "A lot of miners developed lung problems from their work," he said, "and I think I heard the ghostly sounds of their suffering."

A young woman told us that she had a chilling experience one night during a full moon as she walked by an older hospital farther down on Cleopatra Hill. In retrospect, she told us that she felt as if she were being drawn to the place, as if something within was telling her that she needed to have a certain kind of experience for her spiritual growth. "At first I heard the sounds of people breathing heavily," she said. "Then I could hear sighs and moans."

Even though she had a flashlight with her, she felt that she should not turn it on. There was enough moonlight filtering in through the windows for her to see quite clearly the dim shapes of several bodies lying covered with blankets in a hallway. She could see doctors and nurses rushing around the bodies, bending over them. The whole scene, she estimated, lasted only ten or twelve seconds, then it was gone.

> Headless Charlie, the ghost of a miner who was decapitated in a gruesome mine accident, has been seen by quite a number of Jerome residents....

"I knew that there had been accidents in the mines," she said, "but when I did some research on the history of Jerome, I read about the awful influenza epidemic that struck around 1917 and '18—and I had an inner knowing that I was seeing a scene from that terrible time."

Headless Charlie, the ghost of a miner who was decapitated in a gruesome mine accident, has been seen by quite a number of Jerome residents, as has the shade of a prostitute, who, legend has it, was knifed in the old red-light district. Especially when the moon is full, people see the ghostly hooker walking from where the crude shacks of the prostitutes used to be to within a few feet of the Little Daisy Hotel—where she disappears.

Before we left the mining town that had once been called the "wickedest city in the West," Sherry felt as though it was important to climb Cleopatra Hill one more time and to train her camera lens on the doorway of a building near the old Episcopal church. Later, when the developed film was returned, Sherry saw what appears to be a figure standing in the doorway, thus providing us with our own ghostly memento from Jerome.

FULL BODY APPARITIONS AT SULPHUR MOUNTAIN

Our friend and colleague Paul Dale Roberts, founder of Halo Paranormal Investigations (HPI), which is currently one of the most active and professional of the "ghost hunting" groups in the United States, told us of a very haunted mountain near Los Angeles called Sulphur Mountain. On May 9, 2009, Roberts and Telly Blackwood, a member of HPI, drove down to the area to check out some reports of Indian spirits.

"We interviewed Roger Tinsley, who owns a lot of property at Sulphur Mountain," Paul said. "He has lived here for 16 years and is now 50 years old.

He tells me that the Mountain Chumash Indians used to live on this land and their presence is very strong on this mountain. Their spirits can be felt heavily from McGoo Rock to Point Conception. This was a spiritual place for the Indians and may have been considered as sacred ground. Many people have claimed to have seen full body apparitions throughout the woods on Sulphur Mountain. People can hear them, people have seen them, and many people have found pictures of ectoplasm on their photographs. When looking at the photographs closer, the ectoplasm at times looks like Indian faces."

He Felt the Spirits of the Sacred Artifacts Cry Out

R.O., a designer who presently lives in California, is of Ojibway (Chippewa) heritage. When he was a college student in the summer of 2000, he did an internship at the Smithsonian Institution's National Museum of the American Indian.

"The first time I was brought into the area known as the Cultural Resource Center's storage area, I began to cry," he told us. "I started to cry because I felt the spirits of the artifacts that were being housed there. I felt that the objects were being imprisoned, kept from living out their intended life and purpose. As with everything, we have a physical beginning, a middle, and an end. These many objects were taken from their intended or sacred purpose years ago—in some cases, over 100 years ago. I was filled with a very intense sadness. I felt my soul cry. I felt my heart scream out for freedom for these items."

An Increasing Number of Reports of Native American Spirits

Our research indicates that it is not only the psychic energy surrounding ancient tribal artifacts that cries out to be seen and heard by contemporary men and women who now occupy lands once held sacred by the native people, it is the very spiritual essence of the tribal members themselves that wishes to be acknowledged. Since the late 1960s, there have been increasing numbers of encounters with Native American ghosts.

Mrs. G. S. told John Pascal, a writer for *Newsday* (August 4, 1972), that she had been seeing a ghost in her Long Island home. She described the spirit as looking like an Indian. "It makes sense if the ghost is an Indian," Mrs. G.S. theorized, "because my home is built on an old Indian burial ground." She then handed Pascal three Indian artifacts, explaining that she had found the carvings in her backyard.

Had They Confronted the Ghost of Mingo?

On August 28, 1972, the *Patriot Ledger* carried a story reporting that Edward A. confronted the ghostly figure of a man in a cloak on Harland Street in Quincy, Massachusetts. He joined what appeared to be a group of Native Americans in spirit form.

Edward and Jacklyn B. thought almost immediately that they had seen the ghost of Mingo, who died in 1763. In 1898, when Mingo Street was cut off of Canton Avenue, the graves of five Indians were unearthed by excavators.

Jacklyn B. told Richard Kent of the *Patriot Ledger* that "the man in the cape appeared to have piercing red eyes." She guessed that an Indian from the Colonial period would wear the type of clothing—such as a cape—that she saw. She theorized that the ghost was that of the Indian Mingo.

One story about Mingo was that he was a member of the Ponkapoag tribe that lived—and still survives—in eastern Massachusetts and whose members were converted to Christianity.

NATIVE SHAMANS SAY THE SPIRITS OF THEIR DEAD ARE BECOMING RESTLESS

"The spirits of the dead seem quite busy and restless on the other side; as a Cherokee chief pointed out to me once, such experiences are not at all uncommon among American Indians," recalled Brent Raynes, editor of the excellent *Alternate Perceptions* online magazine. "He described to me how his mother, who had died four years earlier, had appeared to him on three separate occasions, and that she looked to him as real as she had been in the flesh. He even added that he had kissed her!

"Back in the mid-1970s, I was directed by an Ohio 'contactee,' who was part Iroquois, to a Susquehannock medicine man in Pennsylvania who had greatly impressed her. She recalled, for example, one time how he had helped conduct a successful rain-making ceremony in which four human-like figures appeared in the sky. 'One looked almost like a half bird, half human,' she explained. 'they did not look Indian.' Then there followed a downpour of rain.

"I visited the medicine man a couple of times at his home. He described a variety of personal experiences with spirits, elementals, and star visitors. A few years later, he passed away. His wife wrote us shortly afterwards, describing how his spirit had appeared to her in very dramatic ways. In fact, she said that he had appeared to her in one instance in a solid way as well.

"One night as she had lain down in her bed she felt something pulling her cover from her right hand. Then, she explained, she felt a warm and firm hand take hold of hers, and looking up she wrote that she was looking into the eyes of her smiling husband.

"'He didn't say a word as he enveloped me in his arms,' she wrote. 'these too felt warm and good to me. My heart beat like it did when we first met and that is exactly how he appeared, young again.' She added, 'I got up and wrote down my experience in short terms, but, oh, I do remember more than I wrote down.'"

A Journalist Discovers Amerindian Spirits Are Active

In the "California Living" section of the October 13, 1968, issue of the *Los Angeles Herald Examiner*, respected journalist Wanda Sue Parrott interviewed a Mrs. Potter, who said that her husband had many encounters with an Indian ghost before their marriage. Mrs. Potter's first encounter came in 1961 when she suffered from a serious illness.

"He came to warn us of danger ahead," she told Parrott, "and he protected me."

We established contact with Wanda Sue while on a promotional tour in 1973, and we have remained good friends. She has had many experiences with paranormal phenomena, but in spite of a life filled with psychic encounters she remains an objective researcher about planes beyond the psychical.

Once, after she had interviewed us for the *Herald Examiner*, she told how in 1968 she had been given an assignment to interview people in Los Angeles who claimed to have seen or to have encountered the spirits of American Indians.

"I was nearly finished writing my article when I went to bed about 11 P.M. one night in June," she told us. "I fell into a very deep sleep, but as I had drifted off, I had been wondering how an Indian spirit would manifest if one should come into my room. Would I be able to see or hear him? Would I be scared?

"Suddenly a loud banging sound awakened me. Someone or something was knocking loudly on the center of the door. It was the full moon, and I could see the door shaking in the moonlight.

"Then the banging stopped, and the gold-colored knob started turning. First it turned one way, then the other. It was so noisy, such a rattling sound that I knew my husband would wake up. I was not frightened. I watched the doorknob in fascination. But when my husband did not wake up, and when the door did not open, I decided to open it myself. I did. I peered into an empty hallway, as I knew would happen.

"I then went to my five-year-old son's room. He was fast asleep, as I knew he would be. He could not have been pounding on the door or trying to turn the knob."

Wanda Sue was left with a strong feeling that someone was trying to reach her, desperately trying to alert her to something or get a message to her.

The next day, she received an urgent message from a cousin from whom she not heard for four years. Wanda made a telephone call and somehow she seemed to know exactly the right words to say to solve the cousin's crisis.

"I entered a new phase of my professional life," she told us. "I was suddenly writing quite a few Indian stories and meeting many Native Americans from different tribes and reservations. As my new interest area continued to become more and more active, I was made an honorary chief of the White Buffalo by a symbolic spiritual group embodying the Native spirit of all surviving tribes."

ANN MILLER'S NEW HOME UPSET A HOPI GUARDIAN SPIRIT

Although it was not generally known, actress-dancer Ann Miller (1923–2004), star of such classic motion pictures as *Kiss Me, Kate* (1953), *On the Town* (1949), and *Easter Parade* (1948), was the great-granddaughter of a Cherokee medicine woman who was esteemed for her psychic abilities. Those who knew Ann well knew that she possessed a great deal of psychic sensitivity. Later, she would write a book about her psychic talents, *Tapping into the Force*, with a friend of ours, Dr. Maxine Asher. But being part Cherokee and being psychic did not prevent Ann from being frightened by the ghostly appearance of a scowling Indian warrior.

We received a call from Ann early in 1990, shortly after she had moved into a home that she had purchased as an investment in Sedona, Arizona. Her accountant, Joan G., was sleeping in the guest room, and Ann was in the master bedroom. Sometime during the night, Ann told us, she was awakened by the figure of a fierce Indian brave glowering at her.

"I was frightened by his appearance, and I thought at first that I might be having a terrible dream," she said. "I shook my head and took a sip of water—but he was still there."

When the angry ghost at last disappeared, Ann found the courage to leave her bedroom and walk into the front room to investigate. "There, glaring at me through the front picture window, was a coyote—with the same fierce look that the Indian brave had fixed on me! I felt that I was not wanted in that house."

Sherry had spent a good deal of time with the Hopi teachers and medicine people in northern Arizona and had been invited to

After the Hopi warrior disappeared, Ann saw a fierce-looking coyote outside her bedroom window.

Haunted: Malevolent Ghosts, Night Terrors, and Threatening Phantoms

participate in ceremonies closed to all but spiritual teachers. After some discussion about who might be best able to help Ann, Sherry came up with a name of an accomplished shaman.

Ann told us that as soon as possible she had dinner with the Hopi medicine teacher and his wife. The shaman explained to her that it was possible for spirits to assume the form of coyotes or other animals. After a few moments in silence, he went on to say that the son of the pioneer Arizonian who had built her house had been killed during its construction. The grieving father had asked a medicine priest and a tribal chief to bless the house and to help his son find peace. A fetish had been placed in each corner of the house, and a special blessing had been bestowed upon the *kiva*, a small house used for religious ceremonies situated behind the larger house.

Somehow, unknowingly and innocently, Ann Miller's purchase of the house had not set well with a guardian Hopi spirit that had been placed there long ago by the medicine priests and their blessing ceremonies.

All ended well for Ann. An accomplished exorcist did a complete and total cleansing of the house and the *kiva*. "No more ghosts with fierce expressions wake me up in the middle of the night," she told us.

Chief Seattle, who led the Suquamish and Duwamish peoples, was famous for his concern for the environment.

CHIEF SEATTLE WARNED THE WHITE MAN THAT THE DEAD ARE NOT ALTOGETHER POWERLESS

We suggest that a clue to these continuing manifestations of native tribal phantoms may be found in the prophetic warning of Chief Seathe (Seattle) to the white men who cheated his people out of their lands with the Treaty of Point Elliott in 1855:

Our religion is the traditions of our ancestors, the dreams of our old men, given them by the Great Spirit, and the visions of our shamans, and is written in the hearts of our people....

Every part of this country is sacred to my people. Every hillside, every valley, every plain and grove has been hallowed by some fond memory or sad experience of my tribe.

Haunted: Malevolent Ghosts, Night Terrors, and Threatening Phantoms

When the last red man shall have perished from the earth and his memory among the white men shall have become a myth, these shores shall swarm with the invisible dead of my tribe.... At night when the streets of your cities and villages shall be silent, and you think them deserted, they will throng with the returning hosts that once filled and still love this beautiful land.

The white man will never be alone … for the dead are not altogether powerless. Dead, did I say? There is no death, only a change of worlds.

Chief Seattle's malediction has proven correct. "Every hillside, every valley, every plain and grove," together with homes, hotels, national parks, and the quiet streets of the cities after dark, have proven to be haunted by "those spirits who loved this land."

And those tribal spirits are far from being alone. Those ghosts who so loved this land are joined nightly by a host of entities fitting all manner of descriptions and possible origins. The Spirit World that is always near us visits us with a seemingly endless nocturnal manifestation of ghosts, phantoms, night terrors, things that go bump in the night, and otherworldly visitors from other dimensions of time and space.

THE DEVIL RIDER OF CHISHOLM HOLLOW

The first settlers of the central Texas hill country were Scotch-Irish families who had migrated from the states of Kentucky and Tennessee. They considered themselves God-fearing folk, but their heritage also gave them a healthy respect for the supernatural. When the native people of the area decided to avoid a small valley because of a strange apparition that appeared on horseback, they agreed among themselves that there was plenty of land to go around without offending the inhabitant of the little hollow. Besides, those whose curiosity lured them near the hollow had reported hearing strange sounds, like metal striking metal.

As the story goes, a rancher named McConnell tracking a vicious pack of wolves that had been tearing at his herd found himself following a trail that led to the hollow. Deciding without hesitation to brave the mysterious hollow in an effort to track down the marauding pack of wolves, McConnell ignored all the warnings of a ghostly inhabitant.

He had not ventured far when he was astounded to see a strikingly tall armored rider on a magnificent coal-black steed thundering down the hollow directly at him. McConnell galloped out of the hollow, praying the armored apparition would not catch up to him.

Word of McConnell's sighting was quickly circulated among the settlers and the tribes of the area. The more spiritually minded of the people noted that the incident of the rancher's encounter had occurred shortly before the army of General Zachary Taylor had crossed the Rio Grande, igniting the beginning of the Mexican–American War. From that time on, the people of the central Texas hills have believed that a sighting of the Devil Rider of Chisholm Hollow has predicted every major conflict in which the United States has become embroiled.

Fifteen years after McConnell's encounter with the Devil Rider, Emmett Ringstaff was passing the hollow on April 10, 1861, when the phantom horseman came by him at a steady trot. The horse that he rode was taller than any raised by the settlers of the area, and even though many of the local folk believed the horseman to be a manifestation of Satan, Ringstaff remained calm enough to share a description of the entity: He was wearing some kind of armor, and he carried a shield. Iron gauntlets covered his arms, and he wore a helmet of Spanish design. Two brass pistols dangled from a buckler that appeared to be gold and bore symbols of a crown and a lion. The pistols were of an eighteenth-century design and had the appearance of fine craftsmanship about them.

Judging by Emmett Ringstaff's description, the armor worn by the Devil Rider resembled that of a sixteenth-century Spanish conquistador.

Shortly after Ringstaff had reported seeing the apparition, the first guns of the Civil War were fired at Fort Sumter.

Gradually, the fear that the rider was a manifestation of Satan gave way to the theory that he was the spirit of one of the Spaniards who had been killed near the hollow by Comanche Indians during the massacre of a Spanish garrison around 1700.

Before the Spanish–American War, the rider was seen by three men—Arch Clawson, Ed Shannon, and Sam Bullock—who said that the armored spirit seemed hostile to them. Emotions emanating from the rider had never before been reported.

Then, when the Spanish–American War broke out in 1898, the settlers in the area began to wonder if the rider was sensitive about his heritage. Strange things began to occur around the central Texas hills, and although the rider had been neutral in previous conflicts, this time it seemed as though his loyalty lay with Spain. Although Texas had better than average rainfall in 1898, in the hill country wells and creeks went dry. Cattle died of thirst, and a strange and unexplainable disease began killing horses.

The Devil Rider's next appearance was made in January 1917. A group of young deer hunters, scoffing at the superstitions of their elders, tempted the unknown by entering the hollow to look for sign of deer. When the armored rider thundered out of nowhere, his armor glinting in the January sun, the previously bold and doubting young men scattered and ran.

On February 3, 1917, the United States, which had been teetering on the brink of war, severed diplomatic relations with the German Empire and shortly thereafter was sending armies across the Atlantic.

The world was hypertense in 1941. Europe had been a battlefield for a year and a half, and the Western Pacific had been subject to Japanese aggression for even longer.

Not insensitive to the precarious position of the United States in this world setting, the people of the central hills of Texas had gathered to pray for peace on Sunday, December 7, 1941.

> When the armored rider thundered out of nowhere, his armor glinting in the January sun, the previously bold and doubting young men scattered and ran.

Following the services, as a number of families were driving past Chisholm Hollow on their way home, one of the drivers stopped, claiming that he had heard a horse. After a few seconds, the Devil Rider charged onto the road, stopped broadside to them for an instant, then passed off the road, and disappeared in the cover of trees on the opposite side.

Terrified, the group of men and women hurried home, where they waited impatiently around the radio as the tubes warmed up. The first word they heard was of the bombing of Pearl Harbor.

Although the Devil Rider has not been seen prior to the "police actions" of Korea and Vietnam, nor before the Iraq conflict, some of those who claim prophetic insight have speculated that the spirit waits to herald Armageddon.

THE ANCIENT HORSEMAN OF BOTTLEBUSH DOWN
by Nick Redfern

This section of the book would not seem complete without a ghostly account of one of the ancient spectral horsemen of the United Kingdom. Our friend Nick Redfern works full time as a writer, lecturer, and journalist. He writes about a wide range of unsolved mysteries, including Bigfoot, UFOs, the Loch Ness Monster, alien encounters, and government conspiracies. Nick has written forty-one books, writes for the Mysterious Universe web site, and has appeared on numerous television shows on the History Channel, National Geographic Channel, and SyFy Channel.

In October 1995, the U.K.'s *Cannock Mercury* newspaper reported on a series of very weird events that were then occurring in the midst of Beaudesert Old Park, which is situated near Castle Ring, an ancient Iron Age fort on the south side of central England's Cannock Chase. It's an area noted for its wide range of paranormal and near-magical "things" seen in and around the dense woods. The list includes Bigfoot-type beasts, large black cats, ghostly black dogs with blazing red eyes, werewolves, and Mothman-like creatures. Home to a camp for both scouts and guides, Beaudesert Old Park was the site of repeated, strange, ghostly activity in the late summer and early autumn of 1995. Not only that, but a group of scouts was going to stake out the area in a careful and dedicated bid to try and get to the bottom of the spooky mystery once and for all.

The *Cannock Mercury* revealed: "Wardens and assistants have reported strange noises, screams and eerie goings-on around the camp." Indeed, they had, including encounters with a dark-cloaked figure and a ghostly child roaming the woods and haunting the local roads by night. Steve Fricker, the assistant leader of the 2nd Rugeley Hillsprings Scouts, related at the time: "It is said that the ancient horsemen of old are now seeking revenge for the disturbances they have had to face for several years from these excitable youths."

Newspaper staff added: "Scouts will be camping out to 'confront' the spirits and attempt to restore peace. They will be staying awake from Saturday evening (October 28) until dawn on Sunday, entertained by wardens' tales of the hauntings."

The Beaudesert house was (mostly) torn down in the 1930s, when the royal Paget family could no longer afford its upkeep. This is the south wall of the Great Hall, which is near the more ancient Castle Ring fort in an area of Staffordshire known for eerie occurrences.

Haunted: Malevolent Ghosts, Night Terrors, and Threatening Phantoms

Ultimately, however, the ghostly "horsemen of old" did not make a showing, but, maybe we have an eerie and uncanny precedent for just such a prehistoric horse-rider, and one that may help to explain at least some strange sightings of ghosts of a very ancient kind in the wilds of the British Isles.

A respected authority on prehistory, R. C. C. Clay, had just such an encounter while driving at Bottlebrush Down, Dorset, England—an area strewn with old earthworks—during the cold winter of 1924. The story, however, did not surface until 1956. That was when Clay decided to share the details with an expert on all things ghostly and spectral. His name was James Wentworth Day. He penned such titles as *Here Are Ghosts and Witches*, *A Ghost Hunter's Game Book*, *In Search of Ghosts*, and *They Walk the Wild Places*.

The location of the extraordinary event that Clay related to a captivated and enthralled Wentworth Day was the A3081 road—an old road between the old Dorset villages of Cranborne and Sixpenny Handley on farmland known locally to one and all as Bottlebrush Down. It was while Clay was driving home, after spending a day excavating in the area, and as the daylight was giving way to the magical, twilight hours, that he encountered something extraordinary. Maybe even beyond extraordinary.

At a point where the new road crossed with an old Roman road, a horseman, riding wildly and at high speed on the back of a huge and muscular stallion, seemingly appeared out of nowhere. But there was something wrong about this man, something terribly wrong. In Clay's very own words to a captivated Wentworth Day: "I could see that he was no ordinary horseman, for he had bare legs, and wore a long loose cloak. His horse had a long mane and tail, but I could see neither bridle nor stirrup. His face was turned towards me, but I could not see his features. He seemed to be threatening me with some implement, which he waved in his right hand above his head."

It is deeply fortunate that the witness in this case was Clay—a man with an expert and profound knowledge of English history, folklore, and the people of times long gone. There was no doubt in Clay's mind that, having kept the rider in careful sight for around three hundred feet, his clothing and weapon firmly identified him as nothing less than a denizen of the Bronze Age. Incredibly, this would have placed his origins at some point between 2100 and 750 B.C.E. Not surprisingly, with darkness now falling fast, Clay hit the accelerator and headed for home, somewhat shakily but decidedly excited, too.

His interest most certainly piqued, Clay began to make careful and somewhat wary inquiries—of an understandably tentative and tactful nature—in the area, to determine if anyone else had ever seen the ancient, ghostly hunter of the Downs. As it so transpired, they actually had.

An old shepherd who had worked in the fields his whole life said: "Do you mean the man on the horse who comes out of the opening in the pinewood?" When an amazed and excited Clay replied, "Yes!" and proceeded to ask further questions, it became clear to him that he was not the only person to have seen the enigmatic old rider of the ancient landscape.

And, a couple of years later, while still investigating the strange affair, Clay learned of yet another encounter with the ghostly man and his horse. In this case, the witnesses were two teenage girls. They were cycling from Sixpenny Handley to a Friday night dance at nearby Cranborne and were plunged into a collective state of fear by the presence of what sounded like the very same character Clay encountered back in 1924.

As Clay told Wentworth Day in 1956, he knew of no more recent encounters with the horseman. Clay theorized, however, that what he had been fortunate enough to see was the spirit form of a Bronze Age hunter and his horse. Clay believed that the pair had probably died under violent circumstances on the Downs, and—for a while, at least—roamed the very same old hunting grounds that they had called "home" during their clearly turbulent, physical lives.

Phantom Hitchhikers

As we explore the paranormal, we find that most types of phenomena appear to be universal, the individual circumstances of the accounts fitting themselves to the unique cultural interpretations of whatever area in which they manifest. Certainly, stories of phantom hitchhikers constitute one such category of ubiquitous tales, having been reported around the world.

Resurrection Mary Has Been Hitching a Ride for Ninety Years

Chicago's Resurrection Mary has been hitching a ride and spooking motorists since the 1930s. Said to be the spirit of a beautiful, blond Polish girl, Mary has been picked up by smitten young men at dances and asked to be taken home. The problem is, "home" always turns out to be Resurrection Cemetery on Archer Avenue on the Southside of Chicago. On occasion, the phantom hitchhiker has been bold enough to open car doors and get in, explaining to the startled driver how she desperately needs a ride into the city. Once again, as the car approaches the cemetery on Archer, Mary bolts from the car and vanishes at the gates.

The Pretty Bridesmaid of Blue Bell Hill in Maidstone, England

Since 1965, dozens of drivers have slammed on their brakes to avoid hitting a pretty young woman in a flowing white dress standing in the road on Blue Bell Hill in Maidstone, England. The phantom is said to be that of Judith

Lingham, who was to have been a bridesmaid for her best friend when she died in a car crash the night before the wedding. Her spirit appears still dressed in her flowing bridesmaid's gown, still attempting to get to the wedding.

The Prom Dress Hitchhiker (aka the Niles Canyon Ghost)

Paul Dale Roberts contributed accounts of the Niles Canyon Hitchhiker, the Northern California variation on the vanishing hitchhiker archetype.

There are many different variations of this story, but all accounts include a girl being involved in some sort of motorized vehicle accident on February 26 (the year often changes). One version of the story includes a girl being involved in a car crash on Niles Canyon road (off the 680 freeway in Sunol, California) on the way to her prom. The girl died on impact and to this day is said to haunt Niles Canyon road every February 26.

Another aspect of the haunting is that people traveling along Niles Canyon road (now Highway 84) on the night of February 26 will see a normal-

Stories of ghostly hitchhikers, especially young, pretty women, have become common in cultures all over the world.

looking high school-aged girl walking along the road in a prom dress (many people have said it is white). Travelers along the road (mostly those who are alone) have said they stopped and offered the girl a ride. She accepts the ride, giving the driver an address across the bridge (either Dumbarton or Bay Bridge, depending on the storyteller). Once the driver gets to the beginning of the bridge, the girl will disappear. Sometimes people have gone to the address to find that a girl matching that description once lived there many years ago.

Today, many people will travel along this treacherous dark road in the hopes of catching a glimpse of the Niles Canyon ghost. The latest report was in 2013 when Michael T. of Newport Beach, California, said that he saw a girl in a white prom dress walking alongside the road. He slowed down his car to get a better look at her, and she turned around and gave Michael a sinister grin. Michael calls her the Prom Dress Hitchhiker, because she did have her thumb out. Michael says that her grin brought chills down his spine. When he looked in the rear view mirror, she was gone.

Hitchhiking Jesus

Author and researcher Paul Bartholomew reminds us of the reports of the Jesus hitchhiker that became so popular in the 1980s. This story comes from the October 31, 1980, issue of the Rutland Daily Herald in Vermont.

EKENASSJON, Sweden — The "hitchhiking ghost," reported in Arkansas earlier this year, has turned up in southern Sweden where he is making reckless drivers out of local folk.

Police said Thursday many drivers have reported picking up a young man who talked about the second coming of Christ.

Then, without opening the door, the hitchhiker suddenly disappeared without a trace, drivers said.

As a result of these reports, drivers are speeding down roads without regard to traffic signals, police said.

Or they go miles out of their way to avoid a spot they call the ghost's favorite intersection for catching a lift.

Police have been flooded with calls asking about the mysterious traveler, but have yet to start an official probe.

However local priests are taking it seriously and pursuing investigations.

Alcohol is not suspected by the police as Sweden's drunken driving laws make it an unlikely cause of the mysterious appearances.

In Arkansas earlier this year, motorists reported picking up a similar hitchhiker who said he was Christ, and who disappeared from their cars.

THE BOUNCING FLASHLIGHT AND A TALE OF LOST LOVE

Paul Dale Roberts, always the careful and cautious investigator, offers a disclaimer with the following two stories. Although he has not personally investigated them, the accounts came into HPI's Paranormal Hotline with both callers attesting the validity of their experience.

The Bouncing Flashlight

June 6, 2016: Dwayne Johansen of Monterey was driving down Highway 1 near Big Sur, California, when Dwayne's younger son spied a bouncing light behind the car. The light got closer and closer to the back of their car and the son alerted his father. Thinking it was a motorcycle, Dwayne sped up a bit to get away from the bouncing light, but the light just seemed to get closer and closer to his back bumper.

His wife began yelling at Dwayne to slow down, as the curves were very dangerous. The time was about 10:30 P.M., and the bouncing light seemed to get brighter. Finally, Dwayne had enough and slowed down his car. The light went out and Dwayne and his family heard a woman emit a terrible scream. The experience was traumatic for the family, and it was hard for them to get it out of their mind.

Lost Love

July 7, 1954: A couple named Lorna and Tom had enjoyed a long visit at Pfeiffer Big Sur State Park. They had a nice picnic on the beach, and later when

the sun went down, Lorna told Tom that she wanted to jog up and down the beach. Tom couldn't run with her because he had recently sprained his ankle. Tom gave Lorna a flashlight and told her to keep it on so he could keep an eye on her. Tom had his own flashlight ready so he could signal Lorna as she ran.

Lorna started running with her flashlight, and the illumination from the flashlight would bounce up and down while Tom kept his flashlight light trained on her as she ran. When Lorna came close to Tom in her run, she would raise her flashlight high in the air, and Tom would do the same thing.

Lorna did her first lap and told Tom that she would do one more lap. Lorna began her second lap, and Tom again kept his flashlight trained on Lorna.

Highway 1 along the California coastline near Big Sur is a twisting road that can be dangerous, especially when it comes to rock slides.

Lorna was at a good distance, but Tom was able to see her bouncing light. Then all of a sudden the light went out. There was nothing but pitch darkness in the area where Lorna was. Tom couldn't understand what was going on because the flashlight had new batteries. Tom went to investigate but Lorna was nowhere in sight. Tom spent the whole night on the beach looking for Lorna but still no Lorna. When the sun rose, Tom went straight to the police.

The police conducted a search, but Lorna was never heard from again. The police suspected Tom of murder, but it was never proven. No one ever discovered what actually happened to Lorna on that summer day in 1954.

Tom claimed that he had reoccurring nightmares of Lorna being abducted by a shadowy looking man who was hiding behind a rock. Tom could hear Lorna in his nightmare yelling: "The Man, the Man, he is going to get me! Help!" The nightmares became worse, and Tom would wake up in a cold sweat. Four years after this incident, Tom had a massive heart attack and died.

People who stay on the beach during the evening hours have claimed that they have seen a bouncing light going up and down the beach, and at times a light can be seen going along Highway #1. Could that bouncing light be Lorna?

GHOST GIRL IN THE MIDDLE OF OLIVE STREET

On June 12, 2017, two reports came into HPI's paranormal hotline of four apparitions seen near Olive Avenue in Olivehurst, California.

The first report: "Hi, my name is Carol, and I saw a ghost girl in the middle of the street at Olive Avenue in Olivehurst, California. It was about 1:00 A.M., and the girl ghost ran toward my car and went through my car. At first I thought it was a real person and I was scared to death. Then I realized it had to be a ghost because it went through my car and then I got even more scared. Have you had any reports of ghosts in Olivehurst?"

Second report: "My name is Dwight, and I live in Marysville. It was about 2:00 A.M., and my buddy and I were driving around McGowan Parkway in Olivehurst. Out in the field, we could see four shadowy figures. We slowed down the car to watch because we thought it was very unusual for people to be walking in the field early in the morning like that. As we watched, the figures just vanished. So freaking weird."

There is a dedication to the four people who died in a Memorial Park on McGowan Parkway. This is a tragedy that the residents of Olivehurst will never forget.

With a little research, Paul Dale Roberts discovered that on May 1, 1992, three students and one teacher were shot dead by Eric Houston. He burst into Lindhurst High School and started shooting with a 12-gauge pump action shotgun. Not only did he kill four people, but he also wounded many. There is a dedication to the four people who died at Memorial Park on McGowan Parkway. This is a tragedy that the residents of Olivehurst will never forget. Olivehurst is right next to Marysville, a town known for its haunted activity. Some of the ghosts from Marysville may be "bleeding" over into Olivehurst. Here are some of the haunted places in Marysville:

Mary Aaron Museum: Caretaker Frank Aaron died at this museum and his apparition is sometimes seen in one of the back rooms. Frank may have caused a portal to open up at the museum because other apparitions have been seen in the museum. Voices and footsteps are also heard in the museum.

Silver Dollar Saloon: I have investigated this saloon with radio personality Lori Schulz. Legend has it that serial killer Juan Corona once owned this saloon and that there may be a few dead bodies buried there. What we do know is that Corona murdered twenty-five migrant workers. The Silver Dollar Saloon was also once a brothel, and some of the ghostly ladies of the night are seen sporting their nineteenth-century floozy garb.

Marysville Cemetery: Full bodied figures are seen roaming the cemetery and glowing lights have been observed. A home near the cemetery is where I saw my first full body apparition of a woman walking from one loft to another loft. At the same house, I captured a large red orb on my camera. The orb moved from one side of the loft and down the steps, right into my camera.

GHOST LIGHTS

Old Brit Bailey's Light Still Shines in Brazoria County

Brit Bailey's dying request was that he be buried standing up. He proclaimed that he had spent his whole life stomping over the Texas prairies, and he didn't aim to stop when he died. They buried old Brit in 1833, but residents in the area of Bailey's Prairie, five miles west of Angleton, Texas, in Brazoria County, claim that the early settler has kept his vow to continue to stomp around on the prairies.

The Thomases, who moved into old Bailey's place after he had been planted erect in the sod, were the first to bear witness that the old-timer's ghost did not wait long to start prowling around. In her diary, Ann Rainey Thomas made a record of her sighting of old Brit when his ghostly face looked at her through the window one night. Her servant girl, Melinda, reported that the ghost chased the hired hands away from the cows during evening milking.

All members of the household swore to have heard old Brit's shuffling footsteps moving around in the house after dark. Once, when Mr. Thomas lay ill, he claimed that he clearly saw Brit Bailey in the room with him.

It was not until about the early 1850s that Bailey's glowing, ghostly image began to be seen on the prairies. Colonel Mordello Munson and several of his guests saw an eerily glowing ball of light drift slowly past his home early one evening. Saddling their horses, the colonel and his male guests gave the strange globe of glowing light a hardy pursuit but were unable to capture it or clearly identify it. From that night on, "Brit Bailey's Light" has drifted across the Texas prairies that the old settler was so reluctant to relinquish.

Alsate's Ghost Light Haunts the Chinati Mountains

Since pioneer days, night travelers in the area of the Chinati Mountains in the Cienegas Range of southwestern Texas have seen a peculiarly glowing orb about the size of a basketball that materializes, moves about, splits into twin spheres, reforms, and runs a range of light intensity varying from a mere twinkle to a blinding glare. According to area residents, the best spot for observing the ghost light is along Highway 90 between Marfa and Alpine.

Local legend attributes the source of the spook light to the spirit of the Apache chief Alsate, who was tricked into offending a tribal manitou (spirit) after he had been betrayed by some Mexican soldiers. As his eternal punishment, according to the old story, Alsate was condemned to wander the Big Bend Country of Texas, and it is the chief's glowing spirit that people see when they witness a manifestation of the spook light of the Chinati Mountains.

Some observers of the ghost light have attributed the source of the eerie illumination to the reflection of the moonlight on deposits of mica in the cliffs and crags of the mountain. However, this theory does not explain the brightly glowing ball that appears on nights when the moon is hidden behind thick cloud banks.

Some residents maintain that the spook light is seen under only two conditions: either just before or just after a rain. But others argue that they have seen the light dozens of times when the country was bone dry.

For those demanding a rational explanation for the manifestation, some clever individuals came up with the theory that the mystery light was caused by the reflection of automobile headlights coming down Paisano Pass. But others countered that hypothesis by asking how the spook light maintained a steady glow for several hours if it had to depend on the headlights of an occasional motor vehicle that may speed by? And then there is the troublesome fact that the earliest settlers and travelers in southwestern Texas mentioned seeing the ghost light. Covered wagons and stagecoaches were not known for having powerful headlights.

Whether the enigmatic light of the Chinati Mountains is caused by certain unique climatic conditions working on mineral deposits peculiar to that area or whether observers really are seeing the glowing spirit of Chief Alsate, one indisputable fact remains: the spook light is there.

The Persistent Mystery Lights of Brown Mountain

Nestled far from the nearest city of Hickory, North Carolina, the Brown Mountain region has been the dwelling place of mysterious glowing lights for well over two centuries. From sunset until dawn, globes of various colored lights, ranging in size from mere points to twenty-five feet in diameter, can be seen rising above the tall trees and flickering off again as they fall to the mountain passes below.

Brown Mountain first received national attention in the works of Charles Fort, who described how the lights would chase early settlers along the various trails that lead to the sparsely placed cities.

One of the many legends that have sprung up about the origin of the lights is that they are caused by the spirits of Cherokee and Catawba braves who search the valley for the maiden lovers they left behind when they were slain in a big battle hundreds of years ago. Some area residents believe the battle still rages between spirits of the two tribes, for they claim that they have seen the lights fighting, butting into each other, and bouncing around like extra-large basketballs.

Bizarre lights at night over Brown Mountain in North Carolina have baffled even scientists for years. Recently, a theory has sprung up that radioactive minerals beneath the mountain are the cause. There are many skeptics to this theory, however.

In 1916, skeptics tried to explain that the lights were reflections caused by the headlights on locomotives or cars running through a nearby valley. However, during the spring of that year, all bridges were knocked out by a flood, and the roads became too muddy for cars to travel—yet the Brown Mountain lights were seen in greater numbers than before.

Since the early 1900s, people have attempted to devise scientific explanations for the Brown Mountain lights. And since that time, thousands of men and women have witnessed, photographed, and had bizarre encounters with the mystery orbs. In more recent years, in addition to Native American ghosts, certain researchers have attributed the eerie lights to entities from UFOs.

It Takes Three States to Hold the Spooksville Ghost Light

One of the most famous of all ghost lights is located in the tri-state corner of Missouri, Arkansas, and Oklahoma. Spooksville's ghostly light is even advertised as a tourist attraction.

The ghost light resembles a bright lantern. Often, the light dims before the spectators, then bounces back over the mountains in a brilliant blaze of light. Hundreds of firsthand encounters with the mysterious ghost light are on record. These accounts demonstrate actual experiences with the unknown— sometimes frightening, but always interesting.

During World War II, the U.S. Corps of Engineers scoured the entire area, using the latest scientific equipment. For weeks they tested caves, mineral deposits, and highway routes, exhausting every possible explanation for the origin of the mystery lights. They finally left, confounded.

Louise G. reported coming home in a school bus from a school carnival in Quapaw, Oklahoma. A ghost light perched on the rear window of the bus as though attempting to enter. Everyone in the bus was thoroughly frightened, and several of the women were screaming. In *Ghost Lights*, a pamphlet written by Bob Loftin, Louise said that the light was so bright that it temporarily blinded the bus driver and he had to stop the bus. Just as the driver stopped, the light went away.

Chester M., a farmer near Quapaw, said that when the weather got intolerably hot, he liked to do his plowing in the evening. Chester recounted the night that the ghost light "felt real neighborly" and hovered over the field where he was plowing. Chester thought it was a good idea until the light suddenly darted directly at him. He said that he "absolutely froze stiff" to the tractor until the light sailed out of sight.

Visitations by Malevolent Spirits

Cornia recalled the time that she first encountered a shadow man when she occupied "the house from hell" in Capulin, Colorado: "There are many Hispanics and Catholics living there, and many claim that the La Lorna and shadow people also inhabit the region. A familiar saying is, 'the Devil walks the roads of Capulin.'"

Cornia said that she and her husband moved into a very old farmhouse outside of Capulin by the Conejos River. The house had very old doors without locks, and they would put knives on the door to hold it shut. Her life, she recalls, was the worst it had ever been.

"I was sitting on the sofa watching television when I heard someone open the door and walk in the kitchen," Cornia said. "I got up real quick to see a man dressed in black with a black top hat standing facing me. He just stood there and pointed at me and walked out dragging his feet out the kitchen door. I flipped the light on and went into the kitchen. No one was there. The doors were still locked with the knives."

Cornia summoned the Capulin Catholic priest to bless their home. "A nun came with him, and when she entered, she went pale and said that there was something evil in the house. She excused herself and went back to the car. The priest blessed the house, but he said we should leave the house because death was upon us."

Behave or the Cucuy Will Get You!

In the October 31, 2005, issue of the *Brownsville Herald*, Kevin Garcia writes that in the Texas border towns of Brownsville and Matamoros, mothers keep their children in line by warning, "Behave or the *cucuy* will get you."

The Cucuy has been described as a small, humanoid creature with glowing, red eyes. (Art by Bill Oliver.)

According to social sciences professor Manuel Medrano, the cucuy is a small humanoid entity with glowing red eyes. "Some lore has him as a kid who was the victim of violence ... and now he's alive, but he's not. He is childlike with red eyes and somewhere between life and death," said Medrano, citing Xavier Garza's 2004 book, *Creepy Creatures and Other Cucuys*.

Medrano also discussed the legend of La Llorona, referring to the popular ghost story. "Some people say she has blond hair and a skeleton face. Others say she has black hair and a horse face."

THE DEADLY MOJAVE DESERT SAND STORM SPECTER

Paul Dale Roberts has said that the Mojave Sand Storm Specter is one ghost you do not want to encounter. No one knows where this ghost came from or who this ghost once was as a person. All everyone knows is that this ghost is evil and may have come from the deepest depths of Hell.

On September 19, 2002, Darren Westlaw, a hunter, told Roberts that he saw three dust devils spinning through the desert. Darren found the dust devils entertaining and sat for a spell looking at them. When the dust devils finally dissipated, a wave of sand started heading his way. From the sand storm, a nightmarish cowboy stepped out of the swirling sand and proceeded to strangle Darren. The choking lasted for a few seconds but seemed like an eternity to Darren. When the cowboy ghost was gone, Darren found himself on the ground, holding his throat and heavily coughing.

Another hunter who does not want to be identified told Roberts that he encountered the murderous specter after a small dust storm. This happened on August 11, 1998. The hunter said the ghost wore a cowboy hat and his face was hideous. The ghostly cowboy placed his hands on the hunter's shoulders, and the man felt a tingling sensation throughout his body.

When the ghostly encounter was gone and everything was back to normal, the hunter felt weak. He felt as if his energy was completely depleted and drained. One week after the encounter, the man still felt weak and decided to go see a doctor. The doctor diagnosed him with stage 4 lymphoma. The hunter feels he was cursed when he encountered the Mojave Desert Sand Storm Specter. Fortunately, after extensive chemotherapy, the hunter survived his cancer ordeal. But he said he will *never* hunt in the Mojave Desert again.

THE GHOST-GODDESSES LA PHANTASMA AND LA LLORONA

By Theo Paijmans

For this book, we called upon Theo Paijmans, one of Europe's top para-normalists and investigators of the strange and the unknown to provide a detailed exploration of La Phantasma and La Llorona.

The gods are older than man, and there are ghosts older than the mortals who encounter them. When the conquistadors invaded Latin America, they were greeted by presences already ancient long before the Spanish Armada had been built. Not all ghosts are spiritual remnants of a human existence. Not all phantoms are echoes of man. Gods can become ghosts, too. And nowhere is their presence more felt than in that enchanted land of dreams and endless deserts where the dead are well remembered, the borders between Mexico and America.

Somewhere down an intersection of two dusty Texan highways, the quiet little town of Falfurrias is nestled. Hardly five thousand souls live there, and nobody knows how the town got its name and what it means. Each year hundreds of Mexicans trek to Falfurrias. They go there to honor Don Pedro Jaramillo, a Mexican *curandero* (faith healer) who died in 1907. Don Pedro is buried just outside the little town, and his shrine is a place of devout pilgrimage.

A little farther up state but still in the southern part of Texas is the bustling city of San Antonio. Many strange tales linger there. Not everyone encountered on its busy streets is of flesh and blood.

The city is old, and the air is filled with the spectral tales it tells. It is said that there was a suicide tree where the rustling was not always of the leaves. Many houses are haunted—a sudden sigh, a faint whiff of perfume, half-finished sentences whispered in empty rooms with peeling paint and plaster. There are cellars far from the light with secrets underneath the dust and the floorboards.

San Antonio is a place of ghosts and of darker things. Generations of its children have heard about the Donkey Lady, a horri-

Faith healer Don Pedro Jaramillo helped save his people in San Antonio from the lethal visit of La Phantasma.

bly disfigured woman living somewhere in a ramshackle shack in northwest San Antonio at the end of a strangely curved road. It is not pleasant to see her contortions, nor is it pleasing to hear her. She cannot speak, and her screams are terrible to endure.

One night many years ago an even more frightening thing tried to claw its way into the homes of the Mexican residents of the West Side neighborhood in San Antonio. Its arrival, it was said at the time, was predicted by Don Pedro in a letter he wrote to warn the community. And when it was averted, the apparition returned the next year.

Wednesday night, the third of May 1905, was an ill-fated night for the Mexican section of San Antonio. There was not a door without a hastily painted sign of the cross on it. The Mexican residents of West Side were in a state of fearful anticipation. The Phantasma was heading their way. It would visit all the Mexican families that same night. The unclean spirit had a terrible fate in store once it entered their homes.

The first crosses appeared before dark. They were painted and chalked up on the doors, fences, and gates in the entire Mexican section of the city. Crosses were also designed in ashes and lime on the walks that led to the door from the streets. In some places they were made of the holy palms that had been reverently carried home from the churches on Holy Palm Sunday.

La Phantasma was a terrible sight to behold. The spectral figure was ghostlike, yet more than a ghost. It was partly formless. Below the waistline there was nothing more than a vapor-like cloud. But from the waist up the mist coagulated into the shape of a tall, lean woman dressed entirely in black. But her face was hidden; her head was tightly wrapped in the folds of a black mantilla. It was said that two tired-looking children accompanied her. The Phantasma brought death and ill fortune.

Some claimed that they had seen the ghost in several sections of the West Side that night, going from door to door, drifting away when it beheld a white cross as it approached a gateway. That not everybody had seen la Phantasma, the Mexicans argued, was because she was invisible to the people who did not have a protective cross on their doors.

An old Mexican woman told a reporter from the *San Antonio Express* how a man from the westernmost part of the city had received a letter from Don Pedro. The letter had warned that la Phantasma would come to San Antonio and that the ghost woman would scatter death in her path.

As another Mexican woman explained to the reporter: "Was it not said in the letter from Pedrito that the Woman in Black would be here tonight? And has the Pedrito not always told the truth? The Phantasma is coming. The Woman in Black will this night pass the street."

Don Pedro was a highly respected spiritual beacon and source of relief for the Mexican communities. He died in 1907, two years after the reign of terror of la Phantasma. Today, he is still known and revered as the faith healer of Los Olmos Creek, and many flock to his shrine each year.

Don Pedro discovered his miraculous healing powers after he had broken his nose in an accident. On the third day of his self-administered treatment, a disembodied voice told him that God had granted him the power to heal.

All who knew him agreed that he was a good man—honest and sincere—who devoted his entire life to relieve the suffering of others. La Phantasma left, but in January the following year the Mexican section of San Antonio was again in panic. A second visitation of the wraith was expected.

Again, crosses appeared on the houses as protection. The stories of the Mexicans who had seen the woman in black were so convincing that the city police department believed them but did not know what to make of them.

There are ghosts that are remnants of things and forces older than man. La Phantasma is one such example, as is that other horrible presence, la Lllorona, the Weeping Woman. La Llorona has been known for centuries throughout California, Texas, Arizona, Mexico, and parts of Latin America. La Llorona is forever searching for her two children, whom she herself had drowned.

More than a century ago, Thomas Janvier, writing about the legends of the City of Mexico, was told: "As is generally known, señor, many bad things are met with by night in the streets of the city; but this Wailing Woman, la Llorona, is the very worst of them all…. Seeing her walking quietly along the quiet street—at the times when she is not running and shrieking for her lost children—she seems a respectable person, only odd looking because of her white petticoat and the white reboso with which her head is covered, and anybody might speak to her. But whoever does speak to her, in that very same moment, dies!"

Collecting stories about la Llorona in Mexico City, Janvier noted that such tales have been told since the sixteenth century. Around 1585, for instance, Fray Bernardino de Sahagún admonished Mexican converts to Christianity: "Your ancestors also erred in the adoration of a demon whom they represented as a woman, and whom they

An actress is shown here portraying La Llorona facing down the U.S. border patrol.

gave the name Cioacoatl. She appeared clad as a lady of the palace (clad in white). She terrified, she frightened, and cried aloud at night."

And before that, in 1550, the Weeping Woman was first heard in Mexico City, especially on moonlit nights, where a wailing figure dressed in white would vanish in a lake, folklorist Betty Leddy noted.

La Phantasma and la Llorona are no mere ghosts. They represent the terrible, mighty gods and forces older than man. Perhaps man has forgotten what was already ancient when it built its first cities, but the gods surely have not.

In his *Legends of the City of Mexico*, Janvier notes that la Llorona is a direct survivor from very ancient times. La Llorona stems from Aztec mythology. She is an ancient, powerful goddess living on, "her power for evil lessened, but still potent—into modern times." La Llorona is part of the ancient Aztec pantheon with an early, pre-Columbian body of feminine spirits and goddesses.

> Aside from descriptions of a woman with a horse's head, others hold that she is a woman dressed in black with long hair, long, shiny metal-like fingernails, and a skull face.

Nor are these ghost-goddesses confined to Latin America. Already in the sixteenth century, some very old stories were circulating in Germany of Die Weisse Frau, the White Woman, who had many similar features as la Llorona. The majority of the tales feature la Llorona as a woman clad in white. But there are quite a few intriguing accounts from around the Austin, Texas, area, where la Llorona appears in many other shapes and forms.

Two men found that out one night. They were on their way to their favorite saloon when they noticed that a very attractive woman was walking just ahead of them. They decided to follow her, but they couldn't catch up with her. When it seemed that they were coming up even with the woman, she suddenly seemed to get about half a block ahead of them. Finally, the men gave up, saying a good night. The woman whom they had followed turned around. She had the face of a horse, and her fingernails were shiny and made of a metallic substance. She gave a long and piercing cry. It was la Llorona.

Aside from descriptions of a woman with a horse's head, others hold that she is a woman dressed in black with long hair, long, shiny metallic fingernails, and a skull face. "A few believe that she is a vampire that sucks its victim's blood. The majority insist that she is a woman dressed in white with long black hair, long fingernails, and the face of a bat," Wilson M. Hudson wrote in *The Healer of Los Olmos and Other Mexican Lore*.

There are many stories of horribly disfigured donkey ladies living in labyrinthine cul-de-sacs, of horse-headed wraiths with metal claws accosting drunken stalkers, and of shrieking spectres in white or black running through the endless night. The terrible ghost-goddesses la Phantasma and la Llorona occupy contrasting niches in these tales. La Phantasma does not weep or wail, but la Llorona does. Two children accompany la Phantasma. La Llorona, however, perpetually searches for what la Phantasma has captured: two little lost souls.

In this pantheon, where the ancient gods have transformed into twentieth-century demonic monstrosities, la Phantasma and la Llorona claim their rightful and unique places. In modern times, we often tend to forget what came before and what lies beneath. These ghost-goddesses—powerful presences from another world—remind us of that uncertain but precious place we briefly occupy, lodged between the eternal night and the abyss of time.

CAN A PARANORMAL ENCOUNTER LEAD TO SERIOUS PHYSICAL HARM?

The report of the following bizarre case may provide a warning for any "ghostbuster" to exercise caution in seeking to become a participant in any paranormal scene.

Scott Corrales, founder of the Institute of Hispanic Ufology, learned of a strange and disturbing case in Peru from a Peruvian physician named Raul Rios Centeno. Reportedly, Centeno had a thirty-year-old patient who had experienced very unusual symptoms and told a peculiar story describing how the onset of those symptoms had occurred. Centeno, in his own words, wrote:

"It was a very strange case of hemiplegia, since upon examination with a CAT (computerized axial tomography) scan, there were no areas showing bleeding vessels nor any traumatic lesions. When I began asking questions about the case, the patient told me the following: 'I was at a campground in the vicinity of Marcahuasi (the famous stone forest located some 56 km [35 miles] east of Lima) when I went out exploring late at night with some friends. Oddly enough, we heard the strains of music and noticed a small torch-lit shack. I was able to see people dancing inside, but upon getting closer I felt a sudden sensation of cold, which I paid little attention to, and I stuck my head through an open door. It was then that I saw the occupants were clad in seventeenth-century fashion. I tried to enter the room, but one of my girlfriends pulled me out.'

"The patient was tugged out by one of her friends, and her body became paralyzed precisely as she was drawn out of the 'shack.' My conclusion is that the probable cause behind the hemiplegia is unknown. No medical test was able to ascertain its cause. Nonetheless, an EEG was able to show that the left hemisphere of the brain did not show signs of normal functioning, as well as an abnormal amount of electric waves."

Regarding the CAT scan results, Centeno also shared with Corrales the following: "Intact intracranial regions without any specific area having been compromised. There is neither swelling nor color changes, which may suggest some manner of trauma. The clinician certifying this exam cannot find a justified cause for the hemiplegia in the left hemisphere, due to the fact

Marcahuasi is a volcanic plateau in the Andes Mountains famous for its many formations resembling human heads and animal figures.

its vascularization and irrigation fall within parameters considered to be normal. The EEG shows areas evidently paralyzed due to the lack of electric current transmission. These tests lead me to believe—and this is my personal opinion, since my colleagues have simply catalogued it as an 'unknown affliction'—that the dimensional shift, or 'partial entry' of this person into this anomalous zone, (was) able to produce a change in the energy flow existing in her nervous system, or perhaps even a change in the type of energy. Given that the cranial area is where our nerve impulses are contained—in other words, the right cerebral hemisphere controls the left side of the body and vice versa—this could be the reason why the left hand autonomous nervous system did not at all affect the operation of crucial organs such as the heart or the stomach, which are governed by the right cerebral hemisphere."

A DISRUPTIVE SPIRIT
MADE ITS HOME IN THE ELEGANT CHAIRS

Graham D. M., who now lives in Canada, recalled an incident when he was a boy in London, England, when his mother came into the possession of some elegant chairs that brought with them a very disruptive spirit.

"After my mum was given some antique, embroidered, silk, high-back, Victorian armchairs, it was soon evident why they were given away," Graham said. "An old man had obviously owned the chairs in the past, as my mum and I both saw him sitting in the largest of the chairs. Ghostly events went on with the chairs for some time, and concluded with my mum being thrown from one of them across the room."

Graham ran straight away to the vicarage and brought back the vicar. When he returned to their residence, the vicar at his side, they found Graham's mother upset and a little bruised. And, he noted, the chairs were still banging on the floor.

The vicar sent Graham back to the vicarage for the night. Graham admitted that he went gladly. The vicar's wife and his housekeeper set him up for the night, and he slept in front of the fire on rugs with an eiderdown blanket on him.

"When I returned home," Graham recalled, "the two chairs were in the spare bedroom. My mum was fairly tight-lipped about the entire ordeal and simply said, 'the vicar solved the problem.'"

Graham noted, however, that the chairs continued to gently bang the floor for about three more weeks before they suddenly stopped.

A PORTAL WHERE SPIRITS OF THE DEAD WAIT TO ENTER

N. M. writes about an eerie situation that keeps cropping up with his daughter Selina (not her real name), whom he describes as "eleven years old, very bright, and very gifted spiritually." Selina had been able to see people's auras for years, but recently she claimed to be able to see a "portal" situated in the bathroom at the northern end of their house. According to Selina, spirits of the dead lined up in order of their death and wait to enter the portal to "who knows where."

"I believed that she really was telling the truth, N. M. said, "and really was seeing something that I could not."

Then, one day in May 2004, Selina came running to her father after arriving home from school to declare that the portal had changed. The "people" didn't have to wait and jump into the portal; now the portal just sucked them in as they approached it.

> The "people" didn't have to wait and jump into the portal; now the portal just sucked them in as they approached it.

The father and daughter went immediately to the bathroom, where Selina said she could clearly see the people lined up awaiting their turn to be drawn into the portal. Selina said that the people could see her just as she could see them, but verbal communication was impossible.

Shortly before N. M. sent his account of the mysterious portal to us, his wife had encountered a young woman, dripping wet, standing in front of the door to the bathroom. It was as if some force prevented the spirit of the woman from entering the portal at that time.

N. M. and his wife were chilled by the thought that the ghost of the woman could have been one of those murdered on their property many years before their occupancy. They had always suspected that not all of the bodies of the victims of a murderous rampage had been found. The police had wanted to continue to dredge the nearby lake years before, but they had abandoned the effort because of the blackness and depth of the water.

Perhaps sometime soon, the apparent victim of the murders on the property will be permitted to enter the portal that exists in the home of the N. M. family.

SUZETTE FOUGHT OFF AN ATTACK BY MALIGNANT SPIRITS

Suzette B. told of a frightening encounter with malignant spirits one morning that began as usual with her husband getting up for work at 5:30 A.M.

She had decided to stay in bed a bit longer, and as she was drifting off to sleep, she heard strange sounds coming up and around the bed.

"It sounded like the snorting and snuffing sounds that pigs make when they have found a special treat to eat," Suzette recalled. "It sounded like there were five or six of them. I felt them climb onto the bed. The sheets depressed, and I could feel the weight of them on the bed. I tried to move and push them away."

The next thing Suzette was aware of was a "sharp, blinding knife flash of pain" in the back of her head. She screamed at her invisible attackers to leave her alone.

She struggled and pushed her invisible attackers aside as she sat up and looked around to an empty room. It was 6:03 A.M. Her head hurt where she had been struck, and the spot was tender for several days. Her husband didn't know what to think when she told him of her frightening experience.

Suzette's evaluation of her encounter was that she had a suffered a psychic attack.

"I did some research and realized that my life had changed in a negative way during the past year or so," she said. "I used to pay attention to visualizations, prayer, and protective white light, but my spiritual life had begun to slip away. The whole experience was a real wake-up call.

"In retrospect," she concluded, "the frightening encounter had a positive effect. I had a daylight exorcism of sorts, a real opening of all my blocked emotion gates, when I was attacked by an evil entity that tried to take over my persona. My husband helped me through it, and I actually felt a spiritual and physical lift in my body. My attitude toward people in general is like I used to be. No more harboring dark thoughts."

THE SOCIETY FOR PSYCHICAL RESEARCH BEGINS IN LONDON, 1882

Although people have been reporting seeing ghosts and the spirits of the dead since our earliest historical records of human activity, the first organized effort to study such phenomena occurred in 1882, as the first major undertaking of the newly formed Society for Psychical Research (SPR) in London. By means of a circulated questionnaire, the SPR asked whether its recipients had ever, when they believed themselves to be completely awake, experienced some kind of visual or auditory phenomena. Of the 17,000 people who responded, 1,684 answered "yes." From this, the committee members who were conducting the survey estimated that nearly ten percent of the population of London had undergone some kind of paranormal manifestation, and they sent forms requesting additional details to all those who had indicated such encounters. Subsequent investigation and interviews enabled the early psychical researchers to arrive at a number of basic premises regarding ghosts.

For example, the committee was able to conclude that although ghosts are connected with other events besides death, they are more likely to be linked with death than with anything else. Visual sightings of ghosts were the most common, and of such cases reported, nearly one-quarter had been shared by more than one percipient. Those who answered the second form of the questionnaire requesting more information stated that they had not been ill when they had witnessed the paranormal visitations, and they insisted that these manifestations were quite unlike the bizarre, nightmarish creatures that might appear during high fevers or high alcoholic consumption. Of those cases in which the percipients had experienced auditory phenomena, such as hearing voices, one-third were collective, that is, witnessed by more than one percipient at the same time.

The logo of the Society for Psychical Research in London, the first nonprofit organization of its type in the world.

After the findings of the research committee had been made public, the SPR began to be flooded by personal accounts of spontaneous cases of ghosts and spirits. In order to aid the committee in the handling of such an influx of information, the SPR worked out a series of questions that could be applied to each case that came in. Among the questions were the following: Is the account firsthand? Has the principal witness been corroborated? Was the percipient awake at the time? Was the apparition recognized? Was the percipient anxious or in a state of expectancy? Could relevant details have been read back into the narrative after the event?

And today, 135 years after the British Society for Psychical Research began its earnest efforts to chart and categorize ghosts, what percentage of London's population believes in ghosts? According to a survey released on March 20, 2000, by television station GMTV in London, 42 percent believe in ghosts, and almost half of this number said that they had seen or felt the presence of a ghost.

SO YOU REALLY WANT TO BE A GHOSTBUSTER?

On the oppressively hot Saturday of May 17, 2008, an HPI ghost hunter-in-training we will call Mae came all the way from San Jose, California, to Paul Dale Roberts's home to do some ghost hunting in the small town of Ione.

Their first stop was the Ione Hotel, where they introduced themselves to Jennifer Leigh Collado, the hotel manager and head housekeeper. Jennifer was willing to take them on a grand tour of the hotel. The hotel was built in 1877, she said, and she had worked there since February 2008 and loved her job!

"The short time that she has worked here," Roberts recalled, "she had already experienced strange things. Once she was locked in Room 2. She heard the door click behind her, and after twisting the doorknob a few times, she knew she was trapped in this room. The hotel staff below came running up the stairs to help her, and no one could get the door open. She was trapped in this room for two hours and finally had to go out the window. Once, while walking down the hallway, the lights would either get dimmer or brighter and seemed to follow her down the hallway. She has seen shadowy figures run past her. In Room 4, the chandeliers spun around on their own accord."

> Room 13 is a strange room and Jennifer told them how two guests woke up and found themselves speaking in a strange language.

Jennifer told Paul that the hotel had caught fire in 1884 and 1893. George Williams, a guest of the hotel, died in one of the fires, and some patrons believe that George still patrols the hallways of the hotel. Another victim of the fire was the baby of Mary Phelps, who got caught in the fire and screamed for her baby to be saved.

Jennifer opened up Room 13 and showed them the infamous "upside down black rose" that is on the wall. Hotel personnel have tried to wash the upside down rose off, but it still appears. Room 13 is a strange room, and Jennifer told them how two guests woke up and found themselves speaking in a strange language.

Mae and Paul were now parched and decided to inhale some sodas at the Pizza Factory before making their next move. "After we quenched our thirst, we headed over to the Preston Castle to meet Marie Nutting, president of the Preston Castle Foundation," Roberts said. "Marie explained that the castle was the first correctional youth facility in California."

"The place does look like a castle," Roberts wrote in his report. "I have seen many castles in Europe, and this building can be compared to some European castles. It was built in 1894. Some people think that this castle has about three or four ghosts residing inside. One of the stories is that an employee was kicked to death by an inmate during the '50s. Her ghost may be one of the resident ghosts. Many inmates have died here, and not too far away is an inmate cemetery with about twenty-three graves. Many people have felt strange things when entering this castle."

THE VICIOUS SPIRIT WHO SOUGHT TO KILL

There can be no malevolent spirit more horrible than one that physically attacks individuals, tries to hold them down and smother them, and seems only to want to create violence and horror. Sherry and I were privileged to know personally a number of the principal investigators in this remarkable haunting that echoes the terror wrought in the film The Entity with Barbara Hershey (1982) and to interview them after their ordeal.

On August 8, 1989, television cameraman Barry Conrad was asked to accompany respected psychical investigator Dr. Barry Taff and a number of other researchers to a reputed haunted house in San Pedro, California. Conrad accepted the assignment in the hope that he might be able to capture some authentic paranormal phenomena on videotape. He ended up getting far more frightening footage than he could have foreseen in his wildest imaginings.

When the group of researchers arrived at the alleged haunted house, Jackie Hernandez, the woman who had requested the investigation, told them of lamps and other objects flying across rooms, the apparition of a decaying elderly man in the children's bedroom, and a ghostly, disembodied head in the attic.

Conrad considered her accounts to be a bit unbelievable, and Jeff Wheatcraft, the photographer he had brought to assist him, proclaimed him-

In addition to the floating head in the attic, a rotting elderly man was haunting the children's bedroom in Jackie Hernandez's home (not an actual photo).

self a complete skeptic of things ghostly and otherworldly. Disbelief and skepticism would soon disappear.

Shortly after Wheatcraft ascended into the attic opening by standing atop a washing machine in the small laundry room at the rear of the house, all those assembled below heard his screams of terror. *Something*, he declared after he had jumped down from the attic, had pulled his Canon 35mm camera from his hands.

Despite his fright and his decreasing skepticism, Wheatcraft joined Conrad in another foray into the attic. The two photographers crawled up into the overhead space, videotape rolling, ready to record anything between heaven and earth that might be occupying the darkened recesses of the attic.

Then, as Conrad states in his report of the haunting, without warning, his camera went dead. Although he quickly replaced the batteries, the camera remained inoperative. "Usually when a battery goes out, the green pilot light will change to red with the picture gradually fading to black," he noted. "In this case, the pilot light failed altogether, a highly unusual occurrence."

Wheatcraft found the camera that had been "taken" from him in a dusty old grape box in the northwest corner of the attic. Eerily, though, the lens had been removed and placed in a space just behind the trap door to the attic.

Just then a foul stench permeated the attic space, and Wheatcraft emitted another scream that something was touching him, and he stumbled toward the attic's trap door. Somehow the two photographers managed to get down from the attic to safety below without falling and injuring themselves. Shaken, Wheatcraft stated that what felt like a bony hand had applied tremendous pressure to his lower back.

Once downstairs, Conrad's camera began again to function, and he was able to record what sounded like the heavy footsteps of an angry giant thundering across the attic floor. When Wheatcraft stood on the washing machine to peer into the attic crawlspace, he shouted in awe that he was seeing three brilliant flashes of light and then an eerie black mass "the size of three adult men standing side by side."

According to Conrad's report, for days afterward Wheatcraft continued to suffer pain in his lower back from the pressure that had been applied by the "bony hand," and when he visited a chiropractor, it was confirmed that his lower back had indeed suffered massive internal bruising.

Nearly a month later, on the evening of September 4, Conrad received a desperate call from Hernandez. She said that she was undergoing a vicious poltergeistic siege in her home. A soft drink can had been thrown at her while doors opened and slammed closed of their own volition. The night before, she claimed, an "invisible force" had held her down on the floor for several minutes and attempted to smother her.

Wheatcraft and another friend, Gary Boehm, happened to be visiting Conrad at his apartment when they all heard Jackie's frantic call. They decided that they must leave at once for San Pedro and do their best to help the beleaguered woman and her two small children.

The men arrived in San Pedro around 1:00 A.M. At first, everything in the bungalow seemed to be calm. Then Wheatcraft wanted to show Boehm the grape box in the attic, where he had discovered his camera after it had mysteriously vanished from his hands.

Conrad remained downstairs in the laundry room with Jackie and her neighbor, Susan. Then, Conrad said, "A bright orange comet of light suddenly flashed before us and flew through a small door that led outside."

A loud moan emanated from above them in the attic. It was Wheatcraft's voice crying out that he had to get out of there. *"It's put something around my neck!"*

"My heart almost froze with fear as I noticed a weathered clothesline cord dangling from my friend's swollen neck as he stiffly emerged from the [attic] hole above,"

In this reenactment of the dangerous experience, Jeff Wheatcraft found himself hanging by the neck in the attic of the Hernandez home. Fortunately, he was rescued before it was too late.

Conrad wrote in his report of the harrowing experience. "It was at this instant that we all felt the pangs of incredible disbelief."

According to Boehm, who had come to Wheatcraft's rescue, something had wrapped a clothesline cord tightly around Jeff's neck and then hanged him on a nail protruding from one of the rafter beams. "If I had not been there," Boehm said, "Jeff would have been strangled in that attic. He didn't know what was going on, and the cord was wrapped so tightly that it was very difficult to get him down. I had to bend the nail in order to release him."

Wheatcraft was left with red friction burns encircling his neck as a result of the attack by the vicious entity. Later, when Conrad examined the tapes of that evening, he was startled to observe a "bright comet of light" traveling through a doorway behind Wheatcraft shortly after the bizarre hanging episode.

"Another orb of light can be seen buzzing over the top of Jeff's head while standing in the living room discussing his ordeal," Conrad said. "And yet another light was found zooming across the kitchen above Susan moments after Wheatcraft had descended from the attic space."

"In the history of paranormal research," Dr. Barry Taff has observed, "there have only been a handful of cases in which phenomena have deliberately and maliciously attacked human beings. And [the San Pedro poltergeist case] is one of them."

ARE THERE ALWAYS MALEVOLENT CREATURES LYING IN WAIT TO CAPTURE THE INNOCENT?

Growing up in a small town in Iowa as I did, one's classmates on his or her first day in school remain largely consistent all through the years from elementary school, to junior high, to the momentous senior year. A few kids move out of town with their families, a few move in from country schools or other areas, but, essentially, the scholars with whom you began the quest for knowledge are still standing beside you in your caps and gowns on graduation day.

A friend we will call Clarice was a quiet girl—modest, sincere, and kind. Although she was shy and seldom spoke in groups, she always had a smile to share with everyone.

Our community was composed of nearly 100 percent Scandinavian Americans, with a couple of German American Roman Catholic families thrown into the mix. Clarice was a particularly devout person, and she confided in me that she wanted so much to become a Lutheran pastor, but, back in the 1940s and 1950s, the bishops had not made the societal-religious leap that would permit women in the pulpit. Clarice graduated from college, married a professor at a local university, and sublimated her yearning to serve the Lord by working as a librarian at her church.

When Clarice learned that Sherry was an ordained Lutheran minister and a former staff member of the Lutheran School of Theology in Chicago, she had to meet my bride as soon as possible.

We lived in Phoenix at that time, and arrangements were made for the three of us to go out for dinner when Clarice arrived from the Midwest.

Shortly before dinner, our daughter returned from school and in a panic wondered why Sherry didn't have the makings for the backyard cookout prepared. Although neither of us recalled that the high school cheer squad was arriving at our home for a barbeque, Sherry had no choice but to switch quickly into mother mode and begin preparing for the onslaught of teenaged girls.

Clarice was visibly disappointed when I arrived with Sherry, but, true to her always polite and loving nature, she quickly recovered her always calm composure, and we were soon all laughing about old memories of our hometown.

However, after a half hour or so of "catching-up," she became very serious. Not only did she wish to speak to Sherry about the possibilities of entering the clergy, she had to tell us something that she could contain no longer. She knew that we sometimes wrote about spooky and weird subjects, so she was certain that we would not laugh at her.

Clarice and her family lived on a farm that had quite a luxurious growth of trees, berry bushes, and other flora. When she knew that she was alone at home, she would go out to their grove, climb up on a tree trunk, and practice giving sermons. Even as a young girl, the power was in her, and she would praise the Lord to all of nature.

Then, late one afternoon when she was filled with the Holy Spirit, she saw a strange rustling in the bushes. Before her disbelieving eyes, she beheld strange and hideous creatures emerging from behind trees and under fallen trees, and also from peculiar holes in the ground. Their faces were grotesque, resembling reptiles the likes of which did not slither through Iowa fields. Their voices made horrible grating, growling sounds.

Then it became obvious to Clarice that they were beginning to surround the tree trunk on which she stood. Their open mouths displayed awful fangs and long tongues.

Clarice jumped from the trunk and began to run for their farmhouse. She now regretted that she waited to begin her sermon until she was home alone. She was somewhat relieved when she noticed that the sunlight appeared to halt the demonic creatures at the edge of the grove. Soon she was safe inside the house.

> Then, late one afternoon when she was filled with the Holy Spirit, she saw a strange rustling in the bushes. Before her disbelieving eyes, she beheld strange and hideous creatures emerging from under fallen trees....

When she had completed recounting her misadventure with the creatures of darkness, I agreed that she had most certainly had a dangerous adventure that could have ended very badly.

The story admittedly will border on the fantastic to many, but I have known Clarice since I was five years old. Not once did I ever hear her recount some wild and crazy story. In fact, I don't think I ever heard her tell a joke. And not in a hundred years could I imagine her telling a lie.

Could it have been her purity of soul that attracted these hideous, uninvited creatures from the dark side and prompted their rage at a young, innocent girl shouting her praises to God?

Night Terrors
That Shake the Psyche

Suzanne R. grew up in a very haunted funeral home and saw spirits constantly as a girl. Although she went through some frightening experiences, today she is a medium, and spirits seek her out to convey messages to her loved ones.

Understandably, as a child, Suzanne said that she was terrified of her ghostly encounters. "There were some unsavory entities that had taken up residence in the funeral home," she recalled. When I used to practice out-of-body travels, I discovered a plane of existence that one must pass through that is filled with these types. I learned how to bypass that place, but I believe that I was shown the psychic location so I could understand the face of its existence."

As she grew older, she was able to read books on the paranormal, but she never met anyone with her deep interest in the spirit world or who shared her abilities until she was in her twenties.

"When I was fourteen," Suzanne told us, "I was diagnosed as paranoid schizophrenic and placed in an institution. There was a woman worker there who recognized that I was psychic and had me released. She was able to comprehend that I was seeing auras, and she even taught me about them. She confirmed that predictions that I was foreseeing taking place in the institution had actually occurred. Thank God for that woman!"

Although today she has an understanding of the phenomena that occurs around her and has very little fear of any encounters, there are occasions when she must draw upon her mediumistic abilities.

"Recently, on a paranormal investigation, a disruptive entity followed me home," she said. "It was extremely oppressive and it took a long time to rid me of its influence. Back in my twenties, there was a spirit in the house where I lived that tried to choke me."

Suzanne has learned to handle the "nasties" in the other dimensions and accepts that she has been blessed with the supernatural gift of grace and the ability to receive it. "The majority of the time," she said, "I can see the interconnectedness of all things and understand that I am part of the Divine."

THREE TROUBLESOME ENTITIES AND A DARK PRESENCE

HPI Paranormal Investigators present: Deborah Baughman, Kathy Foulk, Angelita Reyes (psychic), and Gwen Johnson (freelance reporter). Lead investigator: Paul Dale Roberts.

Betty F. and Cassandra B. moved into a home in Sacramento and discovered that the home was haunted by four entities. The four troublesome entities were a mother and daughter, a small dog, and a dark presence.

They had lived in this home for three months, and in the first week, they felt a haunting presence. Betty felt there was something wrong with the home before they even moved in. Some of the problems they endured in this home were:

1. Lights would dim and go completely off on their own.
2. The bedroom door would shut closed by itself.
3. Messages were erased from the telephone answering machine.
4. The occupants were touched.
5. Woman entity was seen; she was thin and had gray hair.
6. Woman entity had a daughter and the daughter seemed sad and depressed.

Among the many paranormal activities at the house, clock hands would spin around inexplicably.

Note: They learned from their neighbors that an older woman who lived in this house had died from a terminal illness and that her daughter, in her thirties, committed suicide by a possible drug overdose. The neighbors told the occupants that the mother and daughter lived in the home for twenty-six years. The neighbors said that they had a small dog that had died in this home, too.

Other tenants who subsequently lived in this home did not stay for very long. There were tenants who ran out of the home late in the evening and packed up and left. One of the tenants was screaming when she ran out into the street.

Other paranormal activity they reported:

1. Clock hands spun around.

2. Dishes slammed down to the floor.

3. Growling noises were heard.

4. Plumbing sounds were heard in the bathroom. It sounded as if plumbers were working on the pipes. The sound emitting from the bathroom was very loud.

Betty has been threatened by the dark presence. She felt like she was pushed down while walking in the kitchen. She had a hard time breathing. Another night, she was lying in bed and her cane lifted up and was pointed to her face. She could see a black mass on the ceiling. Again, she had a hard time breathing.

Betty said that a dark entity had been with her for thirty years and that this had all started in Reno. The dark entity wore a black trench coat. Its face was in shadows and it wore a black brimmed hat. Betty felt this dark entity was protective, and she does not believe it is the same dark entity that had been attacking her in a home in Sacramento.

The worst event in this home happened on the night when Betty felt that she was attacked by the dark entity. She felt multiple stabbing pains from the being. Another note for this story was that the paranormal activity increased during the renovation of this home.

First Session Evidence Gathered: Before she learned that there was a dog entity in the home, Angelita picked up on the little entity and felt it nipping at her leg. Deborah felt an invisible presence touch her while she was in the kitchen. A dark shadow anomaly showed up in one photograph.

Second Session Evidence Gathered: An electronic voice phenomenon (EVP) sounded like Darth Vader talking from another dimension, trying to say complete sentences, but words were inaudible. More shadowy anomalies were seen in photographs. Angelita, Deborah, Kathy, and Gwen were sitting on the master bedroom bed, and the bed felt as if it was breathing, moving up and down. A spirit box was used, with such words as *suicide* and *cancer* heard when asked, "How did

A spirit box captured the voice of someone who sounded like Darth Vader if the Sith lord were speaking from another dimension.

you die?" When asked how many entities were in the house, the answer was twelve, and this was said three times. *Note:* We do not regard a spirit box as substantial evidence. Angelita channeled the mother entity, who, through Angelita, asked, "Do you want to feel my pain?"

Third Session Evidence Gathered: Paul Dale Roberts took a series of pictures in the front yard and in one part of the backyard. Suddenly, he felt a quick suffocation and he snapped a picture. There was something half in darkness and the other half was in light. A second and third shot was taken.

"The third picture was normal," Paul said, "and I felt no suffocation. Most of the investigators felt they were touched one way or another. Even I felt like a ghostly finger stroked my forehead. A Catholic blessing was conducted to cleanse the home and send any entities into the light."

Note: The email below has been edited somewhat for spelling and grammar to make it more readable for audiences.

————Original Message————

From: airbrain3@aol.com

To: timewalker2@netins.net

Sent: Saturday, January 19, 2008 11:11 PM

Subject: Erica from (De) Paranormal Help

Mr. and Mrs Steiger:

I know you may not remember my call from the Radio show on Saturday 19th of January because it cut off right before I was getting to my question, and I really hope this message gets to you both. I think you might be able to give me some advice on my problems with the paranormal activity in my home. And if you talk with Grant and Jason please tell them that I'm sorry. Also my phone loves to cut off, and e-mail seems to go astray when I try and speak out about my experiences because it's done this more than once (with no certain cause) I guess I have a bit of bad luck. Also now that I think of it … bad things seem to happen when I talk about it. So, now back to my problem, which I really hope you both can help with. I've tried so hard to get help, but it seems to return quite often.

Well I guess I should start from the beginning. A few years back my sister and I were "playing" with a Ouige (sorry about the spelling) Board. and well we thought it was just a game, but soon found out that it really wasn't. That was mainly ignorance on my part. When shortly after weird occurrences began to happen. It was little at first, Like footsteps in the hall and on the ceiling. They would be loud thuds, like someone wearing boots or heavy shoes. Or hearing wind chimes inside the house when we knew it was impossible because we had no wind chimes in or outside for that matter. Then things start to get more strange.

I remember one night while I was in bed I started to stare into a dark corner of my room. The light from the hallway casts a shadow in a certain corner of my room. Now I was fine with it and I was about to close my eyes when I noticed that the shadow began to get darker and darker. I couldn't quite understand what was happening so I just continued to stare. Then the shadow almost took up the entire corner and I could see a silhouette of a person. Fear sunk in at this point, and I could feel him staring right through me. Like he struck the fear within me. I know that may sound strange but you seemed like a very understanding man [Brad] on the show, so I think you might understand me here. Anyway ... I then saw this "shadow" man step out into the light and everything was visible except for the features of his face. It was "blacked out" so to speak. From what I could tell about his clothing (from researching) was that he was a revolutionary officer. I could remember everything about what he wore down to the golden buttons. Then he walked right past my bed and out into the hallway. He seemed like an intelligent sort of shadow person or spirit. I was extremely scared, and didn't tell anyone about it for a while.

I'm not sure whether it's the same "shadow" person or not but since then I've seen it quite often. Sometimes in the living room and it even ran across what is now my room (while the room light was on). My sister was the one that was in the back room and yelled for me just when it happened. I see him or it mainly in the daytime or while the lights were on. To be honest I can't explain it as hard as I try to debunk this. And he seems to be a common occurrence.

I also saw a figure to a woman in a white gown float down my hallway. My sister has also seen her once. We don't know how to explain it, but to say it was a spirit or a ghost. I'm sorry I don't go into much detail about it but there are a lot of things that I would like to discuss and I don't want to take up too much time.

And also a little boy and girl have been see in my home. The boy mostly, but they both seem harmless, and I do not hate that they are in the house. I just live with it. I have personally seen the boy in my niece's room and he was knelt alongside a doll house that she had at the time (almost as though he were playing with it.) The boy has also been seen outside of the house by my sister's boyfriend. He was standing by her boyfriend's car as if he wanted to take a ride inside of it. I've also heard both the boy and girl laughing together from the hallway. My sister's boyfriend has heard the girl giggle while he was in the bathroom. I think that made him more uncomfortable about the house. Also, in regards to the children like spirits I've heard my nieces Gameboy playing as if someone was playing it, but as soon as I would get the Gameboy the noise would stop just as I saw that it was off the whole time. As in regards of the girl I was watching TV one day and I caught something out of the corner of my eye. When I turned I saw a blue ribbon floating freely coming from my parents' room. I blinked a couple times, but it was still there. But when I turned to the TV just when I heard a commercial coming on and turned back it was gone. I went in to investigate and there was no sign of this ribbon that I have seen.

I've also had my hair lifted up while I was in the shower. It caught me off guard but by that time I was used to and accepted that I lived alongside these spirits. Things have also moved and lights flickered on and off. Now when these things happen I don't panic I just accept it, but there are things … that are harder to accept.

The darker things began only a couple years ago and things seemed to spike after a horrible but extremely vivid nightmare I had. It was worse than any nightmare I could ever have. I didn't know what fear was until the end of that "dream" I won't go into too much detail unless you would want to know (it might help it might not it's up to you both). But in the dream there was a desert and when I woke up I could feel the sand still on my face. Now I don't panic from dreams. I'm a very grounded person, or try to be, and I've never done that before then and I was honestly trying to convince myself that it was just that. A dream. But it proved to me that it was more than that after something touched my face right after the dream. It's a long story and I think it would make more sense if you knew the dream, but to make a long story short I honestly couldn't get over it. Especially after the fact that after the dream for about 5-6 days straight I would see shadow creatures (from the dream) follow me in the house. I know this sounds like I'm crazy and that's what I honestly thought, and believe me I've been through the "am I crazy" stage a few times.

Then I would be out in public places and see people with no whites in their eyes. Their eyes would be totally black. It scared me at first and I've learned just to ignore it in order to keep me sane. Then after I began to doubt that demons or dark spirits exist worse things would happen. I would see candles bleed, but when I looked at them later things would be fine. I just thought it was my imagination, and then one night I was in the shower and I said that enough was enough, that "demons did not exist." All of sudden I began choking. I was extremely afraid. It felt like I was being choked from the inside out. (if that makes any sense) It would not stop until I said that "they did exist." Another time I was sitting down and in the house by myself and just out of nowhere it felt like something reached into my chest and began to squeeze my heart. I thought I was having a panic attack or heart attack, but I've actually experienced a panic attack before, and this was different. It felt like something was trying to pull my heart out of my chest. I'm trying to say this with as much seriousness as possible, and I can only hope you believe my story. My heart beat slowed, and my view turned dark for about 5-10 seconds straight. I honestly thought that this was it, and I asked for God the great spirit to spare me. I begged him and as soon as I said that the pain started to subside.

Also once I was woken to a loud hissing growl coming from the middle of my room. I turned but nothing was there. I then heard scratching on the wall at the head of my bed. I didn't know what to make of it. Another night I was about to go to sleep and heard people screaming as I closed my eyes. I could hear two people screaming and two people in the foreground arguing. I was speechless. I couldn't explain it. Everyone was asleep that night ... so I thought it was my imagination, but I knew that it wasn't.

I later went to the doctor about the pain in my chest and about how I became so pale and weak (when this darker sort of activity started to take place.) He ran some tests and looked me up and down. He told me afterwards that I was fine. And that the pressure or pain could be acid reflux disease. It didn't explain any of it in my eyes. I then did my own research and couldn't find any disease that corresponds medically with what was happening with me. I took the medicine and it quite honestly didn't work. After trying to explain this medically for all this time I've had no real answers. Please I come to you both, Jason, and Grant as a last resort. I've tried some of the advice that people have given me from the message boards on the TAPS website and some of it seems to work for a little bit and then it seems to come back. I would take any advice you both would give or even if you could get in touch with Jason and or Grant again and tell them my story. It would've been the one I would've told on the radio but in fewer words and less detail. I'm just worried about these things and I hope that nothing will happen to my niece. I try to be her protector.... I'm like her mother figure, and If I can't protect myself from this dark entity I don't know if I'll be able to protect her. Please I hope you get this message, and I hope you understand and have insight for my situation.

Sincerely,
Erica Ansbach

Ghosts Invaded Her Dream House

Our late friend Rita Gallagher (1921–2004), a popular romance novelist, was a charming expression of positive energy personified. She was crowned Miss Michigan at age nineteen and never stopped achieving accolades. She and several other highly recognized romance novelists—Rita Clay Estrada (her daughter), Parris Afton Bonds, Sondra Stanford, and Peggy Cleaves—created the Romance Writers of America, holding its first-ever conference in 1981 at The Woodlands, Texas.

In late September 1984, Rita moved into an old Victorian mansion in the small central Texas town of Navasota. For years she had made no secret of her desire to establish a writer's retreat, for in addition to being the author of such novels as *Passion Star*, *Shadows on the Wind*, and *Shadowed Destiny*, Rita was a highly respected teacher of writing. She knew that her students would love learning in the rambling old mansion, so she leased the house with an option to buy.

Regretfully, no one at the real estate agency bothered to tell her that the house hadn't been lived in for more than ten years—or that it was haunted.

Her first night in the old mansion explained why the lease price had been so reasonable. Shortly after 3:00 A.M., there came a rustling sound in the back hall. Then she heard slow footsteps, with one foot dragging, making their way from the front hall between the bedrooms and descending the main staircase.

Rita said that she peered up and down the corridor—and even ventured out to the bannister—but she saw nothing. There were only the sounds of an invisible presence descending the broad staircase.

And then suddenly she was looking into the sad eyes of a young man with shaving cream on his face—who then promptly disappeared.

Recalling the startling occurrence in a diary that she later sent to us, Rita said, "I wouldn't have been afraid if he had stayed and talked with me. But his sudden appearance and disappearance made my first night in the house a terrifying one."

When morning came, Rita tested the steps. "The third one down was a creaking one. A board on the top landing had a different sound, and the fourth step above the lower landing creaked more loudly than the others."

Navasota, Texas (city hall shown here), has been called the "Blues Capital of Texas." Romance author Rita Gallagher would discover the peaceful town is also no stranger to ghosts.

The next evening, shortly after 3:00 A.M., when the creaking sounds came again, Rita was able to determine the location of the ghost's descent to the main floor.

"The ghostly walk ended in the kitchen," she said. "Until dawn, the sound of rattling pots, pans, and dishes echoed faintly throughout the house. Then the ghost made the trip back upstairs and, with a rustling sound, vanished into the back hall."

Ghost or no ghost, Rita could not afford to lose her investment. And she had a book to write. She decided to work around the ghost and live out the lease.

The next day, she tried to hire a maid and was informed in no uncertain tones that there wasn't a maid in town who would even enter the house, much less work in it.

Haunted: Malevolent Ghosts, Night Terrors, and Threatening Phantoms

Rita slept very little in the next two weeks. Then she realized that the ghost's pattern never really changed and that it never walked until shortly after 3:00 A.M.

And it never entered her room. She could sleep until that time each night without disturbance.

With clockwork regularity, after 3:00 A.M. the halls were given over to the ghost. And then, one night, Rita discovered that she had to make that plural. Other footsteps, separate and distinctive from the familiar ghostly tread, had manifested. Now, after the rustling sounds, the footsteps of what seemed to be an elderly woman wandered the hall, descended the main staircase, and walked back to the kitchen.

> **S**ometimes after the female ghost reached the kitchen, the rest of the house was silent. Other times, it seemed, her walk evoked further manifestations.

Sometimes after the female ghost reached the kitchen, the rest of the house was silent. Other times, it seemed, her walk evoked further manifestations. Now and then Rita heard an intermittent, murmuring conversation between a man and a woman, just low enough so that words were indiscernible. Every so often a woman's heartrending sob lasted barely a full second.

Occasionally, there were knockings and heavy sighs, and once in a while there came the tinkle of glasses, faint piano music, and laughter. Shortly before dawn Rita was frequently awakened by the sound of something heavy being dragged over the third floor above her room.

In mid-October, Rita went to Beaumont, Texas, for the Golden Triangle Writer's Guild Annual Conference. On the way she planned to visit a friend, a fellow writer who lived in San Antonio.

When she arrived, she found her friend in tears. Jupiter, her beloved German shepherd, had inexplicably changed from a good-natured, obedient pet to an angry, unpredictable behemoth. He had bitten neighbors, friends, meter men, and the postman. Just a week before Rita arrived, he had broken free of their home by chewing up the back door frame. Then he proceeded to dig up the roses in the neighbors' yard and run down the street knocking over garbage cans, threatening anyone who came near him. Jupiter's record at the county dog pound convinced the authorities that he was a dog gone bad, and Rita's friend's husband had promised that he would put the dog down while she was at the writer's conference.

It had been less than a year since Rita's beloved cockapoo, Cleopatra, had died of old age. Rita had never met Jupiter, but she knew that he had registration papers that recorded nine champions in his bloodline. She also knew that the first four years of his life had passed without incident.

Rita felt a strong compulsion to save Jupiter. She told her friend and her husband that since she lived two hundred miles from San Antonio, she would take him far away from the place where he had gotten into so much trouble.

The German Shepherd, with its heavy ruff of fur around the neck, began growling and whining once it was in her home. An unseen presence was clearly disturbing the dog.

"I must admit that the mere size of the magnificent animal was intimidating," Rita said. "He had a great, leonine head and a regal bearing. He studied me through intelligent, golden eyes, and I stared back at him. It was love at first sight. He walked across the room and placed his giant head in my lap. We were meant for each other."

It was three in the afternoon when they arrived at Rita's haunted house.

"Jupiter walked into the enormous hall, and I followed him through the loftily ceilinged parlor into the dining room, and across the main hall into the library," Rita remembered. "When we entered the back hall, he paused a moment at the foot of the steep servant's staircase. Staring upward, he sniffed, raised his head abruptly, and whined."

As Jupiter ascended the servants' staircase to the second floor, Rita was right behind him. Then, as the big German shepherd continued up the narrow steps to the third floor, she waited below.

"Just before reaching the opening landing, Jupiter stiffened, and his ruff came up like a lion's mane," Rita said. "With an earsplitting howl, he backed swiftly downstairs and, staring intently upward, sat down and pressed against me."

Rita saw nothing, but she felt the same presence that she had noted on her first night in the old mansion. At the immediate foot of the stairs there was a small room that Rita—for no reason she knew then—called the nursery. Jupiter wasn't moving. He sat firmly at Rita's feet, alternately cocking his head, staring, and whining. Deciding to test him further, Rita opened the door to the nursery.

Curious, Jupiter poked his head into the room. Then, turning quickly, he threw himself against Rita and literally pushed her from the back of the house into the main hall.

"He had found his place," Rita said. "For the rest of our time in that house, he spent his days gazing at the passing scene. That night, and every night thereafter, he slept on a rug beside the bed in my large second-floor room."

Jupiter's first night in the house was an uneasy one. When the old lady began walking, Jupiter leaped to his feet, nails clicking, and walked across the polished floor to stop just inside the doorway. Cocking his head, he looked out at the dimly lit hall, first one way, then the other.

As the footsteps came closer, Jupiter's ruff stood straight up. Then, front legs moving like pistons, he slid backwards on his rump over the floor to his rug, where he put his paws over his eyes and gave a low whine.

When the ghost of the elderly woman walked on Jupiter's second night in the mansion, he left his rug and went to the foot of Rita's bed. As the eerie sounds disappeared into the rooms below, he went back to his rug, put his paws over his eyes, and whimpered.

On the third night when the spectral footsteps passed their door, Jupiter merely raised his head, then went back to sleep. "It was as if he were saying, 'Oh, the hell with it,'" Rita observed.

> But one late summer afternoon, Rita discovered that she had been wrong. Something menacing did exist in the old mansion.

Over time, Rita had become convinced that there was nothing to fear from the ghosts that walked the halls of Inspiration House. Except for her encounter with the young man with the shaving cream on his face during her first evening in the old mansion, none of the other entities had ever been seen.

Although the auditory manifestations were obvious as they moved about the mansion, Rita observed that "for the most part, they seemed to be on a never-ending soundtrack, each entity performing intermittently. There seemed to be nothing threatening at all in the old house."

But one late summer afternoon, Rita discovered that she had been wrong. Something menacing did exist in the old mansion.

The house had been completely "ghost-free" during the daylight hours ever since Rita moved in, but on this particular afternoon, while she ran errands, Patricia, one of her students, was terrified to hear the sound of heavy footsteps thudding up the back servants' staircase. She had been seated in the seminar room, evaluating manuscripts, when the disturbances began; and even though Jupiter lay at her feet, she was badly frightened by the manifestation.

With a low, deep, warning growl, the big German shepherd chased after the unseen intruder. Summoning her own courage, Patricia followed Jupiter until the footsteps suddenly ceased in the middle of the main hallway on the second floor.

Jupiter whimpered and sat down abruptly. His invisible quarry had vanished, leaving him puzzled and confused.

In the days that followed, the heavy footsteps sounded spasmodically through the halls. But Jupiter chose not to give further pursuit of the invisible intruder. He would only whine and nestle close to Rita's feet.

One afternoon, with Jupiter beside her as usual, Rita was seated with Patricia and the bookkeeper in the large room that they had established as an office. While Patricia marked manuscripts and the bookkeeper made ledger entries, Rita busily edited the last chapter of her book.

Then, all at once, Rita felt as though she were engulfed in a pillar of ice: "It was hard to catch my breath, and my heart felt like a large, heavy rock in my chest. I could neither move nor speak. Patricia went on writing; the bookkeeper went on working; and I was terrified!" she recalled.

But Jupiter, snarling menacingly, scrambled to his feet. Ruff standing straight up around his neck, he sank his teeth into my heavy slacks and literally pulled me from the chair toward the door.

As soon as I was pulled from the icy pillar, she said, I could breathe again. But the pain in my chest lasted into the next day. It took even longer to get rid of the chill. It was then that I realized that something in the house was far from benign.

Two days later, while Rita was writing upstairs with Jupiter at her feet, the bookkeeper was the one who became enveloped in the deadly chill. This time, however, it was Patricia who pulled the woman free from the icy spell.

"Ministers, priests, and psychic investigators who came to Inspiration House all confirmed what we had already determined," Rita said. "There were multiple hauntings in the old mansion. There was the old woman, the young man, a younger woman, a child, and the heavy man whose footsteps sounded intermittently throughout our afternoons.

"And then there was the threatening, chilling entity that seemed determined to snuff out my life and that of my bookkeeper."

More than a thousand writers and others associated with the publishing world visited Inspiration House during the two and a half years that Rita and Jupiter shared their turf with eerie interlopers from the spirit world. In spite of the rumors about Inspiration House being haunted, student writers, editors, and literary agents came there to participate in various writing programs sponsored by Rita Gallagher.

"Some students left after the first night and thereafter only came for daytime tutoring," Rita said. "Others, traveling from greater distances, stayed at a nearby motel."

Having at last completed her book, Rita realized how much energy it had taken just to live in the haunted mansion. Jupiter had lost a great deal of weight. He slept little, and now and then appeared to be tormented by something unseen. Although the veterinarian said that Jupiter's health was good, Rita knew that he was suffering.

"Our last two weeks in the mansion were dreadful," Rita said. Old-fashioned push-button light switches were turned rapidly off and on. Water ran intermittently. Toilets were flushed. Doors slammed. In broad daylight, books were lifted from their shelves, hoisted two or three feet in the air, then dropped to the floor.

In late March 1987, Rita, Patricia, and Jupiter moved to Conroe, Texas. This time, instead of an old, haunted Victorian mansion, the new Inspiration House was a modern fifteen-room home with maids' quarters, wide lawns, trees—and no ghosts!

A Shadow Person Visited a Paranormal Investigator

Even experienced paranormal investigators can be taken off guard by shadow person-type entities. Here is an account from Robert A. Goerman of the Nonhuman Research Agency.

We keep our master bedroom cool, very dark, and quiet.

At 2:20 A.M. on October 7, 2008, I snapped awake to the presence of a silent and shadowy someone in our darkened bedroom. I had retired alone as I awaken at 4:45 each morning for work. My wife is a "night owl" on the com-

puter in the living room and retires much later. I remember thinking to myself that although she was being ever so quiet and trying very hard to not disturb my sleep, she really should just turn on the light so that she does not trip over anything or stub her toes on the furniture.

I propped myself on one elbow and was about to speak when the shadow fled straight through the east wall of the bedroom, dramatically knocking over a pile of paperback books in the process. The books were stacked atop a low box against the wall. The stack measured about two feet high. That wall was seven feet from my bed.

Whatever the thing was, it stepped or floated over our dog's food and water dishes on the floor during its escape and did not disturb those obvious obstacles. This particular eighteen-inch-wide area of east wall is flanked on the left by a heavy wooden rocking chair and on the right by a huge bookcase. A narrow escape, indeed. From

Paranormal investigator Robert Goerman.

the moment that I awoke to the tumble of the pile of books took only seconds. The bedroom door was still closed.

Raven, our aging black mongrel, her eyesight and hearing much diminished, was fast asleep in the living room, which was located at the opposite end of our home. My wife was busy on the computer and had not entered our bedroom.

During the course of my research for the Nonhuman Intruder Project, I found a similar case.

Lyssa from Festus, Missouri, was having a restless night on March 20, 2008, in the top bunk of the bedroom that she shared with her sister. The room had high shelves nailed up on three of the walls that were filled with different glass figures of dragons, wizards, and fairies. She kept waking up to what sounded like wheezing and the glass figures being bumped. This puzzled her because the shelves were too high up for anything to get bumped. She leaned over the railing and saw that her sister was sound asleep.

Then she saw a tall, black, foggy something. It was in the shape of a man and what looked like feet that never touched the ground. As it passed near the shelf, one of her sister's dragons was bumped. The shadow wheezed and floated right through the wall. After this happened, our witness pulled the covers tight over her head and fell asleep.

In both incidents, the shadow entity was "real" enough to be seen and disturb physical objects one moment (books in my case and glass figurines in Lyssa's) and then "ghostly" enough to instantly depart by passing through a wall the very next second. This ability to be real/unreal is one trademark of the "bedroom encounter." When discovered, the entity escapes by passing through solid matter or vanishing in plain sight. There is precious little time to find a camera or even try to communicate. Are these beings where they are for a reason? What do they want? Why do some entities flee while others force the witness into deep sleep?

What Is a Ghost?

Robert A. Goerman, Nonhuman Research Agency

A ghost is an inference. The presence of a ghost implies that the astral essence of a human being survives physical death.

A ghost can be sensed when meaningful coincidences follow the death of a loved one. This proof of survival often takes very personal forms.

A ghost can be seen. Folks encounter apparitions (some recognizable) of varying degrees of completeness and solidity. Some phantoms are initially thought to be living persons.

A ghost can be felt. The caress of a specter can be nice or not so nice.

A ghost can be photographed. More convincing than just orbs and luminous or dark blobs, ghostly persons occasionally appear in photographs. These individuals were not visibly there when the snapshot was taken.

A ghost can be heard. Discarnate voices and compelling electronic voice phenomena remain unexplained.

Genuine ghost encounters are often what they appear to be. Do not confuse ghosts with ghostly phenomena. Some poltergeist activity may or may not be ghosts at all. People awaken to the presence of entities in their homes that depart like ghosts by fleeing through walls or vanishing in plain sight. Not everything that touches you in the dark is a ghost. Sweet dreams.

Ghosts are the astral essence that survives the death of a human being (not an actual photo).

THE NONHUMAN INTRUDER PROJECT

By Robert A. Goerman, Nonhuman Research Agency

I created the Nonhuman Intruder Project in 2013 and originally examined eighty cases of paranormal home intrusions, extracted from diverse sources, and selected on the basis of geography, chronology, and relevance. These accounts were evenly divided between domestic and foreign locations to compare the impact of cultural differences. Sightings spanned the years 1914 to 2011 to explore parallels and variations.

Documenting how these nonhuman intruders entered the homes had been thwarted by the fact that nearly every witness was asleep at the time. How these trespassers departed offered us tantalizing clues.

This March 6, 1975, encounter from Chantilly, France, was typical of seven cases. Suzanne was startled awake by the sounds of dishes breaking. (Note: Sounds resembling breaking glass, tearing paper, and riffling of playing cards might be related to the energy involved.) She and her husband investigated, but they found nothing. He went back to sleep. Before long, she noticed a light in the hallway and got up to check. She discovered a tall and beautiful humanoid, with wavy blond hair, wearing a long yellow outfit. The figure floated just above the floor. They exchanged glances. The interloper seemed surprised and escaped through the solid wall.

In another twenty-two cases, these nonhuman intruders simply vanished before the eyes of the startled witnesses. One March night in 1999, a

Georgia homemaker was suddenly jerked from sleep by the terrifying thought that someone else was in her bedroom. She sat bolt upright and saw an extremely tall being dressed in a flowing white garment. Its right hand was raised to its temple in a gesture that she could only describe as surprise, as if she was not supposed to have awakened and seen it. The home invader just vanished in the blink of an eye.

I always ask myself, "When these nonhumans disappear in plain sight, have they really gone or are they just no longer visible to us?"

How did our nonhuman intruders exit most of the time?

We do not know.

However, we know precisely why we do not know.

In 1991, a North Lauderdale, Florida, man woke up in the middle of the night to see a bright light in the living room. The witness leaned over his sleeping wife to see a small individual wearing a grayish-blue cloak standing at a counter with its back to him. The witness then heard a voice in his mind that told him to go back to sleep. He did lie back down for a moment, then sat up a second time, and again heard the mental voice telling him to go back to sleep. He went to sleep.

Mr. and Mrs. Michael Rutherford of Scotland were sleeping peacefully on July 20, 2004, when Michael awoke to the presence of a glowing figure in their bedroom. He shook his wife several times, but she would not awaken. By this time, he was beyond terrified. When the luminous being drew near, Michael suddenly blacked out and did not wake up until morning.

On July 16, 2011, a married couple was on vacation and staying at a bed-and-breakfast along Beach Avenue in Cape May, New Jersey. The husband awoke to find two beings standing at the foot of the bed. There was sufficient light coming in from the street to see they were identical in every way. Both wore dark, form-fitting suits with snug hoods that resembled scuba diving gear. He propped himself up on his elbow and was about to say something when he got this very clear thought, "Something is wrong. He sees us." The man suddenly became extremely sleepy and tried to fight the urge to lie back down, but it was no use. He felt his eyes closing and that was it. The next thing he knew it was morning and he was awakened by the sunlight streaming in through the balcony door.

The obvious manipulation of consciousness plays a huge factor in these accounts. In more than 60 percent of the original eighty cases, the witness inexplicably fell asleep or was compelled to sleep. Something is at work here to deepen slumber. Potential corroborating witnesses in the same room often do not awaken, despite sometimes-frantic attempts by the primary witness to rouse them. These paranormal prowlers repeatedly express surprise or annoyance when folks unexpectedly wake and experience "accidental awareness" during a home invasion. We are not meant to observe these clandestine activities.

Have you ever awakened to sounds or sights in your home that made you decide "I have to check this out!" and the next thing you know it is morning? You distinctly recall exactly what it was that aroused your curiosity. You can kick yourself for falling asleep. The fact that you fell asleep is most often the weirdest aspect of the entire situation.

Reports continue to trickle in. Bedroom encounters are fleeting and leave the witness confused. Where can you report your experiences? These episodes seem to be of little concern to enthusiasts who focus on UFOs, monsters, or ghosts.

Case 63119 from the Mutual UFO Network database reveals the February 4, 2015, experience of a gentleman from Suffolk County, New York. Awakened by a weird buzzing, he turned over in bed and saw a five-foot-three creature standing silently in his bathroom doorway, staring at him. He reported that the entity had "a sad look on his face and it appeared like its skin was very wrinkled or had a melted-like appearance." At this point, the witness screamed in terror, scared for his life, and tried to get away, but he found that he suddenly could not move. In his words: "Then I immediately passed out, which I'd never do if I'm facing something like that…. I think it knocked me out somehow, even though he just stood still and didn't move towards me. I woke up about five hours later and it was gone."

> Have you ever awakened to sounds or sights in your home that made you decide "I have to check this out!" and the next thing you know it is morning?

Genuine bedroom encounters are not innocent hallucinations associated with Awareness during Sleep Paralysis (ASP). The entities move physical objects and can inflict pain or injury. Pets react with fear. Many witnesses are compelled to sleep against their will. The Nonhuman Intruder Project Classification System below both summarizes and categorizes the rich diversity of the "bedroom encounter" experience.

- GHX: entity exits through solid matter
- VAN: entity vanishes in plain sight
- ZZZ: other people in room do not or will not awaken
- TKO: witness falls asleep during encounter
- WP: witness temporarily cannot move
- MW: multiple witnesses
- MP: multiple witnesses temporarily cannot move
- TALK: some manner of communication noted

Glowing entities or objects receive the classification of GLOW under the Nonhuman Intruder Project Classification System. Makes sense.

- DARK: shadow entity
- GLOW: glowing entity and/or unexplained light phenomena
- TOUCH: entity touches witness
- PAIN: witness suffers pain without visible physical damage
- INJURY: witness suffers physical damage to the body
- FIGHT: physical struggle with entity
- MOVED: objects physically moved by entity
- DOG: animal (identified) reaction
- HEAT: abnormal heat felt before, during, or after encounter
- COLD: abnormal cold felt before, during, or after encounter

These incidents merit immediate and serious study. Valuable information is lost when genuine encounters are dismissed as ASP-induced hallucinations by eyewitnesses who are comforted by this advice, whether this counsel originates with the medical community or comes from a book or website on ASP. It is less upsetting to believe that "it was all just a dream," rather than confront the fact that these entities can violate our homes with impunity.

SLEEP PARALYSIS OR BEDROOM ENCOUNTERS

By Robert A. Goerman, Nonhuman Research Agency

Do you lock your doors at night?

How often do paranormal prowlers carry out their agenda in your home while you sleep peacefully in your bed? Men, women, and children everywhere awaken and discover that they are not alone. Many cultures have tales of non-human beings that terrify vulnerable humans at night. Science today uses two words to debunk these nocturnal encounters: sleep paralysis.

What exactly is sleep paralysis? When dreams occur, your body shuts down most muscle activity. This protective REM atonia is a natural mechanism that prevents you from hurting yourself when you are dreaming. While sleep paralysis occurs in the typical sleeper practically every night, the phrase itself has become synonymous with Awareness during Sleep Paralysis (ASP).

ASP is another matter entirely. ASP occurs when you become conscious while your body is still immobilized. Your brain is in the transition state between dreaming and waking up. Imagine awakening to discover that you cannot move a muscle! Able to see and hear, you find yourself virtually frozen in bed. You might fear that you are suffocating or dying due to a crushing weight on your chest. Mortal terror sets in when you realize that you are not alone. Some ASP experiences are accompanied by a "sensed" presence or even wild hallucinations projected on physical surroundings. There are very few things more terrifying than being helpless while unspeakable horrors stalk you in the night.

> According to medical science, all reported nocturnal intruders are nothing more than ASP waking nightmares superimposed upon our real world.

According to medical science, all reported nocturnal intruders are nothing more than ASP waking nightmares superimposed upon our real world.

This is not always true. Understanding the five classic symptoms of ASP will finally enable experiencers and researchers to distinguish between ASP and genuine paranormal home invasions.

1. Waking paralyzed: The crucial, never-changing symptom of ASP is waking up paralyzed. If you do not awaken paralyzed, then you are not experiencing ASP. (Less than 25 percent of our witnesses to genuine encounters mention an inability to

move. If the witness is initially able to move upon awakening, those encounters involving later paralysis should not be automatically dismissed.)

2. Unseen presence: One of the more commonly reported symptoms associated with ASP is that of the "sensed" presence. Nothing at all is ever seen. (This invisible or "just out of sight" presence is at odds with our reports of visible nonhuman intruders. Genuine encounters deal with eyewitness sightings.)

3. Folklore symptom: During ASP, few muscles of breathing are active. Many people have a sense of suffocating and chest pressure, as if something is standing or sitting on their torso. Various societies mistakenly interpret this signature chest pressure in supernatural terms based upon their local folklore. (None of our witnesses to paranormal home invasion reports this folklore symptom of chest pressure.)

4. Extreme terror: Terror plays an integral role in ASP. Sufferers can feel horrific fear unlike anything they experience in waking life. (Some folks who meet real nonhuman intruders manage to remain quite calm and curious.)

5. Dream overlap: Auditory hallucinations are the most common. Many people hear sinister or taunting voices. Others hear gibberish. There may be the perception of whispering, screaming, and laughing. Some people hear breathing, footsteps, or knocking. There might be feelings of floating or levitation. In a distinct minority of cases, dream overlap can result in wacky or scary illusions projected upon actual physical surroundings. It often seems as absurd and ridiculous as it does real. The "visual" hallucinations evaporate when the sufferer regains movement. (ASP figments of the imagination and paranormal home invasions are two very different things.)

A Skeptic Who Didn't Believe in Ghosts

Whenever the topic of ghosts came up in his presence, Mr. K of Spokane was often heard to say that he didn't believe in them and that even if he saw one he wouldn't believe it. Somewhat pompously he often declared that he would not accept the reality of any so-called supernatural entity until it had been dissected in a laboratory, distilled in a test tube, and stamped with the scientific seal of approval.

A successful businessman, Mr. K felt that he had managed a "smoking deal" when he moved his wife and three kids into a practically new, two-story home in a fashionable suburb. The original owner had moved out after seven months of occupancy. A young couple had signed a six-month lease, but they vacated before the lease expired. Mr. K credited his ability to drive a hard bargain to the fact that he had acquired the house for several thousand dollars less than the FHA appraisal.

Unexplainable events, such as dishes breaking on the kitchen counter, began to occur after the family moved in to the newly constructed home.

But then, almost immediately, the K family was confronted with a series of events with which they were unprepared to deal, and which Mr. K found impossible to fit into the scientifically ordered scheme of the universe upon which he insisted. Footsteps went up and down the stairs when all members of the family were accounted for elsewhere in the house. Television sets changed channels without anyone touching the controls. Dishes rattled in the cupboard, and some dinnerware smashed itself on the kitchen counter. Billiard balls chased themselves across the table when Mr. K squinted down the cue for a shot.

Somehow, a man of iron will, he managed to convince himself that the bizarre manifestations in his home were the result of his working too hard at the office. They were all caused by his fatigue, clumsiness, and stress. They were all illusions.

One late afternoon when he was parking his car in the driveway, Mr. K was surprised to see at the living room window an elderly couple dressed in very old-fashioned clothing. He entered the front door, announced his arrival, and then asked his wife the identities of their dinner guests.

When his puzzled wife wondered what "dinner guests" to whom he might be making reference, her invitation to step into the living room made it obvious to both of them that no elderly couple had come for dinner. That was when Mr. K unburdened the whole dossier of bizarre occurrences that he had been attempting to rationalize away into "working too hard at the office."

Mrs. K was relieved to hear her husband's confession and admitted that she had begun to fear that she was losing her mind. A few weeks earlier, she had been waxing the floors when suddenly two men—dressed in very old-fashioned clothing—walked out of the closet, down the hall, and into one of the children's bedrooms.

Shortly after Mrs. K's encounter, their older daughter, a college student, arrived home for a two-week vacation. Her parents had left her at home before

At first suspecting Mr. K of rigging the table as a joke, his friends checked the table for wires or magnets, but they could find no evidence of trickery of any kind.

a roaring fire while they took advantage of her being home to keep her younger siblings company. When they returned home, they found their daughter pale and shaken. She had already packed her suitcase, and she informed them that she was leaving to spend her vacation time with a classmate in a nearby city.

Stunned and stung by their daughter's behavior—but fearing that she had had an encounter with their ghostly housemates while they had been dining out, the Ks reluctantly allowed her to leave without protest.

It was not until two years later that their daughter revealed the reason for her sudden departure. She had been sitting by the fire, enjoying its warmth and crackling logs, when a strange man walked out of the closet right through a closed door and made his way down the hall and into the bathroom. And that door had been closed, too.

She had run outside and stood on the lawn for two hours, shivering with fear and cold. She had at last convinced herself that she had been studying too hard and resolved to leave the next day so that she would not burden her parents with fears of her mental fatigue.

Although the ghosts did not show themselves when Mr. K and his sons played billiards, they did enjoy rolling the balls around on the table top. Interestingly, the spirits never rudely ruined anyone's turn to sink a ball in a pocket.

One night, Mr. K decided to reveal the phenomenon to some of his closest friends—those who might at first scoff at the very suggestion of such manifestations but who would not laugh at the percipients. The K's invisible housemates were not at all shy about performing in front of strangers, and they rolled the billiard balls about in a lively manner.

At first suspecting Mr. K of rigging the table as a joke, his friends checked the table for wires or magnets, but they could find no evidence of trickery of any kind. Curious and wanting more information about the Ks' personal ghosts, Mr. K declared that he had no rational explanation. Most of the time, the spooks liked to have fun, but on occasion, for no reason the family could comprehend, the beings seemed to become angry and smash plates, tip furniture, or even pinch or punch Mr. K or his two sons.

On one occasion that the Ks found more than a little unnerving, they clearly saw the indentation of a human body on the smooth bedspread of their king-sized bed just as they were about to retire. As they watched, the indentation began to move, as if someone were sitting up.

The Ks' two boys, who were still in high school, quickly adjusted to the members of the household who were usually invisible. On more than one occasion, they were startled by the man who entered their bedroom without opening it. The most irritating action of the ghosts to the teenagers was when they would find the bathroom door locked. They would hear water running as if to cover the sound of their shouts that they had to use the room. After a few moments, the door would swing open, and an invisible entity would leave, ostensibly clean and refreshed.

Eventually, Mr. K contacted the original owner of the home, who would only admit to noting that the house, although new, had an "old feeling" to it. After some discussion, he also admitted that some strange things had begun to happen just before they moved.

The young couple were much more forthcoming and admitted that they couldn't wait to get out the door.

Mr. K, however, held fast to his scientific indoctrination. He said that he still does not believe in ghosts. What they encounter in their home is "some kind of strange energy."

A "strange energy" that rolls billiard balls across the pool table, that sometimes breaks plates and moves furniture, and that on occasion appears as two separate male occupants and a charming, elderly couple who from time to time comes to visit. Sounds an awful lot like a ghost to us.

Possessed Houses

Whether or not actress Joan Crawford dabbled in Satanism, it seems that her home somehow became a center for demonic negativity. Sherry and I visited the Crawford home after mysterious fires had broken out repeatedly in the master bedroom. The current owners of the house had called in the Reverend Rosalyn Bruyere of the Healing Light Center to exorcise the house. Rev. Bruyere found many spirits in the house and picked up that at one time there had been strange rituals conducted in the home.

Christina Crawford, Joan's adopted daughter, told us that Joan's relationship with men was extremely violent. Christina said that she had always seen and felt strange things in the home: "Now, evidently, the walls are starting to catch fire! Other people have heard children's cries in the walls! Every single owner has had trouble.… She built the majority of the house. It was a small cottage when she bought it, but most of the house she built. Every single family that has lived in that house has had horrible things happen."

Christina said that the last words that her mother uttered were to a woman who was kneeling at the foot of her bed, praying for her. "As she was dying," Christina said, she "opened her eyes and said directly to the woman, 'don't you *dare* ask God to help me!' … and then she died."

It was such arrogance, Christina said, that she believes is a major part of the difficulty with the seemingly accursed house. "She was capable of real evil," she said. "If you have never experienced that *look* from another human being, it is almost impossible to believe that such an experience could even exist! I think perhaps that's why so many people are unwilling to deal with the shadow side because they can't really get themselves to believe that such a dimension exists. My brother and I were absolutely terrified of her. In fact, there is a passage in *Mommie Dearest* that describes 'the look' on her face when she tried to kill me when I was thirteen. We all saw *that look*. My brother and I talked about it extensively … it was not of an ordinary human being!

A GHOSTLY ENCOUNTER AT GREYSTONE MANSION

Paul Dale Roberts recalled the ghostly encounter that may have inspired him to become a full-time paranormal investigator: In Beverly Hills there is a Tudor Revival mansion called Greystone Mansion. It has also been called Doheny Mansion. Greystone Mansion is a smorgasbord of horrific deaths, making this picturesque mansion one of the most haunted in the world.

Some history about this mansion. It was a gift from oil tycoon Edward L. Doheny to his son. According to Wikipedia:

> On February 16, 1929, four months after Ned Doheny, his wife, Lucy, and their five children moved into Greystone, Ned died in a guest bedroom in a murder-suicide with his secretary, Hugh Plunkett. The official story indicated Plunkett murdered Ned either because of a "nervous disorder" or inflamed with anger over not receiving a raise.

There is a lot of mystery that surrounds this supposed murder-suicide. There have been witnesses who see a pool of blood on the floor. As soon as they see this pool of blood, it disappears instantly. The ghosts of Doheny and Plunkett have been seen in this mansion.

The Greystone Mansion in Beverly Hills, California, was the site of a murder-suicide involving oil tycoon Edward Doheny and his secretary.

In 1971, the Greystone Mansion became a city park and has been added to the National Register of Historic Places. The mansion is also used often in television and motion pictures—the descending staircase, especially. *Arrow, Alias, Dark Shadows, Ghostbusters,* and *Garfield* are a few TV shows and movies in which Greystone Mansion has been featured. In 1978, I visited Greystone Mansion with my psychic cousin from Anaheim. We were sitting outside, and I was talking about the stories of its ghosts when he started yelling.

I asked him what he was yelling about, and he said his back was raked three times with sharp fingernails. Of course, I didn't believe him, but when he raised up his shirt, he had scratch marks running up and down his back. He told me that he saw a ghostly elderly woman with an evil smile, wearing a long, blue dress.

I was staying with my cousin in Anaheim and tried out for the *Gong Show* and *American Bandstand.* I was a professional dancer at the time. I got to be in a couple of commercials and that's about it. I knew it was time to head home.

On the last night at my cousin's house, he screamed in the middle of the night, around 1:00 A.M. I asked him what was wrong and he told me that the ghostly elderly woman that he encountered at Greystone Mansion followed him home and attacked him again. He claimed that the woman sat on his chest and was trying to take his breath away. My cousin's father was a preacher and blessed him and prayed over him. The entity finally left.

A ghost hunting group called LASH (Looking for Apparitions and Seeking Hauntings) said it captured many electronic voice phenomena (EVP). Some of the EVPs said: "Misery is all mine." "Death follows." "Go to Hell." LASH claims the EVPs were Class A EVPs. LASH said when shadow figures appeared in its pictures that one of the investigators felt a hand on her neck. Her neck was squeezed three times. This investigator was so scared that she is no longer a ghost hunter.

HAUNTED HOUSES SOAKED UP EMOTIONAL UNPLEASANTNESS

Psychoanalyst Dr. Nandor Fodor theorized that genuinely haunted houses were those that had soaked up emotional unpleasantness from former occupants. Years, or even centuries, later, the emotional energy may become reactivated when later occupants of the house undergo a similar emotional disturbance. The "haunting"—mysterious knocks and rappings, opening and slamming doors, cold drafts, appearance of ghostly figures—is produced, in Dr. Fodor's hypothesis, by the merging of the two energies, one from the past, the other from the present. In Dr. Fodor's theory, the reservoir of absorbed emotions, which lie dormant in a haunted house, can only be activated when emotional instability is present. Those homes that have a history of happy occupants, the psychoanalyst believed, are in little danger of becoming haunted.

Psychic investigator Edmund Gurney put forth the hypothesis that the collective sighting of a ghost is due to a sort of telepathic "infection." One percipient sees the ghost and, in turn, telepathically influences another person, and so on.

THE RED-HEADED MAN IN THE CLOSET

Charlie told us that in the mid-80s he bought a 200-year-old farmhouse that, unbeknownst to him, contained an unpaying boarder.

Some records came with the house, so we had an idea of some of the changes and remodeling done over time. The oak pantry door had once been the main entrance to the house, but it was remodeled at the turn of the century. It latched with a three-inch iron thumb-latch. We often found it open when we came in or in the mornings. I blamed my wife for not shutting the door; she blamed me.

Finally, it got so annoying we put a chair against it to keep it closed.

For a couple of weeks it stayed closed.

One night, preparing for company, I was mopping the floor in an unused room with another old main doorway. This door was never used and was bolted from the inside, yet I found muddy bootprints coming from the door across the room.

In the kitchen a bit later, I told my wife about the bootprints. She joked that it must be the guy who was coming in the pantry door and we had locked him out. Looking toward the pantry, she said, "It's OK, if you prefer this door, go ahead and use it."

Immediately the latch clicked open and the door opened, pushing the chair aside. Needless to say, cold chills ran up both of us. We never worried about the pantry being open again and never saw anything else.

But, maybe someone in the house did. Sometime later our then three-year-old son came downstairs and told us he'd been talking about farming with the red-headed man in his closet. Many kids have an imaginary friend, so we gave it no thought. He continued to talk about the red-headed man, who told him about farming, wagon making, and to be careful around the river.

Fresh bootprints were found in one of the unused rooms of the farmhouse, which was once owned by a bearded man who built buckboards for a living.

When we asked about him, he described him as short, with a red beard, and stooped over with a limp.

A couple of years later, while doing research to register the home with the National Register of Historic Places, I discovered that the man who lived in the home before the turn of the century was short, bearded, red-headed, built buckboards for a living, and walked with a limp due to an accident.

Immediately after his death, his son did the remodeling involving the pantry door and turned a southern-facing sleeping room into the upstairs closet.

He had also had two children drown in a river a mile away.

LAWSON'S LAW: NEVER BUY A HOME BUILT OVER A MASS GRAVE

When the Lawson family (Patricia, wife and mother; Cliff, husband and father; Teri, 16, Christie, 13, and Kim, 10, daughters) moved into a home that was only two years old and had been constructed on the outskirts of a picturesque village in Vermont, they certainly didn't expect it to be haunted.

What they discovered after the manifestations began was that a portion of the house had been constructed over a mass grave that contained the bodies of nearly one hundred men, women, and children from a Native American tribe that had been deliberately infected with smallpox in the early 1800s. Since such communicable diseases as smallpox had been unknown in the Americas prior to the European invasion, it was a common ploy of inhumane settlers to trade tribespeople blankets that had been infected with smallpox. With no generational immunity to such diseases, entire villages would quickly fall prey to the epidemic. Such had been the case in the mass burial site that now lay beneath the recreation room of the Lawsons' new home.

Before the Lawsons had learned that a portion of their home had been constructed on sacred ground, their daughters had complained of strange things occurring in the family room. The overhead lights, as well as the television set, the CD player, and the computer, would turn on and off without anyone being near any of the switches. The same was true of the faucets in the bathroom.

The girls started complaining that the house was haunted, but Patricia and Cliff did the practical, rational things of checking the wiring, the switch boxes, and the plumbing. The trouble was, they found everything to be fine and in order.

About twelve days after they moved in, Kim and Christie screamed that they had seen shadows moving across the walls of the recreation room. When Patricia went to investigate, she saw what appeared to be the shadows of two or three people moving in a repetitious pattern that she eventually decided was a dance of some kind.

The next night, as if to accompany the dancing shadows, the entire family could hear, very faintly but completely discernible, the sound of a far-away flute, drums, rattles, and singing or chanting. They all saw and heard them, and at first the girls were really frightened.

And then a strange thing happened. According to Patricia, the girls began to move rhythmically and to mimic the movements of the shadow dancers. Within a few minutes, their actions were so fluid and seemed to come so naturally to them that she and Cliff feared that they had become possessed by the spirits of the dancers.

When they attempted to pull their daughters out of the recreation room and away from the mesmerizing shadows, Cliff and Patricia were startled to see the hazy image of a Native American man dressed in full tribal regalia standing in the doorway as if to block their escape.

"I just closed my eyes and gritted my teeth and pulled one of the girls behind me and charged right through the ghost of the Indian in the doorway," Patricia said. "Cliff and the other two girls were right behind us."

After the girls had been calmed and put to bed, Cliff and Patricia discussed the bizarre situation in which they found themselves.

Patricia had always been open to the idea of spirits and ghosts, but the whole haunting business was blowing Cliff's mind. He was having a very difficult time dealing with what they had just seen and heard. And it didn't help him one bit to calm his nerves when the sound of the drums seemed to come from all around the kitchen and living room.

After the Lawsons managed to get through that incredible night of visual and auditory manifestations, they decided that they would ask around about the place and check any old records available that might give them some clue to the eerie spirit phenomena that they had experienced.

> The more they talked to some of their new neighbors, the more they heard stories of people who had encountered Indian spirits in the vicinity of the burial site.

That was when they learned about the terrible deed that had been worked upon a tribal village that had once occupied the area along the river. After the smallpox epidemic had done its awful work on the villagers, the bodies of the victims were dragged to a trench and unceremoniously dumped in. That trench, the mass burial site, was on their land, and the corner of the house containing the recreation room had been built over a part of it. The more they talked to some of their new neighbors, the more they heard stories of people who had encountered Indian spirits in the vicinity of the burial site. And a good number of folks said that they had heard the sound of drums and rattles on certain nights.

When word got around the area that the Lawsons had experienced strange phenomena at their home and were asking questions about the grim history of the mass burial site, a woman who claimed she had psychic abilities invited herself over to have coffee with Patricia.

"According to this lady, these manifestations have been happening around this burial site for years," Patricia said. "She suggested that there was some kind of psychic vortex that had been created because of the cruel way that the Native American tribe had their lives cut so short. She believed that the whole area around the house, the river, and the land where the village had once stood had been saturated with negative vibrations."

Patricia invited the psychic-sensitive to return that evening with some of her study group. "Around eleven o'clock, one of the group was drawn to a particular spot on the lawn," she said. "According to the psychic, this was a power place caused by the spirits in the burial site. As we looked back toward the house, we saw incredible projections all over the place. We saw ghostly images of the Indian villagers, moving about as they must have in life—some of them dancing, some of them seeing to cooking, preparing food over fires. It was an absolutely incredible experience."

Two nights later, the psychic-sensitive returned to the Lawsons' home, bringing with her a friend, a tribal medicine priest, along with certain members of her study group. "They held a cleansing ceremony for the spirits of the dead," Patricia said. "They prayed and chanted and sought to bring peace to the troubled spirits who had been buried in that mass grave without the benefit of their death songs or prayers. After that ceremony, the thuds, noises, and other disturbances in our house stopped."

Patricia stated, however, that on nights when the moon is full—especially in August, September, and October—they could still hear the faraway sound of drums, flutes, and rattles. "None of our family finds this manifestation frightening or disturbing," she explained. "I guess, if anything, it gives us a kind of reassurance that life continues beyond the grave."

THE WHALEY HOUSE: AMERICA'S MOST HAUNTED MANSION

Old San Diego is the birthplace of California. On Presidio Hill, Father Junípero Serra established the mission of San Diego de Alcalá on July 16, 1769. In the early 1820s, a small Mexican community was formed that by 1835 had evolved to El Pueblo San Diego. Because it was the site of the first permanent Spanish settlement on the California coast, San Diego is as significant to the Pacific heritage of the United States as is Jamestown, the first English settlement in Virginia Colony, to our Atlantic ancestry. The first U.S. flag was raised on Old San Diego's tree-lined plaza in 1846.

Not only have Sherry and I found Old San Diego one of the most haunted places in North America, but the Whaley House, constructed in 1857, just might be one of the most haunted mansions. June Reading, the amicable and knowledgeable director of the Whaley House who has since passed on, told us when we were researching the mansion that immediately after its completion by Thomas Whaley, the mansion became the center of business, government, and social affairs in Old San Diego. The oldest brick house in Southern California, the Whaley House served as a courthouse, a courtroom, a theater, and a boarding house, as well as the family home of Thomas and Anna Whaley and their children. Located at 2482 San Diego Avenue in Old San Diego, the Whaley House has been restored and it is now owned and operated by the San Diego Historical Society as a tourist attraction.

Although guests can no longer stay overnight in the Whaley House, it is still possible to tour the mansion in the early afternoon. No one is allowed in the Whaley House after 4:00 P.M., but police officers and passersby say that someone—or something—keeps walking around half the night turning all the lights on. Often, while conducting tours through the old mansion, members of the society have heard eerie footsteps moving about other parts of the house when the rooms were visibly unoccupied.

Almost every facet of haunting phenomena has been observed or encountered in this mansion. Footsteps have been heard in the master bedroom and on the stairs. Windows, even when fastened down with three- or four-inch bolts on each side, have opened of their own volition, often in the middle of the night, triggering the burglar alarms.

As they tour the mansion, people have often smelled cooking odors coming from the kitchen, sweet scents from Anna Whaley's perfume, and the heavy aroma of Thomas Whaley's favorite Havana cigars. Screams have frequently been heard echoing through the upstairs rooms, as well as the sound of girlish giggles and the rattling of doorknobs. Once, a large, heavy china closet toppled over by itself. Many people have heard the piano playing in the mansion's music room and the milling and shuffling about of ghostly crowds in the courtroom. The ghostly images of Thomas and Anna Whaley have been seen on numerous occasions.

Numerous individuals have sensed or psychically seen the image of a scaffold and a hanging man on the south side of the mansion. According to Mrs. Reading, ten years before Thomas Whaley constructed his home on the site, a renegade sailor named Yankee Jim Robinson had been hanged on the spot of what would later become the arch between the music room and the living room in the mansion. Whaley had been an observer when Yankee Jim kept his appointment with the hangman.

In the fall of 1966, a group of reporters volunteered to stay in Whaley House to spend the night with Yankee Jim. Special permission was granted to

The Whaley House in San Diego's old town district is one of the most haunted buildings you will ever see. One notable ghost there is "Yankee" Jim Robinson, a sailor who was hung on the property for grand larceny in 1852.

the journalists by the historical society, and the ghost hunters settled in for their overnight stay. The wife of one of the reporters had to be taken home by 9:30 P.M. She was badly shaken and claimed that she had seen something on the upper floor, which she refused to describe. The entire party of journalists left the house before dawn. They, too, refused to discuss the reason for their premature departure, but some people say that they were confronted by the ghost of Yankee Jim, still protesting the horror of his death.

In addition to the sightings of the primary spirits of Thomas and Anna Whaley and Yankee Jim, Mrs. Reading said that the other ghosts most often seen include those of a young girl named Washburn, a playmate of the Whaley children; and "Dolly Varden," the family's favorite dog. Some visitors to the Whaley House have reported seeing a gaudily dressed woman with a painted face lean out of a second-story window. In Mrs. Reading's opinion, that could well be an actress from one of the theatrical troupes that leased the second floor in November 1868.

The Court House Wing of the mansion is generally thought to be the most haunted spot in the Whaley House, due to the violent emotions that were expended there in the early days of San Diego. Many individuals who have visited the old house have heard the sounds of a crowded courtroom in session and the noisy meetings of men in Thomas Whaley's upstairs study.

Haunted: Malevolent Ghosts, Night Terrors, and Threatening Phantoms

According to many psychic researchers, the fact that this one single mansion served so many facets of city life, in addition to being a family home, almost guarantees several layers of psychic residue permeating the environment.

Many sensitive visitors to the Whaley House have also perceived the image of Anna Whaley, who, some feel, still watches over the mansion that she loved so much. And who, according to a good number of those who have encountered her presence, deeply resents the intrusion of strangers.

> Many individuals who have visited the old house have heard the sounds of a crowded courtroom in session and the noisy meetings of men in Thomas Whaley's upstairs study.

Numerous photographs of spirit phenomena have been taken over the years in the Whaley House, and many are on display in a glass case in the mansion. As a matter of fact, Sherry was able to capture a rather startling image on film. When we returned home and developed the photographs taken during our research trip of the Whaley House, we discovered to our amazement a ghostly materialization of the noose that hanged Yankee Jim Robinson. Sherry had photographed the arch between the music room and the living room, the site where the renegade had been executed before that portion of the Whaley House had been constructed. There at the top of the room, the location where Yankee Jim swung, one can see a phantom noose hanging from the ceiling.

Sherry also captured several other odd materializations that showed up on the developed photographs. In two locations of the house, where many have reported the lights being turned on when no one is there, the lights were "on" in the developed pictures—even though the lights during our daytime interview with Mrs. Reading were clearly "off."

DRIVEN OUT BY THE ANGRY GHOST OF AN OLD LADY

The magnificent and ornate Victorian house that stood atop a forested hill had seemed like their dream home in the country. If they hadn't been so excited over finding what they believed to be their perfect new home, David and Mary might have asked the real estate agent why it was that the house had sat empty and uninhabited for so many years. If they hadn't been so eager to move into the place, they might have taken more time to walk through the old house and sensed the dark and ominous presence that dwelt within its shadowy corridors.

David and Mary, both in their early forties, had grown up in the same city in upstate New York and had lived and worked there all their lives. Idealistically, they envisioned this sprawling house in the country as the perfect place to bring up their kids, eleven-year-old Mark and eight-year-old Alice. As two realists, however, they decided to take advantage of the fact that the place had sat empty for several years and make an offer to rent with an option to buy. After all, neither David nor Mary could be absolutely certain that either they or their children could adjust to country life. It would be unwise to invest all their savings and their immediate financial future in a move that might not work out for them. The real estate agency did not hesitate to accept their offer to rent—and the house of their dreams soon turned into a waking nightmare.

It was on a Sunday afternoon, just two days before the movers would arrive with their furniture, that they first experienced a strange, eerie presence in certain rooms.

Mary, an accomplished illustrator of children's books, was trying to decide whether one of the upstairs rooms that had especially good natural light would serve as her studio or be one of the children's bedrooms. Out of the corner of an eye, she thought she saw someone moving in the hallway. When she called out, she received no response—but a few minutes later, she felt a firm, solid hand on her left shoulder.

At first, the old woman just seemed like an eccentric neighbor to the family who had moved into the Victorian home, but after a couple visits she became more violent and frightening.

Expecting to turn around and face her husband, Mary could not suppress a startled scream when she saw that she was alone and there was no one behind her. She was suddenly overwhelmed with a sensation of cold that chilled her to her bones.

At about the same time, David was experiencing a similar phenomenon as he was using a tape measure to mark off an area on a wall where he intended to place bookcases. He remembered seeing what he could only describe as a strange kind of shadow that seemed to be moving toward him from the hallway. Later, he said that the very sight of the dark presence made him feel as if he had been suddenly drenched with ice water.

Two sensible, modern individuals who prided themselves on their lack of superstitious beliefs, Mary and David attributed their strange experiences to tricks of shadows and light, fatigue over working long hours packing their household belongings for the move to the country, and a general case of nerves over their big decision to move from the familiar environment of the city to the unfamiliar trappings of rustic living.

Haunted: Malevolent Ghosts, Night Terrors, and Threatening Phantoms

"I think we both knew that there was something strange going on in that old house," David wrote in his report of their experience with the supernatural for the *Steiger Questionnaire of Mystical, Paranormal and UFO Experiences*. "But we had made such a major commitment in renting the place and packing up all of our stuff that we stubbornly wanted to see it through. Although neither of us was the least bit superstitious, I think at that point we were willing to battle ghosts or monsters for the place."

However, it did not take very long after they had made their move to the grand old Victorian mansion that their resolve to fight against the unknown began quickly to weaken, especially when whatever was in the house started to trouble their children.

"We had been in the place only two days," Mary said, "when we were awakened late one night by little Alice crying that someone was in her room. After we managed to calm her, she said that an ugly old witch had come out of her closet and stared at her."

By that time, Mark had left his own bedroom and had joined his parents in Alice's room. He told them that he had seen an old woman with a cane in the upstairs hallway on the first night they moved in. Unfamiliar with country living, the boy had assumed she was a nosey old neighbor who had come to check them out.

When he approached her and asked if he could help her with anything, she had stared at him and walked down the backstairs. Mark went on to say that he had seen her on two other occasions—once looking in at him from an outside window as he watched television, and another time, standing at the outside gate, looking up at his room.

"When we asked Mark why he hadn't said anything before," David said, "he shrugged and reminded us that we had lectured him about getting along with their new country neighbors. He had seen some television programs where it appeared that countryfolk just dropped in to visit one another without invitation. He assumed that the stern-looking old woman was just an eccentric neighbor lady who from time to time would wander into the house without being invited."

> The next night, the "eccentric neighbor lady" got downright mean. Alice cried out in pain, shrieking that the "ugly old witch" had pulled her hair.

The next night, the "eccentric neighbor lady" got downright mean. Alice cried out in pain, shrieking that the "ugly old witch" had pulled her hair. Awakened by his sister's screams, Mark told his parents that he had had a nightmare in which the old woman had appeared in his room and had shaken her cane at him in a threatening manner.

"We tried so hard to convince the children—and ourselves—that they had simply had some bad dreams," Mary said, "but we remembered our eerie experience with the cold, chilling shadows before we moved into the old house."

Two days later, as David was standing on a ladder, stretching to hang a picture on a living room wall, he felt a sudden, stinging blow across his back, as if someone had swatted him smartly with a stick—or a cane. "I actually had a red welt across my back where the invisible object had struck me," he said.

That same evening, Mary went to her studio to find that her easel had been tipped over and the canvas on which she had been painting had been ripped. "I knew that neither of the children would do such a thing," she said. "They regarded my studio as sacrosanct, and they would not have been playing in there and accidentally knocked over the easel. They loved watching me paint—and they understood that this was Mommy's way of helping to pay the family's bills."

Later that night, as the family lay sleeping, they were awakened by the sounds of someone—or *something*—pounding on the walls of their bedrooms and the hallway. "The sharp, striking blows sounded for all the world like someone hitting the walls with a stick or a cane," David said. "When Mary and I rushed out to the hall to investigate, we clearly saw the image of an old woman with a cane staring malevolently at us. She was surrounded by an eerie, greenish glow, and we heard her tell us in a high-pitched shout to leave the house at once. It was her home, she screamed, and she did not tolerate interlopers."

According to the report, they attempted to stick it out in the old house for another few weeks before they could no longer endure the psychic and emotional stresses caused by the ghost of the angry old woman. "Our kids were on the brink of hysteria, and they would never be anywhere alone in the house," Mary said. "They insisted on sleeping with us, and they seldom left our sides."

When David and Mary were forced to accept the grim truth that they had encountered something beyond their previous beliefs and understanding about the boundaries of reality, they knew that they had to leave the place and return to the city. "We crowded into a two-bedroom apartment for nearly a year before we could afford a larger place," David said.

"Before we left the old house in the country," David said, "we learned from some of the neighbors that many years ago, around 1917, a young woman had inherited the place from her father. Although she had been engaged to be married at the time, her fiancé was killed in the trenches during World War I. Heartbroken, she had never married and had become an embittered woman, walking about with a cane after she had injured her legs in a fall down the backstairs. She had died in 1972, and the very next family to inhabit the house soon moved out, insisting that it was haunted by the ghost of an old lady with a cane. Ever since that time, the house had only occasional short-term occupants, who always moved out after a few weeks, complaining that the place was haunted."

"We had to bite the bullet and accept the loss of our moving expenses and the first and last month rental deposit," David said," but the real estate agency did waive the remainder of the contract. Thank God, we didn't buy the place, for in all conscience, we could never have sold it to anyone, and we probably would never have recovered from that financial drain. As it was, we just hope and pray that Alice and Mark will recover psychically and emotionally from the experience of sharing that old mansion with a very inhospitable ghost. And as far as that goes, Mary and I still wake up some nights thinking we hear that old lady hitting her cane against our bedroom wall."

LEAVE MY HOUSE ALONE OR LEAVE MY HOUSE

I first entered the home accompanied by a friend, who was very psychically sensitive. "Someone died here," he stated bluntly as soon as we crossed the threshold into the dining room.

The woman whose home we were in the process of purchasing appeared startled by my friend's immediate announcement. When he quickly added, "A man died in the room across from the kitchen," she became visibly upset.

I strongly felt a presence in the house, and I was concerned about the children, since the energy that I detected did not seem to be hospitable.

The pleasant, two-story farmhouse already had a resident when they moved in, a spirit that caused sounds like explosions to be heard all over the house!

Haunted: Malevolent Ghosts, Night Terrors, and Threatening Phantoms

The outside of the farm home was a solid, two-story dwelling with an inviting front porch. It sat atop a grassy hill and was flanked by majestic pines and backed by a dwindling number of oak and walnut trees. At the foot of the hill was a picturesque creek with a small but sturdy bridge. Across the lane from the barn was a cabin said to be one of the very oldest pioneer homes in the county. The sturdy Iowa farmhouse seemed an ideal home in which our family might attempt an experiment in country living.

Shortly before we were to move in, a cousin of the vacating family approached me with an amused smile. "Well, Brad, you should really be happy now," he said. "What more could a writer of all those spooky books want than a haunted house of his own? Now you don't have to chase around the nation going after ghosts. Now you can share a house with one. A very active one."

When I pressed him for details, he only shrugged. "Grandpa was a stubborn Norwegian when he was alive, and I guess he's just as stubborn now that he's passed on. You should have some interesting evenings ahead of you."

Within a few days we had the whole story. The granddaughter of the late owner worked in Trollheim, the ice cream and magazine store that we owned in the village, and she had brought her mother with her to explain the idiosyncrasies of "Papa." Her father had in his day been a well-respected church and community leader. However, his "day" had been in the 1920s and 1930s, and he had steadily grown more reclusive and more strongly opposed to modern technology. Papa's distrust of modern times extended to storm windows, electric lights, and running water. Life with Papa had been a rugged existence.

He had yielded to electric lights sometime in the 1940s, and he loved to sit in his room and listen to the radio—one of his few concessions to the contemporary world around him. He had not permitted running water in his house during his lifetime, and the plumbing we now saw for the toilets had been only recently installed. There still was no drinking water in the home, however, and we would have to get our water by carrying buckets from the well near the barn.

As I evaluated the situation, we had a problem. If we truly were dealing with the earthbound spirit essence of a man who had been a pious church leader and a fervent opponent of progress, just how would he take to a family moving into his home that was headed by a psychical investigator with four lively kids who would immediately begin playing stereos and television sets? And how would the impressionable psyches of the kids, aged eight to sixteen, respond if the spirit became antagonized?

An immediate problem lay in my past. I had spent the first years of my life without electricity, indoor toilets, or running water. To heck with Papa. I was digging a well near the house, and we were having drinking water inside the house flow into our glasses with the twist of a faucet. No carrying water from a well many yards away from the house.

I was the first to undergo retaliation from an angry ghost.

I was alone in the house on a Sunday morning shortly after our move, having some tea and toast while I read the newspaper. My wife, Marilyn (who died in 1982), had gone to the village to open Trollheim, and all the kids had gone with her. One moment things were as idyllic as they could be—the next, my tranquility was shattered by a violent explosion that seemed to come from the basement.

Fearing that the oil-burning furnace had somehow exploded, I opened the basement door, expecting the worst. I could hear what seemed to be the walls of stone and brick caving in on the washer, the dryer, and the other appliances. I expected to be met by billowing clouds of thick black smoke.

> **B**ut the instant I stepped onto the basement landing all sounds of disturbance ceased. The furnace was undamaged. The walls stood firm and solid. There was no smoke or fire.

But the instant I stepped onto the basement landing all sounds of disturbance ceased. The furnace was undamaged. The walls stood firm and solid. There was no smoke or fire.

Before I could puzzle the enigma through, I was startled by the sound of yet another explosion coming from somewhere upstairs.

I had a terrible image of the old brick chimney collapsing, and then I was running up the stairs to investigate.

The attic was as serene as the basement had been. I shook my head in confusion as I studied the sturdy beams and the excellent workmanship that held the roof and the brick chimney firmly erect and braced. The house had been built by master carpenters and bricklayers. It could probably withstand a tornado, I thought to myself as I attempted to understand what was happening around me.

A massive eruption sounded from the basement again. I slammed the attic door behind me, fearing the awesome damage that surely must have really occurred this time.

But before I could run back down the stairs to inspect the extent of the destruction, I heard what sounded like someone tap dancing behind the door to my son Steven's room. I knew that Steven did not tap dance and that I was home alone.

Then I thought of Reb, our beagle. I laughed out loud in relief.

The sound of "tap dancing" had to be the clicking of the dog's paws on the wooden floor. He must have been shut in the room by accident.

But why wasn't Reb barking to be released? He was never shy about expressing his wishes, frustrations, or irritations.

I hesitated with my hand on the door-knob. I felt an even greater hesitation when I heard Reb barking outside.

He was out back by the kitchen door. I had become so engrossed in the mystery of the strange disturbances that I had forgotten I had let him out. It was cold out that morning, and Reb was wanting to come back into the warm house.

Who—or what—was still merrily dancing behind the door to Steven's room?

I twisted the knob and pushed open the door.

The room was empty. And the dancing stopped as suddenly as the explosions had when I had swung wide the basement and attic doors.

Another detonation roared up at me from beyond the basement.

It sounded as if the ghostly intruder was actually tap dancing on the other side of the door, but when he opened the door—silence.

It was then that I sensed the game plan behind all of this. I was now supposed to dash down the stairs in puzzled panic, desperately seeking the cause of the violent "explosions."

I could almost hear the laughter of an unseen prankster.

I resolved not to play the silly game. I walked purposefully back to the kitchen table, where I had left my tea, toast, and Sunday newspaper.

Then it sounded as if the attic roof was being torn from its anchoring beams. The basement walls shuddered and collapsed in what seemed to be another wrenching explosion.

During my career as a psychical researcher, I had become well versed in the games that certain entities like to play with people. I decided to do my best to ignore the phenomena.

The tap dancing was nearer now. It was coming from the music room, the room that the previous owners had kept locked and unused—Papa's room.

When we had moved into the home, I had placed the piano, television, and stereo in the room and had repainted the walls and ceiling with two coats of paint. We had blessed the room and announced that it would henceforth be a place of love and laughter.

I was determined not to glance up from my newspaper. I was not going to play the game.

Within about twenty minutes the disturbances stopped. I was relieved that I had guessed the secret. It appeared that the invisible pranksters did not enjoy playing tricks on someone who remained indifferent to such a grand repertoire of mischief.

Since I did not wish to alarm the rest of the family and was totally immersed in working on a new book at my office in the village, I did not mention the incident to anyone.

About three nights later, when I was working late at my office, I received an urgent telephone call from my older son, Bryan. The panic in his voice told me that I must drive out to the farmhouse at once.

"Dad," Bryan told me, "Reb and I are in my room. Someone is coming up the stairs. I can hear him move up one step at a time!"

It had snowed earlier that day, and I prayed for no ice on the highway. My prayers were heard, and I managed to shave four minutes from the normal twelve-minute drive to the farmhouse.

The doors were locked from the inside, and Bryan was still barricaded in his room with Reb. I offered silent thanks that the boy hadn't blown any holes in himself or the walls with his .12 gauge shotgun.

Bryan had been alone at home watching television in the music room. He heard what he assumed was the sound of other family members returning home. He listened to the familiar noises of an automobile approaching, car doors slamming, voices and laughter, and the stomping of feet on the front porch.

Then he was surprised to hear loud knocking at the front door. Everyone in the family had their own keys, so why would anyone knock? And why would they be pounding at the front door when they usually entered through the back door in the kitchen?

Bryan begrudgingly stirred himself from his television program and went to admit whoever it was on the front porch. He was astonished to find it empty.

Just as he was about to step outside in an attempt to solve the mystery, he heard knocking at the back door. Uttering a sigh of frustration, Bryan slammed the front door and began to head for the kitchen. He had taken no more than a few steps when the knocks were once again at the front door.

And they were joined by every one of the downstairs windows—of which there were many—rattling noisily as if they were about to leave their sills.

By now Bryan knew that someone was playing a joke on him. He figured that it must be half of his high school class coming to give him a scare.

He turned on the yard light so that he could identify the jokesters' automobile. He gasped when he saw that his car was the only one there.

Fists were now thudding on both doors, and Reb was going crazy, growling and baring his teeth.

Bryan next became aware of an eerie babble of voices and short bursts of laughter. Someone very large was definitely leaning against the kitchen door, attempting to force it open.

That was when he called me.

I showed Bryan that there were no footprints in the freshly fallen snow. There was no evidence of tire tracks in the lane. No human had visited him, I explained, but rather some nonphysical intelligences that would initiate a spooky game with anyone who would play along with them.

Later that evening I gave all of my children instructions on how best to deal with any ghostly mechanisms of sound or sight that might frighten them. Basically, the strategy was to remain as indifferent and as aloof to the disturbances as possible. In a good-natured way, one should indicate that he or she simply did not wish to play such silly games.

The entity that was quite likely causing the spooky activity in the home, Papa had been a strong-willed man who didn't care much for progress and newfangled inventions. He never would have approved of his daughter and son-in-law selling the place. He had died in the room that we had named the music room. His family had kept the room locked and had never used it again while they lived there, since things just hadn't felt right in there.

I told the children that under no circumstances should any of us become defiant or angry or threatening. The laws of polarity would only force the tricksters into coming back with bigger and spookier tricks in response to the negative energy that had been directed toward them.

Whether we were dealing with Papa's restless spirit in limbo or a repository of unknown energy that somehow mimicked human intelligence, I felt that I had given the kids some sound advice.

Bryan had experienced the phenomenon firsthand, so he was now better prepared to confront it should the situation arise. Steven reported that he had been reluctant to go to his room at night, because just as soon as he made himself comfortable in bed, the rocking chair in his room began moving back and forth. Kari, who had strong mediumistic abilities, seemed very aware of the disturbances and had often heard her name being called from the shadow of the attic. She had declined their invitation to come upstairs to play with them. Julie had also heard her name being called but had always run downstairs to escape them. Marilyn, who had listened quietly to my discussion with

> Bryan slammed the front door and began to head for the kitchen. He had taken no more than a few steps when the knocks were once again at the front door.

the kids, told me when we were alone that she had witnessed balls of light that had moved around the outside of the house.

The most frightening of all for Marilyn came later when I was away from home lecturing. She had awakened to find the ghost form of an old man on the top of the bed covers attempting to molest her. She had fought him off with blows and prayers until he disappeared.

Marilyn was very conventionally religious, and she found such confrontations with spirits to be very troubling and difficult to fit into her previous reality construct. She had married me with the understanding that I was going into the Lutheran ministry and that she would then be the choir director and a good pastor's wife. She had never accepted my decision to undertake a kind of ministry that was completely nondenominational and totally universal in its philosophical parameters.

The varieties of paranormal experiences that were worked upon our family became a little too awesome for eight-year-old Julie to understand. Whenever she was left alone in the farmhouse, the entities would gang up on her, and I would return to find her standing at the end of the lane or seeking refuge in a neighbor's home. In each instance she complained of having heard strange voices, laughter, and weird music.

Early one evening just as I was entering my office to do some work on my book, I heard the telephone ringing. It was Julie. She had been calling the office ever since I had left home, and she was in tears. A dramatic manifestation had begun within minutes after I had left her at the kitchen table eating cookies and drinking milk. She was home alone. Marilyn was at work, and the older children were involved with school activities.

This time it had begun with laughter from the music room.

There was a noisy blur of voices as if several people were trying to speak at once. Then came some "funny piano music" and the sound of a drum.

Valiantly, Julie had tried to practice what I had told her do: remain calm, act aloof, and not play the game with whatever it is that likes to play such spooky tricks on people.

When the rhythmic tapping of the drum suddenly gave way to blaring horns and trumpets, Julie's indifference melted.

They held a series of séances in a final effort to remove the spirit from their lives.

Haunted: Malevolent Ghosts, Night Terrors, and Threatening Phantoms

I had not been gone for more than two or three minutes, but Julie knew that I was headed for the office. She just let the telephone ring until I answered it.

Shortly after that incident, Deon Frey, a medium friend of mine from Chicago, visited for the weekend, and a series of séances and cleansings managed to calm the phenomenon considerably. Within another few weeks, it had largely dissipated. According to the medium, I had, in fact, angered the spirit of the original owner by bringing in running water, television and stereo sets, and adding insulation, modern windows, and modern toilets. I had simply "ruined" his home—and he didn't care very much for my attitude, either.

It was years later, but Julie finally identified the music that she had heard coming from the music room on the several occasions when she had been left alone to deal with the phenomenon.

"When I was a senior in high school," she said, "some girlfriends and I were just driving around one night, and we had on one of those radio stations that play nostalgic music from the 'good old days.' We were talking about how different some of the music used to be, when suddenly I just about freaked out. It was a good thing that I wasn't driving! It was the same music that I had heard coming from that spooky room, and all those terrible memories came back to me."

Julie had heard Glenn Miller's "In the Mood."

Incredibly, it had been music from the 1940s that had so frightened Julie. To this day, whenever she hears Benny Goodman, Duke Ellington, or Glenn Miller, she gets a cold shiver, for it was their old records that she had heard playing from the darkened recesses of the music room.

Although she grew up in a home where we enjoyed eclectic musical taste, I must confirm that the tunes of the 1940s would have been foreign to Julie at that time of her life. The family had classical, folk, motion-picture themes, rock, pop, and Broadway show tunes, but we had no big-band records from the 1940s in our collection.

Papa might not have cared much for most of the instruments of progress, but he accepted radio. And he probably tolerated the music of the 1940s, the years when he would have been having some of the most meaningful experiences of his life.

Although it has now been over forty years since we shared those encounters in our very own haunted house, there is never a time when the family gets together that the conversation does not eventually turn to the subject of "that place"— and each time I learn about some eerie experiences that the children had endured and had never before shared with me.

ONE OF MY FAVORITE GHOST INVESTIGATIONS

This particular haunted house and its lively ghost will always be one of my favorite investigations because of the vast number of witnesses who saw the spirit forms for themselves. The manifestations were so profuse that one almost expected the principal ghost to carry a tin can in which he would hustle the price of admission to view another dimension of reality.

In July 1970, my friend and associate Glenn McWane had received a lead on a haunted house in a Midwestern college town. Before the house had been vacated, two elderly sisters had lived there alone. According to a number of police officers, who had themselves witnessed the appearance of a ghost, nearly every night a glowing *something* would manifest in the lane, walk to the house, enter it, and converse with the sisters.

On several occasions, the police had received calls from frightened neighbors who had seen the thing. These people thought the police should do something about the spook light, but the officers who responded to the call really didn't know quite how to handle a ghost. They would just sit in their squad cars outside the house and watch the two elderly ladies talking with the glowing ghost. After one of the sisters passed on and the other was taken to a nursing home, the ghost light continued to make its appearance. Now, however, there were at least two entities, and some of the officers assumed that the man's deceased daughter had joined him.

It was midnight when we arrived at the lane of the once elaborate and well-maintained estate. The headlights picked up the image of a wooden gate bearing a warning to any trespassers to keep out or to risk being prosecuted.

Glenn said that he had arranged for the caretaker to meet us at the estate the next day. He had also requested a police officer to accompany us just to be certain a passing squad car didn't pick us up as vandals.

In our group was the late, famed, Chicago seeress Irene Hughes, who noted the thick, drooping branches of untrimmed trees that virtually blanketed the narrow lane. Glenn said that from our present position we wouldn't be able to see more than the edge of what had once been one of the city's loveliest estates.

I don't remember who first saw it, but no one had to point out the sudden glowing intruder upon the dark and quiet scene. There appeared to be a very large mass of light moving in front of us down the lane.

Glenn turned off the headlights, and the strange orb glowed brightly in the total darkness.

The moon was covered by clouds that night. The nearest street light was a vapor-light, completely cut off from the old estate by the thick wall of trees.

Haunted: Malevolent Ghosts, Night Terrors, and Threatening Phantoms

As we watched, the orb of light—that had by now assumed the shape and dimensions of an average adult male—moved toward the old house. Everyone turned to look at Irene, who was seated in the middle of the backseat.

"Shall we go right now and investigate whatever it is?" someone wondered.

"No," Irene answered firmly, breaking her silence. "Not tonight. I have a very bad feeling that it would not be good for us to walk down that lane right now."

There was a certain tone to her voice that indicated that she meant exactly what she said. Her psychic impression told her that the time was not right to invade the darkened lane and approach the shimmering orb that seemed more and more to be moving toward the deserted house.

"Let's leave … *now!*" Irene said suddenly.

No one argued with her.

American psychic Irene Hughes was a popular figure who often appeared on television programs such as *The Merv Griffin Show.* She joined the other spirits in 2012.

When we visited the estate on the second night, we had the caretaker and a policeman with us in the station wagon. This man was not the same open-minded police officer who had accompanied us that afternoon and who been one of the officers who had previously witnessed the glowing entity in the lane. This fellow had joined us earlier that evening and had been openly skeptical, even mocking, toward our efforts of investigating haunting phenomena at the mansion.

We opened the gate and drove cautiously down the lane. When we were adjacent to the old house, Glenn stopped the car.

"Let us just sit quietly for a few moments, and permit me to gain some psychic impressions of the house by night," Irene requested.

As our medium sat in meditation, I glanced absently out the windshield. Then I blinked my eyes rapidly. There was a glowing, mist-like substance forming directly in front of the station wagon's hood. The ghost was beginning to take shape right before my eyes.

"What is *that?*" asked the police officer sitting beside me in the front seat.

Because he had announced himself as a professional disbeliever in such things as ghosts, I could not resist having a bit of fun with him.

"What is what?" I asked blandly. "I don't see anything."

"There," he said in a harsh whisper. "Right there in front of the car! What in hell is that?"

I started to deny seeing anything one more time but decided against further teasing the officer when I saw that he was nervously brushing the strap that held his service revolver in its holster. It was clear to me that this man was now dealing with something that was not covered in the police manual and that he was having an extremely difficult time fitting the reality of the materializing entity into the world view that he had only moments before held so sacrosanct.

At that moment, Glenn whispered over our shoulders in response to our overheard conversation. "I've been watching it for a couple of minutes now," Glenn said. "At first it was just a wispy tendril that seemed to come from that clump of bushes over there. Then it stopped directly in front of the car and began to take form."

By now everyone in our research group was watching the glowing, mist-like thing, and we all sat in silence for a few moments, as we observed the orb grow larger and denser and begin to assume a humanlike form. We decided to get out of the car for a closer inspection.

It was a very warm evening, but as I extended my hand into the midst of the glowing mist, I felt its very cold interior.

Such a bold act may have been considered very rude by the entity, for suddenly the glowing image vanished.

Before we could speculate on this ghost's rapid disappearance, Irene whispered loudly from the other side of the station wagon: "There are some people coming through the bushes by the house!"

Members of our research team swore that they could hear the approach of two or more people coming toward us.

Then the footsteps stopped, and one of our group directed everyone's attention to the reappearance of glowing images between two trees. But before any of us could approach it, the lights winked out as rapidly as if they had been extinguished candle flames.

"I swear the ghosts looked real to me, more than spirit," Irene said.

Perhaps Irene's greater sensitivity enabled her to see images where we could only see the glowing mist and orbs.

Irene suddenly put her hands to her ears and said that she heard the terrible sound of a woman screaming. "There! There in the bushes," she directed us. "Can you see her head?"

Glenn and I told her that we could see a glowing orb, but we were apparently not sensitive enough to tune into the vibrations on the estate and see distinctive features on the entities.

"Well, there are plenty of vibrations around here to tune in to," Irene remarked. "This place is just drenched with psychic vibrations."

Every member of our party, including the police officer and the caretaker, had seen the ghostly glowing orbs, but only Irene Hughes had been able to adjust the fine tune mechanism within her psyche clearly enough to pick up distinct images of the forms that had been preternaturally recorded on the grounds of the old estate.

Approximately one calendar year after our visit to the mansion, Glenn and I were conducting some follow-up research on the place. We pulled into the lane about midnight in the company of three investigators, only one of whom had visited the place on a prior occasion.

We took careful notice of a wire stretched across the lane. Someone, undoubtedly the caretaker, had strung a number of white and red strips of cloth from the line. We switched out the headlights, got out of the vehicle, and prepared to await the ghost, which had been sighted by Glenn and a university professor just a few nights before.

We did not have long to wait before a column of light about the size of a human being of average height appeared off to the right of the automobile and made its traditional trek down the lane toward the old mansion.

We viewed the glowing orb until it disappeared inside the house; then, satisfied that the phenomenon continued unabated, we turned to walk back to the car. As we were approaching the automobile, we were startled to see that a three-tine pitchfork had been shoved into the ground just a few feet in front of the vehicle.

We all knew that the pitchfork had not been there before we had switched off the headlights and began to walk down the lane. The pitchfork had been driven into the ground just in back of the white and red stripes of cloth on the wire that stretched across the driveway entrance.

If that shimmering column of light had truly planted that pitchfork before us, then I must admit that I was becoming concerned that we may have worn out our welcome at the haunted estate.

Three years later on Halloween, Glenn learned that the old mansion was about to be torn down and replaced by a new home. We drove out to the estate for a farewell viewing, and on that particular occasion, even though it was Halloween, we saw nothing out of the ordinary. We joked that the glowing entity must have learned of the imminent destruction of the mansion and had at last moved on to a higher spiritual plateau.

Later that evening, we were invited to stop by a Halloween party in which a number of police officers were in attendance. Egged on by one of the officers who had experienced the haunting at the mansion on many different occasions, Glenn and I began to regale the partygoers with some spooky Halloween stories about our encounters with the glowing ghost.

The next day, before I left the city to return home, Glenn and one of the police officers stopped by the motel where I was staying to share the perfect capper to the haunting at Sinclair mansion. It seems that a couple of the police officers who had attended the Halloween party the night before had been highly skeptical of our accounts of the glowing ghost. Since they had to go on duty after the party, they decided to take the squad car out to the estate to see for themselves.

Amidst howls of laughter, Glenn told me that the two officers had sat drinking coffee in the squad car, commenting derisively about our abilities as ghost researchers. Then, to their utter astonishment, the glowing entity materialized directly in front of their squad car. Begrudgingly admitting their terror, the two men confessed to their fellow officer that they had burned rubber getting out of the lane. They went from cynics to believers in ghosts in a matter of seconds.

Poltergeists—Teenagers
and the Supernatural

Journalist Jane Hamilton reported that on August 8 and 9, 2016, police in Rutherglen, South Lanarkshire, Scotland, were stunned when they witnessed clothes flying across a room, lights going off, the lampshades turning upside down, and oven doors opening and closing.

A chihuahua that was playing in the garden was discovered sitting on top of a seven-foot hedge.

The family who lived at the property had called the police in a panic. They had endured two days of the bizarre occurrences before moving out of the property.

The situation was discussed at high levels within Scotland police, with senior officers perplexed as to how to best handle the incidents.

A police source said, "These were incidents that were witnessed by our own officers. Incidents that are not easily explained. One problem we've got is where we go from here as no crime has been established, so what else can we do but deal with any reports of disturbances?"

"But officers with more than twenty years' service are saying they've never seen anything like this. It really is something that down-to-earth police officers are having trouble getting their heads round."

"How do you handle what, despite us liking to use the word, has been described as a poltergeist?"

The family at the center of the disturbances were devoutly Catholic, and police did seek assistance from the church. A priest went to the house on Stonelaw Road and performed what has been described as a "blessing" at the property.

The supernatural saga unfolded when the family—a woman and her son in his early teens—contacted police to report "disturbing incidents" in her home. The woman and the teenager, described as extremely distressed, had been experiencing violent and unexplained circumstances and in desperation contacted police.

A police source told reporter Jane Hamilton that the officers arrived, expecting it to be a mental health issue, but they witnessed the lights going off, clothes flying across the room, and the dog sitting on top of the hedge.

With no reasonable explanation for what they had witnessed, police, acting with the support of the family, contacted the Catholic Church, who sent a priest to bless the house.

No one was harmed, though the family chose to leave the house. They are understood to be living with relatives.

The source added: "The main concern is with the family's welfare and well-being but with no crime committed and no culprit we are at a loss how to proceed with it. Inquiries are ongoing but it's difficult to know where to go with it."

TERRI'S POLTERGEIST PLAYED GAMES WITH HER FOR YEARS

Terri S. told us that when she was a teenager of thirteen she was entrusted by her parents to sit with her younger brother and sister on the night when Mom and Dad went bowling. One night after she had put her siblings to bed and she was taking a bath, Terri heard footsteps in the hall. Her brother

The mischievous spirit scattered Terri's clothes around the room after she had neatly folded them.

and sister were sound asleep. She checked the house from kitchen to basement, but she found no sign of an unwelcome invader.

Weird things continued to occur as Terri grew older. She would iron her clothes on the board in the basement and leave her freshly laundered and ironed outfits to await her return in the morning before school.

"In the morning," she said, "I would go down to the basement to get dressed and find my clothes messed up, scattered, and sometimes even with items missing. I knew my mother, father, or brother and sister would not do such a nasty thing—and sometimes an item of clothes would be missing for days, even a week, before it was returned."

By her mid-teens, Terri had begun reading about the paranormal, and she chalked up the somewhat irksome phenomenon to a poltergeist playing games with her.

Terri's encounters with an inconsiderate and messy poltergeist reminded us of a similar instance that occurred to a teenaged girl in Wisconsin. She, too, would prepare the outfit that she would wear the next morning to school before she went to bed. When she awakened and prepared to get dressed, her clothing would be wrinkled and scattered throughout her bedroom.

After enduring such irritating ghostly visits for several nights, a daring idea entered her mind. She left her clothes messy and lying carelessly across chairs and a dresser. When she awakened the next morning, the poltergeist had fallen into her snare. All of her clothes were neatly arranged and ready for her to put them on and get ready for school.

POLTERGEISTS: SPIRITS OR PSYCHIC UPHEAVAL?

In common parlance, any violent and disruptive haunting is said to be caused by poltergeists. In the view of many psychical researchers, such phenomena are born not in the machinations of a ghost or spirit entity but rather in the psyche of a living being who is undergoing some kind of stress, psychic upheaval, or severe and dramatic psychological adjustment. Such an individual (most often an adolescent) expresses unconscious aggression toward others through dramatic manifestations of psychokinetic power (mind over matter), such as the overturning of furniture and the propelling of objects through the room. In some cases we have investigated, poltergeist phenomena have interacted with the haunting manifestations that already existed in the home, thereby producing intensely negative and disruptive energy.

In his book *The Poltergeist Phenomenon: An In-Depth Investigation into Floating Beds, Smashing Glass, and Other Unexplained Disturbances*, Michael Clarkson reviews seventy-five notable cases and talks to the victims and eyewitnesses to one of the most intriguing and baffling areas of paranormal research. It is Clarkson's conclusion based on his research that "we are dealing with haunted people, not spirits or buildings.

"Poltergeist energy (recurrent spontaneous psychokinesis or RSPK) usually revolves around a person in the room, most often a young person going through puberty. In only about 5 percent of the 75 cases I reviewed, a spirit was reportedly involved and perhaps acting through a young person to move objects. [I]t seems a number of components must come together for a 'perfect psychic storm,' and that's one reason RSPK is rare. There is usually stress or repression in a house and the poltergeist agents seem frustrated and have no other way of expressing themselves. As well, the agents often have unusual brains and the ability to tap into nearby energy sources to move things unconsciously with their minds."

Researcher Michael Clarkson noticed that poltergeists occurred around people with remarkable brains, and, therefore, the spirits seemed to emanate from "unusual brains."

We are in general agreement with Clarkson that a poltergeist is a psychokinetic (mind influencing matter) projection of energy that finds its explosive center often in the hormonal surges of adolescence, a teenager's frustrated creative expression, and sometimes the stresses of marital adjustment. The poltergeist, therefore, quite likely emanates from the living, rather than the dead. The poltergeist (pelting or throwing ghost) is a ghost only in common parlance, which links the two because of the "spooklike" nature of the poltergeist that causes the invisible pseudo-entity to prefer darkness for its violent exercises of tossing furniture, objects, and people about the room. On occasion, though, hauntings may precipitate poltergeist activity, and the energy of the poltergeist may in some cases recharge dormant memories and set a ghost in motion.

A MESSY, SADISTIC, UNINVITED GUEST

When the poltergeist is at its peak, the host family may be beleaguered to the psychological breaking point. Psychoanalyst Dr. Nandor Fodor maintained that the poltergeist was unquestionably sadistic. Dr. Fodor theorized that such projected aggression through unknown biological factors is the one way in which an adolescent can release hostility against his parents and other figures of authority and still maintain his conscious innocence.

Between January 14 and February 8, 1960, the Edgar C. Jones family in Baltimore, Ohio, were the unhappy hosts of an uninvited guest that proved to be very messy.

The poltergeist activity began when a row of Mrs. Jones's prized ceramic pitchers exploded one by one. Then, while the startled family watched in bewilderment, a flower pot lifted itself from a shelf and smashed through a nearby window pane. A sugar bowl floated up to the chandelier and scattered its contents in the candle holders. Pictures were tossed off the walls, and a brass incense burner became airborne and sailed six feet off a bookshelf.

Once when Mrs. Jones and her married daughter, Mrs. Pauls, were preparing a meal, a string of glasses danced off the shelf in the cabinet and shattered on the floor. No sooner had the women cleaned up the shards of glass when two dirty ashtrays flew into the kitchen and dumped their refuse on the floor.

A suddenly animated table on a stairway landing came bounding down the steps to splinter itself at the foot of the stairs.

The home-wrecking poltergeist did not ignore the basement in its domination of the Jones household. A case of soda bottles popped off their caps in a series of explosions that sounded like a string of firecrackers on the Fourth of July. A well-stacked pile of fireplace wood erupted in violent bursts of energy that sent bits of bark and pulp flying across the floor.

No one received any real physical harm (and it is seldom that anyone ever does during a poltergeist attack) throughout the period of the psychic siege, but Mr. Jones was struck on the head by a falling can of sauerkraut as he stooped to pick up a can of corn that the invisible, rambunctious ghost had thrown. The can of sauerkraut barely bruised him, but Jones felt true anguish when he saw some of his most valued pieces of furniture rudely destroyed by their violent and unbidden guest.

None of the Jones household—Mr. and Mrs. Jones, their daughter, Mrs. Pauls, and their seventeen-year-old grandson, Ted—were injured in any appreciable way, but they all suffered terrible mental and emotional pain during that three-week period of siege under the attack of the poltergeist.

Many researchers have noted that, in addition to the sadism of the attacks directed upon authoritarian persons (parents, older siblings, police officers, clergymen), the psychic "eye of the storm"—the individual who serves as the poltergeist's energy center—may receive such attacks as the appearance of stigmata on the flesh, the painful puffing up of the body, or the appearance of writing on walls or various personal objects that relate vile and obscene threats. Whether such abuse is due to unconscious feelings of guilt is difficult to assess. It would seem that, in at least some cases, the agent of the poltergeist is subconsciously aware that he or she is responsible for the psychic storm that has been unleashed in the home.

Dr. Fodor was able personally to investigate the Jones case in Baltimore. He learned that the police department's crime laboratory could find no trace of any volatile substance having been placed in any of the moving or exploding objects. The city engineers had been there to test for earth tremors with a seismograph, but they had found nothing. A radio repairman had developed a theory that high-frequency radio wavelengths had been responsible for the weird occurrences, but his sophisticated equipment could find nothing to substantiate his thesis. A local plumber claimed the ghost was nothing but suction coming from the hot-air furnace, but none of his tinkering did anything to hinder the activities of the noisy demon in the Jones house.

Newspaper reporters, television crews, press photographers, and radio interviewers stomped through every inch of the home and photographed the

Poltergeists find their energy most often in adolescents who then generate the ghostly visions. Sometimes this is done consciously, sometimes unconsciously.

Haunted: Malevolent Ghosts, Night Terrors, and Threatening Phantoms

phenomena from every conceivable angle. Kooks, cranks, and cultists had plagued the Joneses, each with his or her own time-tested method of ridding a home of an unwanted ghost.

Dr. Fodor felt that he had discovered the poltergeist with little effort at all. Seventeen-year-old Ted was a shy, brooding youth, who had left school at the legal age because he said that his classes bored him. He liked to sit alone in his room and read. He confessed to the psychoanalyst that what he wanted most to do was to write short stories.

Dr. Fodor put the ghost to rest by encouraging the teenager to do what he most desired: write fiction. A very simple exorcism, indeed, but it worked. When the youth realized that he had found a sympathetic audience for his opinions and someone who would listen to a recitation of his ambitions and goals, the poltergeist activity ceased.

Dr. Fodor had come to alter an earlier opinion that poltergeist phenomena only occurred in prepubescent children. The psychoanalyst believed that the mechanics of poltergeist activity were accomplished by what he termed "psychic dissociation." Dr. Fodor theorized that the human body is capable of releasing energy in a manner similar to atomic bombardments. Through such psychic bombardments, a projected energy force was apparently able to enter soda bottles and to burst them open from within.

Sacheverell Sitwell is another writer who expressed his opinion that the poltergeist most often finds its energy center in the psyche of an adolescent who performs the ghostly effects, both consciously and unconsciously, "being gifted for the time being with something approaching criminal cunning. The particular direction of this power is always towards the secret or concealed weaknesses of the spirit … the obscene or erotic recesses of the soul. The mysteries of puberty, that trance or dozing of the psyche before it awakes into adult life, is a favorite playground for the poltergeist."

Perhaps Dr. Fodor said it simplest when he told the press during his investigation of the Jones case that a ghost haunts a house and a poltergeist haunts a person. In his opinion, the poltergeist was very often not really a ghost but rather "a bundle of projected repressions."

SPOKANE'S HOME ON THE EDGE OF HELL

It began one night in November 1986 in a suburb of Spokane, Washington, when Donna Fencl was awakened by the sounds of what she thought at first was someone dragging some heavy furniture across the attic floor. She nudged her husband, Vernon, awake and told him that someone was after the antiques they had stored in the attic.

Grumbling at first after being awakened from a sound sleep, Vernon sat upright and was soon wide awake when he, too, heard the peculiar noises issu-

> **T**hey were no sooner back in their own beds when Amy's screams brought them once again rushing to her bedside.

ing from above their bedroom. He grabbed a baseball bat he kept at the side of the bed and a flashlight from the nightstand drawer and cautiously began creeping up the attic stairs, ordering Donna to stay by the telephone, ready to dial 9-1-1.

They were both relieved when Vernon returned to report that there was no sign of burglars or any indication that any furniture had been moved. What had awakened them, he theorized, was air locks in the pipes of their old hot-water heating system. Perhaps, Vernon speculated, it really was time to install a new furnace with forced-air ducts.

Air locks in the pipes seemed a satisfactory answer, and after checking to see that their twelve-year-old daughter, Amy, slumbered undisturbed, the Fencls went back to sleep.

But the next evening the sounds returned, much louder than before and unmistakably in the attic directly above their heads. Once again, it sounded as though a crew of furniture movers was at work, but when Vernon went upstairs to investigate, there again were no intruders to be seen and nothing had been moved.

However, on this occasion, Donna and Vernon were summoned to Amy's bedroom by her screams of terror. According to their daughter, she had felt something moving in her bed. When it had brushed up against her, it had seemed to her to feel both cold and furry. She imagined it to be some animal, such as a rat.

Although they had never been bothered by rodents in their home, both Donna and Vernon carefully searched Amy's room for any signs that it was serving as an unwilling host to a rat or a mouse. They found no visible traces of any such creature in her room, so they assured Amy as best they could that she must have been dreaming.

They were no sooner back in their own beds when Amy's screams brought them once again rushing to her bedside. This time she said that something had lifted the end of her bed and slammed in back down several times in succession. For the second time that evening, they did their best to pacify her and assure her that she had been having a troubled dream, perhaps caused by her hearing the odd thumps and knocks caused by the air locks in the pipes of the heating system.

Two nights later, when Donna and Vernon were returning from the movies, they were barely inside the door when the eighteen-year-old girl they had hired to sit with Amy met them with the frightening accusation that their house was haunted. She would never sit for them again.

When the Fencls calmed her and asked what she was talking about, she told them how the television set had gone off and on when no one was near it. Footsteps had sounded upstairs, and doors had opened and closed in second-floor bedrooms while she and Amy had sat cowering downstairs in the living room. Amy had refused to go to her room and was sleeping on the sofa.

Vernon paid the sitter double to compensate for her anxiety, but he couldn't accept her analysis of their home as haunted. As he drove her home, he tried to explain about the knocking sound in the pipes and how they could have sounded like footsteps walking around upstairs.

Rushing to help Amy, Donna saw a "gray, shadowy figure coming down the stairs...."

"Hey, Mr. Fencl," she told him as they pulled up in front of her house, "I know what I heard and what I saw. You've got a spook loose in your house."

Vernon could see that she could not be persuaded otherwise, and he chalked the "ghost" up to two young girls alone at night permitting themselves to become frightened by strange noises and allowing their imaginations to run wild. But when he drove into the driveway of his home, he was surprised to see the upstairs lights blinking on and off. Rushing inside, he found Donna sitting ashen-faced on the stairs, a sobbing Amy huddled next to her.

"I saw it with my own eyes," Donna said. "A gray, shadowy figure coming down the stairs toward us. I screamed with fright, and the thing vanished. But it's been turning the lights on and off upstairs ever since."

Over the next week, the shadowy figure was seen frequently, moving about in different rooms of the house. Vegetables and cooking utensils would go flying around the kitchen. Appliances would mysteriously turn themselves on and off. Doors would open and shut of their own volition.

The morning after some invisible force snatched Amy out of bed and spun her across the room, the Fencls summoned a priest to bless their home and drive away the evil entity. In the opinion of Vernon and Donna, their household had been invaded by a demonic entity and their home had somehow been moved to the edge of hell.

After the visit by the priest only seemed to provoke even more violent disturbances, Vernon called a friend of his, Karl Liekweg, a former policeman, and beseeched him to come to spend the night with them and be their bodyguard, so to speak.

"Ghostbuster had never been in my résumé," Liekweg wrote in his report of the haunting, "but I have an interest in the paranormal and I was curious to see if the kind of things that Vernon described to me were really happening, so I agreed to come."

Liekweg was dozing in the big armchair that had been moved to the foot of the stairs. At around 3:00 A.M., he was awakened by noises from above. As he moved to investigate, he noticed that the air in the house had taken on an eerie chill.

With his flashlight in hand, he moved toward the bedroom occupied by Amy, the room from which the sounds were emanating.

"When I opened the door and scanned the room with my flashlight, I saw little Amy curled up in bed with her back to the headboard, horrified by the weird demonstration going on before her," Liekweg said. "The furniture was dancing. The girl's bed was elevated. Dresser drawers floated across the room as if they were filled with helium. Dolls, books, and other objects were spinning around the room. As soon as I turned on the overhead lights, the spooky shenanigans stopped."

After Vernon and Donna entered the room to calm their daughter, Liekweg followed through on police procedure and checked the furniture and other objects that he had seen in motion. He found no wires, no strings, no pulleys.

"I know that I myself was not strong enough or dexterous enough to make all the furniture move about as I had seen it dancing around the room, so I could not perceive how a slight twelve-year-old girl could have done so," he said. "It seemed to me like a genuine poltergeist case with the girl, Amy, providing the energy center. As discreetly as I could, I inquired of her mother about any onset of puberty, and I learned that Amy had been quite upset and frightened with the advent of certain of her new bodily functions."

Familiar enough with the literature of the paranormal to recognize that so often the energy of the poltergeist is set free by a girl entering puberty, Liekweg suggested that Mrs. Fencl explain to her daughter in greater detail and with a lot of tender loving care the hormonal and other changes that came with her womanhood. He also wisely suggested that the entire family take a few days away from the house on a holiday.

"I spent a night in the house after the Fencls were away," Liekweg wrote, concluding his report of the poltergeist haunting, "and there were no manifestations of any kind. I did a follow-up check after the family returned, and I was pleased to learn that everything was quiet once again in their home. The poltergeistic energy had been spent, and once Amy had come to terms with adolescence and that things that were happening were all right and normal, the haunting had ended."

IDENTIFYING THE WORK OF A POLTERGEIST

As we have seen, many contemporary researchers argue that such invisible housebreakers are really not messy and rude ghosts but rather berserk bundles of uncontrolled psychokinetic energy, the direct action of mind on matter. Such investigators also attribute the often violent poltergeist activity to the sexual changes and adjustments that accompany puberty, the early stages of a marital union, or feelings of inadequacy or frustration accentuated by some traumatic experience.

While there may be many instances in which the outbreak of poltergeist phenomena might be associated with puberty and the dramatic changes that adolescence brings to a child's psyche, many of the classic cases of noisy ghosts throwing objects and severely disrupting the normal flow of things occurred where no adolescent was on the scene. If the extrasensory ability of psychokinesis—mind over matter—can somehow cause an individual to become an unaware participant in haunting phenomena, then we may have to expand our theory of the poltergeist to include those instances in which the human mind, under stress, fatigue, sleep deprivation, and so forth, may release uncontrolled spontaneous energy that has the power to activate and to interact with dormant spirit forces.

Poltergeist or Haunting Activity?

By Stephen Wagner
(updated April 1, 2017)

Determining the difference between poltergeist activity and ghosts or haunting activity can be difficult. While ghost and haunting activity is the result of spirit energy, poltergeist activity—also known as recurrent spontaneous psychokinesis (RSPK)—is the result of psychic energy generated (usually unconsciously) by a person, referred to as an agent.

But how do you know if there might be poltergeist activity in your home? Most often, you'll know because it is out of the ordinary and pretty obvious: sounds, movements, and odors of unknown origin.

Below are seven of the most common types of poltergeist activity. Let me be clear, however: Because you experience—or *think* you experience—one or more of the activities listed below does not automatically mean that it definitely is poltergeist activity. There could be more mundane, everyday causes for the activity. For example, smells of unknown origin could be wafting in from an open window, or lights flickering on and off could be the result of faulty wiring.

You should always seek logical explanations before jumping to the conclusion that it is poltergeist activity. Although it is a well-documented phe-

In addition to making objects disappear, poltergeists enjoy levitating or throwing objects around the house, too.

nomenon with many real cases, true poltergeist activity is relatively rare. A professional investigator might be able to help you to determine the cause of what you are experiencing.

Here are the seven signs of poltergeist activity.

1. Disappearing Objects: You put your set of keys or your cell phone down in the place you always put it. You turn around a minute later and it's gone. You and your family search high and low for it, but it cannot be found. Later—sometimes days later or longer—the object mysteriously reappears in the very place you always put it. Or, more bizarrely, you later find it in a ridiculous place, like high on a bookshelf, in a shoebox in the closet, or some other spot where you'd never put it in a million years.

2. Objects Levitating or Thrown: You're sitting there watching TV, totally engrossed in a dramatic movie, when suddenly the bowl of popcorn you've been munching from rises from the coffee table, floats through the air a few feet, then drops to the floor. Or, you're having a loud argument with your teenage daughter, and as she storms out of the room, books and knick-knacks come hurtling off the bookcase, as if reacting to the young girl's anger. The movement of physical objects like this can be quite dramatic and can be as slight as a box of Tic Tacs sliding a few inches across a table top or as amazing as a heavy refrigerator levitating off the kitchen floor.

Ivan T. Sanderson (1911–1973), world-famous zoologist, natural historian, and investigator of the unusual, once told me when I visited him at his estate in New Jersey that one should not use the term "throwing" when speaking of the poltergeistic manipulation of stones. "The stones are not thrown; they are dropped or lobbed or just drift around," Sanderson insisted.

Sanderson went on to declare that such cases are within the realm of physics rather than psychical research. Stone-dropping, he said, is a purely physical phenomenon and will, in time, be completely explained as connected to some physical principles, though not necessarily on Newtonian, Einsteinian, or any other principles that concern our particular space-time continuum.

Sanderson told me that he had "played catch" with flying rocks in Sumatra. "If somebody would measure their speed of fall on arrival," he maintained, "it might be demonstrated that they are obeying some law or, at least, following some pattern that is not entirely random. "They might be obeying some other so-called 'law' of dynamics. If we could establish this, we would have at least two principles of dynamics in our space-time continuum."

3. Scents and Odors: No one in your house smokes, yet on occasion, the distinct smell of cigarette or cigar smoke can be detected in the bathroom. Or as you're dressing for bed, suddenly the overpowering scent of lilacs fills the room. As stated above, all kinds of smells can enter your house from the outside, even from a passing car, so such scents might not necessarily mean they're from a poltergeist. Such scents and odors can also be a sign of ghost activity as they might be associated with a spirit or residual haunting.

4. Electrical Interference: Johnny is having a tough time in school, and sometimes when he enters the living room with that scowl on his face, the overhead light and lamps flicker. Or it's 3 o'clock in the morning and you're shocked out of sleep by the stereo in the den turning on full blast and it doesn't have a remote control that could have set if off accidentally, either from inside or outside the house.

5. Power from Nowhere: That antique clock on the fireplace mantle hasn't worked in years, but it's a family heirloom and you like how it looks there, so you've kept it. Quite suddenly, it begins to chime and the second-hand resumes moving, even though the clock hasn't been wound in ten years. Maybe it's 9:15 P.M. and the little kids are sound asleep in bed when suddenly Billy's little choo-choo train begins to chug across the living room floor. Thinking there's something wrong with the switch, you open the battery compartment to remove the batteries … but there are no batteries in it!

6. Knocks, Rappings, Footsteps, and Other Noises: You're in your office trying to balance the checkbook, but you find it hard to concentrate when your husband is in the other room banging on the wall for some reason. You go to investigate, but then remember your husband is out bowling—he isn't even home. No one else is. So where's that knocking coming from?

7. Physical Attacks: Twelve-year-old Alyssa can't stand how her parents are always fighting. The constant yelling and screaming are driving her crazy. She sits on the floor in the corner of her room, crying with her face in her hands. She winces from a sudden pain on her back. When she checks it in a mirror, she finds fresh scratches.

AN ENDLESS POUNDING ON THE WALLS

Police Sgt. Daniel G. told of me of an encounter with a poltergeist that he and three fellow officers had in an apartment in a large Midwestern city.

The officers had no idea what to expect when they received the call around eleven o'clock on the night of October 12, 2000. All Sgt. G and his partner Les H had been told was that a lady had complained that someone was banging on her walls.

"We didn't know if we were going to have to quiet some noisy party animals in the next apartment or some cranky neighbor who might somehow be annoyed because he or she thought the woman was making too much noise in her apartment," Sgt. G said.

At first, the knocking sound on the wall sounded like a person's knuckles, but it became louder, more like a hammer pounding insistently.

When the two officers arrived at the address that had been dispatched to them, they quickly discovered that the complaint had been filed by a woman who lived on the third floor. That meant no one could be making noise above her, because she was on the top floor.

As the officers walked down the hallway toward her apartment, they could hear nothing that could qualify as raucous party sounds. Maybe they had lucked out, and the complaint of a disturbance had taken care of itself.

But the minute the two officers stepped inside the apartment of Mrs. C and her eleven-year-old daughter, Sophie, they could hear terrible pounding sounds that seemed to be issuing from all around them.

As Sgt. G stated in his report of the incident: "Mrs. C appeared on the brink of nervous collapse, and her daughter was curled up on the couch. It was incredible.

You stepped back out into the hall, and you couldn't hear a thing out of the ordinary. Yet the second you moved back into the apartment, you could hear what sounded like someone pounding the walls with a hammer. I told Les to check up on the roof while I tried to calm Mrs. C and her daughter."

Mrs. C told Sgt. G that the disturbance had begun as they were finishing the evening meal about six o'clock. They had been discussing some problem that Sophie was having in school when the pounding had begun. Not so loud at first, kind of like someone knocking on the wall with his knuckles. They knew that they had raised their voices to some degree, and they thought that they might have disturbed the elderly man who lived in the next apartment. When the pounding got louder, Mrs. C called her neighbor to see why he was so upset with them, and he said that he had no idea what she was talking about. It surely was not he pounding on the wall.

"I felt along the walls, but it was the strangest thing," Sgt. G stated in his report. "The pounding didn't really seem to be coming from the walls at all. I couldn't really tell where the sounds were originating [from]. Les came back down from checking the roof and said that he could find nothing up there that could possibly make such noises. I told him to call officers B and L to come and help us go through the apartment house. I thought right away that maybe someone had rigged some kind of electronic device in Mrs. C's apartment as some kind of cruel prank. Such proved not to be the case."

When officers B and L entered the apartment, the phenomena dramatically increased in scope and intensity. As all four police officers watched, the dinner plates, which were still on the kitchen table, lifted themselves into the air and smashed against the wall. As Officer B rushed forward to examine the unexpected and unexplained mess, a kitchen chair scooted across the room, slamming into his knees and nearly tripping him.

"And all this time," Sgt. G said, "the infernal pounding kept right on, not missing a beat. When the plates and the chair started to move, Sophie began to scream hysterically that she wanted to leave the apartment. At the same time, Officer L covered his ears with his palms and said that he had to get out of the room. There was some kind of weird vibration in the place that was making his eardrums feel that they were about to explode."

Sgt. G could clearly see that officer L was in extreme distress. His face was ashen, and he appeared about to faint. "I ordered him to go down to the basement and check the heating to determine if there might be anything there to account for the strange disturbances," Sgt. G said. "When officer L hesitated, I could tell that he was genuinely afraid to go alone, so I told Les to go with him. Officer L is a big, tough guy, but he was scared of something in that apartment."

Officer B called Sgt. G's attention to another kitchen chair slowly moving backward. As the two officers and Mrs. C watched, the chair did a complete flip, then set down gently again in its former upright position.

Sgt. G concluded his account: "I asked Mrs. C if she had someplace that she could go for the night. She said that she had a cousin who lived across town. I suggested that she call the cousin and request a night's sanctuary, pack a few things in a bag, and I would have Officer L drive her and Sophie to wherever they needed to go. All this time, Sophie had been whimpering and crying, and, from time to time, emitting this hellish scream."

Once Mrs. C and her daughter left the apartment, Officer H, Officer B, and Sgt. G stayed and puzzled over the continued sounds of the pounding and did their best to come up with some kind of rational explanation for what they had experienced that night. They remained for another fifty minutes or so. The pounding became quieter and less frequent.

"But approximately every ten minutes or so, the entire apartment would seem to tremble, as if we were experiencing an earthquake," he said. "And then the disturbances stopped altogether."

The officers checked everywhere in the apartment building for some kind of ordinary physical explanation for the things they observed and came up blank.

"From what I have read on the subject," Sgt. G said, "a young person, especially a female, can serve as the center for these kings of weird disturbances, and I wonder if Mrs. C and her daughter had been experiencing an emotional conflict of greater duration than an argument about school over dinner that night. Officer Les H stepped into a number of apartments around and below the C apartment, and neither he nor any of the occupants could detect any unusual sounds—certainly not the terrible pounding that we had experienced in the C apartment. Officer L pointed out that there was a large cemetery across the street, and he admitted that he thought that he had seen and felt spirit presences in the C apartment. Later, I learned that Mrs. C and her daughter had moved out, because Sophie refused to return to the apartment. I think they also moved out of the city soon afterward."

Guarding against Spirit Parasites

We used to be as dogmatically opposed to the concept of demonic posses-sion as any modern investigator is supposed to be. However, many years of research and encounters with entities that are unabashedly evil have con-vinced us that homes in which murders or other violent physical deeds have been committed may become repositories for nonphysical leeches of the soul that we prefer to call "spirit parasites." These beings are hideous and grotesque in appearance, often manifesting as reptilian-like entities. When humans make themselves physically and spiritually vulnerable through drug and alco-hol abuse, promiscuous sex, and other excesses of the physical body, they may not be aware of spirit parasites in their presence that are capable of possessing and manipulating them.

Paul Dale Roberts sees these "parasites" a bit closer to their traditional character but adds a very contemporary element:

> Demons are entities that never had a mortal, human form. Ori-gins: Extraterrestrial. Why? If you believe that God and his angels are from the "heavens," that would make them extrater-restrial. If Satan and one-third of the angels rebelled against God's Kingdom, then Satan and one-third of the angels that became demons are also extraterrestrial. That is why they never had mortal human form. Einstein said that $E = mc^2$. Energy can be converted into matter and matter into energy. Demons are pure energy entities. They are described in three different ways.
>
> 1. As angelic, a being of beauty that will manipulate the person to commit something that is sinful or out of the ordinary.

Demons are not always frightening, ugly creatures. They can appear as very beautiful and seductive, as well.

2. Horrific, evil looking. Some people claim they have seen demons that are incredibly hideous to look at. I believe demons do this for a scare effect; they know what we fear and this is not their true appearance.

3. Black mist, black fog, black shadow, black smoke. In most demonic hauntings, the occupants claim to be followed by black mist or black fog.

The demons' main purpose is to cause chaos and havoc upon humankind. Demons are deceivers and they manipulate our society towards social upheaval. Demons seek out our destruction. Demon cases are extremely rare. To handle demonic cases, it is essential that a blessing of the purest kind is conducted on the person or home.

BROTHERS OF THE SHADOW AND THE TRICKSTER

In metaphysical works, these entities are sometimes referred to as the Brothers of the Shadow. Whoever or whatever they may really be, there is an aspect of their appearances that is suggestive of the Trickster figure that is common to all cultures and well-known to ethnologists and anthropologists. The Trickster plays pranks on hapless humans, but often at the same time he is instructing people or transforming aspects of the environment for the good of his human charges.

Most cultures view the Trickster as a supernatural being with the ability to change his shape at will. Although basically very clever and wily, he can at times behave in a very stupid, childish manner and may often appear to end up as the one who is tricked. The Trickster does not hesitate to lie, cheat, and steal. Often he seems to be the very essence of amoral animalism.

The Trickster figure frequently manifests in the guise of a culture hero. To the Native Americans of the Southwest, he appeared as the wily coyote. To the Norse and the Greeks, the Trickster manifested often in the role of a mischievous, but not really demonic, god. We have the ability, however, to exorcise the negative aspects of the Trickster by refusing to play its silly games, thereby allowing us to concentrate on the positive aspects that he can bring to us.

BROTHERS OF THE SHADOW MAY BE FALLEN ANGELS

Some researchers have theorized that such spirit entities as the Brothers of the Shadow might be angels—with the emphasis on *fallen* angels, the non-material beings who serve evil, rather than good, and who try their best to ensnare humans in their nasty plans to supplant our species. An angel (*angelos* in Greek; *malach* in Hebrew) is a messenger, one who is sent to accomplish whatever mission has been assigned to him or her. In relation to God, the Supreme Being, the obedient angels of righteousness stand as courtiers to a king. They themselves are not gods but rather are created beings, as subject to God's will as are humans. In spite of an age-old misconception, humans do not become angels when they die. The angelic ranks were formed long before humankind was scooped from the dust of Earth.

Although angels are frequently called spirits, it is often implied in the Bible that they can possess corporeal bodies when seen on Earth and that they have throughout history been mistaken for ordinary humans when judged by their appearance alone.

In the teachings of Islam, there are three distinct species of intelligent beings in the universe. There are first the angels (*malak* in Arabic), a high order of beings created of Light; second are the *al-jinn*, ethereal, perhaps even multidimensional, entities; and then human beings, fashioned of the stuff of Earth and born into physical bodies.

According to Persian and Chaldean tradition, the *Ahri manes* are the fallen angels, who out of revenge for being expelled from heaven continually torment the so-called apex of God's creation, the human inhabitants of Earth.

The old legends have it that the Ahrimanes finally decided to inhabit the space between the Earth and the fixed stars, which is called *Ahrimane-Abad*.

Humans are constantly being seduced into doing the work of the nether forces because they simply do not acknowledge that such forces exist, let alone recognize how they work *into* and *upon Earth life*.

For centuries, the Ahrimanic entities have held as their goal the total enslavement of humankind. If they are unopposed, they will overwhelm humanity and take evolution wholly under their control. We must realize that in the struggle for mastery of Earth, we human beings and our souls are at once the goal of the battle and the battleground itself.

THE DARKLINGS

As we have been warned by many shamans and native magicians in our research and in our travels, for those under the influence of the Spirit Parasites and prophets of evil, objects that are familiar to us may take on different shapes and sizes. They also reveal the qualities in various objects that are truly paranormal and actually supernatural in their nature.

As the mystic Norma Gainer once told us, "Call it evil or the work of the devil, but the inanimate becomes alive in the black of night. The dark-

Darklings are often described as humanoid beings that do not reflect light; they are shadowy beings with no facial features. Despite this, they can somehow bite people.

Haunted: Malevolent Ghosts, Night Terrors, and Threatening Phantoms

lings, the shadows, the dead sneak near to you as you breathe evenly and [are] sound asleep."

Accounts of "the dark" describe them as being deep, nonreflective, black, humanoid or creature-like silhouettes. Sometimes these creatures have no discernible mouths, noses, or facial expressions, though at times those features might be all that you actually see in the darkness.

Many lurid accounts also exist of these entities being child-sized humanoids or shapeless masses that sometimes change to more human-like forms or animals. The eyes are usually not described as being discernible, but some reports mention glowing red, white, or blue eyes. The color of the eyes, if any, is typically given as red. Their specific form is described variously as either a two-dimensional shadow or a vaporous or distorted three-dimensional body (as though made out of smoke, fabric, water, or steam).

Movement is often described as being very quick and disjointed. Some witnesses describe this movement of the shadow entities as resembling a kind of dance from one wall to the next, or as moving around the room "as if they were on a specific track."

Rarely, they are seen "standing" in the middle of doorways or by a wall. Often they are described as being seen staring at the floor. Some accounts describe what appears to be the outline of a cloak, and in some instances the outline of a 1930s-style fedora hat. This last type is referred as the "Dark Hatman" or "The Darkling King."

The Dark has also been called "The Wight," which is from the Middle English word used to describe a creature or a living being. It is akin to the Old High German *wiht,* meaning "a creature or thing."

In terms of the Darklings, their evil over the centuries is based on Shadow people (also known as shadow men, shadow folk, or shadow beings), supernatural, shadow-like creatures of both modern folklore and traditional Native American beliefs. These creatures are known to pull you violently out of your bed at night, strangle you, or rape you.

The Darklings can also bite you, hit you, hurt you, and are known to poke your eyes out as you sleep.

They have been known to kill infants as they sleep in their mothers' arms or suckle at their breast.

They can scratch you to the bone, and tales of them even tell of their stealing kidneys (thought to be what they love most to eat) from sleeping victims.

Darklings are best known to take the shape of cats, especially large, black ones. They can roam highways and slip into to your home and kill all who live there.

In the darkness, they are the strongest paranormal entity you can encounter. They can change shape and even talk to you in the thick, black night.

According to folklore, they appear as dark forms in the peripheries of people's vision as they begin to haunt them. If they find no reason to haunt you, then they seem to disintegrate or move between walls when noticed.

> Darklings have been known to hide at the sign of any type of light. Their favorite spots to hide are in dark cracks or inside a child's toys (dolls, stuffed animals) or closets.

Reports of shadow Darkling people occupy a similar position in the popular consciousness to ghost sightings, but they differ in that shadow people are not reported as having human features, wearing modern/period clothing, or attempting to communicate.

Witnesses also do not report the same feelings of being in the presence of something that was once human. A Darkling has never walked the earth as a human. Some individuals have described being menaced, chased, or, in some rare instances, attacked by shadow Darklings. There have also been reports of huge, menacing Darklings appearing in front of witnesses and lingering for several seconds before disappearing. Witnesses report that encounters are typically accompanied by a feeling of dread.

Darklings have been known to hide at the sign of any type of light. Their favorite spots to hide are in dark cracks or inside a child's toys (dolls, stuffed animals) or closets.

In New Orleans, Voodoo Darklings are creatures that prowl the city looking for innocents to possess. They will take a person and turn them into someone they are not. They who are possessed by a Darkling have been known to kill or hurt their family members during daylight hours. Since the late 1800s, they have been aptly called the Dark Darklings.

The great voodoo queen Marie Laveau described them as the evil thoughts that good church people have but don't act upon that come to life. They carry out evil deeds no sane person would do!

The actual belief is that the Darkling enters people through their mouths as they sleep and are trapped inside them until they fall asleep again.

Small children between the ages of 3 and 9 are more apt to encounter these beings and see them clearly. Those who have psychic powers have been known to see them as sparkling, dark shapes.

SPIRIT PARASITES WHO COMMAND HUMANS TO KILL

While those spirit parasites that seek to possess and to enjoy sexually the physical bodies of mortals are evil and demeaning enough, even worse on the scale of degradation are those fiends who invade the psyches of men and women and command them to maim, mutilate, or murder their victims. These monsters are not werewolves or vampires or cat people—they are real men and women who could be friends, relatives, or the neighbor down the street—any one of us who hears demon voices that demand unquestioning obedience.

If you believe such demons exist only as a superstitious throwback to the Middle Ages, pay attention to what Dr. Morton Kelsey, an Episcopal priest and noted Notre Dame professor of theology, has to say: "Most people in the modern world consider themselves too sophisticated and too intelligent to be concerned with demons. But in thirty years of study, I have seen the effect of demons upon humans."

Dr. Kelsey maintains that demons are real and can invade the minds of humans. Demons are not the figment of the imagination but are negative, destructive, spiritual forces that seek to destroy the possessed host body and everyone with whom that person comes into contact.

The Rev. James LeBar, an exorcist for the Archdiocese of New York until his death in 2008, commented in September 2000 that there had been a "large explosion" of exorcisms in recent years. In New York alone, he said, the number had accelerated from none in 1990 to a total of 300 in the early 2000s. Rev. LeBar said that as men and women have diminished self-respect for themselves and decreased reverence for spirituality, for other human beings, and for life in general, one of Satan's demons can move in and "attack them by possessing them and rendering them helpless."

Dr. Ralph Allison, senior psychiatrist at the California state prison in San Luis Obispo, commented: "My conclusion after thirty years of observing over one thousand disturbed patients is that some of them act in a bizarre fashion due to possession by spirits. The spirit may be that of a human being who died. Or it may be a spirit entity that has never been a human being and sometimes identifies itself as a demon—an agent of evil."

Dr. Wilson Van Dusen, a university professor who served as chief psychologist at Mendocino State Hospital, was another health care professional who boldly stated his opinion that many patients in mental hospitals are possessed by demons: "I am

The Episcopal priest Dr. Morton Kelsey has asserted that demons are real and can invade the human mind—in other words, they can possess people.

totally convinced that there are entities that can possess our minds and our bodies," he said. "I have even been able to speak directly to demons. I have heard their own guttural, other-world voices."

And all too often, those hellish guttural voices have commanded their possessed hosts to kill, to offer human sacrifice to Satan.

In a report released by the American Psychological Evaluation Corporation, Dr. Andrew Blankley, a sociologist, issued alarming statements about the rise in contemporary sacrificial cults, warning that society at large might expect a "serious menace" to come. According to Dr. Blankley, human sacrifice constitutes an alarming trend in new religious cults: "Desperate people are seeking dramatic revelation and simplistic answers to complex social problems. They are attracted to fringe groups who provide the ritualistic irrationality that they crave. In the last ten years, fringe rituals often include the sacrifice of a human being."

> The monstrous voices that command men and women to kill others are not those of mortals.

Dr. Al Carlisle of the Utah State Prison System has estimated that between 40,000 and 60,000 humans are killed through ritual homicides in the United States every year. In the Las Vegas area alone, Dr. Carlisle asserts, as many as 600 people may die in demon-inspired ceremonies each year.

Mutilated bodies of hitchhikers and transients are being found in forested regions, beside lonely desert roads, and alongside river banks—their hearts and lungs removed and strips of flesh slashed from their bodies.

Devil-worshipping rites are being held in our state and national parks. Human blood is mixed with beer and drunk by all participants. Human bone fragments, teeth, and pieces of flesh are discovered in the ashes of campfires.

The terrible power that drives and compels those obsessed with sacrificial murders is something so much more insidiously evil and complex than can be created by the distortion of creeds, ecclesiasticisms, or belief structures. The monstrous voices that command men and women to kill others are not those of mortals. Those who have fallen under the deadly spell of the possessing entities claim to have been controlled by something outside of themselves—usually personified as Satan or one of his demons. And those demon voices—whether you prefer to identify them as symbolic of some strain of psychopathology or as literal, perverse, and evil entities—can utter the command to kill to a quiet, conventionally reared individual just as readily as to a disheveled disciple of the iconoclastic.

Perhaps these demonic entities are the archetypal, shapeshifting monsters that have inspired countless generations of mortals to protest that grotesque reptilian creatures or hideous, half-human, animal-like monsters have forced them to commit horrible crimes.

Here is only a sampler of recent cases of men and women who were possessed by demons and commanded to kill:

- On January 5, 1990, authorities searching an Ohio farm commune found the slain bodies of a family of five—all victims of human sacrifice. Jeffrey Lundgren, a self-declared prophet of a new religion, had decreed the sacrifices necessary to persuade the "forces" to present the cult with a magical golden sword.

- Daniel Rakowitz couldn't quite understand whether or not the voices said that he was actually Jesus reborn, but he knew that they were insistent that he was a messiah. The voices also told him to form a new satanic religion to be named the Church of 966, thereby discarding the old and familiar 666 label. To insure his messiahship, in September 1989, he sacrificed his girlfriend.

- Once people accepted Satan as their savior, heavy metal, grass, and sex parties just weren't enough. Soon the demon voices ordered Terry Belcher, the young high priest of a cult, to sacrifice Teresa, one of his followers, in January 1988.

- When the jury passed sentence on Richard Ramirez in 1985, he was convicted of twelve first-degree murders and thirty other major offenses of rape and burglary. Throughout his trial, the infamous "Night Stalker" flashed the devil's pentagram scratched into his hand or placed his fingers to the side of his head to fashion demon's horns. Defiantly, he declared his worship of Satan.

- On June 11, 1998, taking the stand against his lawyers' advice to make statements concerning the killing of two students and the wounding of seventeen in Hattiesburg, Mississippi, in October 1997, Luke Woodham told the astonished courtroom that his involvement in Satanism had given him power over many things. Woodham went on to declare how he had been able to cast spells and send out demons to accomplish various tasks for him. "I've seen demons," he said. "I know what I was dealing with. I felt like I had complete control, complete power over things.... It's real in spite of what people think."

- The voices told Herbert Mullin that California was about to be destroyed by a cataclysmic earthquake and a giant tidal wave unless he immediately began sacrificing human life to Satan. The voices nullified Mullin's squeamishness by declaring that the sacrificial victims would actually be grateful for being given the opportunity to serve the greater good of California. Before he was stopped on Feburary 13, 1972, Mullins had sacrificed thirteen victims to, in his mind, become the Savior of California.

- In May 1983, Michael and Suzan Carson went on trial in San Francisco for obeying their demonic visions and hunting down and killing three victims that the voices they heard identified as witches that must be slain to set California right.

- While other households in the borough of Queens in New York watched the Thanksgiving Day parade on November 22, 1990, Joseph Bergamini honored the satanic promise that he was immortal by stabbing and killing his mother and wounding his father.

- As a teenager, Mark David Chapman had experienced a vision of Jesus that led him to become an advocate for the common man. When the visions later revealed that the popular music idol John Lennon was no longer a working-class hero but rather a prosperous businessman, the voices decreed that the former Beatle must die on the night of December 8, 1980.

- In June 1988, Jason Rose and John Jones were indicted for the ritual sacrifice of nineteen-year-old Melissa Ann Meyer. The two satanists had cast their own fate in the form of life imprisonment when it was revealed that they videotaped their human sacrifice.

The list of demon-possessed killers goes on and on:

- January 1986: Satanic priest Harold Smith and four disciples were jailed following a series of murders in Houston.

- February 1986: Dana Jones, an admitted member of a sex magic cult founded by Aleister Crowley in 1907, was arrested for the ritual mutilation-slaying of a man in Denver.

- March 1987: Inspired by the vampire movie *Lost Boys*, Tim Erickson and other Minnesota teenagers decided to form a vampire cult. They murdered a drifter and drank his blood.

- July 1991: Jaime Rodriguez was convicted and sentenced to life for beheading a teenage runaway as a sacrifice to Satan. He also severed one of her fingers to wear as a charm around his neck. Augustin Pena, a fellow Satanist, kept the girl's head in his refrigerator.

- April 1994: Cary Grayson and three others murdered a female hitchhiker in Birmingham, Alabama. Police stated that the victim was mutilated in an apparent ritual that involved cannibalism.

- May 1996: Three satanists in San Luis Obispo tortured and murdered a fifteen-year-old girl. The demon-possessed trio told arresting officers that they hoped the sacrifice of a virgin would put them in good standing with Satan.

- December 2000: Prosecutors charged a man in Great Falls, Montana, with killing a ten-year-old boy, butchering him, eating his flesh in specially prepared dishes, then feeding the remains to his unsuspecting neighbors. A psychiatric evaluation revealed demonic fantasies about cannibalism and the taste of human flesh. Encrypted writings found in the suspect's home revealed a list of recipes involving the bodies of small children.

Musician and song writer John Lennon (pictured) was killed by a young man named Mark David Chapman, who was later convicted of murder on grounds he was criminally insane.

POPE FRANCIS SUPPORTS EXORCISM

At a large gathering of priests in December 2016, Pope Francis called on priests to contact "exorcists" when their parishioners are facing spiritual crises linked to "supernatural" causes.

Any such exorcists, however, should be chosen with "great care and prudence," the pontiff cautioned.

Pope Francis offered his advice to hundreds of priests attending a Vatican seminar on dealing with sins of the faithful recounted in the sacrament of reconciliation, or confession.

A priest needs to take action when he is confronted with "real spiritual disorders," the pope advised, according to Agence France-Presse. When such crises are caused by "supernatural" forces, he added—presumably referring to the Devil—a confessor "must not hesitate to refer to exorcists." Priests must take care, however, to differentiate between mental illness and demonic possession.

The Vatican also holds training sessions for exorcists, who are charged with expelling the Devil from people thought to be "possessed." It's not a Catholic practice often openly spoken about by church leaders because it's highly controversial and disdained by skeptics who doubt the existence of devils and view the practice as based in ancient superstition.

A 90-page document issued by the Vatican in 1999, "De Exorcismis," updated church guidelines on the practice. It acknowledged that some appar-

Pope Francis has supported the employment of exorcists to help Catholics tortured by demons and other supernatural beings.

ent demonic possessions are actually mental illness, and, if necessary, psychiatrists should be consulted. But the report also noted that the devil also possesses individuals, describing Satan as a "lion looking for souls to devour." Signs of possession can include superhuman strength, speaking in unknown languages, and a visceral aversion to God, according to the document.

The pope has referred to the Devil a number times and in 2014 recognized the International Association of Exorcists, an organization of 250 priests around the world who have been prepared to conduct exorcisms.

DARKLINGS, DEMONS, OR DEVILISH SPIRITS

The Bible records many awesome appearances of angelic beings that indicate that at least some of the heavenly messengers are not the beautiful entities depicted in the accounts of many of the men and women who have reported angelic encounters. The entities described by Ezekiel and identified as cherubim certainly border on the grotesque. As the Old Testament prophet beheld the "Living Creatures," their outstretched wings touching the corners of the square that encased them, he perceived that each cherub appeared to have four faces—that of a man, a lion, an ox, and an eagle. Regardless of whether Ezekiel actually saw four separate visages on a single head or was simply using figurative language to describe a single face combining the attributes of human, lion, ox, and eagle, the beings who delivered this particular prophetic vision would have had most people trembling in fear and revulsion.

The figures seen by Ezekiel are very suggestive of the manner in which the ancient Mesopotamians depicted their spiritual guardians, the *lamassu*, as rather grotesque creatures that often appear as lions or bulls with human faces and large wings. Such monstrous images were placed at the entrances of temples to ward off evil, and the common people of Mesopotamia cherished them as very accessible guardian spirits.

After he was spared from a royal death sentence in a lions' den by a heavenly being who sealed the big cats' mouths closed, the prophet Daniel probably felt that he was in no position to complain about the angel's physical appearance. Later, when Daniel perceived a heaven-sent messenger beside him at the Tigris River, he beheld an entity dressed in linen and wearing a solid gold belt, who had a face like lightning, eyes like flaming fires, and a voice like the roar of a crowd.

The prophet Ezekiel described cherubs with four frightening faces—those of a lion, an ox, an eagle, and a human being.

Throughout our many years of research and our interviews with hundreds of men and women from cultures and countries around the world who have claimed angelic or spirit contact, it has seemed to us that the beings have always manifested to each individual witness in a form that is most acceptable to him or her. We long ago came to believe that the physical appearance of the manifesting angel or spirit guide depends almost completely upon the witnesses' personal cosmology—that is, their religious background, their cultural biases, and their level of spiritual evolution.

KEEPING SPIRIT PARASITES AT BAY

After many years of conducting our own private war with spirit parasites, we have come to believe that we can practice certain techniques that may help us to create the proper attitude of acceptance that may encourage the participation of a spirit teacher in our life and may bring about a clearer vision of our path on our Earthwalk. We also believe that the disciplined practice of certain meditation or visualization exercises may enable us to "hear" more clearly the soft whispers of angelic guidance and to perceive more completely the full meaning of the spiritual messages that are sent to us.

We would very strongly urge you to experiment with the following techniques with an attitude of respectfulness to the sacredness that is inherent in the act of communication with your spirit teacher or spirit guide. And you should definitely not practice these exercises with the goal of hoping to see your guide manifest physically in your presence.

Truly, the best attitude to take is that you are going to enter a state of relaxation and tranquility whereby higher levels of awareness—perhaps from your *own* individual higher self—will present themselves to you in a manner that will enable you to get in deeper touch with important aspects of yourself.

Surrounding Yourself with a Positive Energy Field

If you should sense the presence of negative entities in your environment, practice this exercise.

Immediately visualize yourself slamming shut a door between you and the negative presence.

Next, visualize a golden energy of light moving upward from the bottoms of your feet to the top of your head. See it moving over your legs, your hips, your chest, and your neck, right up to the top of your head. Then see the energy cascading down around you in sparks of golden light, as if you are being enveloped by the shimmering, sparkling outpouring of a Roman candle.

Impress upon your consciousness that those "sparks" of golden light represent a new, positive energy field that surrounds you and forms a vital protective shield against all discordant and negative entities.

Visualize the Golden Light of Protection

If you have sensed an unseen presence that has left you feeling frightened and alone, immediately visualize the Golden Light of Protection forming itself around you. Calm yourself by saying, as you inhale, "I am." On the outbreath, say, "Relaxed." Repeat this process a number of times until you feel yourself becoming calmer and more centered.

"I am" asserts your sovereignty and your uniqueness as an individual entity. "Relaxed" positively affirms that you have no fear.

A Prayer for Renewed Strength and Energy

Many people who have encountered entities from the dark side have suddenly felt themselves feeling drained of energy. If you should sense or perceive a negative entity in your environment and experience a sudden energy drain, say the following:

> Beloved Light Being [or the name of a holy figure or your angelic guide], fill me with your great strength.
>
> Charge me with your light and your love.
>
> Rejuvenate each of my vital body functions with strength and energy.
>
> Empower me with your might.
>
> Keep me now and always sensitive to your guidance and your direction.

What Is the Nature of Fairies?

Among the 30,000 men and women who have returned *The Steiger Questionnaire of Mystical, Paranormal, and UFO Experiences*, a remarkable 19 percent claim to have seen elves, fairies, or some form of nature spirit.

Sherry and I both observed the *Fae* as children, but her relationship playing with them amidst the flowers in her family's backyard was much more storybookish than mine.

When I was a month or two from turning five, I caught a fairy looking in the kitchen window and seemingly spying on my parents. When he became aware that I had seen him, he gave me a look that was less like Tinker Bell's and more like Captain Hook's. And there was nothing Disney-like about him. I had obviously caught him at a most inopportune moment, but whatever his purpose, it activated what would be a lifelong interest in the paranormal and a lifelong involvement with a prankster from a much larger reality.

I must have really ticked him off because he has been playing tricks on me for over seventy years now. Nearly once a day, Sherry and I will shout out, "Nisse [Scandinavian for a house elf], give my pen back now!" or "Nisse, where did you hide the keys?"

Give the rascal a few minutes, and the missing object suddenly materializes in plain view in a place where neither of us left it.

MUCH AKIN TO HUMANS

In most traditions, especially in the British Isles and Scandinavia, the wee people, the fairy folk, were thought to be supernormal beings who inhabited magical kingdoms beneath the surface of the earth. Fairies have always

In many European traditions, fairies are tiny people living in magical kingdoms below the surface of the earth. (Art by Bill Oliver.)

been considered to be very much akin to humans, but they have also been known to be something more than mere mortals and to possess powers that humankind would consider to be magical.

It is interesting for those of us who study cross-cultural accounts of angels and paranormal phenomena to note how certain activities once attributed to such entities as fairies in so-called "pagan" times often became elevated to manifestations of angels with the advent of Christianity. Good deeds that were an important element of the repertoire of the fairy folk became the province of heavenly beings, and kind nature spirits were replaced in the newly converted people's mass consciousness by benevolent angels. Local gods and goddesses, as well, very often became transformed into saintly humans with extraordinary powers, while mischievous entities were transmogrified into imps.

THE SIDHE SAY THEY ARE CATCHING UP "HEIGHTWISE"

Recently, some theorists have suggested that the fairy folk may actually have been the surviving remnants of a past civilization populated by a species of early humans that were of diminutive stature compared to modern *Homo sapiens*. These little people may have been quite advanced and possessed a technology that seemed to be magical compared to the primitive tools of the migrating hunter-gatherer humans who later became the established residents of the area. The little people may have died out, they may have been assimilated into the encroaching culture by interbreeding, or they may largely have gone underground, emerging topside often enough to be perpetuated in folklore and legend.

From time to time, we receive emails from those who declare that they are the "real fairies," the *Sidhe*. They claim that they are the descendents of an ancient species of hominins, much shorter than contemporary *Homo sapiens* but "otherwise superior in every way."

Some say that they are "catching up" height-wise, and that a number of their species, both male and female, serve in the armed forces of their respective nations. According to one of our interesting correspondents, the average height of a male Sidhe is now close to five feet, three or four inches, and the females are around five feet. Interestingly, I would estimate the Sidhe that appeared to me as a child to be at a bit over three feet tall.

It should be noted that they favor the armed forces to assist them in their assimilation to human society, not to form armies to conquer us. From their perspective, they are an older, wiser species of hominids who have been forced to live in the shadows of newcomers and exist by their wits and their magic. Now, they say, the technology of humans has begun to equal their ancient skills, and they wish to blend into the dominant society, rather than coexist with it.

All of the ancient festivals are still observed, and Sidhe royalty reveal themselves at each of the major celebrations. Although still possessed of what humans would consider magical powers, most of their "wicked ways," such as their kidnapping of children, have been completely abolished.

If the contemporary Sidhe are truly the descendents of an ancient species of hominins as they claim to be and those claims can be substantiated, then the entire study and science regarding our evolution is set spinning desperately to define an entirely new order of things.

Until such claims can be substantiated, however, we tend to maintain that the considerable body of fairylore that exists worldwide demonstrates that fairies are entities that belong solely to the realm of spirit. Many of the ancient texts declare that the fairies are paraphysical beings, somehow of a "middle nature betwixt Man and Angel."

FAIRIES AS FALLEN ANGELS

Some biblically inspired authorities have sought to cast fairies as an earthly incarnation assumed by the rebellious angels who were driven out of Heaven during the celestial uprising led by Lucifer. These fallen angels, cast

A 1911 painting of the Tuatha Dé Danaan, or Sidhe, the supernatural race of Irish mythology.

from their heavenly abode, took up new residences in the forests, mountains, and lakes of Earth. As fallen angels, they now existed in a much-diminished capacity, but they still possessed more than enough power to be deemed supernatural by the human inhabitants of the planet.

The fairies are said to be able to enchant humans and take advantage of them. It is often related that they can marry humans or—if they wish no lasting relationship—they can cast a spell on a likely lad or lass and have their way with them against the mortal's will. Those careless or disrespectful humans who trespass on forest glens, rivers, or lakes considered sacred to the fairy folk may suffer terrible consequences—even cruel deaths. Those entrepreneurs who wish to desecrate land whereon lie fairy circles or mounds in order to build a road or construct a commercial building may find themselves combating an unseen enemy who will accept only their unconditional surrender.

NEVER DISTURB A FAIRY MOUND

The countryfolk of Ireland and Scandinavia take their fairies seriously, and they know that to disturb the mounds or raths (ringforts and other circular structures) in which they dwell is to invite severe supernatural consequences upon oneself.

The trouble at the fairy mound outside the village of Wexford began on the morning when the workmen from the state electricity board began digging a hole for the erection of a light pole within the parameters of a rath. The villagers warned the workmen that the pole would never stay put because no self-respecting community of fairy folk could abide a disturbance on their mound.

The big city electrical workmen had a laugh at the expense of the villagers and said some uncomplimentary things about the level of intelligence of the townsfolk of Wexford. They finished digging the hole to the depth that experience had taught them was adequate, then they placed the post within the freshly dug opening and stamped the black earth firmly around its base. The satisfied foreman pronounced for all within earshot to hear that no fairy would move the pole from where it had been anchored.

However, the next morning the pole tilted unattractively in loose earth.

The villagers shrugged that the wee folk had done it, but the foreman of the crew voiced his suspicions that the fairies had received some help from some humans bent on mischief. Glaring his resentment at any villagers who would meet his narrowed, accusative eyes, the foreman ordered his men to reset the pole.

The next morning the same pole was once again conspicuous in the long line of newly placed electrical posts by its weird tilt in the loose soil at its base. While the other poles in the line stood straight and proud like soldiers on parade inspection, that one woebegone post reeled like a trooper who had had one pint too many.

The foreman had endured enough of such rural humor at his expense. He ordered the crew to dig a hole six feet wide, place the pole precisely in the middle, and pack the earth so firmly around the base that nothing short of an atomic bomb could budge it.

Apparently fairies have their own brand of nuclear fission, for the next morning the intrusive pole had once again been pushed loose of the little people's rath.

The foreman and his crew from the electricity board finally knew when they were licked. Without another word to the grinning villagers, the workmen dug a second hole four feet outside of the fairy mound and dropped the pole in there. And that was where it stood as solid as the Emerald Isle for many years.

DON'T TREAD ON SACRED FAIRY GROUND

In 1962, the new owners of a herring processing plant in Iceland decided to enlarge their work area. According to Icelandic tradition, no landowner must fail to reserve small plot of his property for the Hidden Folk, and a number of the rural residents earnestly pointed out to the new proprietors that any extension of the plant would encroach upon the plot of ground that the original owners had set aside for the little people who lived under the ground.

The businessmen laughed. For one thing, they didn't harbor those old folk superstitions. For another, they had employed a topnotch, highly qualified construction crew who possessed modern, unbreakable drill bits and plenty of explosives.

But the bits of the "unbreakable" drills began to shatter one after another. An old farmer came forward to repeat the warning that the crew was trespassing on land that belonged to the Hidden Folk. At first, the workmen laughed at the old man and marveled that such primitive superstitions could still exist in modern Iceland.

But the drill bits kept breaking.

Finally, the manager of the plant, although professing disbelief in such nonsense, agreed to the old farmer's recommendation that he consult a local seer to establish contact with the Hidden Folk and attempt to make peace with them. After going into a brief trance-state, the seer returned to waking consciousness to inform the manager that there was one particularly powerful member of the Hidden Folk who had selected this plot as his dwelling place. He was not an unreasonable being, however. If the processing plant really needed the plot for its expansion, he would agree to find another place to live. The Hidden One asked only for five days without any drilling, so that he could make his arrangements to move.

The manager felt a bit strange bargaining with a being that was invisible—and as far as he had previously been concerned, imaginary. But he looked over at the pile of broken drill bits and told the seer that the Hidden One had a deal. Work on the site would be shut down for five days to give him a chance to move.

After five days had passed and the workmen resumed drilling, the work proceeded smoothly and efficiently until the addition to the plant was completed. There were no more shattered bits on the unbreakable drill.

WINNING THE FAVOR OF THE FAIRIES

Throughout the long history of interaction between humans and fairies, there are those men and women who have somehow managed to win the favor

When one is on good terms with the fairy world, the wee ones might be inclined to help humans from time to time.

of the fairies through a process beyond the kin of mortal men. On behalf of such humans, the wee ones can materialize to help a poor farmer harvest a crop and have it in the bins before a storm hits, or they can clean a kitchen in the twinkling of an eye to ease the stress of an exhausted housemaid. If they see fit to do so, the fairies can guide their favored humans with their ability to divine the future, and they will stand by to assist at the birth of a special couple's child, whom they will tutor and protect throughout his or her lifetime.

Betty Kirkland, who now lives in a suburb of Chicago, told in her questionnaire how she had acquired fairy helpers when she was just a child of three. "I am now 33, married, with two little girls, eight and six—and I think they, too, have received fairy guardians, for I have seen little sparkles of light above their heads when they are sleeping."

Betty recalled how, when she was three years old, she first saw the Wee People on the farm in central Illinois, where she spent her childhood. "I saw a little man and little woman picking apples that had fallen from the trees in our orchard. They were taller than I was at that age, so I thought at first they were just some very short people that my mother had allowed to enter our orchard. What really caught my attention is the way they were dressed. With their conical hats and bright green and red costumes, I thought they wore very strange clothing for farmers."

When Betty approached them, they just smiled at her and went on picking apples and placing them in colorful cloth bags. "But when in my childish curiosity and bluntness I asked them what their names were, they looked shocked," she recalled. "The little man's mouth dropped, and the woman gasped in a shrill, tiny voice, 'Oh, no! She can see us! She's not supposed to be able to see us!'"

And then, Betty said, the man began to laugh in a high-pitched giggle. "Sure she can see us," he told his companion, "she's got the gift. See the glow around her wee head?"

Betty remembered that the woman asked the man if "the child is a changeling." Although that term meant nothing to her at the time, Betty later learned that a "changeling," according to fairy lore, is a hybrid fairy-human child that the fairies sometimes leave in place of a newborn infant that they "borrow" to take with them to their underworld kingdom.

The male fairy introduced themselves as fairies—himself as Acorn, his companion as Fluff. "She made a little curtsy when Acorn introduced her," Betty said. "I thought it was so cute when she did. I had never seen a woman do that before. Later that night, when my mother asked me to wash my hands and face for supper, I curtsied. Mom laughed and wondered where I had learned to do that. I told her that a fairy named Miss Fluff had shown me how, and Mom just laughed harder."

Once her two fairy guardians distracted an angry bull from butting eight-year-old Betty when she inadvertently crossed the pasture during a bovine mating ritual.

Betty enjoyed the company of Fluff and Acorn throughout her childhood. "They would usually just appear seemingly out of nowhere," she said, "so it didn't take me long to figure out that they were invisible to human eyes most of the time. Some evenings I would look out the window of my bedroom and see the 'fairy lights' of Acorn, Miss Fluff, and other fairies mixed in with the fireflies and dancing and swirling around in the darkness."

Once her two fairy guardians distracted an angry bull from butting eight-year-old Betty when she inadvertently crossed the pasture during a bovine mating ritual. Another time when she was ten, Acorn and Fluff chased off a stray dog that had invaded their farm and was likely rabid. It had approached Betty, growling, foaming at the mouth, about to charge, when sparkling lights swirled around its head and pulled it away by its floppy ears.

"Less than a year later, they saved me from drowning in the creek that ran near our farm," Betty said. "I had seen some older neighbor kids jumping off the banks into the water, and I had incorrectly assumed the depth as being much less than it truly was. And to make matters worse, I was alone that afternoon."

She was soon sputtering, threshing about in the water, panicked that she could not touch the muddy bottom with her toes. "I would surely have drowned if Acorn and Fluff had not hovered over me and pulled me to the bank. There was no one else to help me, but my fairy guardians were there."

As she grew into her teenage years, Betty saw her fairy friends less and less. "But when I was ill or sad or depressed, I would first see sparkling lights swirling around me … and then I would hear their delightful laughter and know that everything would be all right," she said. "And so it has been throughout my adult years, as well."

THE LUMINARIES

James Neff, a talented artist and the very able webmaster for popular radio talk show host Jeff Rense's website, told of sighting a mysterious, luminous object on an old country road north of Little Rock, Arkansas, on December 4, 1997. It was a very dark night with overcast skies, and his wife, who was driving at the time, his stepdaughter, and Neff were all leaning forward to watch for deer in the road.

Suddenly, about 100 feet in front of them, a strange sphere of light seemed to jump out of the thick yellow weeds and reeds along the roadside. Neff recalled that the object was self-luminous and resembled "a large dandelion head … composed of light or energy of some kind." The object did not roll across the road, but rather seemed to glide.

"Inside this slightly luminous shell were very defined, lighted spires or veins, only very straight, radiating in all directions from a very bright point of light at its core," Neff wrote in his report of the mysterious encounter. "It seemed that where these veins or spires touched the outer-edge of the translucent shell there was a slight 'burst' of light."

Neff estimated the dimensions of the luminous object to be about six to eight inches in diameter. Strangely enough, it "scurried like an animal" across the road, speeding up as their automobile approached it. The object "jumped" into the weeds and high grass on the right side of the road and disappeared from their sight.

Neff said that all three of them had shouted in amazement the very moment that the glowing orb had first appeared on the left side of the road. "We definitely all three saw and described precisely the same thing," he stated. "This object was truly material and crystalline in quality and was not a trick of reflected light."

And it impressed all of them that it was alive. Its movements as it scurried across the road, Neff said, were "typical of any nocturnal creature that we often see darting across the road in our headlights."

Luminaries are fairy folk who actually glow as they scamper about the forest.

Later, Neff came to realize that what they had seen was a classic fairy or sprite: "What the Irish called 'luminaries,' the little people or beings that glow and scamper around in the deep forests. My stepdaughter commented that it looked very much like 'tinkerbell.'"

James Neff concludes his report by affirming that he had never believed in fairies, goblins, leprechauns, or sprites. "Now I think I do," he mused. "At least I may have seen what thousands of others have seen and described in much the same way we did: self-luminating, alive, animal-like, seemingly conscious of us—a fairy!"

A GOOD TIME TO SPOT NATURE SPIRITS

S. B. told us that when she lived in Nevada she had seen nature spirits several times. One night she had a particularly good sighting when she was driving home from her waitress job at 3:00 A.M. She knows that some folks will scoff and say that she was too tired to be able to see anything clearly.

"I may have been a bit tired," she acknowledges, "but I was wide awake and sober as the day is long. I witnessed a Wood Spirit riding on the shoulders of a large jackrabbit [as it ran] across the highway."

On another occasion, S. B. was with her husband and young son when they saw a water sprite throwing leaves into the water from the river's edge. "It was a very magical experience," she said. "The light of day became 'different,' much more luminous and bright. We followed the sprite up the stream as it flitted in and out of sight. Finally, the sprite waved at us and slipped into a hole at the base of a large tree near the water's edge."

POLICE CAUTION MOTORISTS TO AVOID PUKWUDGIES

The Freetown, Massachusetts, Police Department notified area residents on April Fools' Day that they had posted new signage cautioning motorists that they may encounter a small, troll-like entity known as a "Pukwudgie."

The diminutive beings have long been linked to the Freetown State Forest, which sits at the heart of the infamous paranormal hotspot known as the Bridgewater Triangle.

In a posting on its Facebook page announcing the news, the police department noted that "the danger the Pukwudgies present to the motoring public is that they can appear and disappear at will by using [their] magical powers."

Additionally, it was noted that Pukwudgies also allegedly possess the ability to transform into "a walking porcupine," create spontaneous fires, and control the dead.

Author and researcher Christopher Balzano applauded the police department's effort to warn the public about Pukwudgies, telling WBSM that "they are far more dangerous than any of the other creatures in the forest and people need to be aware of [them]."

No doubt concerned about possibly causing a panic among visitors to the town who are not aware of the local legend, the police department stressed that the signage will only be used during Pukwudgie mating season.

NATIVE AMERICAN TRIBES TAKE THE PUKWUDJIES SERIOUSLY

When the Miami and Delaware tribes settled in the territory that is now the state of Indiana, they soon discovered that they were sharing the forests with some very peculiar neighbors. These people were only about two feet tall, with white skin and light-brown hair. Their clothing was woven together from long grasses, bark, and tufts of fur and feathers. Some of the little tribespeople built small huts out of grass and tree branches, but most of them lived in caves along the riverbanks. But the strangest thing about these little men and women was that they could vanish right before one's eyes, as if they were somehow beings between humans and spirits.

The Miami called them *Pa-i-sa-ki*, and the Delaware referred to them as *Puk-wud-jies*. Both names translate as "little wild people of the forest."

> But the strangest thing about these little men and women was that they could vanish right before one's eyes....

Researcher/writer Tim Swartz passed along an old Indiana story that tells of a Methodist minister who, in the early 1800s, decided to put an end to the pagan tales about the Puk-wud-jies that had enthralled a good many of his congregation. He set out with ax in hand to chop down the tree that, according to local tradition, sheltered the entrance to the little people's underground kingdom. The minister had struck the huge tree only a couple of whacks when a hole opened in its base, and he suddenly found himself surrounded by a large group of small, angry men. Although the Puk-wud-jies threw him to the ground and cut his throat with a flint blade, the minister managed to survive the terrifying ordeal—but he never again scoffed at the tales of the little forest people.

LITTLE VANISHING PEOPLE

It is interesting to note that the Algonquin dialect, which was in extensive use throughout many of the northeastern tribes, called the wee inhabitants in their forests *Puck-wud-jinies* , which translates as "little vanishing people." These tribes, as well, spoke of the entities as being able to disappear, as if they were of a substance somewhere between human and spirit.

And now one begins to wonder if the elves' name for themselves might well be something very similar to "Puck" or "Puke" or "Pooka." In Shakespeare's *A Midsummer Night's Dream*, Puck is the very personification of the woodland elf, the merry wanderer who declares what fools we humans be. And then we must consider the similarity between Puck and the old gothic *Puke*, a generic name for minor spirits in all the Teutonic and Scandinavian dialects. Puck/Puke is cognate with the German *Spuk*, a goblin, and the Dutch *Spook*, a ghost. Then there is the Irish *Pooka*. So now we have Puck, Puk, Puke, Spuk, Spook, and Pooka—names from the forests of England, Ireland, Scandinavia, Holland, Germany, and the northeastern and central United States, all describing a little vanishing person, an entity somewhere between human and spirit.

PAUL DALE ROBERTS DUELS WITH KRAMPUS AND LIMEY

Paul Dale Roberts gets many strange calls on his paranormal hotline, and one of the strangest occurred on November 23, 2015. A family who resides in Massachusetts made the claim that they were haunted by Krampus and his little gnome friend named Limey. After the family had seen the preview of the movie *Krampus*, they felt the urge to tell their story to the paranormal hotline. The family wants to remain anonymous, and they make the claim that this incident happened many years ago. The family is of German descent.

The Krampus is a creature from European folklore that is half goat and half demon. The antithesis of Santa Claus, the Krampus punishes bad children at Christmastime.

The family has three children: two boys and one girl. While in her teens, the girl played around with a Ouija board with her two girlfriends. The board started answering their questions, and the girls got really freaked out about it. When they asked the entity what his or her name was, the name it spelled out was Krampus. The family realizes that Krampus is a fictional character, but they feel there is either an entity out there that calls itself Krampus or there is actually a real Krampus.

Their daughter was misbehaving and using acid (LSD) with a boy in the neighborhood, and the entity said he would punish her for her misdeeds. The entity told the daughter that she would first be visited by a gnome named Limey. Perhaps under the influence of LSD, the daughter started seeing a misshapen gnome creature running about the house. Limey had scrawny legs, feet with pointed slippers, a slight hunchback, and facial skin blisters. He was hideous to behold.

There was a time when the daughter opened the closet, and Limey jumped out and scurried off. The mother of this family saw Limey only once while watching TV. With her peripheral vision she saw a small, shadowy creature dart off and run underneath the kitchen table.

While lying in bed, the daughter heard thumping sounds coming from underneath her bed, and when she rolled over and looked underneath the bed, the little gnome creature poked her in the eye with a sharp object.

The daughter's eye was bleeding profusely. The mother was about to rush her daughter to the hospital, when all of a sudden, the bleeding stopped and the eye was normal as if nothing had ever happened. This was the last time they saw Limey.

Now here comes Krampus. The two sons, who slept in a bunk bed, heard a knocking on their closet door. The boys kept watching the closet door as the pounding became louder and louder.

The father of the family went to the boys' room to investigate. When he got there, he opened up the closet door. Two large, red eyes came flying out, and he felt a chilling cold breeze go right through him.

The next incident occurred on Christmas Eve, when the daughter confronted a large entity with horns and red eyes. The entity held the daughter down on her bed and slapped her five times. The daughter had to be hospitalized because the experience produced psychological issues.

The family was very stressed out from the paranormal experiences in this home and decided to go on vacation to Florida for a week. When they returned, they discovered that their home had burned to the ground. There was no explanation for the fire. The paranormal activity experienced by this family has ceased, and they now live in a new home in another state.

ROBERT GOERMAN DISCUSSES FAIRIES

From Minnie (her last name withheld) to Robert Goerman, founder of the Nonhuman Research Agency:

This happened in Roswell, New Mexico, in the summer of 1997. At about 5:30 A.M., I took my cup of coffee outside to a picnic table in the backyard. My chihuahua, Bella, followed me. At first, I thought my neighbor had bought a dog—a little schnauzer. Taking a better look, I noticed it was not a dog but a "little man."

Bella thought it was a dog also as she ran to the fence to get a better look. We both noticed a little man about 12 inches tall, with stocky build, bushy eyebrows (gray), and a beard. He was wearing a gray woolen-type shirt (no buttons) and gray pants with a rope for a belt. He had brown boots that looked like socks.

Bella ran back into the house and under my bed, shaking, and remained there most of the day. The little man had a funny walk from side to side and quickly ran into a big chinaberry tree and disappeared. I could not see a door or entrance, but the little man disappeared into the tree. I will never forget this as long as I live.

Robert Goerman responded:

Minnie's testimony is a sobering reminder that, even in our techno-wondrous society of wireless laptop computers and cellular telephones, people can still report being startled by the sudden appearance of diminutive creatures, generally in humanoid form.

Tales of "wee people" have been recorded by most, if not all, cultures throughout human history. Some of our ancestors called them fairies. Medieval fairy-faith populated our world with a puzzling array of visitors (elves, gnomes, goblins, leprechauns, pixies, and others) from the fairy realm or fairyland.

It was the actual sightings of these beings that created the fairy-faith, not the other way around. Little people were believed in because they were seen!

Sightings continue today even without an accompanying "superstitious" belief in fairies. Two dozen "tantalizing and mysterious" stories of encounters were gathered from people living and vacationing within the region of the Catskill Mountains in New York for author and colleague Ron Quinn's *Little People* (Galde Press, 2006).

In two separate cases, 1949 and 1955, these little bandits were caught red-handed "borrowing" eggs and fruit. There were meetings where the wee folk left behind not only tiny footprints in haste but also a teeny hat and, in still another episode, a miniature fishing pole.

Usually only one little man was seen, but occasionally two or more have been reported. Sightings of little women were rarer still. In one nocturnal encounter, the little man's eyes displayed eyeshine and reflected light from a flashlight beam. Their spoken language was most often described as foreign or weird.

Quinn submits a snapshot that he received from a Kingston, New York, woman that purports to show a "little man" making off with a sock stolen from a box of old clothes sitting outside. She overcame her surprise in time to snap one 35mm photograph with Kodak ASA 400 film using a Nikon point-and-shoot "One Touch Zoom" camera. The photographer wishes to remain anonymous to avoid unwanted publicity.

For centuries now, hundreds of thousands of men and women have claimed to have seen the fairy folk—and many serious-minded scholars and researchers have felt that they have accumulated convincing proof that the Wee People truly do exist. Call the entities fairies, brownies, nisse, leprechauns, the good folk, the Hidden Folk, the gentry, or personify them as Puck, Robin Goodfellow, or Queen Mab. An incredible amount of folklore and anecdotal material has been built up around the accounts of the Wee Folk.

Heavenly Beings, Spirit Guides, and Multidimensional Teachers

Joan from Louisville, Kentucky, said that her eleven-month-old son, Jason, was in his playpen in the family room. His dad was watching a ballgame on TV in the same room. Everything seemed normal and peaceful.

"Jason had his normal Fisher-Price toys all around him to keep him from getting bored," she said. "I was upstairs working on the laundry when I decided to lie down on the bed for a few seconds to rest. While I was almost ready to doze off, a clear voice spoke to me and said, 'The baby is choking, go now!'"

Joan got up immediately and ran down the steps to the family room. She saw Jason standing up in his playpen smiling at her. Then she noticed her husband eating potato chips and drinking a coke. He turned around and asked her what was wrong.

Joan said, "Jason is choking."

Her husband looked at the seemingly calm child and said, "You were dreaming. He's fine. Go back upstairs and rest."

Joan couldn't let the strong command that she had heard go unchecked, so she went over to Jason, put her finger in his mouth, and pulled out half of a plastic Fisher-Price key from a play keychain. He was seconds away from swallowing the large object he had bitten off and it surely would have choked him to death.

Joan became weak and she fell to her knees.

"I began thanking God for sending a message from Jason's angel that was meant to protect him from harm. I have the broken key set in his box of memorabilia, and I look at it every few years just to remind me to always be on my guard when I receive a command that urges me to take action. It may be a life-saving experience for me or someone I know. I always praise God for his angels. Their messages are directly from the Throne of Our Father in Heaven and they are sent to keep us in His care."

MARCIE WAS CONVINCED THAT GOD PICKED ON HER

When we conducted two- or three-day seminars, we often found our-selves nearly surrounded by attendees at a local restaurant where we would go to have dinner after a long day at the lectern. Often when this occurred, with the permission of the owner, we told the attendees to bring their chairs to our table.

We remember well when Marcie joined us. She wondered why God was picking on her and just how much more she could possibly endure. To her inter-pretation, God seemed to be an ancient tribal god—fierce and demanding.

Her vitriol upset many of those sitting around our table, as she went on to declare, "I know that God must have judged me guilty of something, but I just can't figure out what it is that I have done to so arouse his wrath against me."

Sherry and I were disappointed when Marcie didn't return the next day to continue the seminar, but miracles do occur: Two weeks later, we received a wonderfully positive update of the troubled young woman's spiritual well-being.

Marcie told us that she had been considering some of the teaching that we had begun sharing at the seminar, and she had read one of our books on angels. Then, after nearly a week of study and prayer, she was awakened in the early, pre-dawn hours by a bright light shining in her eyes. When she opened her eyes, she saw a sphere of light about four feet in diameter floating in her room.

"It was about six to eight feet from my bed," she said. "It looked like a luminous, wispy fog, and it was swirling within itself, very gently rotating from my right to left. I was immediately filled with a sense of great peace and tranquility. All of my troubled feelings immediately vanished. And then this sphere of light spoke to me."

A clear, soft male voice asked her if she was afraid.

"I was nearly overcome because he was radiating something of unspeakable beauty," she said. "I felt his light envelop me and flow through me. It was a light which was not limited by boundaries of physical matter. It was a light of great gentleness and compassion beyond words. I told him that I had no fear."

She saw a sphere of light floating in the room; it was luminous, foggy, and seemed to swirl in on itself.

"You are loved unconditionally," he said. "The Creator Spirit is not filled with wrath and vengeance. What you humans have mistaken as punishment from your fierce concept of God is nothing more than the effects of your own actions."

"At this point," Marcie said, "the light coming from the celestial being went through me—and I experienced unconditional love for the first time in my life. It was searing—and exquisite. It was as though I was being bathed in a light which entered every cell in my body and filled everything it passed through with love.

"As the light washed through me, it removed all traces of fear, anxiety, guilt, and loneliness—and I felt clean and profoundly at peace. I began vibrating, as though to the sound of light—and I suddenly became aware of each cell in my body, and I felt love and compassion for them."

The Light Being bade her to open herself and to fill herself with the energy that was emanating from him.

She did as the being instructed her.

> The Light Being then stated that humans were neither judged nor punished by the Creator Spirit. Hatred, anger, prejudice, and ill will were creations of humankind....

"Incredibly, as I allowed more of his light energy to flow through me, I felt filled—but knew that I could never truly be filled," she said. "And although he was filling my being with this incredible love, his own brilliant light was not diminishing. When I saw this, I knew the light was coming from a source that was endless and was equally available for all people. I knew that I was not being singled out. This same love was available for all of creation. And this realization only added to my elation because there was great comfort in discovering that I was not a single entity that I was a part of all creation. I was feeling joy, relief, peace, love beyond any level I ever thought the human body was capable of achieving."

Marcie was aware that she was sitting on the edge of her bed, tears running down her face, a smile on her lips.

The Light Being then stated that humans were neither judged nor punished by the Creator Spirit. Hatred, anger, prejudice, and ill will were creations of humankind and directed by those of low awareness toward their fellow men and women.

"And then he was gone," Marcie told us in her email. "But I know that he is always somewhere teaching others in his universe of love."

CHARLIE KNOWS HIS ANGEL GUIDE IS ALWAYS THERE

In September 1968, Charlie was blown out of a helicopter while it was attempting to land and pick up wounded soldiers at a remote base under attack in Vietnam. The helicopter was struck by a rocket fired from the ground, which severely damaged the vehicle and threw Charlie clear.

Charlie felt an arm around his shoulder, and in his head he heard a voice saying, "Charlie, trust me and lean on me, and I will be there with you always."

He watched the ground rushing toward him 100 feet below. Just before impact, he felt something squeeze him; then everything went black. Charlie was in and out of consciousness for several days. When he returned to full wakefulness, he found that he had miraculously lived through the fall and had suffered no permanent injury.

In 1972, while employed by an Arkansas Police Department, Charlie was riding his motorcycle to work. He had just passed a semi-trailer truck when he had a flat tire. Charlie felt the bike shake and turn suddenly sideways. To his horror, he saw that he was sliding across the interstate toward the semi.

Once again he heard the voice asking him to trust it. At the last second, Charlie's bike moved behind the rear dual on the trailer of the semi, slid onto a curb on the inside lane, sat upright, and rolled to a stop. An unseen "someone" beside him had steered the bike out of danger.

In 1984, Charlie responded to a burglar alarm at a business that had frequently sounded false alarms. It was almost 11:00 P.M., time for a shift change, and Charlie called off the backup unit, assuming that the signal would turn out to be another false alarm. He didn't even unholster his revolver when he arrived to check out the building.

When Charlie rounded the back corner of the building, he saw a hole knocked in the wall and a perpetrator standing there with merchandise from the business. At the same time, he saw the subject was reaching for a gun in his waistband.

Again, the voice: "Trust me, Charlie. I am here for you always."

Charlie will never forget how "something" behind him pushed him down on the ground while the perp drew his weapon. He heard two shots fired by the suspect just before he made his getaway. Later, Charlie found that the burglar's bullets had impacted the wall just a foot to his right.

Charlie concluded his account by stating that the angel's promise to be with him always has come true many times. Any time he ever felt alone or afraid, he has always felt the angel of the Lord beside him—never ahead or behind, but always beside him. Charlie knows without a doubt that his guardian angel will always be there for him.

TOUCHED BY AN ANGEL OF HEALING

By C. Norman Shealy, M.D., Ph.D.

Longtime friend Clyde Norman Shealy, M.D., Ph.D., is an American neurosurgeon and a pioneer in pain medicine. He is credited with the invention of the transcutaneous electrical nerve stimulator, the spinal cord stimulator, and radiofrequency ablation for back pain arising from facet arthropathy.

For over sixty years I have had sudden important "knowings," sometimes as a vision, sometimes as an abstract understanding. Twenty-four years ago, I experienced the first of a few dozen audible contacts with angelic guides. One of the most important took place about sixteen years ago, while I was jogging in the woods in Holland. I suddenly had a vision of a copper pyramid with crystals at the top. I made a sketch of this when I returned to my room. The following night my angelic teacher spoke to me: "Where do you think that image came from yesterday?"

I replied: "I thought it was mine."

My guide said: "I put it there. You need to work with that."

I returned home and received permission to work with seventy-five patients in such a pyramid, activated by a Tesla coil. I treated them daily for one hour, five days a week, for two weeks, twenty-five patients each with rheumatoid arthritis, back pain or depression. Seventy percent were markedly improved within two weeks. But I felt there was no way to get this device approved by the FDA. So for the next twelve years I worked with five other circuits in the human body and developed a specific stimulator, the SheLi TENS, which could reduce pain, as well as selectively raise DHEA (dehydroepiandrosterone), aldosterone, neurotensin, or calcitonin, or reduce free radicals. The guide gave me the physical locations of points; I had to figure out the proper acupuncture points and the neurochemistry. That done, I came to the conclusion that life could be extended to an average of 140 years if people would just activate at least the three energetic rings to rejuvenate DHEA and calcitonin as well as reduce free radicals. I presented this work in my book *Life beyond 100—Secret of the Fountain*. As I spoke in over forty-two cities about this approach, I learned that a majority of people were not willing to spend twenty minutes a day required for the work. And in fact a majority of people were not interested in living even to one hundred years!

Dr. Norman Shealy, an authority on pain management, created a copper-and-crystal pyramid that alleviated pain for many of his arthritic patients.

In January 2007, I awoke at 4 A.M. with the image of that copper pyramid and knew I had not finished the work given to me years earlier! I then tested the effect of the pyramid on telomere rejuvenation in six volunteers. Telomeres are the tail of DNA and are an accurate reflection of longevity. Ordinarily, telomeres shrink an average of 1 percent each year. Within three months, telomeres had regrown an average of 1 percent. As I talked about this, I learned that most people would not put a pyramid in their house. After careful meditation, I realized that the only way this finding might be useful is to convert it to a mattress pad. Integrating another message from twenty years ago—"If you placed crushed sapphire over the heart, it would bypass the need for bypass surgery"—I created the mattress pad with copper and sapphire, connected to a Tesla coil. This can then be plugged into a timer, so that the entire solar homeopathic treatment (a term given me by the angelic guide) can be done while you sleep. Within an additional seven months on this device, the six subjects had had telomeres grow an average of 2.9 percent. This means that rejuvenation of telomeres is proceeding at an average of 3.4 percent each year, instead of declining at 1 percent per year. I have applied for a patent on this approach. It will be my eleventh patent. All have been the result of angelic guidance! Indeed, I consider my entire career guided by angelic wisdom. I have documented much of my 85 percent successful therapeutic approach in over 30,000 patients in a DVD, *Medical Renaissance—The Secret Code*.

AWARENESS OF SPIRIT GUIDES GOES BACK TO PALEOLITHIC AGE

Humankind has been aware that it is part of a larger community of powers and principalities, seen and unseen, physical and nonphysical, since at least the Paleolithic Age (c. 50,000 B.C.E.), when primitive artists painted images of supernatural beings on the walls of their caves. As early as the third millennium B.C.E., the written records of ancient Egypt and Mesopotamia recognized a hierarchy of supernatural beings that ruled over various parts of the Earth, the universe, and the lives of human beings. They also believed in lower levels of entities that might be either hostile or benign in their actions toward humans.

The idea of a spirit guide or guardian angel dates back to the farthest reaches of antiquity. It is unlikely that anthropologists have ever discovered a single aboriginal culture that did not include the concept of a spirit guide in its theology. As early as the third millennium B.C.E., the written records of ancient Egypt and Mesopotamia recognized a hierarchy of supernatural beings that ruled over various parts of the Earth, the universe, and the lives of human beings. The Mesopotamians wanted to be certain that they were well protected by their spiritual guardians, the *shedu* and the *lamassu*.

In the Sanskrit texts of the ancient *Vedas*, the word for angel is *angira*; in Hebrew, *malakh*, meaning "messenger" or *bene elohim*, for God's children; in

Arabic, *malakah*; and in India, multiwinged angels or beings are called *garudas*. The teachings of Islam state that there are three distinct species of intelligent beings in the universe. There are first the angels that are a high order of beings created of Light, the *malakh*; second, the *al-jinn*, ethereal, perhaps even multidimensional entities; and then human beings, fashioned out of the stuff of Earth and born into physical bodies. On occasion, the al-jinn can serve as helpful guides or guardians, but they can also be tricksters.

The scriptures of all the world's major faiths state firmly that angelic beings are not to be worshipped or held as objects of veneration. Even though possessed with ethereal energy and certain powers beyond those of humans, the angels are by no means omnipresent, omnipotent, or omniscient— and neither are they immune from falling into temptation or into error.

A circa 1550 artwork from Iran shows helpful *al-jinn* constructing a wall for Alexander the Great. The jinn could be helpful aids or sinister tricksters, depending on their mood.

The great Socrates provides us with the most notable example in the classical period of a man whose subjective mind was stimulated by the voice of his *daemon*, a guardian spirit who kept constant vigil and warned the philosopher of any approaching danger. In spite of the similarities in spelling, one should not mistake the benevolent guidance of Socrates's tutelary spirit for the evil machinations and perverse guidance of a demon.

True angelic beings will immediately discourage humans who attempt to treat them as minor deities. On the other hand, the fallen angels, the tricksters, and the deceivers—those who were banished from the heavenly realms for their arrogance in claiming divinity—are motivated by their own selfish goals and delight in corrupting humans. All of the principal religious texts warn the wise to be cautious of any manifesting entity and to test it to determine its true motives. There seems to be a general spiritual law that maintains that such negative entities cannot achieve power over humans unless they are somehow invited into a person's private space—or unless they are attracted to an individual by that person's negativity or vulnerability.

Some skeptical psychologists and other researchers have suggested that those individuals who believe in their having an angel to guide and to guard them may be accessing an as yet little-known power of the mind, which

E ven in this techno-
logical, scientific
age, a person of a con-
servative or fundamen-
tal religious persuasion
may tend to behold
angels....

enables one's subjective level of consciousness to dramatize another personality, complete with a full range of personal characteristics and its very own "voice." Such a theory sounds too much like a description of mental illness to those men and women who are convinced beyond a reasonable doubt that they were guided, directed, and protected by a spiritual being. Those who believe completely, without question, that they interacted with a guardian angel stoutly maintain that the reality of a spiritual guide or teacher is so much more than any kind of psychological phenomena.

There is no question that the authors of the books in both the Old and New Testaments considered angels fully capable of becoming quite physical and material—at least long enough to accomplish their appointed mission of rescue, healing, or guidance. Throughout the Bible there are accounts of angels who wrestled with stubborn shepherds, guided people lost in the wilderness, and freed persecuted prophets from fiery furnaces and dank prisons. Jesus himself was fed by angels, defended by angels, and strengthened by angels.

PERSONAL STORIES OF ANGELIC ENCOUNTERS SINCE 1968

Sincere men and women have been sending us their personal stories of angelic encounters for over four decades and beseeching us to share their witnessing of benevolent beings from the unseen world. Since 1968, we have been distributing various versions of the Steiger Questionnaire of Mystical and Paranormal Experiences to our readers and lecture audiences, and of the more than 30,000 respondents, 42 percent claim to have witnessed angelic activity; 52 percent believe that they have a guardian angel or spirit guide; and 38 percent say that they have had an encounter with a benevolent being of light. These percipients generally describe the beings as appearing youthful, commanding, beautiful of countenance, and often majestic and awesome. Manifestations of light often accompany them, which adds to the grandeur of their appearance and the feelings of profound reverence that suffuses those who encounter angelic beings. In many accounts, the angelic beings appear to be paraphysical—that is, they seem to be both material and nonmaterial entities. Although they originate in some invisible and nonphysical dimension, they seem completely capable of shaping reality in our three-dimensional world to suit their purposes.

Even in this technological, scientific age, a person of a conservative or fundamental religious persuasion may tend to behold angels in their traditional winged and robed persona while a member of a more liberal religious expression may be more likely to perceive an angel minus the wings and other sacerdotal trappings. On the other hand, even those who consider themselves avant-garde in many areas of contemporary life may still cherish the tradition-al and comforting angelic images

When spirit mediums speak of their guide, they are referring to an enti-ty from the Other Side who assists them in establishing contact with the spiri-tual essence of deceased humans. The spirit guides of mediums usually claim to have lived as humans on Earth before the time of their physical death and their graduation to higher realms of being. For the more contemporary spirit mediums, who often prefer to call themselves "channels," the guide may repre-sent itself as a being who once lived as a human on Earth or as a Light Being, an extraterrestrial, or even an angel. Regardless of the semantics involved, today's mediums and channels follow the basic procedures of ancient shamanic traditions.

THE LADY IN WHITE

Back in the 1970s, when he was only seven years old, Brady became very aware that he had a guardian angel.

"Our house consisted of three levels," he explained, "a basement, a main floor with three bedrooms, and an upstairs with two bedrooms. When he had first moved in, Mom and Dad slept in the master bedroom and Bobby, my younger brother, and I each had our own rooms. We didn't really use the upstairs."

When Brady's mom became preg-nant, his parents decided that he would move to an upstairs bedroom and his room on the main floor would be converted into the nursery for the new arrival.

Brady emphasized that in no way did he resent the move to an upstairs bedroom. He was eager and excited to do so. The situ-ation was not being forced upon him in any way. His parents were always very loving to him and his brother.

Shortly after he had moved upstairs, Brady was playing with his five-year-old brother on the main floor. They had been chasing each other around the dining room when Brady decided to quit the game of tag and go upstairs to his room.

As he began to walk up the steps, he was startled to see a lady in white standing at the top of the stairs.

The woman was wearing a white dress, something like what one would see at a beauty pageant. She was not scary, but, rather, loving.

"She was wearing a dress that had a strange kind of banner across it," Brady said. "As weird as it sounds, it looked like the kind of banner that someone like Miss America would wear."

Brady recalled that he managed a quick "U-turn" back down the steps. That night, he slept in his brother's room.

"I told my parents what I had seen," Brady said, "but they were understanding and didn't give me a lecture about seeing things or watching too many spooky television programs."

Brady's next encounter with the Lady in White occurred one evening when his parents were out and Bobby and he were at home with a babysitter.

"I was upstairs, sitting on the floor of my room, watching my little television set when I felt something brush against me," Brady said. "Thinking it was Bobby sneaking up on me, I turned about quickly—and there stood the Lady in White."

That was when Brady heard a gentle, soothing, feminine voice tell him not to be afraid. "I know you, Brady," she said. "I know you, and I love you. I know you, and I love you."

> When he told his mom the next day, she said that either Brady was dreaming about his guardian angel or else his angel was paying him a visit.

Brady listened to the Lady in White say those words over and over. Then he managed to get to his feet and make his way downstairs.

He did not tell the babysitter about the mysterious woman in white who had visited him in his room upstairs. Brady slept with Bobby that night, as well.

When he told his mom the next day, she said that either Brady was dreaming about his guardian angel or else his angel was paying him a visit.

Brady saw the Lady in White in his room twice more, but on neither occasion did she speak. She only smiled and made him aware of her presence.

While some people might judge Brady's Lady in White to be the product of an overactive or very creative seven-year-old mind, he feels that he has strong testimony in support of his theory that he did, indeed, receive visits from his guardian angel.

Two years later, when Brady was in the fourth grade, his parents were visiting his classroom during a parent-teacher conference. At one point in the discussion about her son, Brady's mother felt prompted to tell his teacher about the Lady in White.

"My teacher immediately told my mother not to say any more about the Lady until she returned, saying that she would be right back," Brady said.

"When she returned, she brought my second-grade teacher, who still taught at the school and who was also there that evening for parent-teacher conferences.

"I had never spoken a word about the Lady in White to any of my teachers—or to anyone outside of my family," Brady stressed. "My second-grade teacher then told my parents that on more than one occasion while I was in her class, she had seen the apparition of a lady dressed in white in the back of the classroom. And something she said she would never forget: the apparition appeared to be wearing some kind of banner."

The teacher had kept her own counsel about the apparition and had only recently confided about the strange experience to some of the other teachers, one of whom was Brady's fourth-grade teacher.

"That was why as soon as Mom started talking about my Lady in White, my fourth-grade teacher had excused herself from their conference to get my second-grade teacher," Brady said. "When she heard about my guardian angel, she was relieved. She had not been going crazy."

Brady said that neither he nor anyone else sighted the Lady in White after the appearances witnessed by his second-grade teacher. Perhaps, one might theorize, the benevolent entity only wished for another to witness her presence.

THE SPIRIT GUIDE IN SHAMANIC TRADITIONS

In shamanic traditions, the spirit guide serves as an ambassador from the world of spirits to the world of humans and often manifests to the shaman to serve as a chaperone during visits to other dimensions of reality. It seems quite likely that today's mediums and channels are contemporary expressions of ancient shamanic traditions.

Those who follow the spiritual path of the traditional Native American Medicine priests believe in a total partnership with the world of spirits and the ability to make personal contact with individual spirit guides and those physically deceased loved ones who have already changed planes of existence. In the traditional Native American vision quest, the seekers go into the wilderness alone to fast, to pray, to go into the silence of meditation, and to receive a personal spirit guardian, who will connect them with a Higher Being who will tell them what to do and tell them the way that they must help their people, their family, and their tribe.

While the matter of the guardian spirit may seem but a fairy tale to the ardent skeptic, the concept of multidimensional beings materializing to assist humankind in times of crisis appears to be universal.

Dr. Walter Houston Clark, the late professor emeritus at Andover Newton Theological Seminary, once told me that upon those occasions when he had personally explored the mystical consciousness in various Native American rituals, he had assumed that any entities that he had perceived in such

There are shamanic traditions to be found all over the world, including with Native Americans in the United States. A belief in spirit guides is common in shamanism.

states were "symbols created by my unconscious, rather than coming from an intelligence in another plane of being."

Dr. Clark added, however, that he believed that "those who have received messages from cowled figures, angels, or venerable men in dreams or in visions—and then found that these messages contained verifiable truths—should treat these figures with respect, whatever their origin."

Traditional Native Americans treat their guardian spirits with respect, and they use the information given to them in dreams and in visions as lessons about themselves to be used in the most effective performance of their personal worship ceremonies.

In our contemporary American society, one may become rather uneasy in acknowledging a belief in a partnership with the spirit world, especially when we have learned so much about the limitless reach of the human psyche.

You might begin by at least granting the possibility that you may establish contact with those loved ones who have graduated to other planes of existence. You could begin to sit in development circles, remaining receptive to whatever communication might be channeled to anyone within the circle.

Under no circumstances, however, should the situation be forced. A relaxed and tranquil state of mind will best allow the psyche to soar free of time and space and return with images, impressions, messages, and perhaps even a more complete awareness of the presence of a spiritual guide. Each session should begin with each member of the circle praying for guidance and protection.

Once we asked Grandmother Twylah, the repositor of wisdom for the Seneca, how she might answer those people who found it difficult to accept a partnership with the spirit world. She told us, "The first thing I would say to such people is to ask if they had ever had an experience that caused them to wonder if there might not be a possibility of a spirit world. If they were reluctant to discuss this, I would ask them if they feared death.

"If they admitted such a fear, I would ask just what put such a fear into them. Was it their religious teachings? A dread of the unknown? In either case I would say that fear has a great deal to do with the rejection of spirits.

"Then I might ask them if they have ever thought strongly of a loved one who has passed over. Has it ever occurred to them that they may have had that strong thought because that loved one was close to them in spirit at that moment?

"I would suggest that the next time that they had such a sensation that they have a conversation with the person in spirit. I can promise that they will have a wonderful feeling.

"Once a person opens up, the entities, the spirits, will come. Everyone wants proof of survival. So did I. I have now proved many times over the existence of the spirit world to my own satisfaction."

We very much believe, as the Native American medicine priests instruct their students, that a spirit that is called by us and asked to do our bidding will always want something in return. And all too often that seemingly innocent process of barter will turn out to be far from benign. On the other hand, we do believe that we can practice certain techniques that may help us to create the proper attitude of acceptance that may encourage the participation of a spirit teacher in our life and may bring about a clearer vision of our path on our Earthwalk. We also believe that the disciplined practice of certain meditation or visualization exercises may enable us to "hear" more clearly the soft whispers of angelic guidance and to perceive more completely the full meaning of the heavenly messages that are sent to us.

> We very much believe, as the Native American medicine priests instruct their students, that a spirit that is called by us and asked to do our bidding will always want something in return.

We would very strongly urge you to exhibit an attitude of respectfulness to the sacredness that is inherent in the act of communication with your spirit teacher or spirit guide. And you should definitely not practice any spiritual exercises with the goal of hoping to see your guide manifest physically in your presence.

Truly, the best attitude to assume is that you are going to enter a state of relaxation and tranquility whereby higher levels of awareness—perhaps from your *own* individual higher self—will present themselves to you in a manner whereby you might get in deeper touch with important aspects of yourself.

Some contemporary scientists are suggesting that such mystical experiences can be explained in terms of neural transmitters, neural networks, and brain chemistry. Perhaps the feeling of transcendence that mystics describe could be the result of decreased activity in the brain's parietal lobe, which helps regulate the sense of self and physical orientation. Perhaps the human brain is wired for mystical experiences.

While the physical activity of the brain and its psychological state may sometimes serve as a conduit to a transcendent world, we believe that the appearance of the benevolent beings that we most often recognize as angels is far more than a manifestation of a belief in the unknown, a blending of brain chemistry, or a personification of our hope in a spiritual comforter. We believe that there is some spiritual reality that exists outside of us that is interested in our human condition, and with which we may somehow communicate.

ANGELIC NIGHT SCHOOLS

In the mid-1970s, we began to receive an increasing number of emails from individuals who claimed that they were leaving their bodies at night to study with angelic beings.

Caleb told us that he had attended such an angelic night school since he was a young boy and that he has remained in contact with his celestial tutors throughout his adult life.

"At first, two angels would come to me and lift me from my physical body as I lay in bed, but soon I was able to slip out of the body without their assistance," Caleb said. "As soon as I was out of the body, I would receive instruction from angelic teachers. I suppose you could say it was like going to night school. During the day, I went to junior high. At night, my soul body was taken up to a higher plane to attend an angel school."

One of the lessons that the angels taught Caleb was how to heal himself and others.

Caleb continued to use his healing abilities throughout junior high and secondary school. Nothing too dramatic, he said, just minor things, like fixing a teammate's sprained or dislocated shoulder. On one occasion, however, he placed his hands on the chest of an older teacher who was having a heart attack and reversed the episode. Doctors credited Caleb's resourceful use of "massage" with saving the man's life.

"I am often asked if such double schooling wasn't tiring," Caleb said. "On the contrary, I used to awaken in the morning feeling completely refreshed. Now that I am in my forties, I have developed my level of awareness so that I am aware of my guides' presence without leaving the physical body and I have quietly used my healing gifts to help many family members, friends, and fellow employees in my office."

HEAVENLY ANGELS OR SPIRIT GUIDES?

Many contemporary spiritual seekers have begun to wonder if the differences between a spirit guide and a guardian angel are just a matter of semantics. Guardian angels and spirit guides are both nonphysical, multidimensional beings whose mission it is to provide important guidance, direction, and protection for their human wards on the physical plane. Today, more and more spiritual seekers prefer avoiding issues of religious, shamanic, or spiritualist dogma and have begun to refer to any benevolent, compassionate, otherworldly entity as a Light Being.

Some recipients of angelic phenomena have also come to believe that they were visited by benevolent beings from another dimension of time and space rather than a heavenly kingdom. These beings may be members of an ancient teaching order from the past, a spiritual brotherhood/sisterhood from the future, or a fellowship that exists in the Eternal Now. While having no wish to quarrel with traditional beliefs that angels are occupants of Heaven sent on godly missions, we have come to accept the premise that some otherworldly benefactors originate in another plane of reality, another dimension of being.

In recent years, the theory that it may have been the angels themselves who created humankind has become increasingly popular. The seed of life may have been planted by superior beings who had the knowledge, the science, and the technology

The Christian notion of guardian angels is really not all that different from the concept of spirit guides found in shamanistic beliefs.

to fashion planets that could support life and the evolution of intelligent species. Paraphysical entities or beings of pure mind, these "angels" shepherd the planet and monitor its progress.

Mentioned in the apocryphal texts as well as the accepted books of the Bible, the mysterious angelic beings known as the "Watchers" and the "Holy Ones" observe humankind and make certain that the inhabitants of Earth never forget that "the Most High rules the kingdom of men and gives to whomsoever He wills" (Daniel 4:17). It may well be that the Watchers are still on duty.

A Sick Boy Finds Comfort from an Angel

As a child, Jonathan suffered from severe allergic reactions to almost everything. He remembers his mother once sighing in frustration that it seemed as though Jonathan was allergic to planet Earth.

In the account he provided to the *Steiger Questionnaire of Mystical Experiences*, Jonathan said that his sole form of solace came from an angel who always appeared to him as a cowled figure, much like that of a monk. Jonathan remembered the benevolent being's voice as gentle and soothing, filled with wisdom and love. The hooded angel's name was Jedidiah.

Jonathan said that he first met his angel when he was about five years old.

"1 started to fall down the stairway," he said, "and someone reached out and pulled me back to a sitting position on the landing. 1 looked up to see this bearded man bending over me and smiling at me."

Jonathan's twelve-year-old sister, Sarah, who was supposed to be babysitting him, saw him totter at the top of the steps, start to topple, then appear to fly backwards up to the landing. Jonathan clearly recalled his sister's declaration when she ran up the stairs to check on him: "You must have a guardian angel!"

When he turned sixteen, Jonathan was startled one night to see a strange manifestation of a greenish, glowing ball of light that appeared in his bedroom shortly after he had finished saying his prayers.

"The glowing object just seemed to shoot around my room at great speed, yet never hitting a wall, any of the furniture, or the ceiling," Jonathan said. "And then suddenly it seemed as though my spiritual essence was out of my body and racing along beside the glowing ball! Then the two of us seemed to soar up through the ceiling and upward into the dark night sky. The feeling was absolutely ecstatic!"

After that liberating experience, Jonathan found that all his debilitating allergies had left him. It was as if he had left his cocoon of illness and pain and emerged as a butterfly, free of blights and blemishes.

"1 still had the occasional sinus headache, but all in all, I felt wonderful," he said. "I knew that it was Jedidiah, my guardian angel, who had assumed the form of the mysterious glowing ball to set my physical body free of all those restrictive illnesses and allergies."

When Jonathan contacted us, he was a twenty-eight-year-old high school sociology teacher and guidance counselor who was popular and well-liked by his students. "Jedidiah will sometimes enter my consciousness and speak through me to the students," he admitted. "Of course, neither they nor my superiors on the staff know that on occasion I channel an angel during some of my guidance sessions. Jedidiah has a knack for saying what people *need* to hear, rather than what they *want* to hear, so while some of the students might be stung by his initial comments, the truth of his counsel always rings true. And best of all, it always seems to help them."

HEALED BY HOODED BEINGS

Who are these mysterious hooded entities who visit humans to teach and to heal? Are they angels in a less familiar guise? Could they be a special group of "monastic angels" who relay messages of spiritual growth? Or are they members of an ancient order of beings from another dimension of time and space, another world, another universe?

In the account that Douglas sent to us, he wrote that he lived in his youth in Salem, Oregon, in the north-middle part of Oregon's Willamette Valley. It was the summer of 1971, and he was a thirteen-year-old boy. During that summer, the valley was subjected to a major strep epidemic of a form that was very difficult to treat, even with the antibiotics of the day. Douglas knew that he simply was not getting better, and he knew from the conversations in hushed tones by his doctors that he might die.

One night as he lay in the hospital bed, something happened that shocked him and changed his life forever.

"Coming into my room," he told us, "was this 'nurse' with a monk-like, hooded cloak. I interpreted her as a 'she,' though in truth I do not know for certain the gender of the being. She was a bit on the chubby side and stood around 5' 5" in height. Her face was nothing but eyes and a 'V'-shaped ridge for a nose, with only an indication of a mouth. Her skin looked more like plastic sheeting than skin. When she communicated, it was mind-to-mind; I never saw her mouth open."

Somehow she communicated to Douglas that she had a solution to his problem. From out of her overly long sleeve emerged her hand holding a metallic rod, which was very knobby and looked like brushed aluminum. When she pressed the end of the rod against his hip, instead of injecting pain, he felt a sensation like an ice cube pressed against the skin.

By about 11:00 A.M. the next day, his fever broke for the first time, and he started getting better.

Douglas then told us about another very impressive interaction with the hooded beings.

"My mother had been having a series of strokes, which left her totally drained. I was my mother's medical caregiver in those days. I had gotten her to bed and had gone to watch television and to unwind from the day's work. Around 12:45 A.M., about a half-hour after my mother had gone to bed, her bedroom access hall light came on.

Hooded, monklike beings came and healed his mother, who had been sick from several strokes.

"I went to check on my mother, found her quiet and asleep, so I returned to my TV program. About ten minutes later, the light came on again. I got only to the end of our dining-room table when some unseen force caused me to sit down and just look down the hallway. Through the guest bedroom door came three hooded entities who crossed the hall and entered my mother's bedroom. They never opened any door, and they moved in a floating, not a walking, motion. They came back and forth from the guest bedroom, as if it was some sort of staging area, and they carried their equipment in containers colored a flat-finish grey about the size of large facial tissue boxes.

"To describe the beings, they wore hooded monks' cowls, which looked very much like the garb worn by the old Spanish monks. A feature about them that struck me at the time was that they were very thin compared to their height, which was around six feet tall. Their faces were solid black. I could make out some curved dimensions to their faces, but there were no features at all.

"They kept on with their work for what seemed like two hours plus. The next day, my mother was totally better, almost as if she had never had those strokes. Mother stayed that way for around six and a half years, until a major stroke forced her into a nursing home.

"I have no idea whether my mother witnessed any of the activity done for her benefit by the hooded beings. I never talked about the experience with my mother. Interestingly, there was physical trace evidence of Mother's healing. There was caked blood left on her pillow case, which required discarding; and in the guest bedroom from which the hooded beings had come and gone, there was an ozone smell like that of a burned-out electric motor. All I really know is that I have a debt to the hooded ones that I don't know how to pay!"

AN ACCOUNT OF A MIRACLE HEALING BY A HOODED BEING FROM LEE MOORHEAD, WELL-KNOWN PSYCHIC-SENSITIVE AND MEDIUM

I am going to share something that happened to me just after my twentieth birthday.

I had been trained originally to be a high diver, and I was practicing one of my dives when I misunderstood my coach. I thought he was giving me the signal to dive from a thirty-foot board, but the signal was actually for the man who was on the fifteen-foot board. So when I dived off, I looked below and there I saw my fellow diver just below me. We would have crashed and maybe been killed, so I threw my body out of position and ended up away from him, but on my back and unconscious.

I woke up in a hospital and kept drifting in and out of consciousness. They sent me home with my mother, who was a registered nurse, and she continued to care for me. It seems I mangled one of my kidneys, which has not worked since.

But the part of the story I want to get to is that the first day home, my mom had to leave the house to get my prescription filled and I was sleeping. Suddenly I awoke and standing there next to my bed was a hooded being that I felt was male. He was standing there next to me, not saying a word, but I knew that he was reading out of a book, which I have always thought was a Bible. I opened my eyes to look at him, but I kept drifting in and out. The hooded being remained there, reading from this book. I was in a paralyzed state; I could not speak, cry out, or move, but I did not fear him. Then he turned and went away.

Overnight my fever broke, and in a few days I was up and on my feet again. The doctor had told my mother that I should never have children, because I would only have the use of one kidney.

I paid no attention, and I had my family just a few years later. I felt that I was healed by the hooded being, and until this day I have only told a very few people about the experience. Now I am sharing it with you.

THE MISSION OF THE HOODED SPIRIT TEACHERS

Although their original duties may have been assigned to them even before the Earth was fashioned, it seems that the Hooded Spirit Teachers maintain as a considerable portion of their mission the task of guiding us toward ever-expanding spiritual awareness. As well as their having been assigned to be there on occasion in order to give us humans a helping hand, it seems that it is also an integral part of their terrestrial assignment to lead us to a clearer understanding of our true role in the universal scheme of things.

And it seems to be very clear to many humans who have interacted with the Hooded Beings that while these entities cast themselves in the roles of our tutors, they truly favor teaching us by example and inspiration.

It is in this crucial area of noninterference that the good spirits and angelic beings differ markedly from the entities who emanate from the Dark Side. The less benign beings have no compunction about interfering with humankind's spiritual evolution. On the contrary, they appear to delight in their attempts to thwart our spiritual destiny.

The purpose of the Hooded Beings may be to guide us to greater spiritual awareness.

Throughout our human history the benevolent beings have shown us by their examples that the impossible can be accomplished, that the rules of our physics are made to be broken, and that the physical laws of this planet were created to serve, rather than subvert, the human spirit.

A HOODED BEING GIVES BRAD A BOOK IDEA

One evening in the autumn of 1972, I was awakened by an unusual buzzing sound. When I opened my eyes, I was startled to see a dark-hooded figure standing at the side of the bed, waving his arms over me in a peculiar manner.

I felt all of my strength draining from my body. I collapsed in a sprawled heap on the bed.

"Don't be afraid," the hooded intruder said in a deep male voice. "We won't hurt you."

The next thing I knew it was morning. There was no trace of the hooded man nor any sign to prove that he had even been there.

Several times that day I reviewed the bizarre experience over and over in my mind. I knew that I had definitely been awakened by an intruder who had been making some kind of strange sound.

I kept going over the only words that the hooded man had spoken: "Don't be afraid. We [or had it been "he"? Had there been more than one intruder?] won't hurt you."

The next evening I was just falling asleep when I became aware of a peculiar, metallic buzzing sound—the kind of buzz that one might imagine a mechanical bumblebee would make. I realized at once that that must have been the strange sound that had awakened me the previous night just before the cowled man had invaded our bedroom.

I could clearly perceive an eerie, greenish light emanating from somewhere in the stairway. Without question, the strange buzzing sound was coming from a ball of light.

I felt my pulse quicken as I watched the green globe of softly glowing light moving into the bedroom.

The greenish globe hovered over my face for just a moment. I didn't have even a few seconds to attempt to struggle against the darkness that came over me. After a command to listen, the very next sensory impression that I perceived was the light of dawn entering the bedroom windows.

By the afternoon after the second nighttime invasion, I began to get a different view of the whole strange business. Shortly after I arrived at my office, I had the concept of a new book niggling at my consciousness. It occurred to me that I should write a book that would explore the contemporary revelatory experience. Did revelation cease with John the Revelator at the Isle of Patmos in the year 30 C.E.? Of course not! Illuminations, revelations, and mystical experiences were happening to thousands of men and women every day.

As the day progressed, I felt more and more that this idea for a new book on contemporary revelation was connected with the bedroom intruder. I also had a strong feeling that the book must bear the title *Revelation: The Divine Fire*.

As I began to write down some notes about the book, it seemed that they appeared to be coming from some kind of memory of a series of discussions with a learned, older, and wiser friend.

I called Tam Mossman, my editor at Prentice Hall, and told him that I wanted to do a book on the experiences of men and women who claimed to be in spiritual communication with a higher intelligence. Mossman told me to go for it.

The book, *Revelation: The Divine Fire*, published in 1973, proved to be one of the most important in my early career. Reviewers were overwhelmingly responsive and thoughtful. Some were generous enough to compare the work in importance with William James's *The Varieties of Religious Experience*. The book was a selection of many book clubs and published in hardcover, trade paperback, and mass-market paperback editions.

In 1982, a little more than ten years after transmitting *The Divine Fire* to me, the Spirit Teacher manifested in my office in Phoenix when I was working late one evening.

At this time I was the editor of a small publishing company and manager of a recording studio, producing other people's books and cassette tapes— while striving to maintain my own career as an author, lecturer, and paranormal researcher.

Most evenings, after having worked on my duties for the company from ten to five, I would start work on my own writing projects. Many nights, I would often fall asleep at my faithful 1923 Underwood typewriter and spend what remained of the night asleep on the floor beside my desk. Every day, I was forced to deal with the stresses arising from the financial problems of the company, the individual temperaments of the staff, the eccentricity of one of our principal backers, and the fickle demands of the marketplace.

My Spirit Teacher's materialization on this occasion was in sharp contrast to his prior dramatic arrival in a glowing green orb. I simply looked up from my work, and he was seated across from me on the other side of my desk.

He still wore the cowl, but I could distinguish shadowed male features, a rather prominent nose of the type commonly called "Roman," and a salt-and-

Saint Elijah is shown here ascending into heaven. Brad was visited by a benevolent being who appeared to him in the form of this saint.

pepper beard. During his prior appearances, his voice (or the voice I heard) seemed rather androgynous. On this visit, his voice issued in pleasant, rather deep, male tones.

I clearly recall the benevolent being's gray-speckled beard, long hair, and warm, kind, dark eyes. During this meeting, I was able to engage the hooded teacher in conversation, and the wise entity presented me with the precise information that I needed to complete a very important project.

I also got the sense of a name, Elijah, though I cannot be certain if the spirit teacher actually identified himself as such, or if I only somehow "felt" the name. The character of Elijah in the Old Testament had always been my favorite, so he may simply have picked the name out of my subconscious.

The purpose of this visit seemed entirely focused on helping me to decide what my next move should be in terms of furthering my career. He had come to help me evaluate my options.

While the session had begun in my office, we were suddenly transported to his study, a large room with heavily laden bookshelves set against stone walls. I was now seated across from his "desk," a large, coarse, wooden table.

It seemed as though we spoke for many hours, but I cannot be certain if our meeting occurred in linear or other dimensional time. Neither can I recall exactly any nuggets of wisdom to share with others. It was very much like being caught in a memory pattern, wherein one recalls the essence of what was said, rather than exact words.

During the course of our discussion, I was given to understand that he was a member of an ancient order of spirit teachers who manifested from time to time to oversee the fulfillment of certain projects. Since we humans liked to have names for our acquaintances, I sensed that he would be comfortable with "Elijah."

Sometime before the first light of dawn reached through the window shades of my office, he had gone, but he had left me with concepts and information that were acutely necessary to make an intelligent decision regarding the dilemma that had faced me prior to his visit.

Elijah seemed a fitting name for the entity. The parentage of the biblical prophet Elijah is unknown, as if he had just somehow materialized in a time of need. It was said that Elijah could travel from place to place with such speed that it was as if he traveled in a whirlwind. And Elijah was said not to have died: He ascended by fiery chariot. In my cosmology, I could very much accept the proposition that the Elijah of the Old Testament was a multidimensional being.

> In 1986, Elijah brought me together with the one who would prove to be the most important person in my life.

It is clear from an examination of many biblical references and certain passages from the Dead Sea Scrolls that Elijah was regarded as a helper, a guide, who would manifest in time of need. In Matthew 11, Jesus says that John the Baptist was more than a prophet; he was Elijah. In Mark 9:11, after Jesus, Peter, James, and John returned from the Mount after Jesus's Transfiguration, the other disciples asked if it was true that Elijah must return again. Jesus answered that Elijah would return to restore all things. As he hung on the cross during his crucifixion, observers stated that they heard Jesus cry out to Elijah.

In 1986, Elijah brought me together with the one who would prove to be the most important person in my life. I have told the story many times, because it seems in retrospect as if it happened in a motion picture that I was watching rather than a true-life love story that I was living.

A very pleasant lady sat down beside me at a lecture sponsored by a friend and proceeded to tell me that she brought me greetings from Sherry Hansen. Sherry Hansen? A woman that I had admired for years, but whom I had only met when she stopped briefly at my office on her way to England. I knew that she had once had her own school of spirituality and metaphysics, had turned down her own television programs, and lectured at major conventions.

I was astonished further to learn that Sherry was currently living in Phoenix, and I could scarcely wait until the speaker's reception at my friend's house was over to go back to my apartment to check the telephone book for verification that she was in the city and might actually have sent her greetings to me.

It took me two nights to dial her number, but she was really there to answer.

Then the real mystery began. She had not sent me greetings by the charming messenger, and, in fact, Sherry did not even know her.

I found this clear evidence of Elijah's workings behind the scenes to bring us together.

As we grew to know each other more and began to share confidences, I told her of my mystical experience with writing *Revelation: The Divine Fire* and my encounters with the Elijah entity. Astonished, Sherry shared her own experience with Elijah in 1972, which we ascertained would have been precisely when I was working most intensely writing the book.

Sherry had been meditating during a prayer-healing meeting that was being held in her home when she was startled by a voice and vision that was so three-dimensional that she was momentarily confused. In her vision, two sandaled feet began walking toward her, and the closer they came, the more distinctly she could see the edge of a brown, monk-like robe. Then she heard a voice cry out, "Elijah!" Silence. Then another call, this time louder: "Elijah!" And a third call, louder still, a shout: "Elijah!"

The next day it was shown to Sherry how she might combine her interests and backgrounds in nursing, healing, the ministry, and counseling. She saw herself establishing a place of education where one could understand how the body, mind, and spirit functioned and interacted. It seemed clear to her that people needed to perceive the oneness and the interconnectedness of all of life, whether it was the relationship of our minds and bodies to the environment, the planet, or to the universe. In the early 1980s, Sherry gathered as many as forty gifted faculty members and established the Butterfly Center for Transformation in Virginia Beach.

It is our conviction that we should never directly call upon Elijah, nor should we ask him for help or request his intercession. We heed the admonitions given in numerous sacred works that advise against seeking to summon one's spirit guide as inadvertently creating the risk of worshipping the being or encouraging undue reliance upon one's celestial companion. We are, after all, supposed to learn how to accomplish our mission on Earth with as little help as possible from other dimensional allies. Then, too, there is the danger that if we should seek to summon him, we could be opening the portal to an astral masquerader to pose deceptively as Elijah.

On the other hand, on many occasions, I have been aware of Elijah's subtle influence and inspiration in my life and in my work. And who knows, I may even have met him again in one of his many guises as I have continued on my quest. He may have been the strong hand that reached out from the crowd at an intersection and pulled me back just in time to avoid being struck by a speeding taxi. Or he may have been the stranger who claimed to have been the victim of a pickpocket and needed just the exact amount of money that I had in my wallet to buy a bus ticket home to see his wife and kids.

In the spring of 1987, Sherry and I established a business and research association. At midnight during the Harmonic Convergence, August 16/17, we were married by a dear brother, Bishop John Diegel. Serving as witnesses were his wife, Patricia Rochelle Diegel, a beloved friend of many years, Hope Kerruish, our hard-working typist, and the bishop's two cats.

Ghostly Visitations by Loved Ones

A Deceased Grandfather Suddenly Appeared in a Photo

Wendy K. shared an account of a ghostly visitation that resulted in what she will always remember as the best personal experience of her life. She was twelve years old in 1987 when she traveled with her mother to visit her grandmother.

"We were looking through some old photographs, when I noticed one of my grandmother standing by herself. She looked sad, and I asked about the photo," Wendy said. "She said that it was after Grand Daddy had died and she was still upset."

Wendy noticed in the picture that there was a hand on her grandmother's shoulder. "Who is behind you in the picture, Grandmother?" she asked.

When Wendy showed her the image, her grandmother began to cry and shake. "She swore it was my grandfather's hand and that it had not been in the photograph before that night. He always put his hand on her left shoulder, just as it was in the picture."

Later that night, Wendy was sleeping on the couch when she was suddenly awakened. "There, sitting across from me in a chair was my grandfather. I wasn't scared. I felt warm, peaceful, and loved. He never had the chance to hold me when I was an infant before he died. He stood up, walked over to the couch, looked at me, smiled, placed his hand over his heart, and vanished.

"I don't know how long I sat there on the couch, but my mother came walking in the living room. She sat down and started crying. She told me that Grand Daddy had just been in her room and had told her how beautiful his granddaughter had grown to be. Grandmother joined us soon after, and we spent the next couple of hours talking about the events. I will always remember that night's experience as my best personal blessing."

BRENDA VISITED HER DECEASED MOTHER

Brenda A. told us that she had been intensely troubled by her mother's approaching death due to cancer. One night she read a book about a spirit doctor who claimed to be able to perform psychic surgery on someone afflicted of a disease. Brenda followed the instructions the spirit doctor gave in the book regarding the healing process practiced by the medium, and she petitioned him to aid in the removal of the cancer cells that had invaded her mother's body.

"In the middle of the night," Brenda said, "I awakened from a dream in which a face that I presumed to be that of the spirit doctor appeared before me. He simply stated that my mother was dying. That was all he said, but it forced me to accept the fact that her death was to be."

After her mother's death, Brenda said that she had frequent dreams about her. "In these dreams, she was always sick and dying, never dead."

Visions of a dearly departed may persist until one finally accepts their death and allows them to go home.

Then, Brenda told us, one night she spent the entire period of time in the spirit world. "I actually believe this beyond the shadow of any doubt that we were together in another plane of existence."

When dawn came, Brenda and her mother came to her place of internment in the cemetery, and Brenda said goodbye to her beloved mother's spirit self and said. "I guess you have to go back now."

Her mother smiled and replied, "I'm not here now, but I am up there."

From that time on, Brenda said, she never again dreamed of her mother's terrible illness and dying. "I guess that was the moment that I finally accepted her death."

CARY'S GRANDFATHER VISITED HIM IN SPIRIT

Cary F. recalled that his first memorable experience with the paranormal was at the age of thirteen. "My grandfather had passed away, and a couple of days later, while I was lying in the dark trying to sleep, I saw his face at the foot of my bed," Cary said. "This may have been a manifestation of my mind; however, my feeling has always been that his spirit was actually there to visit me. I say this because I remember the vision being very three-dimensional."

DEATHBED VISIONS COME IN ALL SHAPES AND SIZES

Dr. Carla Wills-Brandon, Ph.D., spent over two decades investigating the mystical experiences of the dying and those who were at their bedside. According to Wills-Brandon, who has collected nearly 2,000 modern-day deathbed vision accounts, "Deathbed visions come in all shapes and sizes. As physical death draws near, some people receive visitations from deceased relatives while others encounter angels or other religious figures."

Many of the accounts collected by Wills-Brandon mention seeing a wisp of "something" leaving the physical body of a friend or relative at the moment of passing. "Those who are about to leave will often talk about seeing beautiful landscapes on the other side and then state with conviction that this is where they will be after they pass," she said.

A licensed marriage and family therapist who has been in private practice for twenty years with her husband of twenty-five years, Michael Brandon, Ph.D., Wills-Brandon is the author of *One Last Hug Before I Go: The Mystery and Meaning of Deathbed Visions* and *A Glimpse of Heaven: Spiritually Transformative Mystical Experiences of Everyday People*. Her extensive research has convinced her that deathbed visions bring comfort not only to the dying but also to those who love them. "In most cases, once one has had such a vision, death is no longer something to fear," she said. "This phenomenon is nothing new. It has been described over and over again, across all cultures and religions, for as long as time can remember."

As Carla Wills-Brandon reminds us in *One Last Hug Before I Go*, deathbed visions of the soul leaving the body have been experienced by humans in all cultures and religions; in fact, the existence of the soul is one of the few things upon which the major religions agree. In Judaism, Christianity, and Islam, the soul or spirit is the very essence of the individual, more important to his or her identity than the physical body, which is only a temporary possession that will turn to dust.

The body is the sheath of the soul.

The Talmud (Judaism)

Then the Lord God formed man out of the dust of the ground, and breathed into his nostrils the breath of life; and man became a living being.

Genesis 2:7 (Judaism/Christianity)

And He originated the creation of man out of clay, then He fashioned his progeny of an extraction of mean water, then He shaped him, and breathed His spirit in him.

Qur'an 32:8–9 (Islam)

Now my breath and spirit goes to the Immortal, and this body ends in ashes; OM, O Mind! Remember the deeds. Remember the actions.

Isha Upanishad 17

In Hinduism, the soul is a fragment of the Divine Self, the Atman.

The great Hindu work, the Bhagavad Gita, contains the oft-quoted lines (2:19–25) that tell us that the spirit within is unborn, eternal, immutable, indestructible, immemorial, and unchanging. "As a man abandons his worn-out clothes and acquires new ones, so when the body is worn out a new one is acquired by the Self, who lives within…. The Self cannot be pierced or burned, made wet or dry. It is everlasting and infinite, standing on the motionless foundation of eternity. The Self is unmanifested, beyond all thought, beyond all change."

Buddhism perceives the spirit as the end-product of a life of conditions and causes.

"Behold this beautiful body, a mass of sores, a heaped up lump, diseased … in which nothing lasts, nothing persists. Thoroughly worn out is this body…. Truly, life ends in death…. Of bones is this house made, plastered with flesh and blood. Herein are stored decay, death, conceit, and hypocrisy. Even ornamental chariots wear out. So too the body reaches old age…." Dhammapada 147–51.

The teachings of Seicho-no-Ie, a new religion becoming popular in Japan, state that the nature of human beings is primarily a spiritual life that "weaves its threads of mind to build a cocoon of flesh, encloses its own soul in the cocoon, and for the first time, the spirit becomes flesh. But understand this clearly: The cocoon is not the silkworm; in the same way, the physical body is not man but merely man's cocoon. Just as the silkworm will break out of its cocoon and fly free, so, too, will man break out of his body-cocoon and ascend to the spiritual world when his time is come." Nectarean Shower of Holy Doctrines.

A SURVEY OF DOCTORS AND NURSES ON DEATHBED VISITATIONS

For thousands of years now, many individuals have received personal proof of survival by observing their loved ones at the moment of death. Reports of deathbed experiences have long intrigued investigators of psychic phenomena, and today we have the work of such researchers as Dr. Elisabeth Kübler-Ross, Dr. Raymond Moody, Dr. Kenneth Ring, Dr. P. M. H. Atwater, and Dr. Carla Wills-Brandon to share a greater knowledge of this most personal, and final, of all human phenomena.

Interestingly, however, a systematic investigation of deathbed reports was not attempted until the early 1960s, when the pilot study of Dr. Karlis Osis sought to analyze the experiences of dying persons in a search for patterns (*Deathbed Observations by Physicians and Nurses*, Parapsychology Foundation, New York, 1961).

Dr. Osis selected 640 doctors and nurses as informants, based on their specialized training, their ability to make accurate medical assessments, and their proximity to dying patients. Each of the respondents to Dr. Osis's questionnaire had observed an average of 50 to 60 deathbed patients, totaling a remarkable sum of over 35,000 cases. The initial survey was followed up with telephone calls, additional questionnaires, and personal correspondence.

A total of 385 of the medically trained respondents reported 1,318 cases in which deathbed patients stated seeing apparitions of previously deceased loved ones or ghosts of individuals who were known to them.

Visions of heaven or scenes of wondrous beauty and brilliant color were reported by 248 respondents in 884 instances.

Dr. Karlis Osis is shown here testing his stepdaughter's psychokinetic abilities in this 1954 photograph. Dr. Osis also studied the spiritual experiences of the dying.

The physicians and nurses stated that the experiences left nearly all of the patients in a state of peace or exaltation. In about half of the cases, the spirits of loved ones or religious figures seemed to manifest to guide the dying patient through the transition from death to the afterlife. Those who had visions of the other side seemed serene and elevated in mood. One distinct observation from Dr. Osis's study was that few patients appeared to die in a state of fear.

> **Interestingly enough, the more highly educated patients evidenced more deathbed phenomena than those who were less educated....**

Interestingly enough, the more highly educated patients evidenced more deathbed phenomena than those who were less educated, thus contradicting the allegation that more superstitious people are the only ones to have such experiences.

Those with strong religious beliefs most often identified a saintly figure or previewed Heaven, but even those patients with no religious affiliation reported seeing holy or angelic figures.

Another interesting finding of the study was that deathbed visions, spirits of deceased loved ones, and mood elevations are reported more often in cases where the dying patients are fully conscious and appear to be in complete control of their senses. Sedation, high fever, and painkilling drugs seem to decrease, rather than to increase, the ability to experience these deathbed phenomena. At the same time, cases of brain damage or brain disease were found to be unrelated to the kind of deathbed experiences that were relevant to Dr. Osis's survey.

The study also discovered cases in which there was collective viewing of the apparitions by those who had gathered around the deathbed. There were numerous instances of a telepathic or clairvoyant interaction between patients and their attending physicians and nurses, and there was also a good number of cases in which a physician or nurse had a change in personal philosophy after having witnessed the experience of a dying person.

HIS MOTHER BEGAN SPEAKING TO GHOSTS

Steven Petrow's article in the *Washington Post* on July 22, 2017 ("At the End of Her Life, My Mother Started Seeing Ghosts, and It Freaked Me Out") was likely to contain elements that spoke to many who had recently lost loved ones.

"As it turned out," Petrow writes, "my mother's chat with a ghost was a signal that the end was inching closer. Those who work with the terminally ill, such as social workers and hospice caregivers, call these episodes or visions a manifestation of what is called Nearing Death Awareness."

Rebecca Valla, a psychiatrist in Winston-Salem, North Carolina, who specializes in treating terminally ill patients, commented that such visions are very common among dying patients in hospice situations. "Those who are dying and seem to be in and out of this world and the 'next' one often find their deceased loved ones present," she said, "and they communicate with them. In many cases, the predeceased loved ones seem [to the dying person] to be aiding them in their 'transition' to the next world."

While caring and concerned family members are often clueless about this phenomenon, at least at the outset, a 2014 study concluded that "most participants" reported such visions and that as these people "approached death, comforting dreams/visions of the deceased became more prevalent."

Jim May, a licensed clinical social worker in Durham, North Carolina, said that he "really encouraged people, whether it's a near-death experience or a hallucination, to just go with the flow. Whatever the dying are experiencing is real to them," May said. In fact, he speculates that such experiences may even be very helpful.

Psychiatrist Valla agreed, saying that to minimize, dismiss, or, worse, to pathologize these accounts, may be harmful and can be traumatic to the dying person.

The Manifestation of an Angelic Comforter

Rev. Maurice Elliott and Irene H. Elliott state that they were present at the bedside of a dying woman when an angel-comforter appeared to stand near her and say, "I have come to take you home."

According to the minister and his wife, three other angels and the images of many of the dying woman's deceased friends and relatives were then seen to join the angel-comforter. A white, hazy mist rose above the woman, hovered there for a few moments, and eventually congealed to take on a perfect human form.

After the soul-body had been released from its physical shell, the woman's spirit left in the company of the angels and those dear ones who had already become residents of a higher dimension.

Deathbed Research of Rev. W. Bennett Palmer

During the course of his extended research into reports of deathbed visions, Rev. W. Bennett Palmer commented that in a typical account, a bedside witness sees a mist or a cloudlike vapor emerging from the mouth or head of the dying man or woman. The vaporous substance soon takes on a human form, which is generally a duplicate of the living person—only in most cases any present deformities or injuries are partially or wholly absent. Angels or spirits of deceased loved ones are often reported standing ready to accompany the newly freed spirit form to move to higher dimensions of light.

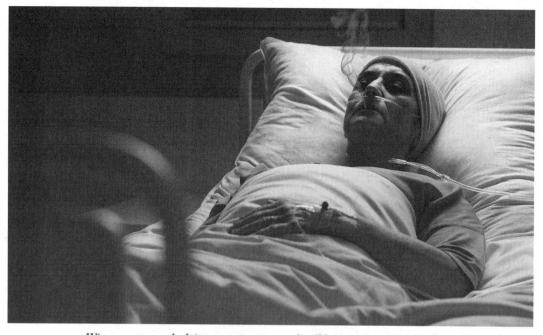

Witnesses to people dying sometimes see a cloudlike vapor escaping the person's mouth as they expire, according to researcher Reverend W. Bennett Palmer.

In numerous reports, the immediate process of death is not witnessed, but the deceased is seen leaving the earth plane for the higher world, most often accompanied by angelic beings. Frequently, such spirit and angel leave-taking is witnessed ascending upward, but this seems to be a mode of disappearance, rather than an indication that Heaven is in any particular spatial area.

"A fact often noted in connection with deathbed visions is that they are quite different from a patient's delerium and are coherent, rational, and, on reflection, apparently real," Rev. Palmer said. "It has also been observed that visions of the dying are different from visions of those who only think themselves to be dying, such as those undergoing a near-death experience. However, visions of the dying are similar to those who claim to have been out-of-the-body during altered states of consciousness.

"Revelations concerning the nature of the future life which are received in deathbed visions seem to be regarded with favor by all churches, and no stigma attaches itself to the deathbed visionary experience," Rev. Palmer continued. "Persons having deathbed visions often claim to have seen the dead—or what is so regarded—and to have had them reveal knowledge of events which could not be known in any normal way. Frequently, the person having a deathbed vision claims to see a person in spirit who is not known to be dead. Later, investigation proves that the person was deceased at the time of the visitation.

Haunted: Malevolent Ghosts, Night Terrors, and Threatening Phantoms

"Another aspect of deathbed visions," Rev. Palmer concluded, "involves visions of angels and other Holy Figures seen by other persons in the presence of the dying."

Bill W. told Rev. Palmer that he saw the spirit of his brother as it was disengaging itself from the dying body. The cloud-like vapor took on human shape, clapped its hands for joy, then passed upward through the ceiling in the company of an angel.

Jerry C. of Denver, Colorado, said that at the time of death of his ten-year-old son, he saw the child's spirit leaving the body as a luminous cloud and rise upward toward the ceiling.

In Rev. Palmer's church in New Port Richey, Florida, two members of the congregation, Mr. and Mrs. S., who were very ill, had been placed in separate rooms in their home to ensure periods of peace and uninterrupted sleep for both of them. One afternoon, as Mr. S. sat back against the pillows of his bed, he saw the form of his wife pass through the wall of his room, wave her hand in farewell, and rise upward in the company of an angel.

In two or three minutes, the nurse came into his room and informed him that Mrs. S. had passed away. "I know," he said, blinking back the tears. "She had enough of this desperate struggle to maintain life. She came to say goodbye and to ask me to join her with the angels."

Mr. S. died two days later.

When Mrs. Ernestine Tamayo entered the sickroom to bring her husband his newspaper, she saw a large, oval light emerging from his head. The illuminated oval floated toward the window, hovered a moment, then was met by a lovely angelic figure. Within seconds, both the oval of light and the angel had vanished.

"I knew that Miles was dead even before I reached my husband's bedside," she told Rev. Palmer. "I had seen his angel guide come to take him home."

His many years of research led Rev. Palmer to record that people who are about to transcend the physical shell often mention a final boundary. After the dying persons have passed that line of demarcation, they cannot return to their physical bodies. In fact, they are sometimes turned back before they can reach it again.

The environment and the scenery described in deathbed visions may be said to be much like the scenery of Earth, only it becomes more beautiful as the spirit progresses. Eventually, the environment becomes ineffable, incapable of description in human terms or in earthly comprehension.

In instances wherein it appears that one has achieved a glimpse into Heaven, the forms of deceased relatives and friends, as well as esteemed or saintly figures, are often seen. Angels are frequently described in the company of

People with deathbed visions have described the afterlife as earthlike but even more beautiful, becoming more beautiful as the spirit travels farther into that world.

deceased loved ones. The angels may come to sing heavenly music, to summon the soul from the dying body, or to accompany the newly released spirit to the other world. Most of the men and women who have perceived spiritual deathbed comforters are able to describe the beings in great detail, including their eyes, hair, wearing apparel, and other attributes and accoutrements.

HE WAS SORRY HE COULDN'T STAY FOR BREAKFAST

Projections at the moment of death betoken that something nonphysical exists within the human body and that it is capable of making a mockery of accepted physical laws and, even more importantly, is capable of surviving physical death. Professor Ian Currie, a former lecturer in anthropology and sociology at Guelph University in Guelph, Ontario, Canada, and author of the book You Cannot Die, shared the following case.

Early one morning a U.S. serviceman who was stationed in Germany showed up quite unexpectedly at his family home in a Detroit suburb.

His mother, who was startled as she prepared breakfast, was overjoyed to set another plate for her son.

"Sorry, Mom," he said, declining the meal with a gentle smile. "I can't stay for breakfast. I just wanted to say goodbye."

The young soldier waved farewell and walked out the door.

His heartbroken mother ran after him, shouting for him to return and stay longer—but she saw that he had completely disappeared.

A few hours later, an officer appeared at their door to inform the family that their beloved son had been killed in a training accident 6,000 miles away in Germany—just a half hour before his mysterious visit.

HER BROTHER APOLOGIZED FOR ALL THE TROUBLE HE HAD CAUSED

Some years ago I was appearing on a radio show on CKTB in St. Catharines, Ontario, when a young woman called in to relate the experience that had provided her with her own proof of survival. She had been sleeping one night for just a few hours when she was awakened by the form of her brother standing at the foot of the bed.

Haunted: Malevolent Ghosts, Night Terrors, and Threatening Phantoms

"I'm sorry, sis, for all the trouble that I may have caused you. I love you," he told her.

Her husband awakened at the interruption of his sleep, but by the time that he had blinked his eyes into full consciousness, the image of his brother-in-law had disappeared.

His wife insisted that she had truly seen her brother standing in their bedroom, and she described in detail what he had been wearing. She had particularly noticed that he was wearing a plaid shirt that she had never before seen him wear.

No sooner had she completed her description of the apparition when the telephone rang, and the woman was given the tragic news that her brother had been killed in an automobile accident.

Later, when they visited the morgue to identify the body, both of them were startled to see the corpse attired in a plaid shirt such as the one that she had described.

KARLA WANTED TO BE REMEMBERED WITH KINDNESS

While he was stationed in Germany in 1972, Stanley met a beautiful girl named Karla with whom he had enjoyed a wonderful relationship. They were both in their early twenties and they discussed marriage many times. Even though he had decided upon a career in the navy, there were times when he thought he might leave it all for the good life with Karla in Germany. Once Stanley went so far as to buy an engagement ring, but he never showed it to Karla. Somehow, the time just didn't seem right to make such a commitment.

When it came time for Stanley to return to the States, the two lovers were faced with the moment of truth. They spent a last weekend together in a lovely old hotel, and they spoke again of marriage as they were finishing what they knew might be their last meal together. As they were slowly sipping cool glasses of Rhine wine, Karla said that she couldn't see herself marrying anyone but Stanley. Stanley admitted that he felt the same way about her.

"Perhaps, then, we should see how we feel after you return to the States," Karla suggested. "Let us correspond. Let us see how we deal with the absence of one another. Let us test our love and see if we should be married."

They touched wine glasses and toasted the concept that Karla had outlined.

After Stanley's return to the United States, the two lovers began a passionate correspondence. Six months later, however, Stanley was finding himself beginning to concentrate more intensely on his navy career. He had opportunities for advancement and that meant putting his spare energy into preparing for exams, not writing love letters.

Stanley conceded that he was the first to begin to slack off on their commitment to maintain an active correspondence. His letters to Karla slowed their pace from a letter a day, to one a week, to one a month.

Karla's letters continued at a more steady pace for a few months, then she began to match his once- or twice-a-month schedule.

About that time, Stanley met Darcy, a navy brat, whose father was a career man. Darcy really understood his love and commitment for the sea.

Shortly after his engagement to Darcy, Stanley wrote to Karla and told her the news about his approaching marriage to another woman.

"I never received an answer to my letter," Stanley said. "I felt bad. I wondered how I would have felt if Karla had been the one to have sent me such a letter. But I couldn't help feeling that I had done the best thing for both of us."

After his marriage, Stanley reported to duty aboard a destroyer based at the Virginia Beach, Virginia, shipyards. Darcy remained in Massachusetts while the ship was deployed to the Middle East and then passed into dry dock. It was Stanley's intention to move Darcy to Virginia Beach as soon as the overhaul of the destroyer was completed.

Late on the evening of June 15, 1975, Stanley was working in his disbursement office, preparing for payday only a few days away. He sat at his desk, typing up the pay roster until about 12:20 A.M. He had just leaned back in his chair to doze for a few minutes when he was awakened by a soft tapping at his office door. Assuming it was the security watch, he rather grumpily opened the door.

Stanley was serving on a U.S. Navy destroyer when he saw Karla standing before him. He later learned Karla had died in a car crash that day.

To Stanley's complete and total amazement, he beheld the image of Karla, standing in the doorway, dressed only in what appeared to be a diaphanous white night gown.

"Karla looked just the way that she had the day that we said goodbye in Germany," Stanley said. "And it hurt me to see that she had been crying."

Stanley was speechless. At last he managed to ask her how she knew where he was and how she had been able to get aboard the destroyer without security stopping her.

She ignored Stanley's questions but spoke directly of other matters. "Stan, I am here to tell you that I understand about Darcy—and I forgive you."

Stanley began to speak, but Karla held up her hand for silence so that she might continue. "I knew that you were right in doing what you did," she said in a soft voice. "So I accepted another's proposal of marriage not long after I received your letter."

Karla blinked back tears and then asked Stanley to promise to remember her always with kindness.

Stanley nodded, choked with emotion. "With great kindness, Karla," he managed to whisper. "And with love."

Karla smiled, turned to leave, then looked over her shoulder and added, "And please be happy in your life with Darcy."

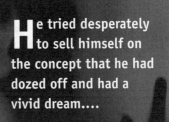

He tried desperately to sell himself on the concept that he had dozed off and had a vivid dream....

Karla stepped away from the doorway and walked quietly and quickly down the passageway until she was out of sight.

Stanley cannot estimate how long he sat quietly in reverie after Karla left him. He does remember being roused by the security watch, who wondered if he was all right.

"Did you happen to see a pretty blonde woman in the passageway a few minutes ago?" he asked the security watch.

"Yeah, right," the man laughed. "I thought you were supposed to be working in here, not dreaming. Are you all right?"

Stanley mumbled something that somehow satisfied the watch, then went back to work on the pay roster.

But whatever had occurred in those incredible few moments in the flow of his normal life experience had completely disoriented him. There was no way that he could remove the incident from his mind. He tried desperately to sell himself on the concept that he had dozed off and had a vivid dream, perhaps partially inspired by the guilt that he still felt toward his breakup with Karla. But such a rationalization was out of the question. Stanley knew that he had seen Karla with his wakeful senses.

Stanley set aside his paperwork and wrote a letter to Karla, detailing his remarkable experience and asking her if she were all right.

"I wanted to know if she might be ill, or if she might have been thinking intently of me at the time that her image had appeared in my office aboard the destroyer," he said.

A few weeks later, Stanley received a reply from Karla's mother, who informed him that Karla had died instantly in a head-on automobile crash early in the morning of June 16. The time of Karla's death was equivalent to about 12:20 A.M. on June 15 in Virginia Beach.

"Mrs. G. told me that she had been looking for my address to inform me of her daughter's death just as my letter arrived," Stanley said. "Only days before Karla's fatal accident, she had spoken of me and said how sorry she was that she had not answered my letter about my marriage to Darcy. Mrs. G. also verified that Karla was engaged to be married at the time of her death. The bond of love that we had once shared had somehow enabled her to bid me a tender and forgiving farewell."

A SPIRIT CAME WITH THE STARTER HOUSE

Terry from Alberta, Canada, told us of an interesting encounter in which the manifesting spirit was not that of a loved one but one whose identity was later established as a former inhabitant of the house.

As Terry tells the story, when she and her husband's daughter Alice was twenty, a realtor friend talked them into putting a down payment on a "starter house" for her.

"Shortly after she got settled in, she was awakened one night to see a man standing in her bedroom doorway," Terry said. "Not being faint of heart, she jumped up and shouted, 'Get the hell out of here!' and proceeded to chase him out. Then he disappeared into thin air."

Their daughter described the apparition as being on the short side of average height, stocky of build, eldering, and wearing a black suit and fedora of the kind that businessmen used to wear.

At that time, Alice was working at a nursing home for the elderly and disabled. An acquaintance of Terry and her husband who lived a few miles away came to visit his parents. Alice couldn't get over the resemblance between her "ghost" and the man, Sam L.

Terry, her husband, and Alice made inquiries and learned that the house had been built in the mid-1950s, and Sam's uncle had owned the house. Sam told them that it was his uncle's habit to wear a suit, tie, and hat, even when he was relaxing at home away from his work. In his later years, after his wife had passed on, the elderly gentleman had quit eating properly and looking after himself and simply wasted away.

Terry wrote that the "ghost" remained in the house, and Alice was frequently aware of his presence. Alice felt that he was a benign spirit, although he was prone to play pranks from time to time.

SEEING MARILYN MONROE'S SPIRIT

Bob Slatzer (d. 2005) told us that he saw Marilyn Monroe's spirit form materialize eleven years after her death.

Slatzer met Norma Jean Baker in the summer of 1946, when she was a young model trying to get work by making the rounds. He was writing some stories on movie celebrities for the Scripps Howard newspaper syndicate, and he kept seeing the pretty blonde at auditions for modeling or movie jobs. Eventually, they struck up a conversation one day and made a date for that evening. Thus, according to Slatzer, began a long relationship that led to their brief marriage in 1952.

While Slatzer's claim of an actual marriage to Marilyn Monroe has been widely doubted and denied by both studio publicists and other writers, he remained firm in his claims until his death, and he wrote *The Life and Curious Death of Marilyn Monroe* (1974) and *The Marilyn Files* (1992) to further his argument. According to Slatzer, he also became a screenwriter, director, and producer, and on one weekend in Mexico, he and Marilyn got married. Although studio pressures and other factors soon ended their marriage, Slatzer told us that they remained close friends until her death in 1962 and that after Marilyn's passing, many strange things had manifested in his life that he associated with his late, dear friend.

In particular, he said, seemingly out of nowhere the pungent smell of roses would fill the air in his home. This manifestation had occurred sixteen or seventeen times from about 1963 until about 1981, then, just as mysteriously, the funereal scent of roses went away.

In 1973, Slatzer met Anton LaVey of the Church of Satan and his wife at the home of a movie studio publicity man. During their conversation, he learned that LaVey was fascinated with Marilyn Monroe.

LaVey believed that about every eleven years astrologically, a cycle would repeat itself and the "dark of moon" would come back on Saturday, August 4, just as in 1962, when Marilyn had died. LaVey needed someone who knew Marilyn very well to help manifest her. Bob agreed to LaVey's making all the arrangements and picking him up about 10:30 P.M. LaVey had received permission from the then-current owner of Marilyn's home to be there. Although she would be closing the gate, they were welcome to sit in the cul-de-sac.

Bob told us that he clearly recalled sitting in the front seat on the passenger's side with LaVey's wife was in the back seat.

Working with Church of Satan leader Anton LaVey, Bob Slatzer testified that he helped bring the spirit of Marilyn Monroe back to the earthly plane.

Anton had a tape recorder with prerecorded songs from Marilyn's films. "At about 11:45 P.M.," Bob said, "LaVey began reading something he had written. It was sort of like tongues or a chant or something. I didn't recognize it. About 12:15 A.M., the night was still. Not one single blade of grass was moving. All of a sudden, a terrific wind came up! It seemed as if we were in a hurricane for three or four minutes, yet nothing else on either side of the road was moving."

Then from out of nowhere the figure of a woman appeared in front of them. Bob Slatzer said it was as if somebody set her there. She had on white slacks with a little black-and-white, splash-pattern top, little white loafers, and I could see a shock of blond hair. She started walking toward the car. The woman was highly recognizable as Marilyn Monroe

Anton's wife had practically turned white and looked almost petrified!

Marilyn hesitated for a minute, her hands clasped. It didn't appear that she was looking directly at the car, but she seemed to be looking at an angle past them. Then she turned to her left and slowly started to walk down the middle of the boulevard. LaVey appeared as if he was frozen and stuck in a fixed position.

Slatzer saw that the spirit of Marilyn Monroe was about three-fourths of the way down the street. He got out of the car and walked as fast and as quietly as he could. When he was about 150 feet away from her, she turned, and as she turned, walked to the middle of the street—and *vanished* into thin air.

No doubt because of the somewhat questionable reputations of the narrators of this account of the ghostly appearance of Marilyn Monroe, readers may make a more skeptical evaluation than they have of other narratives in this book. We can only state that Bob Slatzer seemed open and honest in our interviews with him. He told us that he had repeated the story to only one person besides psychic-sensitive Clarisa Bernhardt—and that was to author Norman Mailer. Slatzer added that Mailer was interested in such matters and told him that he believed Bob's strange experience.

Anton LaVey, in our opinion, was more showman than evil devil-worshipper. In our numerous interviews with Anton, he seemed always direct and forthright in his responses. We may have had vastly different theologies, but he seemed always to keep a somewhat open attitude to his cosmology and always maintained a sense of humor.

Near-Death Experiences and the Spirit World

VIOLET SEES A VISION OF TWELVE STRANGE ANGELS

Violet M. told us that when she was seven, she was ill for several weeks. Concerned family members would take turns sitting at her bedside in the evenings to mark any improvement or worsening of her condition. Violet, remembering seeing her older sister, Rachael, reading a book in the easy chair beside her, then felt herself drifting to a light sleep.

"I remember this strange woman coming into the room," Violet said. She called herself Minerva, and she said that I must go with her. I told her that I didn't know her and I wasn't going anywhere with her. She just smiled, and the next thing I knew I was somewhere in a different dimension and beings of light were all around us."

Violet saw two very tall angels who were seated in a temple library. As she watched them, they brought three scrolls to her.

"One of the angels, who looked more human than the other beings, pointed to the open scroll, and when I looked, I was immediately sucked into it," Violet said. "When I was once again aware of my surroundings, I saw twelve beings of light who were clearly not human. They didn't talk with their mouths, but I knew they were judging me."

The weirdest thing to Violet about the otherworldly scene is that she saw everything in the third person—with herself as a thirty-year-old woman.

"This older version of myself was crying and telling them to send me back," Violet recalled. "Collectively, they were saying that they considered it unwise, that I could not handle life on Earth. I told them that I knew that I could. They agreed to my pleas with two conditions: That I would always show love to my family and number two, when I reached the age that I was shown in the vision, that I must be ready to perform an act of great importance."

Violet woke up cold, shivering, and, according to her sister, with her skin a deep, purplish color.

"All I remember," Violet said, "was that I was glad to be back and wondering why Rachael was crying."

In retrospect, Violet considered the experience to have had a very positive effect on her life. "I was just a kid, and I went to Heaven and recovered from my illness. After this experience, my spiritual eyes were open, and a lot of very strange things happened to me to make me believe in other dimensions and a spiritual side to things."

CLINT WALKER'S REMARKABLE NEAR-DEATH EXPERIENCE

We had for years been intrigued by the near-death experience of Clint Walker, the tall, muscular actor who had portrayed the character of Cheyenne Bodie on the television series *Cheyenne* from 1955 to 1963. Film fans will also remember his roles in such films as *The Dirty Dozen* (1967) and *Yellowstone Kelly* (1959). As it was reported in May 1971, Walker had suffered a skiing

accident in which the tip of the ski pole pierced his breastbone and moved through his heart. Taken as quickly as possible to a hospital, two doctors pronounced him dead on arrival.

Some years later, when he was living in retirement, Walker generously consented to having us interview him regarding his remarkable NDE.

He said that he knew he was in trouble when he fell on the tip of the ski pole with such force that had it not been for the basket being so firmly attached to the pole, it would have gone clear through his body. His sensations of fear and pain were diverted by a most astonishing sight: "I became fascinated with the 'rings' emanating from my wound. There was one ring after another coming forth. The gist of the myriad thoughts in my head was that much of what

Actor Clint Walker, who starred in the TV Western *Cheyenne* from 1955 to 1963, had an NDE after suffering a skiing accident in 1971.

seems to be reality is really a fantasy, and a lot times what we think is fantasy is reality. If we want the truth about life, then we must learn to reason from the seen to the unseen. Our thoughts are the most powerful things in the world."

When he closed his eyes, Clint found that he was not just floating above his body, he was up above the world.

"I saw, too, that time was an illusion. I realized that I had always seen through a glass darkly. For that time I was outside my body, it was as if I could perceive the answers to everything. I understood that I was smaller than the smallest grain of sand on the beach—yet I was also ten thousand feet tall—and both at the same time."

Clint told us that he did not know where he was going, but he felt at peace—and he felt good about his final destination.

"I suddenly became aware that the body is just a vehicle, a garment that we put on for awhile, but the soul goes on forever. It cannot be destroyed."

It was then that Clint Walker was struck by the thoughts of all the things that he wanted yet to do on earth.

"Please, Lord," he said, "I want another crack at life."

And then he was back in his body. He had vague memories of the trip down the ski hill in a toboggan and lying in a hospital three hours later.

Although two doctors had already pronounced Clint dead, a third doctor who just happened to be passing through the room believed him to be alive after taking one glance at the body lying before him.

Next Clint saw himself moving down a long tunnel.

"I asked God to allow me to live, and my prayer was granted."

Afterward, the doctor who had detected life in Clint's body told him that he was a medical miracle. "You should have died," he soberly informed the actor, "or at the very least been left a vegetable."

Clint Walker concluded his interview by telling us that he learned that we are responsible for our thoughts. "One of the most important lessons we can learn is how to slow down the tape loop in our heads and begin to sort out and to understand our beliefs, our feelings, our values—and discover where they came from. With discipline, we can learn to master our thoughts and in so doing we can move closer to the image of love."

NDEs Are Gaining Serious Attention

In the past three decades, there has been a great deal of attention paid to the near-death experience (NDE), both by experiencers and medical doctors. Among the stellar researchers drawn to study NDE have been Dr. Elisabeth Kübler-Ross, Dr. Raymond Moody, Dr. Kenneth Ring, Dr. Karlis Osis, Robert Crookall, and P. M. H. Atwater, Ph.D. Dozens of books have been published that generally describe the phenomenon as occurring when someone appears to have died and is then returned to life, complete with a story of having been drawn down a tunnel toward a light in the company of angels or relatives. Somewhere in their out-of-body travel to the world beyond death, these disembodied souls are told that their time is not yet completed on Earth. They must return to life, often times with instructions to complete a particular mission.

In her 2017 book, *A Manual for Developing Humans*, Dr. Atwater shares a number of her interesting observations of the near-death experience: "During my experience in death, I saw the souls God created as showers of sparks, nuclei of holy fire that spread out and expanded in waves, thought-waves, similar in movement to what happens to the wake caused by a speedboat zooming across a placid lake. The farther afield each wave projected (in a plasma-like 'ocean' of etheric substance or spirit), the more the individual sparks separated from their wave, spinning off into positive and negative poles of energy charge, mimicking what causes the central pulse-beat to oscillate. I observed that the nucleus of holy fire, once divided and freed from its wave, is able to take on any manner or type of existence, shape, or form. Yet no matter what experiences it takes on, the nucleus spark carries within it the urge to attract unto itself that which will unify its charge (the rejoining of its positive and negative poles back into the full nuclei it once was) and fulfill its ultimate purpose (reunion with the original source). *The many ever seek to rejoin with The One....*

> I observed that the nucleus of holy fire, once divided and freed from its wave, is able to take on any manner or type of existence, shape, or form.

"[E]ach and every one of us, all of us, are holy sparks of fire at our core. Our core-self or soul appeared to me as a matrix or mass of pulsing intelligence, sometimes undulating as if wavelike, sometimes flashing or sparkling as if a power grid or circuit board of energetic particles of light. Physically, souls are infinitesimally small, hardly more than a 'wink' in size; yet each contains a power mass so intense, a consciousness so unlimited in function and potential, that it is beyond our ability as humans to fathom either its makeup or design. I saw that what resides within our earthly frame, what we think defines us as human beings, is but a 'finger' of what or who we are—a projection from our soul's mass....

"The will of every soul is to 'outpicture' (project) the Greater Will, and in so doing carry out God's Plan for creation. We are separate from our Source only for as long as we think we are separate....

"I also discovered that the soul sets and experiences growth or learning cycles. These cycles evolve around an overall theme and are planned according to whatever is necessary to carry out and fulfill the theme of the cycle.... Time would not matter, since time has a different meaning to a soul than it does to a human personality.

"These thematic soul cycles can be fulfilled in one lifetime, cover a series of lifetimes, or happen in different or multiple forms of existence on other levels besides that of the earthplane. Results depend on how the soul develops along the way, what it learns."

REPORT TO THE ROYAL MEDICAL SOCIETY, 1937

When the Royal Medical Society of Edinburgh met on February 26, 1937, Sir Auckland Geddes, a medical doctor and professor of anatomy, read a most unusual paper before the august body of medical professionals. A colleague who had requested anonymity had recorded a phenomenon that we today would call a near-death experience, which he wished to bring to the attention of his fellow members of the society. According to this anonymous physician, he had been near death and had at the same time been conscious of being outside his body.

According to his account, one evening, shortly after midnight, the doctor was stricken with acute gastroenteritis so severe that by ten o'clock the following morning he was too ill even to ring for assistance. Although the doctor's body was in terrible agony, his mental processes remained quite clear,

As his body began to die, his spirit became free of the constraints of time and space. His spirit guide or mentor explained that he would be free to travel anywhere.

and he began to review his financial affairs, firmly convinced that his death was imminent.

It was at this point that he realized that he appeared to have two levels of consciousness, one of which was separating from the other. Later, while dictating the experience to his secretary, he labeled these two states of consciousness as "A," his ego—his true spiritual self—and "B," his consciousness that remained with the physical body.

The physician observed that as his physical health deteriorated further, the "B" personality began to fade, while the "A" personality began more and more to embody his complete self. As the process continued, the "A" personality vacated the physical body entirely, and he was able to observe his body lying inert in bed.

Testing his new range of beingness, he soon discovered that he could instantly travel to Scotland or to any other place that occurred to him.

At about this time, he became aware of the presence of a guide or mentor, who explained to him that he was free in a time dimension of space, wherein "now" was equivalent to "here" in the ordinary three-dimensional space of everyday life. The fourth dimension existed, correspondingly, in everything that existed in the three-dimensional space. Moreover, everything in the third dimension also existed in the fourth and fifth. In the present state of his existence, the doctor's guide pointed out, he appeared as a blue-colored cloud.

His spirit mentor, he said, impressed on him that " ... all our brains are just end-organs projecting as it were from the three-dimensional universe into the psychic stream ... and flowing with it into the fourth and the fifth dimensions."

Many more mysteries were revealed to the physician when one of his servants entered the bedroom and discovered with horror his employer's dying body. He watched his servant rush to the telephone and place a hasty call to a colleague

When his colleague arrived, the doctor's "A" consciousness could hear the man think: "He is nearly gone!"

He was able to hear the man speaking to him, but he was unable to respond. He was no longer in the "B" consciousness that resided in his physical body.

The visiting doctor pulled a syringe out of his medical bag. The "A" consciousness of the physician saw this act and became very angry. It did not wish to return to the "B" consciousness.

As the injection flowed into the doctor's body, however, the "A" consciousness once again began to take notice of his heartbeat and gradually

Haunted: Malevolent Ghosts, Night Terrors, and Threatening Phantoms

allowed itself to be pulled back into the physical body. Finally, the doctor became fully aware of himself once again and discovered himself lying in disarray on his bed.

Sir Auckland Geddes completed the reading of his anonymous colleague's near-death experience, stressing that he believed that it held momentous import not only for himself but for every human being. In his own concluding remarks, Sir Auckland told the members of the society that their colleague's experience had helped him to define "the idea of a psychic continuum in which we all exist."

A DOCTOR FROM KANSAS TRAVELS TO THE OTHER SIDE

When Dr. A. S. Wiltse of Skiddy, Kansas, felt that he was dying, he called to his family and friends and bade them farewell. His attending physician, Dr. Raynes, later testified (*St. Louis Medical and Surgical Journal*, 1889; reprinted in volume VII of the *Proceedings of the Society for Psychical Research* [1892]) that for the duration of four hours, Dr. Wiltse lay without pulse or perceptible heartbeat.

"I recollect distinctly," Dr. Wiltse said in his report, "how I appeared to myself something like a jellyfish as regards to color and form."

[*In our research, we have found that many men and women who have projected free of the Earth plane in their near-death experiences discard temporal plane concepts of body image and often report perceiving themselves as a "shiny cloud," a "bright balloon," an "egg yolk," or "something like a jellyfish."*] Brad and Sherry Steiger]

At that point, he gradually arose and expanded himself to the full stature of his regular physical body. "I seemed to be translucent, of a bluish cast, and perfectly naked," he said.

As he reached the door, Dr. Wiltse observed that he was suddenly fully clothed. At the same time, he noted that two of his friends were standing by the door and that they were completely unaware of his presence. With a great deal of surprise and amusement, Dr. Wiltse discovered that he could pass directly through his friends and continue on out through the door. "Glancing around, I noticed that I was attached by means of a small cord, like a spider's web, to my body in the house."

In an NDE the experiencer will often project his or her preconceptions of the other world into their visions—thus, if they believe in Heaven, they will see some kind of Heaven in the afterlife.

Haunted: Malevolent Ghosts, Night Terrors, and Threatening Phantoms

Just as he was relaxing into his newly achieved emancipation from the confines of bodily flesh, however, Dr. Wiltse found himself on a road with steep rocks blocking his journey. He attempted to climb around them, but as he was doing so, a black cloud surrounded him and he found himself back in his bedroom, once more confined to an ill body.

In the Dr. Wiltse case, his near-death experience terminated when he was confronted by steep rocks that blocked his journey. Generally speaking, there seem to be two types of environment for near-death experiences:

1. The environment of this planet Earth in which the projected personality observes the actions of people in faraway places and sees actual occurrences at great distances that can later be substantiated.

2. The environment of other planes of existence or dimensions of reality in which the projected personality may encounter entities that he or she perceives as angels, masters, guides, saints, or the spirits of loved ones who have previously passed away. The geography of these spiritual planes seems to be quite similar to that of Earth, and, depending upon the religious views of the experiencer, is often interpreted as Heaven, Paradise, or a place of eternal bliss.

The "rocks" that halted Dr. Wiltse's advance may indeed have been rocks on another plane of existence or they may have been formed by his own mental machinery as a symbol that he was not to venture farther but was to return to his physical body.

2001 REPORT FROM BRITISH MEDICAL JOURNAL *LANCET*

In December 2001, a study in the British medical journal *Lancet* reported on data acquired from the examination of 344 patients from ten hospitals in the Netherlands who had been successfully resuscitated after suffering cardiac arrest. Researchers spoke to these survivors within a week after they had suffered clinical death and been restored to life and found that 18 percent of the patients recalled some portion of what happened to them when they were clinically dead, and another 8 to 12 percent remembered near-death experiences, such as seeing lights at the end of tunnels or being able to speak to deceased friends or relatives.

AN ANALYSIS OF OVER 2,000 RESUSCITATED PATIENTS

The AWARE (AWAreness during REsuscitation) study, launched in 2008, looked in depth at over 2,000 patients from 15 hospitals in the United Kingdom, United States, and Austria who experienced cardiac arrest and were subsequently resuscitated. Nearly 40 percent of those patients had experienced some kind of "awareness" while being resuscitated, despite being clinically dead.

The study, directed by Dr. Sam Parnia of the State University of New York at Stony Brook, spanned four years. The results were published in December 2016. The scientist explained the modus operandi behind the research:

> Contrary to perception, death is not a specific moment but a potentially reversible process that occurs after any severe illness or accident causes the heart, lungs and brain to cease functioning. If attempts are made to reverse this process, it is referred to as "cardiac arrest"; however, if these attempts do not succeed it is called "death." In this study we wanted to go beyond the emotionally charged yet poorly defined term of NDEs to explore objectively what happens when we die.

AN ANGEL TOLD HER SHE HAD A MISSION TO ACCOMPLISH

Rachael had suffered severe depression for six years. In a moment of torment, she tried to end her life. A relative found Rachael in time to call for medical help, and she awakened in a hospital with the awareness that her spirit essence had traveled to a higher level of consciousness and that she had been in the company of an entity that she later believed to have been her spirit guide.

"I spoke to a man who was so kind, loving, and encouraging," Rachael said. "He kept telling me that I had a mission to complete and that I wasn't allowed to go home yet."

Rachael recalled that she was extremely unpleasant to the kind and gentle man. "After he kept refusing to let me go home, I was told that as soon as I was able I would find a foolproof way to die where he wouldn't have the ability to say no."

It was then that her guide showed her just how selfish Rachael was being and how many people would be affected by her death immediately and in the future. "I can't remember all of what he said," Rachael said, "and he told me that I wouldn't be allowed to recall all of it, but he made his point crystal clear."

When she at last surrendered to her guide's admonishments, Rachael cried for a long time while he watched her without any sign of judgment or pity. When she stopped crying, he asked if she was ready to return to life. Rachael replied that she didn't want to, but she knew that she had to return to a life as Rachael.

When she stopped crying, he asked if she was ready to return to life. Rachael replied that she didn't want to, but she knew that she had to return to a life as Rachael.

Once she had made the commitment to return, she said that she experienced "the most amazing thing ever." She was granted the gift of seeing her life "play out from birth to when I pass over. I saw who I was before, who I really am. I saw the spirit world, the universe and all that is. I cannot remember all that I saw, but I do remember how I felt—alive, free, beautiful, happy, light, blissful, and more."

After having been shown exactly why she was Rachael on Earth at the present time, she thanked her guide for showing her that her soul's path was preplanned before she was born. When she awakened, she knew that she had been granted the knowledge and the proof that life does indeed continue after death and that there are many spiritual beings working behind the scenes to help us through the experience of living on the earthplane.

ANDREW'S NDE AT FIFTEEN RESHAPED HIS LIFE

When Andrew was fifteen, he went into anaphylactic shock for a reason that was never determined. "I died for a few minutes," he told us. "I recall seeing my parents in the room from a vantage point high up and away from my body. I also recall a sense of overwhelming peace, complete freedom from pain, a feeling of infinite knowledge, and a 'presence' that was gentle beyond all imagining. Then I was back in my body. Later I learned that I had been given an injection of adrenaline because my heart had stopped."

The day after his near-death experience, Andrew begged his parents to go to church. During Mass, he recalled, he felt a spiritual connection and depth that he had never experienced before.

"My near-death experience at age fifteen has helped keep my mind open to the possibilities (probabilities, really) of events that transcend normal experience," Andrew said. "I am as certain as a person can be that our being persists beyond the corporeal world. I am also certain of the existence of beings beyond our earthly level. The other dreams, voices, and presences not only help me open [up] to such experiences, they also have helped me to continue a life with meaning."

Andrew explained that he has remained religious, "not out of being convinced that any doctrine or faith is the one truth path, but that these paths are necessary for our spiritual progress during this earthly life. All of this has been extremely important to me since my return from Iraq. I am not certain my healing would have progressed this well if it weren't for these experiences."

Andrew joins the host of near-death experiencers who have told us that their near-death experience has shaped their adult lives. "I have not feared death since that time," he said. "I have, in fact, felt comforted by that experience during some of the darkest times of my life. The 'visits' in my dreams and the feeling of presences at various times have continued to give me not only strength but a degree of hope."

LOURDES OFFICE RECOGNIZES SPIRITUAL VALUE OF NDEs

The head physician of the Lourdes Medical Bureau in France—famed for its painstakingly meticulous investigations of alleged miracles—has issued a ringing endorsement on the legitimacy and spiritual value to Catholics of so-called near-death experiences.

The expert, Dr. Patrick Theillier, said that despite certain back-to-life accounts that may be "of the nebulous New Age," most provide invaluable lessons on what matters in life and the afterlife.

"I noted many similarities between these near-death experiences and extraordinary phenomena such as miraculous healings, Marian apparitions [visions of the Virgin Mary], or events noted among mystics," writes Theiller in the book *Near-Death Experiences Examined*, which carries a positive endorsement by his bishop, Most Reverend Marc Aillet, prelate for Bayonne, Lescar, and Oloron, France.

Dr. Theiller postulates that the need to recognize the miraculous "is especially true in light of an often too radical rationalism stemming from the still very scientific domain of classical science, as well as from a religious domain that is either too conservative (unable to separate itself from its own representations) or too progressive (tempted to close itself off from the scientifically correct ideas of the world)."

The Sanctuary of Our Lady of Lourdes in France includes the Lourdes Medical Bureau facility, where the head physician, Dr. Patrick Theillier, endorsed the legitimacy of NDEs.

Haunted: Malevolent Ghosts, Night Terrors, and Threatening Phantoms

Bishop Aillet expressed his philosophy that "in the face of the inexplicable, it is the greatness of reason to submit oneself to faith. Faith is not the attitude of one who capitulates to the inexplicable; it is the attitude of one who welcomes a higher revelation."

THE DAY BRAD STEIGER BECAME A GHOST

On my parents' wedding anniversary, August 23, 1947, when I was a boy of eleven, my body lay crushed and bleeding, sprawled where the mangling, metallic blades of the farm machinery had dropped it on a field of our Iowa farm. Almost at once my Essential Self, my spirit, left my body and distanced itself from the tragic scene.

Although I could clearly perceive the events taking place below me, I felt only dimly associated with the dying farm boy that lay bleeding in the hay stubble. I felt the concern and panic of my seven-year-old sister who was running for help, but I had no connection to the emotions she was feeling.

I perceived myself as an orange-colored spheroid, intent only on soaring toward an incredibly beautiful and brilliant light higher above me. I felt blissfully euphoric, and I began to glory in a marvelous sense of oneness with a power—an intelligence—that seemed All-That-Is.

And then I discovered that I could be in two places at once. I could exist physically in my father's arms as he carried my terribly injured body from the field; and at the same time, I could be above us, watching the whole scene as if I were a detached observer.

When I became concerned about my mother's reaction to my dreadful accident, I made an even more incredible discovery: The Real Me could be anywhere that I wished to be. My spirit—my soul—was free of the physical limitations that we humans incorporate into our definitions of time and space. I had but to think of my mother, and there I was beside her.

I was a ghost, a spirit. I was able to pass through walls, to soar through the clouds, to be wherever I wished. This was wonderful.

Whenever sorrow over earthly separation impinged on my extended consciousness, I would be shown something that I can best describe as a series of brilliant geometric designs. It was as if these colorful patterns were somehow a part of the great tapestry of life. It was as though the very perception of these geometric figures by my elevated awareness somehow demonstrated in a very dramatic way the order and the rightness of existence. To view this cosmic panorama was somehow to peek into God's notebook and to see that there truly was meaning to existence on Earth. There was, indeed, a Divine Plan. Life on Earth was not simply the result of some cosmic accident.

Yes, I was dying—but that was not really the end of me. Nor was it the end of the world. Life on Earth would be able to continue without me.

Viewing these geometric designs completely removed my fear of death and allowed my spirit essence to move closer to the light. At the same time, the very light itself seemed to be intelligent and to manifest a kind of benevolent presence that brought with it peace and tranquility.

I was in and out of my body during a desperate 140-mile run to a hospital in Des Moines where our family doctor, Cloyce Newman, thought my life might be saved by Dr. Baccodi, a specialist who practiced there at St. Mary's Hospital. Whenever the Real Me would enter the body of the dying eleven-year-old boy, it seemed to reject the choice and return to the dimension of spirit, where there was no pain.

I returned to my physical body just as the surgeons were preparing to operate—and I came back with such force that I sat up, shouted, and pushed an intern off balance. It took the calming tones of love and caring from a Roman Catholic nun to pacify me until the anesthesia could take deeper effect.

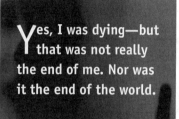

Yes, I was dying—but that was not really the end of me. Nor was it the end of the world.

I now sensed a kind of intelligence or personality within the light itself, and I asked if I might leave the operating room. I was just bobbing around above my body, and I really didn't want to watch the surgery. In answer to my pleas, I remember being taken to what appeared to be a kind of ideal little village, complete with bandstand, ice cream vendors, and friendly people walking about.

During the two weeks of my hospital stay, the nuns seemed to have sensed that I had been "somewhere" and had seen "something," and they asked me again and again about my experience as a spirit being, traveling between the two worlds. A mystery had been pierced, they told me. I would never again have to ask the troubling question about whether we humans survive the experience of physical death. I would be able to testify that there was truly an existence that transcended the material realm.

For many years after my near-death experience, I assumed that my viewing of the geometric designs had to be classified as an ineffable experience, impossible to translate into physical expression. Whenever I attempted to articulate the cosmic panorama and describe the geometric patterns for others, my mind would literally blank out for lack of an appropriate vocabulary. From time to time, I would meet other near-death experiencers who had seen similiar living geometric visions, and they would agree that these awesome messengers of All-That-Is were beyond words.

I finally saw images that very closely approximated what I had been shown during my NDE when, in 1988, Sherry began to conduct healing seminars utilizing computer-derived images of fractal geometry. I was struck with a powerful shock of recognition when she projected these brilliant images during her seminar. Interestingly, the effect on the audience was profound, and many individuals claimed healing experiences after perceiving the images.

THE REMARKABLE DR. JACK HILLER

In April 2012, we received a most interesting email from Dr. Jack Hiller, who stated that he had been prompted to write to us after reading Brad's book *One with the Light* and becoming particularly interested in Brad's near-death experience (NDE) at age eleven.

According to Dr. Hiller:

I had for many years been engaging fruitlessly in trying to understand why there is any world at all, with pure nothingness as a more attractive intellectual circumstance—although obviously an empirically false case. I made some progress a year ago when I realized that the various mentions of NDE and guru experience, in which it is reported that there is no time in the other realm, and that past, present, and future exist all at once, could be found to have a scientific parallel in special relativity (at the speed of light, there is no longer a time clock running and so a photon does not age or experience time change) and in general relativity, infinite mass, as specified for black holes, which likewise creates the condition for time to cease. It turns out that if the original condition of creation is timeless, then the quest for the cause of creation loses all meaning (a logical positivist perspective), because when there is no time, there is no before and after, and thus no causation. The quest for understanding the nature of creation thus becomes meaningless.

Dr. Jack Hiller (seen here with his pal Beaky) concluded that the principles of the afterlife in which time is meaningless might have roots in special relativity.

Dr. Jack Hiller, Ph.D., J.D., has amassed a remarkable list of impressive credentials. Presently, a retired applied scientist and engineer, he earned the Ph.D. from the University of Connecticut Storrs in 1968, specializing in research design, applied statistics, and computer sciences. He earned the J.D. from George Mason School of Law in 1995. He worked as a professor at Southern Illinois University, the University of Maryland, and George Mason University.

Dr. Hiller's primary career was as a research scientist in the U.S. Army for twenty-five years, from bench scientist (GS

13) through lab director (Fed Gov SES4, from 1974 to 1995). He retired from the Army HQ Staff in the Pentagon as director of personnel technologies overseeing human factors engineering design in all major systems and setting policy for all army research and development (R&D) involving man–machine systems design (1995–1998). After retiring from Army R&D, he worked for Northrop Grumman Corporation as a chief scientist providing program management for Ph.D. physicists and electronics engineers (1999–2010). He retired as a fellow of the American Psychological Association and of the American Psychological Society and is a past member of American Mensa.

And most of all from our perspective, Dr. Jack Hiller has become a good friend who has honored us with his 2017 paper on universal consciousness and the near-death experience.

UNIVERSAL CONSCIOUSNESS UNDERLIES ALL OF REALITY
By Dr. Jack Hiller, April 29, 2017

Oh, I have slipped the surly bonds of earth, and danced the skies on laughter-silvered wings; sunward I've climbed and joined the tumbling mirth of sun-split clouds—and done a hundred things you have not dreamed of—wheeled and soared and swung high in the sunlit silence. Hovering there I've chased the shouting wind alongand flung my eager craft through footless halls of air.

Up, up the long delirious burning blue, I've topped the wind-swept heights with easy grace, where never lark, or even eagle, flew; and, while with silent, lifting mind I've trod the high untrespassed sanctity of space, put out my hand and touched the face of God.

—"High Flight" by John Gillespie Magee Jr.

The mind and brain are distinguished by their intrinsic nature in philosophy and psychology, but there are two different dominant schools of thought about how they work together. The materialists, to include most neurologists and other "hard" scientists, do not believe in an immaterial consciousness, but expect research to eventually demonstrate how consciousness is either a brain process, or an epiphenomenon not worthy of continued research. The other school accepts that body and brain process the physical sensory input for conscious perception, but argues that the perception that is realized in conscious perception exists in an immaterial mind or soul; that is the position taken by the Tripartite Domain Theory, but it goes a step further that has not been theorized by any other philosophers or scientists: The Tripartite Theory claims that all of the physical, material world is intrinsically always connected to, or a part of (a subset of), the universal consciousness that is the natural home for the soul in what is defined as the 2nd Domain (the 1st Domain is the pure thought or consciousness, which is God) when not connected to a brain.

The Tripartite Domain Theory analysis of the "spooky action at a distance," demonstrated by entanglement, is what led to the conclusion that the phenomenon of instant "communication," regardless of distance separating entangled elements, could only be explained as characteristic of the instantaneous communication reported by NDE/OBE observers while present in the spiritual world. Thus, it followed that the material objects of our physical world (i.e., the 3rd Domain) also exist in the 2nd Domain, and it is their action in the 2nd Domain of universal consciousness that enables the instantaneous communication exhibited in the 3rd Domain of physical reality.

The bizarre phenomena of instantaneous communication between entangled particles, predicted but unexplained by quantum mechanics and impossible to explain by classical mechanistic physics, is applied by the new analysis presented here to imply that only an energy-free continuum, also free of time and space constraints, may explain it—and we term that continuum the "universal field of consciousness."

A variety of analysts have claimed that materialism ought to be replaced by consciousness as the basic paradigm for science, but "consciousness" defies the cardinal requirement for modern physics of enabling objective observation of phenomena with reliable measurement—as it is by definition and usage unobservable to any but an individual's private mind. However, the entanglement phenomenon (as explained below) provides strong evidence for inferring that the basis for all experience is disembodied consciousness. Furthermore, physics can no longer deny consideration of consciousness as an explanatory paradigm, because it has elevated super string theory to its best hope for developing a "theory of everything" (i.e., a single theoretical framework that includes both relativity theory and quantum mechanics) when the string has a size on the order of the Planck length (approximately equal to 1.6×10^{-35} meters), which is in principle far too small to be directly observed and may only be inferred from indirect evidence, such as this analysis does with entanglement.

The near-death experience (NDE) research literature established that out-of-body experiences (OBE) are reliably associated with the trauma of an NDE; significant reference works include Raymond Moody's *Life after Life*, Jeffrey Long's *Evidence of the Afterlife*, and Pim van Lommel's *Consciousness Beyond Life*. The reality of the OBE, as demonstrated by substantial empirical fact checking, creates a problem for the standard paradigm of modern science, materialism, because consciousness does not follow the laws of standard materialistic physical science.

The OBE Reflects Disembodied Consciousness

The out-of-body experience (OBE) is well characterized by a consciousness separated from the traumatized body that enjoys perception, which is enhanced over normal perception; examples include the vividness of colors; feelings of perfect peace; and often the feeling of being loved without judgment by God. Despite these remarkable reports about disembodied consciousness, substantial evidence for the functioning of human consciousness without a normal brain has been collected and well organized in research reports. A powerful video presentation by Dr. Bruce Greyson (https://www.youtube.com/watch?v=2aWM95RuMqU) cites evidence for disembodied consciousness, such as accurately viewing activities distant from the traumatized body, meeting previously unmet and unknown relatives whose existence was later verified, recollecting former lives with verification of how they reported deaths and injuries; seeing by blind

Substantial evidence and testimony for out-of-body experiences pose a problem for reductionist science that only measures the physical.

individuals who experienced a form of visual perception that was accurate; and traveling made to a heavenly realm where deceased relatives were typically met.

Features of the OBE experience (e.g., time having ceased to run, and all entities appearing to be made of some form of light) were explained to be compatible with Relativity Theory and quantum mechanics in a chapter by the author on Frozen Time Theory (FTT) in *Real Visitors, Voices from Beyond, and Parallel Dimensions* by Brad and Sherry Steiger. In the FTT chapter, it was hypothesized that the baffling phenomenon of quantum particle entanglement (what Einstein aptly termed "spooky action at a distance") might be explained by applying the four-dimensional space-time model of Relativity Theory with time recast as a true fourth dimension.

Entangled Particles Imply Materialism Is an Invalid Paradigm

This note seeks to extend the explanation earlier presented in FTT of how the instantaneous interaction of particles, separated in space, may take place, regardless of their separation distance. It was found to be necessary to replace the materialist paradigm with immaterial consciousness for the entire realm of existence. The implications of particle entanglement drive the need to reformulate our understanding of the nature of reality.

During the development of quantum mechanics, Einstein noticed that its formulation implied the mathematical possibility for the atomic particles of a unified (entangled) system to communicate with each other instantaneously, regardless of how far apart they were, thus violating the stricture of his Relativity Theory limiting communication to the speed of light (EPR paradox, https://en.wikipedia.org/wiki/EPR_paradox). However, empirical research has demonstrated that communication for entangled particles does appear to be instantaneous (https://en.wikipedia.org/wiki/Quantum_entanglement). Instantaneous communication baffles any conceivable explanation by any contemporary materialistic physical theory.

Frozen Time Theory Explains Instantaneous Communication

In the FTT, it was proposed that the apparently separated particles of an entangled system (e.g., an atom or molecule) may communicate instantaneously by being collocated on the time dimension. For this explanation to work, the Schrödinger wave equation that so well defines the formulation of quantum mechanical theory (https://en.wikipedia.org/wiki/Schr%C3%B6dinger_equation) would have to be interpreted to represent particles being manifested as true energy waves extended across space, instead of as merely probabilities for spatial location of a discrete particle. (Whether the Schrödinger equation implies discrete particle spatial location probabilities, or the phases of a wave extended through space, has been an ongoing debate from the days of its formulation; see Particles as Waves in the wiki at [https://en.wikipedia.org/wiki/Schr%C3%B6dinger_equation#Particles_as_waves]).

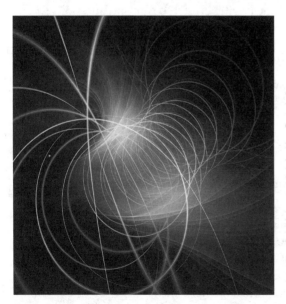

In quantum entanglement theory particles such as photons become connected to each other and influence each other no matter how far apart they are—even if they are billions of light years apart—hence making the limitations of space meaningless.

The Concept of an Energy Wave Defines It to Be Extended across Space-Time

In a wave form, a particle's wave is extended across the manifold of space-time. For simplicity, visualize a two-dimensional Cartesian graph (a vertical y axis by a horizontal t axis) of two separated particles; each particle is plotted separately on the y axis while being set to the same value for the time dimension t. In the FTT, two entangled particles were proposed to be in constant communication by their waves from the instant that the particles were formed as an entangled system. Thus, when one of the particles is "touched" by an observation that measures any characteristic of its existence, such as having a spin in one direction or another, the touched particle is activated into manifesting with either an up or down spin (in terms of the Schröder wave equation, it is said to collapse into one of its possible solutions). The surprising prediction from quantum mechanics was that the second particle would instantly react to the first particle's manifested state by manifesting a complementary spin to keep the entangled system in balance (if the first particle were measured as, say, having an up spin, then its partner would manifest as having a down spin). The results of a considerable amount of experimentation have confirmed that the first particle observed appears to randomly acquire its spin as up or down, and then the second, paired, particle reliably manifests the theoretically expected balancing spin.

Instant Communication between Entangled Particles Implies They Are Not Fundamentally Material Entities

A counter argument might be made that the energy level of waves extended over a great distance ought to be too low to enable any effective communication between such separated particles, and this argument makes sense for the materialistic paradigm. Consider, however, that effective instantaneous communication is commonly reported between spiritual entities during OBE episodes. Thus, an apt conjecture, based on consideration of OBE phenomena, would be that entangled particles communicate by a wave connection that exists in a field of consciousness whose power to operate is continuous throughout its entire field regardless of separation distance. The conjecture that the material particles we may observe also exist as entities in a universal field of consciousness is consistent with the quantum theory hypothesis formulated by de Broglie that all matter is wave-like in nature (https://en.wikipedia.org/wiki/Matter_wave# The_de_Broglie_hypothesis).

> It is proposed here that the light we perceive, which informs us of a material reality, exists in an underlying field of consciousness.

Perception of the Material World Comes from the Mind

It is proposed here that the light we perceive, which informs us of a material reality, exists in an underlying field of consciousness. Furthermore, our ordinary perception of our external reality, the world that we normally see, while informed by the light of objects, is itself a mental construction formed by our consciousness, with our consciousness itself operating in a universal field of consciousness. Our ordinary perception conveys to our minds the existence of a material world of solid objects that we see, touch, and feel. But we have known for over a century that material objects are composed of atoms that are themselves mostly space-separating electrons in orbits relatively far distant from their nucleus of protons and neutrons; thus, the material world we "see" is not really what exists. Centuries ago, before modern physics discovered the atomic structure we now accept for the material world, Immanuel Kant's analysis recognized that human perception was unable in principle to see the world the way it might truly exist; we see appearances of entities, but cannot possibly know them as they truly exist (https://en.wikipedia.org/wiki/Immanuel_Kant).

Existence Is Found in a Universal Field of Consciousness

Analysis of how entangled particles, separated across any vast distances, communicate instantaneously, defies explanation by classical, mechanistic, physical theorizing. Quantum mechanics itself offers no explanation, or even hints at any explanation, for "spooky action at a distance." The explanation proposed here for entangled particle communication instantly across any extended distance was driven to rely on an immaterial concept holding that reality is based on a universal field of consciousness in which time and space do not exist. Our ordinary perception of the world is surely helpful for living and surviving but cannot in principle display the underlying reality. Thus, it may reasonably be speculated that reality consists of a field of universal consciousness. How was this field created? How could it have been created? There are no answers found in ordinary life. Fortunately, the NDE and its OBE have provided reports relevant to explaining Creation.

The founder of analytical psychology, Swiss psychiatrist Carl Jung, proposed that there can be acausal events—occurrences with no apparent initial cause or connections to other events.

Synchronicity Fully Characterizes Activity in the Realm of Consciousness

Carl Jung developed the concept of synchronicity as a concept about acausal events, meaningful coincidences occurring without any apparent causal connections. Interestingly, Jung's development of this acausal concept was informally assisted by the quantum physicist Wolfgang Pauli. However, an analysis of time not running during OBEs, as explained in Frozen Time Theory, implies that all activity in the realm of disembodied conscious spirit is acausal, and thus synchronistic. Where time does not flow, causation becomes an empty concept, because activity does not sequence from one action to the next. Because the realm of consciousness contains no mass (or energy, considering that Einstein proved that mass and energy are interchangeable), it lacks the energy required in our material world to drive activity.

Existence Functions in Three Interrelated Domains

There are three interrelated domains of existence. The first domain is the foundation domain, what is termed here as the "universal field of consciousness." This "field" is God, and included in God are His spirit (human and "other") creations also, as pure consciousness with all connected together as a unitary field. An ordinary definition for consciousness could allude to self-awareness, thought, imagination, and decision making—but these actions are the result of consciousness and not the noumena, as Kant defined for unknown entities that give rise to perception, the thing in itself. Instead, consciousness is basically a primitive term that cannot be defined with words, but may only be known through experience; for example, if we try to define the fragrance perceived from a rose for someone who has never experienced the fragrance, the words would provide meaningless terminology.

The second domain, which is more fundamental than materialistic space-time, is a multidimensional world that is populated by spirit beings that take the form of light, with God also manifesting as light. The NDE/OBE reports are typically about perception within this domain. The second domain is generally referred to as Heaven. Heaven is characterized by uninterrupted love from God, the total absence of stressors, such as produced in the material body for food, clothing, and shelter, and lusts, such as for sex, money, and power.

The third is the material domain we normally perceive while living on Earth, which includes the three spatial dimensions and consciousness of time passing, with a distinctive past and a future. The hypothesized purpose for God creating the material domain is to provide for spiritual development through the experience of stressors, lusts, and the free-will reaction to them. Such spiritual development is impossible in the second domain, Heaven, for lack of stressors and conflicts.

Resolution of Apparent Conflicts between
Morality and Amorality for Life

It is frequently reported from the NDE/OBE, and from spiritually transformative experiences or deep states of meditation, that God does not judge the spirit as His love is given unconditionally. Self-judgement is natural during life reviews subsequent to trauma, and individuals may deeply regret hurtful or immoral behavior, but God is felt NOT to judge. Yet, all cultures and the Judeo-Christian religions are deeply concerned about morality—good vs. evil, and condemn not only immoral behavior but even immoral thoughts or imagination (the precursors to potential action). The Ten Commandments and

Christ's Golden Rule make it clear that the moral dimension of life is paramount, and thus important to God. Thus, there is an apparent conflict between conventional culture and religion and reporting from NDE/OBE and meditative states that good and evil are unimportant to God and reflect a mistake in Western culture and religion. A resolution for this apparent conflict is inherent in the tripartite domain theory.

When individuals are having an OBE or deep meditation experience, the context is the second, Heavenly, domain in which stress and evil do not exist—God would not be judging what does not then exist, although individuals in their life review may typically judge the moral character of their own behavior. However, morality surely applies to the material, Earth, domain by God's design to enable spiritual development. The New Age idea that morality is a false precept from archaic religions fails to recognize that morality is at the core of God's design for life on Earth to enable spiritual development.

The Universal Field of Consciousness Is God

Max Planck, the founder of quantum theory, concluded that consciousness provides the foundation for material reality: "I regard consciousness as fundamental. I regard matter as derivative from consciousness. We cannot get behind consciousness. Everything that we talk about, everything that we regard as existing, postulates consciousness."

Quantum theory founder Max Planck theorized that consciousness is the source of reality not the other way around.

Furthermore, "As a man who has devoted his whole life to the most clear-headed science, to the study of matter, I can tell you as a result of my research about the atoms this much: There is no matter as such! All matter originates and exists only by virtue of a force which brings the particles of an atom to vibration and holds this most minute solar system of the atom together.... We must assume behind this force the existence of a *conscious and intelligent* Mind. This Mind is the matrix of all matter."

The explanation found for creation is that God created the world, that the world created is fundamentally consciousness, and that the world is in fact God's very being. A frequent report from those traumatized individuals returning from an NDE is that, while their soul existed in a spirit form in Heaven or in the direct presence of God, they realized that everything, *every thing*, is connected and actually part of God. Given that God is eternal and all that exists, so too are all of God's creations. Our lives, our experiences, good and bad, harsh and beautiful, are all the play of God creatively exploring possibilities throughout eternity.

OUR RESPONSE TO DR. HILLER'S PAPER

If you should become one of those individuals who undergoes a near-death or illumination experience, a touch of cosmic consciousness, or a revelation from Divine Light, it shall hence forth truly be said of you that by your works, you shall be known.

You will develop deeper qualities of understanding.

You will demonstrate diminished concern about the selfish interests of the world.

You will gain a deep sense of peace and freedom.

You will achieve a powerful sense of wholeness and of Oneness with the cosmos.

You will notice a great shift in consciousness from self to other, from "I" to "thou," from "mine" to "ours."

You will find that your physical health will manifest in increased vitality.

You will develop a much greater patience toward your mission in life.

You will be consumed with desire to fulfill universal laws directed at cosmic harmony.

You will understand that your soul is both individual and universal.

You will become totally aware that there is a higher intelligence from which you may draw power, strength, and inspiration.

And, of course, you will no longer fear death.

Never Become Friendly with Phantoms

When the Bruce Willis film *The Sixth Sense* attained great popularity, we were astonished by how many mothers wrote to us asking for instructions in helping their children to "see dead people," as young actor Haley Joel Osment does in the motion picture. We wrote back stating firmly that such a goal for one's child may not be the very best thing for his or her lifestyle adjustment in contemporary society. If one's child does exhibit tendencies to the development of paranormal talents, he or she should be treated with love and understanding, not encouraged to become a spirit medium.

Most often the response to our counseling of caution was anger and accusations that we just wanted to horde the knowledge of such powers to contact the dead to ourselves or that we chose to teach the techniques only to those select individuals to whom we wished to share the mystical keys to the Other Side. As experienced metaphysicians, we always warn those who wish to take classes in psychic development that their initial attempts at opening higher levels of consciousness could make them easy targets for possession by negative entities. Until they remember always to surround themselves with Light and to apply a disciplined approach to their metaphysical studies, they are easy prey for a molester from the lower planes. Until they develop enough psychic strength and knowledge, their wide-open psyches can attract those aggressive entities who seek always to do harm or enslave humans.

We believe that children are not really more psychic than adults but that their reality has far fewer established borders than their parents or other grown-ups. For instance, watch two young girls receiving dolls for Christmas at a family gathering. Within moments, the girls are "talking" on behalf of their dolls about where they are going to have their hair done or where they will meet for lunch. The little receivers of new friends have quickly entered into a new reality in which it is normal to be talking to their dolls and, perhaps more significantly, talking for them. Later that night snug in their beds with their new dolls beside them, the girls might not be at all frightened to hear another voice speaking to them from the darkness. The girls have already extended their reality to include their dolls discussing social matters with them. What greater leap of consciousness would it require to admit a new "friend" into their ever-expanding universe?

On some occasions we would send those parents set on having a developing psychic in their households or who claimed that they would welcome a mischievous entity into their homes a copy of a newspaper report regarding a ghost called "Larry" and ask if they would really like such a nasty being contacting and tutoring their child.

LARRY THE GHOST LOVED TO PLAY WITH FIRE

It was on Good Friday of 1958 that the Stringers first saw the ghost. It was a milky, fluorescent column of vibrating light about as tall as a man. Shortly after seeing the apparition, the Stringers smelled smoke coming from the baby's room.

The ghost appeared to the Stringers as a column of light about the height of a man. Later, things began mysteriously burning.

There they found that something had burned a hole through the center of a pile of the baby's clothes. It looked just as though a blowtorch had done it. Yet a pair of highly inflammable nylon stockings on the bottom of the pile was untouched.

Graham Stringer explained to a United Press International reporter that the family finally had to call the ghost "Larry," because their four-year-old son kept asking about the column of vibrating light that had moved into their home.

Larry would be benign most of the year, but each Easter season beginning in 1958 the strange entity brought mysterious fires to their home on Trafalgar Avenue in the Peckham district of London.

In 1959, the Easter season once again brought the Stringers Larry, instead of the Easter Bunny. When Graham had a pair of shoes yanked out of his hands, he decided that it was time to call in the experts.

A team of investigators from the College of Psychic Science was not able to achieve a conclusive analysis of the disturbances, but they definitely identified the phenomenon as being poltergeistic in nature. Although the Stringers were prepared for Larry the fiery ghost when he returned in 1960, they were powerless to prevent the murky column of light from burning up another pile of clothes.

Their annual weekend houseguest had also decided to extend his stay a bit longer. Clocks began moving about on the mantelpiece, and objects floated around the apartment for several days after Easter Sunday. Stringer, a freelance photographer, also reported being enveloped in a gray, fluorescent cloud while working in his darkroom.

"The room just lit up," he told reporters. "And there was Larry vibrating and glowing at my side."

In 1961, the Stringers attempted an exorcism with a Catholic priest administering the rites shortly before their annual visitor was due to arrive. It seemed to have worked, but their rejoicing over the ecclesiastical triumph over the ghost proved to be premature. Larry had simply taken a year's sabbatical.

In 1962, the Stringers' living room furniture burst into flames. In addition to losing many pieces in the fire, the harassed family also had their carpet and their son's bed consumed by flames that erupted spontaneously.

On April 21, 1962, a spirit medium disclosed that Larry was in reality Mrs. Stringer's brother, Charles, who had died from burns twenty years earlier at the age of eighteen months. Now that the spirit had made his identity known, the medium promised, he would leave the family in peace.

Whether Larry the ghost actually was Charles's spirit or whether the phenomenon was due to some long-repressed, subconsciously nurtured guilt on the part of Mrs. Stringer, who may, as a child, have considered herself in some way responsible for her brother's death, the Easter poltergeist of Peckham did not return to burn any more clothing in the Stringer household.

SOME TEENS WANT TO SEE SEXY DEAD PEOPLE

For us, the most alarming aspects of the many young people and parents being seduced by the thrill of "seeing dead people" are the young girls in their early teens who begin offering themselves sexually to spirits.

One fourteen-year-old told us how she had stretched out on her bed at night and prayed that a ghostly "boyfriend" would manifest and "make out" with her. A sixteen-year-old said that she had welcomed "Boros" to her bed and that she had cuddled with him until morning. Most alarming were the teens who claimed to have had sex with their ghostly lovers.

Those experienced in paranormal research recognize the otherworldly seductions of the type of demon that has sought to sexually molest human beings ever since our species became "fair" and appeared capable of providing a warm, fleshly body for a spirit being to possess for minutes, weeks, months—or permanently. There are essentially two types of such demonic entities: the "incubi" pester mortal women, and the "succubi" take great delight in seducing human men.

In our more than fifty years of researching the strange, the unusual, and the unexplained, we have come to understand that as much as our materialistic and scientific age might wish it could relegate such supernatural sexual molesters to a much less sophisticated past—somewhere around the Dark or Middle Ages—these demons have not relinquished their grip on the human psyche. According to a good many men and women who swear that they have encountered such sexual offenders from the spirit world, the incubi and succubi are as much a nasty nuisance in the shadow world of our supermarket and space-age culture as they were in the superstition-saturated and sexually tortured Middle Ages.

THE INCUBUS ATTACKS TEENS INSECURE ABOUT THEIR OWN SEX APPEAL

Serious and responsible mediums and occultists have told us that the incubus can appear in many different forms—as an invisible entity; as an image of a loved one, either living or in spirit; as an image of an idealized love partner; or as a hideous gargoyle-like beast.

The incubus attacks the more vulnerable—the lonely, the frustrated, the unloved, the young who are uncertain of their sex appeal. A young woman who lies in her bed at night, tossing, turning, longing for a lover in her arms, sends out vibrations that bring these entities from every dark corner of the etheric worlds.

Sadly, according to our research, perhaps the majority of women who have experiences with the demon in our modern times are not witches, mediums, or occultists, but high school girls, college girls, career women, and young homemakers. Sexual frustration seems to attract these creatures, and although they may *feel* like a human male to these women, if they could view these things as they are, they would see the most grotesque kind of animal-like entities right out of some medieval painting of demons.

WE LIVE IN THE ERA OF THE CELEBRITY GHOST SEX STORY

Sadly, to make matters worse, we live in the era of the celebrity ghost sex story. To name a few who confess to having out-of-body sex:

- Lucy Liu, who stars as "Watson" in the television series *Elementary* and who in an earlier movie was one of Charlie's

Angels, told *Us Weekly* in 1999 that she had a sexual encounter with a ghost while trying to nap on her futon. "Some sort of spirit came down … and made love to me," said the actress. "It was sheer bliss," she recalled. "I felt everything. I climaxed…. Something came down and touched me, and now it watches over me."

- Comedy legend and paranormal believer Dan Aykroyd left audiences with little doubt of the climax of his spooky cuddling spirit sex scene in *Ghostbusters*. In a 2010 *Huffington Post* blog, Aykroyd said that he'd "felt an unseen presence … [i]n my bed no less when we lived in Mama Cass's Hollywood estate."

- Actress Paz de la Huerta, who has starred on TV shows like *Boardwalk Empire* and movies like *Enter the Void*, told the *New York Times* in 2011 that she had sex with the ghost of Elvis Presley on a visit to Graceland. According to her

Actor Dan Aykroyd is well known for being a star in the *Ghostbuster* movie franchise. He has also felt the presence of a ghost in real life.

account, she went to his recording studio because she had been told that sometimes sensitive people feel him in this room. "I stood in this corner and I felt him. What can I say? I felt him touch me. I felt his spirit go through me and give me pleasure."

"SPOOKS ARE BETTER LOVERS THAN REAL MEN"

On November 14, 2015, Jill Foster wrote a piece for the *Daily Mail* provocatively entitled "The Women Who Say They've Had Affairs with GHOSTS: They're Not Mad, but Respectable Twenty-somethings Who Say Spooks Are Better Lovers Than Real Men."

Foster shares the experience of Sian Jameson, a writer, artist, and spiritualist, who told her that "Robert," her "paranormal paramour," began his nighttime visits shortly after she moved into a cottage in a remote part of Wales. She had just broken up with her boyfriend and was lonely when one night the ghostly Robert appeared. "He was very handsome, with beautiful

> **S**ome years ago, I was quite shocked when an elderly female medium whom I had known for many years told me in the strictest confidence that she had had a spirit lover when she was a young woman.

hazel eyes … his body was 'incredibly light,'" yet she could feel his body pressing down on her.

Sian insists that the experience was "not imaginary or stress-induced." She told journalist Foster that "scientists may explain it away, but I'd just say that they didn't experience what I experienced."

BEWARE THE DEMON LOVER

A metaphysical teacher of our acquaintance we will call Cybele said that most of her students would be horrified if an entity jumped into bed with them. "Others would like it too damn much," she acknowledged with a wry chuckle. "I feel a great responsibility to teach my students to exercise control over such encounters, or their chances to enjoy a normal relationship with a fellow human would disappear. There's always an entity hovering about who is all too willing to take care of anyone's sexual frustration."

Some years ago, I was quite shocked when an elderly female medium whom I had known for many years told me in the strictest confidence that she had had a spirit lover when she was a young woman.

"I wish that I had never allowed it to come into me," she said in a hushed voice. "You see, after I had my spirit lover, I could no longer be satisfied by a mortal man. Sexual intercourse with my spirit lover was beyond description. When I got married, I was disappointed. I tried not to blame my husband, but he just couldn't compare."

Her strict advice to any young female medium or occultist was not to get started sexually with any spirit. "It'll ruin your chances for happiness with any mortal man," she said. "A spirit lover might be able to make love like Pan the goat god himself, but he can't keep you warm on cold nights or buy your groceries. It's a terrible thing to judge a man while he's making love to you, but that's what will happen if you've taken up with a spirit lover. And your man will be able to tell by the way you respond that he's way behind in the comparison. So I repeat: Don't start with a spirit lover, or you might find yourself awfully lonely in your old age."

JENNIFER WANTED TO INTERVIEW
THE BEINGS THAT INVADED HER BEDROOM

Endowed with a high degree of spiritual and psychic sensitivity, Jennifer was much better equipped to deal with shadow entities than are many who suddenly find themselves faced with the unknown.

In Jennifer's words: "At a young age, I watched humanoid shadows cross the hallway in my home, moving from one room to another. Often, I could catch the movement out of my peripheral vision and would be staring directly at them when they moved across open space. My brother and mother also witnessed them.

"I ruled out natural causes that may have created a movement of shadows in many of these instances. The shadows moved independently of any backdrop and passed across open space without any distortion of distance or angle."

One night, Jennifer was awakened by two shadows passing over the bed. She *felt* two presences in the room and looked in the direction from which she had felt the movements. She saw two solid-looking, dark, human-shaped shadows standing at the end of the bed.

The moment she saw them, she became paralyzed and felt a weight pressing down on her chest. She emphasized in the recounting of her experience that there was no sense of suffocation—just a weight that would not allow her to get up.

Jennifer was catching glimpses of "humanoid shadows" moving about in her home, and then two appeared in her bedroom and restrained her from moving. (Art by Ricardo Pustanio.)

When she realized that she couldn't move, she became frightened and began to pray.

"I couldn't speak," Jennifer said, "so I prayed loudly in my head. The figures seemed unaffected by my prayer for protection and lingered a few moments before moving toward the back door of the house and disappearing. The pressure and paralysis had left the moment they turned away, but I remained still until they were gone."

Looking back on the event, Jennifer sensed no maliciousness or evil from the shadow men, or shadow walkers, as she began to call them. The experience was terrifying only while she was experiencing paralysis, a sense of inability to act.

"I actually wanted to *ask* questions of the visitors," she said, "but when I discovered I was unable to move, I became fearful of their intentions. Now, I consider it an instructional experience, made forceful because a point was being made, a lesson given that I would not forget: Remain aware of the potential dangers of wandering spirits/entities, and don't leave myself unguarded. Since then, I have taken personal steps toward spiritual protection (primarily deep faith in a higher power) and in my own force of will."

A GHOST OF "PERFECT BEAUTY"?

One of my early heroes in paranormal research was Sir William Crookes (1832–1919), professor at the University of London, editor of the Quarterly Journal of Science, president of the British Chemical Society, one of Great Britain's outstanding scientists, discoverer of the element thallium, inventor of the radiometer and the Crookes tube (which made the later development of x-rays possible), and a physicist and chemist of international repute. He was one of the most thorough and exacting scientific investigators of spirit contact. After many years of painstaking research and experimentation with dozens of well-known mediums, he became convinced that a great deal of spiritistic phenomena was real and indicated proof of an afterlife.

But the details of his "love affair" with the ghost Katie King, whom he described as a "perfect beauty," has always left me puzzled.

When a man of stature, such as Sir William Crookes, announced that he had judged medium Florence Cook's materializations of the spirit Katie King to be genuine, it was bound to spark a violent controversy. Whether or not the "perfect beauty" with whom Sir William chatted and strolled about the seance room was a ghost or a hoax is a question that is still being debated today.

Born in London on June 17, 1832, William Crookes was one of sixteen children of a well-known and prosperous tailor and his second wife. As well as being part of such a large family, William had five stepbrothers and stepsisters from his father's first wife. Although the young man had very little formal education, his keen mind and natural abilities allowed him to enroll in the Royal College of Chemistry when he was only sixteen. Upon graduation in 1854, Crookes became superintendent of the Meteorological Department at Radcliffe Observatory in Oxford. A year later, he gained a post at the College of Science in Chester, Cheshire.

> When she was fifteen, Florence found that she herself was capable of materializing Katie in her own home.

In 1856, when he was twenty-four, he married Ellen Humphrey, and because of the large fortune he had inherited from his father, Crookes was able to establish a private laboratory and devote himself entirely to scientific work of his own choosing. Five years later, in 1861, Crookes discovered the element thallium and the correct measurement of its atomic weight. In 1863, when he was only thirty-one, he was elected a fellow of the Royal Society.

Just when it seemed Crookes faced only a life of one triumph after another, he was grief-stricken when his youngest brother, Philip, died in 1867. Cromwell Varley, a close friend and fellow physicist, who was also a practicing spiritualist, convinced William and Ellen to attend a séance and attempt to communicate with Philip. Whatever spirit messages Crookes and his wife received during a series of séances in 1867, it appears that they were convincing enough to inspire the brilliant physicist to turn his genius toward the exploration of spiritistic phenomena.

Florence Cook, the medium through whom the enchanting spirit of Katie King materialized, first met the attractive entity in séances that she attended as a child. When she was fifteen, Florence found that she herself was capable of materializing Katie in her own home.

After the spirit's first visit in April 1872, when she appeared as only a deathlike face between the gauze curtains of a séance cabinet, Katie began to appear to Florence almost daily. The ghost's control became more and more perfect until she could at last step out of the cabinet and show herself in full body to those men and women assembled for young Florence's séances.

Katie's story was that she had been a girl of twelve when she stood in the crowd that had watched King Charles I of England lose his head at the chopping block. She had been married while very young, but she was much more the violent rather than the domestic sort. She readily confessed that the circumstances leading to Charles's death merited such action, as she, herself, had "done in" several people with her own hands. According to the ghost, Katie had died at a youthful twenty-three.

Crookes no doubt created quite a stir among his more conventional scientific colleagues when he told them that he had walked with a ghost, talked with a ghost, and taken more than forty flash photographs of the specter. And when he went on to describe the spirit as a "perfect beauty" whose "purity of complexion" could not be done justice by mere photography, tongues began to wag that the great scientist had lost all form of objectivity and had grown much too attached to the spirit that he was supposed to be investigating. When a man of stature such as Crookes announced that he had judged medium Florence Cook's materializations of the spirit Katie King to be genuine, it was bound to spark a violent controversy.

It has been said that the spirit of Katie King became almost as if she were a full-time boarder at the Cook household. When Florence married, her husband complained that it was like being married to two women. Katie began to materialize at unexpected moments—and some nights she even went to bed with the medium and her long-suffering spouse.

Many people became thoroughly convinced of the validity of Katie King's existence because of the testimony of the highly respected William Crookes. Others whispered that there was a scandal and made much of the many hours that the physicist had spent alone with Florence Cook and her alleged spirit friend.

A chemist, physicist, and inventor, Sir William Crookes got involved in spiritualism later in life and was a president of Britain's Society for Psychical Research.

Crookes, however, stood firm in his convictions that he had not been duped and summed up his investigations by stating that it was unimaginable to suggest that "an innocent schoolgirl of fifteen" should be able to devise and to carry out such a "gigantic imposture" so successfully for a period of three years.

Crookes pointed out to his critics that in those same three years, the fact that Florence had submitted to any test that might be imposed upon her, that she was willing to be searched at any time, either before or after a séance, and that she visited his laboratory for the expressed objective of submitting to the strictest scientific tests certainly demonstrated her integrity. To insist further that the spirit Katie King was the result of deceit did more "violence to one's reason and common sense than to believe her to be what she herself affirms."

William Crookes's experiments in psychical research did little to prevent his

Haunted: Malevolent Ghosts, Night Terrors, and Threatening Phantoms

receiving the Royal Medal from the Royal Society in 1875 or from being knighted in 1897. He supported the Society for Psychical Research when it was founded in 1882 and even served as its president in 1886, but he conducted no tests of mediumship or any other paranormal phenomena after 1875.

Some scholars of the psychic field have declared the series of experiments that Crookes conducted with the famous medium Daniel Dunglas Home to be the first strictly scientific tests of mediumistic ability. Of one such test, Crookes stated that Home went to the fireplace and after stirring the hot coals around with his bare hands, took out a red-hot piece nearly as large as an orange and "putting it on his right hand, so as to almost completely enclose it, he then blew into the small furnace he had made of his hand until the lump of charcoal was nearly white hot," and then drew Crookes's attention to the flame that was "flickering over the coal and licking round his fingers."

A number of witnesses to the experiment were also able to handle the hot coal without burning themselves after Home had transferred his "power" to them. Those who handled the coal without the transference of energy from Home "received bad blisters at the attempt."

As a kind of summation of his views on the subject, Sir William Crookes once said: "The phenomena I am prepared to attest to are extraordinary and so directly oppose the most firmly rooted articles of scientific belief—amongst others, the ubiquity and invariable action of the force of gravitation—that even now, on recalling the details of what I witnessed, there is an antagonism in my mind between reason which pronounces it to be scientifically impossible, and the consciousness of my senses, both of touch and sight…. It is absolutely true that connections have been set up between this world and the next!"

After Lady Crookes died in 1916, Sir William began immediately his attempts to communicate with her. According to some sources, he did receive messages from her spirit that he felt constituted proof of contact with his beloved wife on the other side. Others say that the alleged spirit photograph of Lady Crookes appeared to have been manipulated in the developing process.

Sir William joined his wife in the Great Mystery on April 4, 1919, survived by four of their eight children.

THE VATICAN REVISES THE CATHOLIC RITE OF EXORCISM

In January 1999, the Vatican issued a revised Catholic rite of exorcism for the first time since 1614, essentially reaffirming the existence of Satan and his unholy legions of demons and advising those priests conducting exorcisms to deal with evil as a force "lurking within all individuals," instead of one that threatens people from without.

In September 2000, headlines around the world announced that "Satan Defeats the Pope in Vatican Exorcism Struggle," and the account that followed such an attention-grabbing declaration told of a demon-possessed teenaged girl who screamed insults in a "cavernous voice," displayed superhuman strength in pushing away Vatican guards, and "sneeringly laughed" at the efforts of the Holy Father and Fr. Gabriele Amorth to exorcise her. Later, papal spokesmen insisted that the pope had been able to calm the girl during her outburst, but that he had not attempted an exorcism. That task had been assigned to Fr. Amorth and Fr. Giancarlo Gramolazzo, who lamented that the nineteen-year-old had been a splendid and pure girl until her terrible case of possession.

> In September 2000, headlines around the world announced that "Satan Defeats the Pope in Vatican Exorcism Struggle" ....

On September 19, 2000, the *Chicago Sun-Times* reported that the Archdiocese of Chicago had appointed a full-time exorcist for the first time in its 160-year history.

In the November 28, 2000, issue of the *New York Times*, an article by John W. Fountain ("Exorcists and Exorcisms Proliferate across U.S.") quoted Rev. Bob Larson, an evangelical preacher and author who heads an exorcism ministry in Denver, as saying that he had forty "exorcism teams" across the nation. "Our goal is that no one should ever be more than a day's drive from a city where you can find an exorcist," said Rev. Larson.

The evangelist questioned why anyone should be "freaked out" by the existence of demons and those of faith who would seek to drive them out of the victims of demonic possession. "It's in the Bible," he said.

If, as some theologians and scholars predict, there is soon to take place a major conflict between the Forces of Light and the Forces of Darkness, one would be well-advised to be wary of those seductive creatures of the shadows who have for centuries sought to confuse us humans into believing that their counterfeit illumination is truly a Guiding Light.

Be Careful "Playing" with a Ouija Board

Very often, the incubi and succubi appear to have been invited into a human's space by someone dabbling in the occult. Curious and previously innocent minds can offer a wide-open portal to this world when some individuals begin "playing" with such devices as a Ouija Board.

Erica told me that a few years back she and her sister were using a Ouija Board when weird occurrences began to happen.

At first, they heard footsteps in the hall and on the ceiling. Then there would be loud thuds, like someone wearing boots or heavy shoes.

Then things began to get stranger. One night while Erica was in bed, she began to stare into a dark corner of her room. She was about to close her eyes when she noticed that the shadow began to get darker and darker. She couldn't quite understand what was happening so she just continued to stare.

If one does not know what they are doing with a Ouija Board, the results of experimentation could be the summoning of a nefarious spirit such as an incubus or succubus.

Then the shadow took up almost the entire corner, and she could see a silhouette of a person.

Fear sunk in at this point, and she could feel him staring right through her. Erica then saw this "shadow" man step out into the light, and everything was visible except for the features of his face. He then walked right past her bed and out into the hallway. He seemed like an intelligent sort of shadow person or spirit. Erica was extremely scared, and she didn't tell anyone about the incident for quite a while. She is not certain whether it is the same "shadow" person or not, but since then Erica has seen the entity quite often.

Erica said that she has had her hair lifted up while she was in the shower. The action caught her off guard, but by the time this incident occurred, she was becoming used to such manifestations and had accepted that she lived alongside spirits.

But there are things that are harder to accept. Darker things began only a couple years ago, Erica said, "When I would be out in public places, I would see people with no whites in their eyes. Their eyes would be totally black.

"I tried to ignore all these things, and I decided that my imagination had gotten the better of me. One night when I was in the shower, I thought that enough was enough and I declared that such creatures did not exist.

"All of a sudden, I began choking. I became extremely afraid. It felt as though I was being choked from the inside out.

"Whatever it was, I sensed that it would not stop until I said, 'demons do exist; Shadow People do exist!'"

Sometime after Erica thought that she had made peace with the entities by conceding their existence, she was sitting alone in the house by herself when "out of nowhere it felt like something reached into my chest and began to squeeze my heart. I thought I was having a heart attack. It felt like something was trying to pull my heart out of my chest. I honestly thought that this was it, and I asked for God/the Great Spirit to spare me. I begged Him—and as soon as I asked for spiritual help, the pain started to subside."

Both Sherry and I have counseled hundreds of individuals who approached a Ouija Board as a game, an adventure, a spooky experience—even as a joke—and suffered unfortunate psychological/spiritual consequences. We have always cautioned those who would listen about the dark side of the paranormal. Most often, we have warned against ill-advised adventures with a Ouija Board.

Now we understand that the board itself doesn't house spirits or demons. We recognize that experienced individuals who practice discernment and discipline and who follow the proper spiritual precautions may cautiously employ the talking board in their research. However, we also know that many earnest and sincere seekers have learned too late how easily the Tricksters and Deceivers can appear as Angels of Light or as Master Teachers.

We are not alone in our concern about this mass experiment conducted over the airwaves. Here are some comments from a group of paranormal researchers whom we surveyed:

All cases where we have been contacted about problems with nasty spirits were a result of using the Ouija board. While the board may not be harmful for some, it just takes one time to open the portals to allow low-level spirits into one's home. We are totally against it, not from a religious standpoint, but from a practical level—it just invites trouble. We believe the living have no power over the dead, so once these low-level spirits enter a home, there is no way to banish them. Every time exorcism is done, the spirits become more angry and still remain in the home, but now they have become more malicious.

—D. O., paranormal researcher

Experimenting with the Ouija Board is not smart at all. I once saw a patient who used the board with her husband and the contact was clear and concise. The party on the other side said they had been stuck in limbo for 200 years and now they could exchange energies with those who were working the board. Asked who that would be who would trade lives with the ones stuck in other dimensions, the party in limbo said, "Why YOU, of course." With that the patient and hubby burned the board and that was that. One should not parachute into lion country wearing a loin cloth.

—J. M., doctor, paranormal researcher

Experimenting with a Ouija Board has the potential for opening a portal for beings that go bump in the night that can't be readily closed. I shudder at the consequences; as with drug experiments, "set and setting" is the "X" factor that has to be managed and monitored closely. To not do so is a form of malpractice and abuse of the airwaves!

—J. J. H., psychologist, author

I have written about our youthful use of a Ouija board, and included a photo that clearly shows us using the board, with a demonic face peering in at us through the window! When a group of us were quietly and intently watching *The Exorcist* at its scariest moment, a Ouija board jumped off a high living room shelf and smashed itself to the floor!

—J. K., psychic sensitive, author, radio/television personality

The board is not the problem; the problem is the host of malevolent spirits waiting for gullible people to open doors that they do not understand. One must always be cautious doing so…. The problem is those ignorant of the dangers and who may not recognize spirits for what they truly are. (Satan's minions often appear as beings of light to mislead people, and such people do not recognize this until it is too late.)

—W. D. A., artist, paranormal researcher

It's not the board, it's the user. Both the board and the word "ouija" have a tremendous amount of "fear consciousness" around them because of the stories and taboos that have arisen though history, and many "undesirables" have linked themselves to that. We will be alert and ready as the "psychic paramedics" if we are needed.

—L. L. M. psychic sensitive

As regards my personal experience with the Ouija board and what I have seen as a result of its use, I would highly recommend against experimenting with the object.

—H. B., physicist and paranormal researcher

While some may argue that a Ouija Board can do no harm sitting on a closet shelf, we are concerned about what it can unleash from the closet of the unconsciousness or what it can activate from the shadows hovering around the psyche from the other dimensions. A so-called harmless instrument can, indeed, be harmful to the indiscriminate and unprepared participant in this most ancient ritual of spirit contact.

Haunted Hotels Where Some Guests Never Leave

THE DISAPPEARING HOTEL

A broadcast journalist I'll call Joan told me of her stay in a most unusual motel. Joan's résumé had been received with enthusiasm by a large radio station in the Southwest, and she had been asked to come in for an interview. Since she was presently employed at a station in a smaller city nearly two hundred miles from the possible new position, she asked her friend Elaine to accompany her on what would be an overnight trip.

Joan said that they arrived in the city quite late and were sorry that they had not made reservations before their departure, for the choices for comfortable accommodations were rather slim.

They were about to resign themselves to spending the night in a run-down motel on the edge of town when they turned a corner and noticed a small, but very attractive, motel directly behind a soft-serve dairy drive-in. The motel had very few rooms, but the place appeared to be clean and well kept, and Joan and Elaine reasoned that the traffic from the drive-in would be minimal at that late hour and would not disturb them.

A quiet, white-haired, rather distinguished-looking night clerk handed them their room key after they had registered and pleasantly wished them a good night's sleep. The crisply clean room had two queen-sized beds, and Joan remarked that she and her friend enjoyed one of the most restful night's sleep that either had had for months.

Joan's interview was set for eight o'clock sharp, so the two women were up early to turn in their key and grab a couple of doughnuts and coffee from the continental breakfast offered by the motel.

The interview went well, and Joan accepted the job offer from the station manager. The man said that he loved her voice and promised her an afternoon talk show in addition to covering special features and doing the early evening news.

Joan was exuberant. She was moving up in her career to a much larger radio station and with a considerable increase in pay over her present position.

On the way out of town, Joan and Elaine decided to drive past the motel where they had enjoyed such a good night's sleep. Joan had paid cash for the room, and the manager hadn't given her a receipt. She should have one for her business records, she reasoned, and besides, neither one of them had seen the name of the motel.

"We drove around and around that corner again and again," Joan said. "but there was no motel to be seen. We knew it was directly behind this dairy drive-in, but now there was nothing but a vacant lot there. We thought we were going crazy. We stopped and asked people about the motel behind the dairy freeze, but no one knew what we were talking about. They definitely thought we were crazy."

At the time Joan told me her story, she had been with the radio station in the city with the vanishing motel for fifteen years.

"Every once in a while," she admitted, "I will still drive around behind the dairy bar and try to sneak up on the motel. It is never there. And according to people in the community, there never has been a motel, inn, hotel, or hostel on that site. Ever. But it was certainly solid and real wherever it really exists.

"Elaine and I know that we didn't sleep on the ground behind that drive-in, and we didn't sleep in the car," Joan sighed, ending her unusual account. "But where did we spend the night? What dimension did two tired women enter that evening and enjoy a wonderful, restful sleep? Believe me, there have been many stressful times since when I have wished that I could hide away under the covers of one of the beds in that motel in the middle of nowhere."

The motel was small but clean, and Joan and Elaine had a nice stay there. The next day, there was no sign of the building. It was gone!

ONE GHOST SIGHTING WAS ENOUGH FOR THE MAID AT THE CLEWISTON INN

On August 11, 2007, Jose Jesus Zaragoza, writing for the *Clewiston News*,

Haunted: Malevolent Ghosts, Night Terrors, and Threatening Phantoms

reported that the Clewiston Inn was haunted. One of the maids who confronted the ghostly figure of a woman turned in her letter of resignation the next day. Chris Hill, the manager of the inn, said the ghost didn't scare her, but she could not explain why the front-desk switchboard light for Room 255 kept lighting up when the room was vacant.

Anita Conklin and her husband had lived in Room 255 for many years. Mr. Conklin, described as a large and affable man, managed the Miami Seaquarium. They appeared to have no family and few visitors, and they spent their evenings reading books. Conklin died several months before Anita passed, and it is their spirits that employees feel haunt the inn. Numerous complaints of a presence touching them and tugging at their clothing have been reported by employees.

Room 118 seems to have no back history to account for a spirit presence, but employees and guests have reported the figure of a woman entering the room, walking very slowly to the window, then disappearing.

"MISS KATE" WATCHES OVER THE SHERIDAN INN IN CASPER

Guests who register at the Sheridan Inn in Sheridan, Wyoming, may complain of a "pocket of cold air" enveloping them, the smell of a lady's perfume that mysteriously appears around them, and a light shining in the window of a room that has no electricity. If any of the above occurs to them during their stay, the guests know that they have met the ghost of Catherine B. Arnold, affectionately known as "Miss Kate," who keeps watch over the inn.

In the October 16, 2007, issue of the *Casper Star Tribune*, staff writer Wes Smalling quoted Della Herbst, a board member of the Sheridan Heritage Center, which was restoring the old hotel, as saying that she definitely feels Miss Kate's presence. "And the worst thing is," she said, "I didn't even believe in ghosts."

The Sheridan Inn was built in 1893 as a place for people to stay at the end of the line. Such illustrious figures of the day as William F. Cody (Buffalo Bill) made the hotel home. Cody bought the business, but not the building, in 1894.

Miss Kate was nineteen when she arrived by train in 1901, and she was hired as a seamstress by the inn. For the next sixty years, she worked as a maid, a front desk clerk, and the main caretaker. She never married, telling her one serious beau that she could not leave the hotel and move to Ohio with him.

She was forced to move out of the hotel in 1965 when the hotel was in such a state of disrepair that it was bought by a developer who planned to tear it down. The Sheridan Historical Society rescued the inn from destruction, and Miss Kate let her request to be cremated and her ashes placed in the building when she died be known. Her wishes were honored when she passed at age

The Sheridan Inn in Wyoming was once run by Buffalo Bill Cody and is registered as a National Historic Landmark. It is also protected by the ghost known as Miss Kate.

86 in 1968, and her ashes were placed in the wall of her favorite room on the third floor.

The National Register of Historic Places placed the Sheridan Inn on its list, and the Rib & Chop House was the proud result of one restoration. Although the inn has not received guests in many years, plans for twenty-two rooms have been added to a restoration project.

Some years ago, the second and third floors were gutted by construction crews. The one thing left undisturbed was Miss Kate's ashes in the wall of her favorite room. Workers have been mindful of her presence, and many of them have captured her wispy image on film and felt mysterious cold spots. Some have refused to work anywhere near where they might disturb Miss Kate.

THE CRESCENT HOTEL
HAS SO MANY GHOSTS IT ATTRACTS CONFERENCES

The Crescent Hotel in Eureka Springs, Arkansas, has so many restless spirits haunting its rooms and hallways that, on March 9 and 10, 2007, members of the Arkansas Ghost Hunters held a conference there hoping to have their own individual sightings of ghosts. According to Laurinda Joenks of the *Morning News* (March 20, 2007), more than two hundred paranormal enthusiasts were drawn to the hotel due to previous reports of locked room doors swinging open by themselves, messages scrawled on bathroom mirrors, and television sets turning themselves on and off. Many of the ghost hunters were rewarded with sightings of glowing orbs of light, mysterious shadows, and clouds of mist manifesting in the hallways.

THE GREEN PARK INN HAS SEVERAL HAUNTED ROOMS

The Green Park Inn, situated on the carapace of the Eastern Continental Divide in Blowing Rock, North Carolina, has experienced numerous ghostly manifestation, but its most-haunted room is Room 318 in which Laura (Laurel) Green died of a broken heart or suicide after being jilted at the altar. Rooms 332 and 333 are more sinister, harboring what has been described by ghost researchers as an entity of pure evil. Although Room 226 had an actual recorded death in the room, researchers who investigated the room in 2007 found nothing foreboding there—only the sound of organ music. Employees at the hotel reported that sometimes guests complain about children running and making noise in the halls—even though no children are registered at the time. (Scott Nicholson, *Watauga Democrat*, October 16, 2007)

"MRS. ADAMS" GIVES PEOPLE THE "WILLIES"

The once-stately (before it was destroyed by a fire in June 2016) Quamichan Inn in Duncan, British Columbia, maintained its always orderly appearance because of a fastidious ghost named Mrs. Adams, a former owner of the establishment. Steven Mugridge says that he saw the ghost of the elegant lady on a number of occasions. "She isn't an angry ghost," Mugridge told Sandra McCulloch of the *Times Colonist* in October 2007. "I am really quite comfortable with her, but she still gives me the willies sometimes."

Robin Duke, who was the owner of the inn at the time, used to come to the place with her parents when she was a child. Not long after she had taken possession of the Quamichan Inn, she felt an invisible somebody walk past her and give her a good scare. The kitchen staff told her that she turned white as a sheet.

A PROTECTIVE GHOST AT
HOMESTEAD RESTAURANT IN JACKSONVILLE

Alpha Paynter operated a boarding house in a cabin that later became the Homestead Restaurant in Jacksonville, Florida. Alpha devoted her life to the place, and when she died in 1962, she was buried in the yard behind the building. According to many of those who have been patrons in recent years, Alpha Paynter has never left the Homestead and remains its protector.

Steve Macri, a former owner of the Homestead, admitted to Michele Newbern Gillis of the Jacksonville *Financial News & Daily Record* (September 22, 2002) that in the twenty-six years that he ran the place, there were many things that he could not explain. In October 2001, just before he closed, there

> A young employee ... ran back in the restaurant screaming that he had seen a woman in the backyard half in and half out of the ground.

was a rash of complaints from women who claimed that an invisible someone was touching them on the shoulders. Macri also mentioned the newly hired dishwasher from out of town who asked who the lady in the long dress watching him from the top of the stairs was. A young employee, who was shooting hoops during his break, ran back in the restaurant screaming that he had seen a woman in the backyard half in and half out of the ground.

A new ownership team, which included Kathy Johansen, whose family owned the Homestead until 1975, reopened the restaurant in September 2002. Although Johansen said that she had never seen the ghost of Alpha, she knew that over the years that her father owned the restaurant many customers and employees had claimed to have seen her. Contractors working alone in the building after hours complain of being touched from behind. Many have left and never returned to complete their work.

According to tradition, Alpha's spirit appears most often in mirrors in various rooms in the restaurant. Many patrons have reported seeing her leaning over the fireplace in the center room.

GENERAL WAYNE INN

Located in Merion, Pennsylvania, on the old Lancaster roadway between Philadelphia and Radner, the General Wayne Inn has been in continuous operation since 1704, when a Quaker named Robert Jones decided to serve travelers with a restaurant and a place of lodging. The land was purchased from fellow Quaker William Penn and was originally called the Wayside Inn. Because of the inn's location near the site of numerous battles during the Revolutionary War, it was renamed the General Wayne Inn in 1793 in honor of a local hero, General Anthony Wayne.

No longer an inn, the three-story stone and timber building is now a synagogue. Over the years, there has been an extensive collection of ghosts—some say as many as seventeen. Wilhelm, the spirit of a Hessian soldier who was killed in the Revolutionary War, likes to stay down in the cellar.

In addition to Wilhelm, there reportedly was a little boy ghost, who cried for his lost mother; two female entities who had worked at the inn and had died young under bizarre circumstances; eight other Hessian soldiers who had once been quartered at the inn and who had died nearby in battle; a Native American who seemed primarily to be observing the others; and an African American who was an entity of very few words.

Ludwig, the spirit of another Hessian soldier, materialized for many nights at 2:00 A.M. in the bedroom of Mike Benio, a contractor who also had

Established in 1704, the General Wayne Inn was originally the William Penn Inn, but was renamed in 1793 after General "Mad" Anthony Wayne, a brigadier general during the American Revolution. Its long history has afforded many opportunities for ghosts to become residents.

psychic abilities. The entity appealed to Benio to unearth his bones, which had been buried in the basement of the inn, and give them a proper burial in a cemetery. Gaining permission to excavate a certain area of the cellar that was under the parking lot, Benio found a small, unknown room that contained fragments of pottery and some human bones. After giving the remains a proper burial, the ghost of Ludwig was at peace and no longer manifested at the General Wayne Inn.

Jim Webb and his partner, Guy Sileo, bought the inn in 1995. Webb was found murdered in his office on December 27, 1996, and Sileo was found guilty of the murder. Felicia Moyse, a twenty-year-old assistant chef, committed suicide on February 22, 1997. Some people felt that the place had added two more ghosts to its roster.

Others recalled that one of the General Wayne Inn's most frequent customers in 1839 would have found the growing ghostly and gory history of the place to be right up his alley. That guest was mystery writer Edgar Allan Poe, who scratched his initials on a window of the inn in 1843.

St. James Hotel, Cimarron, New Mexico

A glimpse of an old guest registry at the St. James Hotel reads like a "Who's Who of the Wild West": Billy the Kid, Pat Garrett, Bat Masterson, Black Jack Ketchum, Doc Holliday, Buffalo Bill Cody....

Almost any room in this 120-year-old hotel—a favorite of gunfighters in the 1880s—will produce an active spirit encounter. According to yellowed newspaper accounts, twenty-six people have died violently at the St. James, and the dining room coiling remains pockmarked with bullet holes. If you should decide to give the St. James a try, it would probably be best to avoid Room 18. Things got a little too wild in that room back in the 1880s, and the spirits there are too hostile and aggressive for most folks.

Bartenders and chefs in the hotel complain that food and crockery disappear from under their noses. Bottles and glasses float in the air and sometimes shatter in loud explosions.

"A lot of gunfighters checked into this old hotel," a bartender exclaimed. "But their spirits have never got around to checking out!"

The Dorrington Hotel, Dorrington, California

The ghost of Rebecca Dorrington walks at night in this hotel in the tiny High Sierra hamlet of Dorrington. The town itself was named for Rebecca, the Scottish bride of John Gardner, an 1850s homesteader who built the old hotel in 1852. Rebecca's eerie nocturnal repertoire consists of banging doors open and shut, flashing lights on and off, and shifting furniture about. Some guests have been "treated" to a ghostly reenactment of Rebecca's fatal tumble down a back stairwell in 1870.

The Brookdale Lodge in the Santa Cruz Mountains

The sprawling Brookdale Lodge (most recently known as the Brookdale Spa and Inn amidst a renovation process), built in 1924 in the Santa Cruz Mountains near Boulder Creek, California, was a popular hideaway for gangland kingpins in the 1930s. Later, the lodge was a favorite of film legends Marilyn Monroe, Joan Crawford, and Tyrone Power. The colorful inn, which features a brook running through the dining room, has a number of "cold spots," which indicate haunted areas. The most frequently sighted spirit entity is that of a small girl dressed very formally in 1940s-style clothing. The ghost is thought to be that of the five-year-old who drowned in the brook sometime in the late 1940s.

Hotel Monte Vista, Flagstaff, Arizona

The picturesque old Hotel Monte Vista provides a marvelous place for an overnight stay on the way to or from the Grand Canyon. Guests who stay there may encounter the "Phantom Bellboy," who knocks on doors and announces, "Room service," in a muffled voice. Others claim to have seen the wispy image of a woman strolling through an upstairs corridor.

HOTEL SAN CARLOS, PHOENIX, ARIZONA

Guests have complained about the noisy children in the halls. When they are informed that there are no children running about unattended, some annoyed patrons have set about trying to prove they aren't going crazy by catching the shouting, squealing, laughing kids who are disturbing their relaxation and sleep. Some frustrated guests who have nearly grabbed one of the little rascals have been astonished to see the child disappear before their eyes.

The only explanation that some investigators have offered for this phenomenon is the fact that the old Hotel San Carlos was built sometime in the late 1920s on the site of Phoenix's first adobe elementary school. Perhaps psychically sensitive guests are hearing and seeing the ghosts of schoolchildren from long ago.

HORTON GRAND HOTEL IN SAN DIEGO HOSTS GHOSTLY DANCES

There are so many ghosts at the historic old Horton Grand Hotel in San Diego that the entities often get together and hold dances. Shelly D., who

Even though the hotel was disassembled and moved to a new location in downtown San Diego, the Horton Grand Hotel maintains a healthy population of spirits who enjoy a good ballroom dance.

lived at the hotel for two years, claimed to have watched a group of fifteen to twenty ghosts dressed in the style of the 1890s have a dance in the third-floor ballroom.

It was only after she had watched them for a while that Shelly realized that there was something very strange about the costumed dancers. No one paid the slightest attention to her. Everyone appeared to ignore her when she spoke. Then she noticed that their eyes were eerie—kind of dark and hollow. The ghostly figures didn't seem to mind the intrusion of her physical presence. Shelly wondered if she was observing the re-creation of a scene that had once occurred in the hotel. She remembered that they swung their partners round and round and seemed to be having a great time.

Room 309 receives the most nominations for "most haunted" in the Horton Grand. Research has revealed that a gambler named Roger Whittaker was murdered in that room in the 1880s.

Dan Pearson, the owner of the Horton Grand, said that he first became aware that there were strange things happening in Room 309 when he brought workmen in to renovate it in 1986. Later, as Pearson walked by the room with a psychically talented friend, the man stopped suddenly and said, "There's something going on in that room! I feel it strongly!"

Three months later, Pearson said that a guest at the hotel staying in Room 309 found her young daughter carrying on an animated conversation with someone else in the room. "Don't you see him, Mommy?" the girl asked incredulously. "Don't you see the man in our room?"

Our son-in-law, John Tyree, a media specialist, was in San Diego a few years ago filming some of the unique architecture of various structures, when one of his technicians shared an experience when he stayed at the Horton Grand.

"He called the front desk to complain that the people above him were making too much noise, as if they were marching up and down the hall," John told us. "The front desk clerk responded, 'Sir, there is no floor above you. Perhaps you should have read the diary on the mantle.' The technician checked and found the diary filled with guest experiences with ghosts through the years at the Horton Grand."

HOTEL DEL CORONADO, SAN DIEGO, CALIFORNIA

In another of San Diego's haunted hotels, the Hotel del Coronado, our son-in-law and his crew were filming a convention. He said that one of his technicians reluctantly admitted that an invisible someone had brushed against him when no one was around. After they had completed filming the function they were assigned to cover, the entire crew heard strange booming noises coming from a balcony loft area where there was no living, visible person.

Haunted: Malevolent Ghosts, Night Terrors, and Threatening Phantoms

The famous Hotel del Coronado located on San Diego Bay opened in 1888. Four years later, the story goes, a woman named Kate Morgan killed herself there. Her spirit continues to haunt the hotel today.

Our son-in-law's technician may have brushed up against Kate Morgan, the Hotel del Coronado's principal resident ghost, who died of a gunshot wound to the head that was officially ruled a suicide. Kate's body was found in November 1892 on an exterior staircase leading to the beach.

Although most of the sightings of Kate have occurred on the beach and in hotel hallways, Room 3327, where Kate stayed, seems to be the center of most of the paranormal phenomena.

KING'S TAVERN, NATCHEZ, MISSISSIPPI

In the late 1700s, Madeline was the mistress of Richard King, the tavern's namesake, until she was murdered by his jealous wife. For over two hundred years, Madeline's restless and angry ghost has been held responsible for every squeak, rattle, and rap in the tavern. Patrons regularly report seeing Madeline's large portrait swing back and forth, and some have claimed to have seen the ghost of a slender woman who stands defiantly before them, her hands on her hips. To add to the color and allure of the haunted tavern, in the 1930s a woman's skeleton was found sealed in a brick fireplace with a jeweled dagger in her chest.

The only guest suite remaining in King's Tavern is on the third floor. After the restaurant section closes, the occupants of the room are left alone in the tavern with Madeline's ghost. According to the proprietors, many guests check in, but few remain to check out in the morning.

THE ROOSEVELT:
OUR FAVORITE HAUNTED HOTEL, LOS ANGELES, CALIFORNIA

We did snuggle a bit in the fabulous top-floor suite of the Hotel Roosevelt (now known as the Hollywood Roosevelt Hotel) in Los Angeles that Carole Lombard shared with Clark Gable, but the ghosts of the two stars of yesteryear would not be tempted to materialize and check out our smooching technique. Lombard's suite in the Hotel Roosevelt, with its elegant décor, is basically the way the ill-fated actress left it. The essence of romantic Hollywood is nowhere more powerful than this glamorous star's favorite hideaway. Numerous guests who have shared the romance of this suite have also experienced an encounter with the gorgeous ghost of Carole Lombard.

The third wife of actor Clark Gable, actress Carole Lombard died tragically in a 1942 airplane crash. Her ghost is said to haunt the Hollywood Roosevelt Hotel, where she and her husband had stayed.

We were not so fortunate, but we did "bump" into the ghost of Marilyn Monroe.

Monroe posed for her first print advertisement on the diving board of the Roosevelt's pool, and she stayed often at the hotel over the years, preferring a second-floor Cabana Room overlooking the pool. Her favorite mirror is on display in the lower elevator foyer, and numerous individuals have claimed to have seen Marilyn's sensuous image near—or superimposed over—their own when they stop to look in the reflecting glass.

In December 1990, while Sherry and I were in the lower elevator foyer taping a *Ghosts of Hollywood* segment for a Japanese television program, a hotel guest, curious as to what we were filming, stopped to watch the proceedings. Suddenly, he stepped briskly aside as if to avoid a collision with some unseen person and stifled a cry of surprise, which interrupted the scene that we were filming.

When the director asked the man what was wrong, he replied, somewhat shaken, "Didn't you see that blonde woman who just brushed by me? If I didn't know Marilyn Monroe was dead, I would have sworn it was her!"

As we quizzed him about his experience, he appeared only mildly interested when we explained that the full-length mirror in the foyer had once been a personal favorite of Marilyn Monroe. "But the woman who brushed by me was solid flesh and blood," he insisted. "She was no ghost!"

The man stalked off, a bit indignant, fixing us with an incredulous glare, when we, together with the director and the camera crew, tried to make him understand that there had been no rude woman visible to the rest of us in the foyer.

Many people claim to have seen the ghost of Marilyn Monroe in the first floor lobby mirror of the Roosevelt Hotel (Brad and Sherry Steiger are shown here with hotel staff employee Kelly Green at right).

Montgomery Clift lived at the hotel for three months during the final stages of filming *From Here to Eternity*. He would often pace the hall outside his ninth-floor apartment, rehearsing his lines, and sometimes practicing bugle calls— much to the consternation of nearby guests, who were trying to get some sleep.

Kelly Green, one of the personable staff members of the Roosevelt, told us of the dozens of guests who had heard Clift's bugle blowing long after his death in 1966. In November 1990, a witness to the ghostly bugle blasts had been interviewed for inclusion on our segment on Hollywood ghosts for *Entertainment Tonight*. In October 1992, Sherry and were asked to return to the hotel and to try to catch the ghost of Clift in the act for ourselves for new "Haunted Hollywood" segments that we would film for the 1992 Halloween edition of HBO's *World Entertainment Report*.

Of course we wanted to participate in the ghost hunt of Clift and his trumpet, but we tried to delay the shooting for a few days. We had been on the road, holding seminars from coast to coast, for two weeks. In addition, the night before the shooting was scheduled, we were lecturing at a local college that had been trying to obtain us as speakers for months. We found out in short order that postponing the scheduled filming was out of the question, so we accepted that "that was show business."

The night before filming, Kelly made arrangements to place us in the room next to Clift's haunted room on the ninth floor. It was our intention to film in the room early the next morning, so Sherry and I were disappointed to hear a variety of sounds coming from Clift's room, as if it may have been occupied by a family with children.

We couldn't imagine that the thoughtful Ms. Green would book guests—especially a family—in a room that we wished to utilize the next morning for filming, but we really didn't feel that we could complain. It was quite enough that she was making the room available for us to film the segment the next day.

Sherry and I went to bed sincerely hoping that the next-door guests would check out very early in the morning—a hope that we increasingly felt was in vain since our neighbors stayed up most of the night, moving noisily about their room. Perhaps it wasn't a family with children next door, for it certainly sounded like a party was in progress with little consideration for the neighbors.

Neither of us seasoned ghost hunters could suppress a small shiver that next morning when we learned that Ms. Green had indeed left orders at the desk for the Clift room to remain unoccupied for the convenience of our filming. The thumps and bumps that we had heard all night had been the ghost of Montgomery Clift and his circle of spooks welcoming us to his portion of Haunted Hollywood.

Later that day, Sherry recalled that she had been awakened sometime during the night by what she had thought at the time was one of the rambunctious kids next door blowing on a horn, but she had been too tired from the seminar that we had just completed at the Los Angeles area college for the eerie significance of the bugle blasts to register fully in her sleep-numbed consciousness.

Encountering Ghosts in Restored Scenes of the Past

Some fields, streams, homes, and other locales are so drenched in the emotions of hate, anger, lust, and bloody violence that it is difficult for the psychical researcher truly to ascertain if there are restless spirits that walk about seeking peace or if the psychic residue of extreme human passions have given birth to ghostly images that remain attached to the area. In other instances, terrible epidemics of pestilence and disease that claimed hundreds or thousands of lives may somehow have impressed indelible images of valiant doctors and nurses and their doomed patients on the environment.

Dogma has no place in the mental toolbox of the psychical researcher. From time to time, the investigator will encounter areas of the unknown that may incorporate many types of phenomena in a single haunting. Within the various manifestations of the general phenomena that we collectively term "ghosts," I believe that there are no spirits or multidimensional entities roaming in search of the Light, but, rather, the psychic-emotional residue left by powerful human emotions.

Although witnesses may perceive the scene of violence or intense emotion from the past as though they were seeing it occur in real time—and may even on occasion feel as if they were participating in the event—they cannot interact with the ghostly tableau, the phantom pageant, any more than they might interact with the actors they observe in dramas being enacted on their television screens. There is a mechanical kind of repetitive action that is observed when one perceives a haunting that is a result of psychic residue—that is, the ghostly figures perform the same acts, walk the same hallways, appear in the same rooms, night after night. While communication with the phantom forms may be attempted, in such hauntings no intelligent contact can be achieved—because there is no intelligence at work. Rather than the spirit of a deceased man or woman haunting a locale, what one is observing is a kind of psychic automaton, an animated image of the deceased caught in some imprinted memory pattern that will continue to repeat its captured moments until its energy eventually dissipates over time.

PEOPLE IN A MODEL T FORD APPEARED TO RESCUE HER

Virginia, a retired schoolteacher, wrote to tell of her strange experience on a late November day in northern Wisconsin. The sky was overcast with heavy snow clouds, the wind had reached gale force, and it was very cold. And then one of the tires on her old Buick blew out.

She fought the wheel and got the car off the road onto a crossroad about ten yards ahead. Then she walked back to the highway, hoping to flag down someone who could stop at the little town that she had whizzed through about five miles back and send a wrecker from a service station.

Fortunately, Virginia was wearing her old army field coat with the liner, but it was getting darker and colder, and she was steadily feeling more helpless. No one would stop to help her, and she didn't know what to do.

The driver of the Model T and his two passengers stopped to assist Virginia, whose car had broken down, but she declined their offer. Something about their strange, outdated dress made her wary that these were not ordinary people.

Then a voice in her head said, "You'd better pray!"

So she did.

Within about three minutes a Model T Ford without a top drove up and stopped. She described the three people in the antique car as "unbelievable." The driver had a beard and wore blue jeans and a denim jacket with an old brown fedora hat on his head. The young man in the back seat was dressed exactly the same and was lounging with one foot resting on the back of the front seat, a silly grin on his freckled face. His carefree attitude suggested that he thought he was riding in a Rolls Royce. The woman who was seated beside the driver wore a light cotton house dress and only a tattered brown shawl against the terrible cold.

"I couldn't understand how she could keep from shivering in the freezing wind," Virginia said. "In fact, all three of them acted as though they thought it was the middle of the summer."

The bizarre trio offered to give Virginia a ride to a service station, but she thanked them and explained that she did not wish to leave her car. The bearded man repeated his invitation, and the woman urged Virginia to get in the Model T and drive off with them.

When Virginia once again graciously refused their offer, they seemed very reluctant to leave without her, but they finally accepted her decision and began to edge the Model T back into traffic.

Virginia remembered that once the antique car got back into the traffic, it appeared to take off at over sixty miles an hour. "I stood there gazing after the strange trio, not believing what had just happened," she said. "Again that voice in my head said, 'You have been talking to angels.' Then, in the blinking of an eye, the Model T and its strange passengers had disappeared from sight."

Virginia had no more than a few minutes to deal with her remarkable encounter with the bizarre motorists when a wrecker pulled off the highway and parked in front of her car. Without a word to Virginia, the man got out of the truck and began to work on the flat tire.

She asked him how long he had lived in the area and if he happened to know the people who drove the Model T, but he didn't answer her. She went on to describe the occupants of the old car and how inappropriately they had been dressed against the bitter wind and cold. But the service attendant seemed unable to hear her—or at least he gave no sign that he did.

"When he finished, I asked him how much I owed him," Virginia said. "He looked at me strangely, as if he had no idea what I was talking about. I finally handed him a ten-dollar bill and told him to take it to his boss. He accepted the bill hesitantly, looking at it as if I had presented him with a great mystery. Finally he nodded, as if understanding the exchange at last, and said,

> S he went on to describe the occupants of the old car and how inappropriately they had been dressed against the bitter wind and cold.

'Oh, all right.' With those few words, I found out that he did possess the ability to speak. He got back into the wrecker, and with a wave of his hand—the first sign he had shown of friendliness—he drove away.

"It has now been many years since that strange experience," Virginia said, concluding her encounter with the unknown, "and I have often wondered if I had got into that old Model T with its mysterious passengers, would I, too, have disappeared along with them?

"If the out-of-place, inappropriately dressed, entities were angels, then I have decided that the truck driver who fixed my tire was also an angel. He couldn't have been sent to me by the first angels in the Model T because he couldn't have arrived on the scene so quickly. And that was probably why he didn't seem to know what I was talking about as I described the other three beings. He had been sent to help me by some other heavenly dispatcher."

THE DISAPPEARING COUPLE IN THE BLACK SEDAN

Mary of Portland, Oregon, said that she was driving east out of Bend on the Bend–Burns Highway early one morning: "The road is raised up somewhat—banked—from the desert and it is a long, easy slope down from Horse Ridge. I wasn't going very fast, just enjoying the drive, when I came up on a black sedan moving slowly. I hit my passing gear and zoomed past. As I passed, I looked in to see if there was anyone I knew in the sedan. There was just an older man and woman who looked back at me."

But when Mary glanced in her rearview mirror, just as soon as she had passed the black sedan, there was no car behind her. "The highway behind me was empty."

Mary had a frightening thought that the older couple had somehow gone over the bank, which, at that point, was several feet high.

"I came to a quick stop at the edge of the road and got out," she said. "I went to the back of my car and looked and looked, but I couldn't see the black sedan anywhere. There were no access roads around or any other cars around. Besides, the car was only out of my sight for a couple of seconds."

As Mary stood there looking around for some sign of the mysterious black sedan with the older couple inside, "a light breeze sprang up and blew across me—and I can tell you that the hairs on the back of my neck and my arms stood up. I jumped in my little car, locked all four doors, and got out of there. I was both frightened and puzzled. I guess I still am. I still get that creepy hair-rising-on-back-of-neck-and-arms feeling whenever I recall the car that disappeared and the breeze that sprang up out of nowhere."

THE OLD CHEVROLET SEDAN DISAPPEARED

Early on a Sunday evening in 1991, Max was driving with his family outside of Albany, New York, when he became impatient with the way in which an old car, which he guessed to be a 1941 Chevrolet sedan, was slowing traffic. Max figured that the car was going or coming to some antique auto show or rally and he wanted to be tolerant, but he was returning from a family outing at Lake George and he wanted to get home to do some paperwork.

"I had to be at work early the next morning with my presentation ready to go, and I had some factors that I needed to sharpen," Max said. "As I approached nearer to the Chevy, I was surprised that it didn't have those special license plates that owners of those old cars are supposed to display. I hated to be a jerk, but I really blasted my horn, something I usually don't do when following a slow-moving vehicle."

Max recalled that he could see the driver of the Chevy turn around and look at him with what appeared to be an expression of total shock.

"I expected an angry, hostile look, and maybe an obscene gesture or two, but this guy looked as if I had genuinely startled him," Max said. "He

A 1941 Chevy sedan much like the one pictured was driving near Albany, New York, when a witness watched it fade away into nothingness.

looked as though he had somehow imagined himself to be driving all alone on the highway."

Then, before the incredulous eyes of Max, his wife, and their three children, the old Chevrolet sedan in front of them began to fade away.

"It was as if it were some old photograph dissolving bit by bit before us, just fading away until there was nothing left to prove that it had ever been there," Max said. "The antique Chevy and its driver had completely disappeared in about thirty seconds."

THE SECRETARY FROM 1963
WHO STEPPED INTO AN OFFICE FROM 1915

On October 23, 1963, Mrs. Coleen Buterbaugh, secretary to Dr. Sam Dahl, dean of Nebraska Wesleyan College in Lincoln, Nebraska, was walking across the campus on an errand for her boss. At exactly 8:30 A.M., she entered the old C. C. White Building, which was used primarily as a music hall, and opened the door to the office of Dr. Tom McCourt, a visiting lecturer from Scotland.

She was struck at once by an almost overwhelming odor of musty air. When she had opened the door to the office, she had observed that both rooms were empty and that the windows were open. But now....

"I had the strange feeling that I was not in the office alone," she later told Rose Sipe of the Lincoln *Evening Journal*. "I looked up, and for what must have been just a few seconds, saw the figure of a woman, standing with her back to me, at a cabinet in the second office. She was reaching up into one of the drawers."

Mrs. Buterbaugh then noticed that she could no longer hear the babble of students in the outer hall as they passed from their classes. She had the eerie, other-worldly feeling that she had suddenly become isolated from present tense reality.

The woman, who appeared to be filing cards so industriously, was tall, slender, and dark-haired. Her clothing was of another period—a long-sleeved white shirt-waist and an ankle-length brown skirt.

Then Mrs. Buterbaugh felt another presence in the office ... that of a man sitting at the desk to her left. But as she turned around, there was no one there.

She gazed out the large window behind the desk, and the scenery seemed to be that of many years ago. "There were no streets," she recalled. "The new Willard Sorority House was not there. Nothing outside was modern."

By that time, she admitted that she was frightened and left the office.

> Then Mrs. Buterbaugh felt another presence in the office ... that of a man sitting at the desk to her left. But as she turned around, there was no one there.

Back at her desk in Dean Dahl's office, she tried to work, but her nervous and shaking fingers refused to obey her. She felt that she must tell her strange experience to someone.

Fortnately, Dean Dahl listened courteously and without comment to her eerie account, then asked her to accompany him to the office of Dr. Glenn Callan, chairman of the division of social sciences, who had been on the Wesleyan faculty for decades. Once again Mrs. Buterbaugh was fortunate to have a listener who heard her out and treated her account with respect.

Together with the aid of a number of old college yearbooks, Dr. Callan theorized that she had somehow "walked" into the office as it had been sometime in the 1920s. Cautiously piecing together a number of clues from her strange encounter and utilizing the yearbooks in the manner of police "mugbook," Dr. Callan and Mrs. Buterbaugh determined that she had seen the ghost of Miss Clara Mills, whose office it had been during that time. Miss Mills had come to Wesleyan as head of the theory department and as instructor in piano and music appreciation. She had been found dead in her office in the late 1930s.

In the 1915 yearbook, a picture of Miss Clara Mills bore the caption: "A daughter of the gods thou art, divinely tall and most divinely fair." The picture and the description, according to Mrs. Buterbaugh, matched the appearance of the tall, dark-haired woman that she had seen in the office.

Psychical researchers Gardner Murphy and H. L. Klemme were intrigued by Mrs. Buterbaugh's experience and employed hypnotic time regression as a means of eliciting further details of her remarkable paranormal encounter.

While in the state of hypnotic regression, she was once again stopped short after entering the office by a very musty, disagreeable odor. As soon as she was stopped by the odor, everything became "deathly quiet." Something drew her eyes to the cabinet along the wall in the next room: "And there she was. She had her back to me, reaching up into one of the shelves of the cabinet with her right hand, standing perfectly still."

In an interview, Dr. Stanley Krippner noted that the forty-one-year-old Coleen Buterbaugh had recalled having had a number of *déjà vu* experiences in her lifetime. "[Such a history of *déjà vu* experiences and predormital sleep paralysis] may have made her susceptible to an episode in which she left the 'here and now' and 'plunged into the past.' The transition from one state of consciousness to another is often favorable to the occurrence of paranormal phenomena, as this case demonstrates."

A FLOATING WHITE MIST IN THE LAGUNA CREEK WETLANDS

By Paul Dale Roberts, HPI Esoteric Detective

In my neighborhood, they know I am a ghost hunter, monster hunter, and UFO hunter. One day a bunch of high school kids came knocking on my

They saw a floating, misty orb in the midst of the Laguna Creek Wetlands in California, which Roberts took as possible evidence of a spirit.

door, and they told me that while partying late at night in the Laguna Creek Wetlands, they saw a floating white mist in the grasslands and heard a small girl's whimpering cries. One of the girls in the group passed out during this scary ordeal.

When I wrote an article about the possible haunting of the wetlands, Manteca Paranormal Shadow Force contacted me and wanted to conduct their own investigation. They obtained orb pictures at the clump of eucalyptus trees, and at the Lee/Wightman Site that was a blacksmith shop in 1865, they obtained an EVP (electronic voice phenomenon) of a horse neighing. Possible residual haunting EVP? It must be, because there are no horses in this area.

So on this night, my HPI Laguna Creek Wetlands Discovery Task Force investigated the floating white mist of the Laguna Creek Wetlands and the giant salamander of the Laguna Creek Wetlands. I was prepared for the giant salamander with night vision goggles in hand.

We were only a few minutes into the investigation when something very strange happened. One of the investigators passed out. This investigator is very healthy and strong with no medical conditions, but for some odd reason the investigator passed out on the trail.

When the investigator revived, he acted as if he were experiencing possession and blurting out strange remarks. I was told that this investigator acted as if he were in a trance before passing out. I am not a medical doctor and cannot determine if this situation was paranormal in nature.

We had to call the investigation off and get the investigator back to Judy's home for his own safety. After the investigator left the Wetlands area, he was back to normal and was unaware that he had passed out and blurted out those strange remarks.

The Wetlands warrants further investigation. One of the theories on the floating white mist and the little girl's whimpering cries is that possibly back in the 1800s a female victim of smallpox was taken to this clump of eucalyptus trees for its medical value and properties.

Eucalyptus is known to open up the lungs and encourages breathing by increasing oxygen in the cells. It also helps to open clogged nasal passages and bronchial congestion. It also kills all types of bacteria and viruses. This multilayered action makes eucalyptus one of the most valued remedies of cold and the flu.

So perhaps—and it's just theory—a young female child was brought to this clump of eucalyptus trees. Her family was trying to save her life, and she may have died on those very grounds in the Wetlands.

AN APPARITION OF A STALWART WARRIOR RACES TRAINS

For decades, ever since the 1940s, those who make the night journey from Minneapolis, Minnesota, to Butte, Montana, have claimed that they have sighted an apparition of a brightly painted Indian brave on his spirited mount. The warrior bends low over the flying black mane of his horse and looks neither to the right nor to the left.

A salesman claimed to have seen the brave and his stalwart horse five or six times in different parts of the Dakotas. "They seem to be solid flesh, but there's a kind of shimmering around them. It's like watching a strip of really old movie film being projected onto the prairie," he explained.

Railroad brakemen, engineers, and construction crews in the Dakotas and Wyoming have spoken of the phantom Sioux warrior and his determined race with the white man's iron horses.

"They couldn't beat the trains when they were alive," said one old-timer, who knew the legend behind the spectral races run by the brave and his horse, "but they seem to have picked up some speed on their way to the happy hunting grounds."

BOW-LEGGED BRIGHAM:
THE GHOST OF AMADOR CENTRAL RAILROAD

Paul Dale Roberts passes on a story from Danielle M. of Jackson, California. She said that she saw a bowlegged man walking along the railroad tracks between the towns of Ione and Martell near Jackson, on August 27, 2016, around 8:00 P.M. Danielle kept her eye on him because she thought that he was acting very suspiciously. The bowlegged man kept looking at the railroad tracks as if he were going to place something on the tracks that would cause a train to derail. As she watched the curious individual, he suddenly disappeared, and Danielle realized that she had been watching a ghost.

Later, Danielle told Roberts this story on the Sacramento Haunted Paranormal Hotline. It was odd to receive her call because two years ago I received a report from Douglas C. in Sonora, who told me that he had once watched a bowlegged man walking along the same area of railroad tracks.

The Amador Central Railroad is a track just shy of 12 miles (19 kilometers) in length near Jackson, California. Along the tracks wanders the spirit of the hobo Bowleg Brigham.

When he told his grandmother of the strange individual, she told him that he had seen the ghost of Bowleg Brigham.

According to Douglas's grandmother, Bowleg Brigham had been an outlaw hobo who had ridden the Amador Central Railroad in 1904. Bowleg was a good friend of Arizona Jack, and they had committed some petty thefts in Wagon Bed Spring, Kansas Territory. When Arizona Jack was lynched for a murder that he had committed during a robbery, Bowleg Brigham decided that it was time to abandon a life of crime and live out the rest of his life as a hobo. His last act of theft occurred when he stole a small satchel of gold and hid it along the railroad tracks in Jackson. If you see Bowleg Brigham walking around the tracks near Ione and Martell, he is still looking for his gold cache.

GHOST TRAIN OF UTAH

In the summer of 1982, the Ryan family was camping out between Green River and Springville, Utah, when they watched a slow-moving train on the nearby tracks. There was no sound from the train, which the family thought was odd.

As they watched the silent train move along the tracks, the air around the train seemed to gyrate. Glare from the sun seemed to bounce off the whirling air around the train, and in the blink of the eye, the train was no longer there. The Ryans were unanimous in their feeling that they had witnessed either a ghost train or some kind of mirage.

GHOSTLY MINERS STILL SEEK WEALTH IN SILVER CLIFF

In the little town of Silver Cliff, in the Wet Mountain Valley of Colorado, ghost lights have been seen in the local cemetery since 1880. The lights can never be approached for a close-up look. As soon as anyone comes too near, the lights disappear, only to pop up again in another section of the cemetery.

Local folklore has it that the lights were first seen by a group of miners passing by the cemetery. When they saw the flickering blue lights over the gravestones, they left the vicinity in a hurry. Since then, generations of residents of Custer County have observed the lights. According to the old stories, the cemetery had become the final resting place for many miners who lost their lives while digging for precious ores. The flickering lights of the graveyard resemble the little lights worn on the miners' caps, and they belong to the restless souls of the miners, who still search for the silver they never found.

In 1880, Silver Cliff boasted a population of 5,087; today it has only a couple hundred inhabitants and has almost become a ghost town. The story of

Silver Cliff, Colorado, was once a bustling silver mining town, but its population has dwindled to fewer than six hundred residents today, not counting the ghosts.

Haunted: Malevolent Ghosts, Night Terrors, and Threatening Phantoms

the ghost lights of Silver Cliff first reached public attention in the spring of 1956, when an article about the mystery appeared in the *Wet Mountain Tribune*. Over a decade later, on August 20, 1967, the *New York Times* carried a story on the phenomenon.

When some observers of the spook lights noted that the bluish-colored illumination could not be seen as clearly on the sandstone markers, many spectators became convinced that the lights were only a reflection of house-lights in the valley. However, Custer County judge August Menzel recounted for the*New York Times* the night that everyone in Silver Cliff and nearby Westcliffe shut off their lights. Even the street lights were turned off, "but the graveyard lights still danced."

Other rational thinkers have believed the Silver Cliff ghost lights to be reflections from the stars. Yet the lights are just as clear on starless, moonless nights. Some have tried to prove that the lights are caused by phosphorescing ore and glowing wood, but the darker the night the brighter the lights. It was suggested that radioactive ores were causing the flickering lights, but geiger counters were employed to cover the entire area, and no radioactivity was discovered.

KNIGHTS FERRY IS A GREAT GHOST HUNTING SPOT

If you enjoy ghost hunting, a favorite spot for Northern California ghost hunters is Knights Ferry, an unincorporated historic community in Stanislaus County, California. Nestled in the foothills of the Sierra Nevada, it is about 40 miles east of Modesto on the Stanislaus River. The Williams Ranch, a California landmark near the town, was one of many filming locations for the television series *Bonanza* and *Little House on the Prairie*. It is home to the Knights Ferry Bridge, which at 330 ft (100 m) is the longest covered bridge west of the Mississippi.

In 1849, Dr. William Knight and John C. Frémont found this place to be a reasonably good river crossing and established a ferry boat at this location. The ferry boat was used by many citizens involved in the California Gold Rush. The ferry boat was a success, and Dr. Knight teamed up with Captain James Vantine to build a hotel and trading post near the crossing.

There is some confusion about how Knight died. Some sources say that on November 9, 1849, Knight was killed in a gunfight on the town's main street. Knight's family believes Knight was stabbed to death in his bed and was buried near the gate of John Dent's home. (John Dent was the brother-in-law of Ulysses S. Grant, who would become U.S. president twenty years later. In fact, in 1852, when he was an army captain in Benicia and Eureka, Grant visited Knights Ferry.)

Some of the hauntings at Knights Ferry are as follows:

- *Abraham Schell House*—This house is built with sandstone. Abraham Schell was the owner of Rancho del Rio Estanislao. There have been reports that Schell is sometimes seen at the doorway of his sandstone home. Sometimes voices are heard through the house. I wonder if the sandstone is an absorber of voice energy from the past and that is why voices can sometimes be heard.

- *Lewis Dent House*—This house was built in 1851 and is the oldest home in the community. While Eugenia Davis was visiting the home, she said that she saw a family sitting at a table, preparing to eat. They were in 1800s garb. As she watched the family, thinking they were actors, the family disappeared in front of her eyes.

- *Knights Ferry Community Church*—Some tourists claim that they have heard a congregation singing when there was no one in the church. This has happened on three separate occasions and usually happens when the sun is setting. The church was built in 1890. The church boasts the original pews, altar, and upper windows. The ghosts of this church are probably residual and nonintelligent.

- *General Store*—Former Wells Fargo agent George Valpey once owned this store. The store was built in 1852 by Albert Wellington Moulton and O. C. Drew. Anuradha Khatri and his wife said they saw a little boy holding a brown cloth bag and running. The little boy ran through a wooden pole as if it were not there. Anuradha and his wife knew they saw a ghost.

- *Millers Hall*—This hall has been around since 1863. At one time the building housed a restaurant and a pool hall/poker parlor on the first floor and a dance hall on the second floor. Workers at this hall claim they have heard music and the sound of shuffling feet and laughter. This sounds like the residual effects of the dance hall, and the sounds of people dancing are replayed over and over again in the atmosphere. They are most likely nonintelligent ghosts.

- *Outlaw Justin "Knights Ferry Kid" Anjo*—Anjo was a California outlaw who was lynched after he murdered a man in cold blood. The Kid's ghost has been sighted by numerous visitors to Knight Ferry, and EVP of his murderous shouts have been made by different ghost investigation teams.

People Who Communicate with Ghosts

In the early summer months of 1972, I was driving across the country with my friend and associate Glenn McWane interviewing Native American shamans with some interesting spirit mediums thrown into the mix. When we arrived in Arizona, we discussed the news that Rev. Kingdon Brown had recently begun to move his Church of Essential Science headquarters from Detroit, Michigan, to Scottsdale, and we decided to make an appointment with the pleasant young man, who had already authored two popular books, *The Power of Psychic Awareness* and *Cosmosis: The Technique and Its Use in Daily Living*.

I was just stepping into Rev. Brown's temporary office on May 27, 1972, when I heard a voice as clear as any utterance of human speech that I had ever heard in my life: "Uncle Frosty just died."

My Uncle Frosty—or Uncle Irwin, as I most often addressed him because of the insistence of Grandma Dina's aristocratic manners—was the family patriarch. He stood six-feet-four and to this day had the broadest shoulders that I have ever seen. He was my father's big brother in so many ways, and he was important in my life.

It had been Uncle Frosty who held my bleeding body in the backseat of the car when my father and Doc Newman made the desperate 120-mile trip to the hospital and the surgeon who would save my life after my accident. It was he who I witnessed toss five brawlers aside as if they were rag dolls when they threatened to disrupt the parade at the county fair. It was he who demanded that every visit to his home included physical tests of strength. Although it took me until I was a junior in college to make him let out a painful yelp while we were wrist wrestling, the smile of approval he gave me will remain always fresh in my memory.

So how could Uncle Frosty have died? What was this ominous voice that so startled me? Uncle Frosty was only seventy-two. If he was really not immortal, he would live at least until he was 120.

However, during my interview with Rev. Brown, troubled thoughts that the mysterious voice may have spoken true kept interrupting my focus. I was now thirty-six-years old, and in spite of my love for my uncle, we didn't keep in touch the way we did when I was a kid. And I really had no idea if my uncle was playing golf at a favorite back home in Iowa, if he was fishing in Canada, or if he was hunting mountain sheep in Alaska. To me, he was the last of the Vikings.

As soon as I got back to my hotel, I called home. My mother told me that Uncle Frosty had died that morning.

That spectral voice had been correct. It had been as if some benevolent spirit being had sought to prepare me for the sad news.

The messenger from the Other Side had fulfilled its assignment, and it had left me with questions that puzzle me still: Can one pick up psychic news concerning one's personal life and loved ones simply by entering the home of someone who is psychically attuned? And was the spirit of Uncle Frosty aware that his only nephew was being notified of his death?

DEFINING A GHOST CAN BE A VERY TRICKY ENDEAVOR

As our friend author-cryptologist-phenomenologist Paul Bartholomew pointed out when he answered our query—"What Is a Ghost, Really?"—the task of defining what a ghost is can be a very tricky endeavor. As Paul said....

There may be no easy answer. The topic is often wrapped in spiritualism and layered in pseudoscience, forming a complicated supernatural riddle.

Many times it can be a case of semantics. One person's terrifying apparition may be another person's demon. As paradigms shift and personal opinions become more refined, being respectful of various cultural perspectives is essential in achieving an accurate understanding of what a ghost really is.

As to be expected when dealing with a common human experience, ghosts may manifest in many forms. While apparitions are witnessed usually leaving no real evidence behind, other forms of ghosts, like poltergeists, have been well documented. It no longer becomes a matter of physical evidence; it becomes a matter of what you accept as physical evidence.

Other times there are residual hauntings in which the ghost or apparition appears to be re-creating the same event over and over. No communication takes place. It is almost like watching a movie and the apparition seems trapped in time and space.

While séances are attempts to directly communicate with the departed, they are usually couched in spiritualism and largely reflect the medium conducting the ceremony. Often the communication is subjective and inconclusive. However, experimentation with electronic voice phenomena (EVP) has yielded interesting results. By using a tape recorder, investigators claim to capture voices on tape, which they can hear when playing the tape back. Sometimes a message is communicated.

Even more intriguing are cases in which people are contacted by phone only to find out later that the person they were talking with had died hours before. Usually the call is brief, the voice is recognized, and the communication short and basic.

Paul Bartholomew points to the haunted Skene Mansion.

While many researchers use a scientific approach to study ghosts, Connecticut's Lorraine Warren and her late husband, Ed, approached it theologically. After decades of investigations, the Warrens worked on numerous high-profile cases. Many times, negative energies had attached themselves to families, houses, and artifacts, thus yielding demonic infestations.

Founding the New England Society for Psychical Research (NESPRA) in 1952, the Warrens traveled the world looking for a way to assist distraught families. Relying on their Roman Catholic faith, they arranged several exorcisms and were sometimes able to cleanse the homes of evil presences. While the Warrens have had many critics over the years, they have many supporters as well. The families who had nowhere to turn were often thankful for their guidance.

To further muddy the waters, Hollywood has been responsible for exaggerating known cases and distorting facts. It has created a cottage industry of theatrical falsehoods that confuse and create fraudulent views of what a ghost and haunting are really like. Hit movies like *The Conjuring* or *Annabelle* are loosely based on the Warrens' investigations, but they are hardly documentaries.

NESPRA's Tony Spera recently commented on this at a gathering in Monroe, Connecticut: "Hollywood is mostly dramatic license. They made up a lot of stuff. Because no matter how dangerous or how scary something is they

Tony Spera of the New England Society for Psychical Research has asserted that most of the events described in the horror film *The Conjuring* are true.

want to make it even more. They want to make sure it is a success. But I can tell you this, *The Conjuring* is 85 percent real."

Experience is vital in the comprehension of the paranormal in general. Researchers who have spent years studying these enigmas often note patterns between various phenomena. UFOs, ghosts, and cryptozoological creatures often share characteristics. For instance, they seem to appear and disappear without explanation. They often yield physical evidence, yet remain elusive to pure scientific scrutiny. Legendary UFO expert and astronomer Dr. J. Allen Hynek theorized about parallel realities and alternate planes of existence.

With recent discoveries of dark matter and advances in studies of quantum physics, we appear to be getting closer to understanding the realities and implications of parapsychology. Hopefully that will help us further define what a ghost really is.

In its simplest form, the ghost encounter is a common human experience that on occasion can be measured and recorded, yielding circumstantial and anecdotal evidence. There may be an unknown energy involved that manifests in various forms and can be perceived by the human mind. It is sometimes positive, sometimes negative, sometimes indifferent, but always fascinating, since it relates to our common human psyche.

THE MYSTERY OF MEDIUMSHIP

Mediums most often relay messages from the other side through the agency of a spirit control or spirit guide, an entity who claims to have lived on Earth and acquired certain skills, knowledge, and wisdom before its own physical death. The concept of a spirit guide dates back to antiquity, and serious scholars and researchers have been asking the same question for hundreds of years: Is this alleged entity, who claims to speak through the medium, really a spirit, or is it the voice of the medium's subconscious?

Some mediums would probably concede that the action of the subjective mind is not entirely eliminated during a trance and the arrival of the spirit control, but from their viewpoint their subconscious is taken over by the guide. An aspect of mediumistic phenomena on which both psychical researchers and mediums will be likely to agree is that there is an intelligence that directs and controls them. Another area of agreement would probably be that this intelligence is human. Once again, the area of dispute would be whether that human intelligence issues from the living or from the dead. Interestingly, spirit communication still requires both a soul and a body—the soul of an alleged deceased human personality and the physical body of the medium.

THE REMARKABLE MEDIUMSHIP OF CLARISA BERNHARDT

While some of our fellow researchers are not enthusiastic about the use of mediums in pursuing an answer to "what are ghosts?" our dear friend Clarisa Bernhardt is the only psychic-medium in contemporary times to predict an earthquake to the day, the location, the magnitude, and even to the *minute* of the event.

The astonishing prediction was made on her radio show *Exploration* and referred exactly to the 1974 Thanksgiving Day quake in San Jose, California. The forecast was also acknowledged and documented in local newspapers and with police departments. As a result, the U.S. Geological Survey in Denver set up a specific program that would be designed to investigate the potential of earthquake prediction. Of some 200 participants in the program, Clarisa was the only one who demonstrated a significant consistency in her forecasts. Through her psi ability, she was able not only to beat out the other seers but the scientists and computers as well.

Of some 200 participants in the program, Clarisa was the only one who demonstrated a significant consistency in her forecasts.

Clarisa has demonstrated an additional use of ESP by finding lost persons and by cooperating with law enforcement as a psychic sleuth. She is regularly consulted by business executives who seek her assistance in making top-level decisions; in addition, she is an extremely gifted medium.

CLARISA TALKS ABOUT MEDIUMSHIP AND GHOSTS

Although many people seem to strongly ignore the subject of ghosts or spirits because of the "undemocratic way" of *not everyone* apparently being able to see them, ghosts can be the subject of heated discussions in many circles or family situations. However, to many, including myself because of personal experiences, it seems ghosts and spirits do exist and, on occasion, can be most helpful.

The subject of ghosts can include both scary and meaningful moments since ghosts are not limited to Halloween. Sometimes when the body wears out, so to speak, and only the ghostly body or spirit body is left, sadly the "ghost" body does not know where to go or what to do, and many spirits become stuck in this reality.

In our more open-minded modern times, important research is being conducted on consciousness and awareness in the afterlife as well as other related subjects. Highly sensitive cameras are now available, and many experts feel that using an infrared camera is a great way to film ghosts.

However, should you have a personal encounter with a ghost or a spirit of someone you know, hold on to your emotions, for they may have an important message that could be helpful to you or they may need your helpful prayers. It is important to remember that prayers and meditations of light do make a difference.

If you have concern, for example, about purchasing a house or moving into an apartment, it is good to have a blessing in the event there were difficult vibrations that may have occurred that attract scary ghostly moments. However, many times the appearance of a ghost or spirit is simply to allow a friend or loved one to know they are okay. And here is an example.

Many years ago, clients who had a farm near Byers, Texas, requested that I assist them in finding out what might be causing Julie, their three-year-old daughter, to cry and be so frightened at night. It seemed that the child felt someone was in her bedroom looking at her as she tried to go to sleep. Every night when it was her bedtime, the young girl pointed towards the bedroom closet across from her bed and started crying loudly, which was most upsetting for everyone. Her parents, whom I will refer to as John and Nellie, simply did not know what to do to resolve their concern. As a result, they contacted me as I was visiting my family in nearby Wichita Falls.

I arrived at their home on a late autumn afternoon, a time of the year when the countryside is especially lovely. I was eager to get the communication underway.

After greeting my clients, who were also longtime friends, I sat with them in their dining room, where they offered me a most comfortable Texas-sized chair. Then I began to proceed with the spiritual contact, which included a prayer of protection for myself and for all.

I comfortably asked whomever's spirit had been in the young daughter's room at night to please communicate so that we might learn about why the child was becoming so upset.

After my first two requests, there was no answer—just silence.

Psychic and medium Clarisa Bernhardt accurately predicted that an earthquake would hit San Jose, California, in 1974. She has also channeled the spirits of the deceased.

Then suddenly there was a startling crash in the short hallway from the dining area where we were seated. Everyone jumped, which was no surprise as we were so focused on this important effort to communicate with an invited spirit who might give us an answer. However, it was good to get some response, especially since there was no object or furniture in the hallway to have caused the resounding noise that had occurred.

And then I said to the spirit, "Who are you? The child's parents want you to leave now, as you are causing the child to be unable to go to sleep at night. Shame on you. Leave."

Then I heard a clear, loud response that boomed "I ain't a-gon-na."

Staying focused, I delivered the message to Julia's parents and inquired of their knowledge of knowing anyone who spoke in that manner or style.

Julie's mother, Nellie, replied with surprise that it had to be the paternal grandmother of the baby, who had died a few months after Julie was born. John instantly agreed that that was the way his mother spoke, using the word "ain't," which she always used to emphasize when she did not want to do something.

As the spirit communication continued, the grandmother explained that she was so happy about Julie's birth and that after she had passed away, she had a choice to leave the earth dimension, but she *chose* to stay earthbound for a while as she wanted to watch Julie grow up.

Julie's parents, John and Nellie, were delighted, but understandably remained concerned about Julie's reaction to the night visitor.

So then I made sure that the grandmother who had chosen to remain earthbound be aware of the family's ongoing love for her and that she, the grandmother now in spirit, was indeed welcome to be around and watch Julie grow up.

I also emphasized to the ghost of the grandmother that the scary moments that Julie had been experiencing because of her visitations must stop immediately. I received the grandmother's enthusiastic communication that she understood and that they would not have to worry.

Just as the contact with her was about to end happily with an agreement of wonderful harmony, I wanted something more. I wanted stronger proof to show without a doubt that I had actually made a definite spiritual contact with the spirit of Julie's grandmother so there could be *no* doubt.

With the family still seated, I spoke once again to the ghostly presence of Julie's grandmother, asking if there was something significant she could tell me that could prove beyond a doubt there had been this communication with her.

To everyone's further delight (especially mine), she replied that there was a storm cellar in which they used to hide from severe Texas storms and tornado alerts. The ghostly presence of the grandmother answered me that *no one* knew it, but some time back, she had placed a beautiful silver kerosene lamp in the wall of the storm cellar on the third step up from the floor. She had meant to tell her family before she passed, but had not.

John and Nellie screamed with delight. John jumped up from the table and said, "Let's go get that lamp!"

Nellie and I eagerly joined him as we went out through the back door to the storm cellar that was conveniently located between their house and the barn. He lifted open the wooden and metal siding door that was the entry to the storm cellar below. John used his large flashlight to help us descend on the wooden, but awkwardly small steps. Nellie was quickly behind him, but I only went part way down so as not to be in the way.

John then quickly dug into the right side of the storm cellar stair wall and at first found nothing. He then decided to try on the left side. Standing on the third step up from the cellar floor, his shovel quickly dug into the cellar stair wall. After about a foot he knew he had found something. He yelled as loudly as he could. In a clear plastic bag was the lamp the ghostly grandmother had told me about in the earlier spiritual communication. A very exciting moment for everyone!

Some months later I heard from Nellie, who enthusiastically told me that there had been no more disturbing ghostly visitations in Julie's bedroom.

The child was getting a full night's sleep, for which they were most thankful.

She added that the grandmother's storm cellar silver kerosene lamp polished up beautifully, and she and John had put it in a very special place to share the story with friends who visited. She added that the silver lamp would also serve as a reminder of the joy they had received from the ghostly presence of the grandmother's visit and how something that at first had been so frightening became so beautiful.

> In a clear plastic bag was the lamp the ghostly grandmother had told me about in the earlier spiritual communication.

CHANNELING SPIRIT TEACHINGS TO THE MASSES

In the 1970s, after the publication of Jane Roberts's books *The Seth Material* and *Seth Speaks*, "channeling" became a more popular name for mediumship, and it remains so to the present day. Jane Roberts received contact with an entity named Seth after undergoing a trance state while Robert Butts, her husband, recorded the thought, ideas, and concepts communicated by the spirit in notebooks. The material dictated by Seth was very literate and provocative, and especially well-suited to a generation of maturing Sixties' flower children and baby boomers. It wasn't long before Seth discussion groups around the nation were celebrating such concepts as the following: 1) We all create our own reality; 2) Our point of power lies in the present; and 3) We are all gods couched in "creaturehood." Nor was it long before "channelers" were emerging in large numbers throughout the land, and individuals such as Jach Pursel, Kevin Ryerson, and J. Z. Knight had attained national and international celebrity status.

Perhaps in the mind of the New Age channelers, the designation of "mediums" conjured up images of the traditional darkened séance parlors and ectoplasmic spirit guides, imagery that had become unacceptable to the modern spirit communicator, who more often relays messages from guides and master teachers in the full light of a platform setting or a television studio and seldom claims to materialize anything other than an engaging performance for the assembled audience.

MEDIUMS OF NOTE

Since this is a book about ghosts and spirits, it seemed most appropriate to me to include brief sketches of the lives of some extraordinary men and women who endured the most exacting tests of the validity of their preternatural prowess that the most famous scientists of their day could devise. I also wished to include these biographies to educate those who choose to begin the study of the paranormal with at least some information about who these unique individuals were and their place in the history of psychical research.

Daniel Dunglas Home (1833–1886)

The clientele of Daniel Dunglas Home was one of the most exclusive that ever gathered around any one medium: Elizabeth Barrett Browning, Mark Twain, Napoleon III, the Empress Eugénie, Leo Tolstoy, and many other notables on both sides of the Atlantic. Home was poked and probed and examined by dozens of scientists, and he graciously submitted to hundreds of tests by psychical researchers. No skeptical investigator ever succeeded in exposing him, and two of the most prestigious scientists of the day, Sir William Crookes and Dr. Robert Hare, stated that, in their opinion, the phenomena manifested by Home were genuine. Home conducted over 1,500 séances and produced phenomena at all times, under all manner of conditions, in broad daylight, under artificial lighting, indoors, outdoors, in private homes, in hotel rooms, and on public lecture platforms.

Born near Edinburgh, Scotland, on March 20, 1833, Home was said to have been rocked in his cradle by unseen entities. Daniel's mother was also said to have had the gift of "second sight," as clairvoyance was called in those

Daniel Dunglas Home was a Scottish medium whose detractors never managed to prove he was faking any of his spiritual feats.

days. Mrs. Mary McNeal Cook, an aunt who adopted Home when he was but a year old, began noticing clairvoyant impressions from the child almost as soon as he began to speak. At the age of four he began having visions that proved to be accurate.

Home was a frail child who contracted tuberculosis at an early age. His early childhood was marked by long periods of convalescence. When he was nine, his aunt and uncle moved to the United States, where they settled in Greeneville, Connecticut.

Home was seventeen when the physical phenomena that was to direct the course of his life began to occur around him. By the early 1850s, his fame had spread, and the teenager was soon beleaguered by scientists, clergymen, and medical doctors, each seeking to be the first to explain his mysterious talents. Home's powers began to grow stronger, and numerous individuals testified to instantaneous healings accomplished by the young medium. At the same time, Daniel displayed an amazing ability to divine the future and to clairvoyantly determine happenings at great distances.

In 1852, when, at the age of nineteen, he made his first trip to New York, Home was eagerly received by those who had been awaiting an opportunity to see firsthand the various wonders that had been attributed to the youthful medium. Dr. Robert Hare, professor emeritus of chemistry at the University of Pennsylvania, attested to the absolute authenticity of Home's strange talents, but the American Association for the Advancement of Science refused to hear the report of its distinguished member.

In 1855, Daniel D. Home set out for England and France. The overseas press had been awaiting the medium's arrival, and so had the greatest hostesses of London society. Home soon captivated England. Those who attended his séances could expect to see spirit lights, to hear raps and the voices of disembodied spirits, and perhaps even to experience the thrill of being lifted into the air by unseen hands.

In Florence, Italy, Home is reported to have caused a grand piano at which the Countess Orsini was seated to rise into the air and to remain levitated until she had completed

> Home ... demonstrated his dramatic control of unseen forces before the courts of Napoleon III, Empress Eugénie, and Prince Murat, and won hundreds of new supporters.

the musical number that she had been playing. Home's mediumship was witnessed by such members of the aristocracy as Prince Murat, Napoleon III, and the Empress Eugénie. During one séance, Napoleon Bonaparte appeared and signed his name, and his grandson attested to its authenticity. The young medium's demonstrations in Florence were of such a dramatic nature that frightened whispers began to circulate that Home was one of Satan's own. Public fervor began to get so heated that Home was attacked and wounded by an unknown assailant.

As he lay in pain recovering from his wound, the spirits informed him that they would remove his powers for a period of one year, beginning on February 10, 1856.

The twenty-three-year-old medium traveled to Rome, where he sought consolation in the Roman Catholic Church, and for a time he considered entering a monastery. The relationship was terminated at the stroke of midnight on February 10, 1857, when Daniel's bedstead resounded with hearty spirit raps and a voice from the other side announced the return of his powers of mediumship.

When Home reappeared on the scene, his elite clientele immediately restored him to celebrity status. He demonstrated his dramatic control of unseen forces before the courts of Napoleon III, Empress Eugénie, and Prince Murat, and won hundreds of new supporters.

Back in Rome, he married Alexandrina, the wealthy sister-in-law of a Russian nobleman. Alexandre Dumas, the famous French novelist, was Home's best man.

It was in the presence of the great Russian novelist Count Aleksey Tolstoy that Home first produced the phenomenon with which he has come to be most commonly associated in the annals of psychical research. In full view of several sitters and with Tolstoy's hands firmly clasping his feet, Home levitated from his chair until he was seen floating above the heads of the members of the séance circle.

Home's wife died in London in 1862. He decided to return to Rome, but he was ordered to leave Italy on the charge of sorcery. Home was forced to leave the country and he returned to Britain in 1864.

The single event in Home's remarkable psychic career that is most remembered occurred on the evening of December 13, 1868, when he was seen to float out of the window of a third-floor home in Ashley House and return through another window to rejoin the men who witnessed the extraordinary act of levitation. Among those who observed the feat were Captain Wynne, the Earl of Dunraven, and the Earl of Crawford, all men of solid character and integrity.

The press was demanding a scientific investigation of such remarkable feats, and Sir William Crookes seemed to be the scientist most likely to succeed in revealing Home's alleged wonders, if hoaxster he be. Crookes, a member of the Royal Society, was a brilliant chemist and physicist, inventor of the x-ray tube, and a scientist eager to test the medium under the strictest of laboratory conditions. Home did not shrink from the challenge. On the contrary, he appeared as eager as Sir William to enter into a full series of experiments and tests.

Crookes found that Home's strange talents were strong enough to resist the antagonistic influence of the laboratory. In one of his reports on the medium, Sir William stated that he was prepared to attest that the phenomena that he had witnessed "are so extraordinary and so directly oppose the most firmly rooted articles of scientific belief—[such as] ... the ubiquity and invariable action of gravitation—that even now, on recalling the details of what I witnessed, there is an antagonism in my mind between reason, which pronounces it to be scientifically impossible, and the consciousness that my senses both of touch and sight—and these corroborated, as they were, by the senses of all who were present—are not lying witnesses when they testify against my preconceptions."

Sir William took extensive notes on all phases of Home's abilities, and a number of his reports were published in the *Quarterly Journal of Science*. However, his colleagues in the Royal Society of Science were immensely disappointed in his affirmation that the phenomena produced by Home were genuine. Most of the members of the prestigious society of scientists had long before made up their minds that D. D. Home was a faker, and they had set Sir

William Crookes to the task of exposing him. The chemist and physicist who had only a short time before been acclaimed as one of Great Britain's most brilliant scientists was now being viciously attacked by his colleagues as a gullible simpleton who had been taken in by Home's parlor magic tricks.

Sir William stood firm, and he challenged his fellow members of the Royal Society to prove his errors by showing him where the errors lay, by showing him how the medium's tricks had been performed. "Try the experiment fully and fairly," Crookes answered his critics. "If then fraud be found, expose it; if it be truth, proclaim it. This is the only scientific procedure, and this it is that I purpose steadily to pursue."

Twenty years later, when Sir William Crookes was president of the British Association for the Advancement of Science, he publicly reaffirmed that his previous assessment of the experiments with Home had been valid and that he found nothing to retract or to alter in his original findings.

In 1871, Home married for the second time, and once again his wife, Julie de Gloumeline, came from a wealthy Russian family. He ceased giving mediumistic demonstrations for the public or for science during the 1870s, and on June 12, 1886, Daniel Dunglas Home died from the tuberculosis that had first assailed him in his youth. If we are to believe one of the most respected scientists of that era, he was one of the most amazing spirit mediums who ever lived.

Eusapia Palladino (1854–1918)

At the time of her death in 1918, Eusapia Palladino had been both the most thoroughly investigated physical medium in the history of psychical research and the most controversial and startling personality ever to confront a team of investigators into the unexplained. She could be at once flirtatious and so suggestive in her conversation that some researchers were embarrassed by her frank sexuality; and at the same time, she dominated her husband so completely that the beleagured man had to take her maiden name as his own when they were married.

Born in Bari, Italy, in 1854, Eusapia's mediumship was discovered by family who employed her as a maid when she moved to

Italian spiritualist Eusapia Palladino was particularly skilled at levitating objects.

Haunted: Malevolent Ghosts, Night Terrors, and Threatening Phantoms

Naples as a young girl. The quality of the phenomena that she produced brought her to the attention of Professor Chiaia, who, in turn, introduced her to the famous Professor Caesar Lombroso. When the great psychologist's initial reports on Eusapia Palladino were published, it was not long before she was sitting with research groups in Paris, St. Petersburg, Turin, Genoa, London, and New York.

In 1908, a special committee was selected by the British Society for Psychical Research for the sole purpose of investigating the claims that had been made by a number of very celebrated scientists on behalf of the celebrated medium Eusapia Palladino. The committee was especially chosen for their skepticism and was composed of Hon. Everard Feilding, Mrs. W. W. Baggally, and Hereward Carrington, each of whom had exposed many fraudulent mediums in the course of their investigations.

Between November 21 and December 19, 1908, the team of professional skeptics spent several weeks in the Hotel Victoria in the medium's native city of Naples and were able to observe an incredibly wide range of spiritistic phenomena. Each of the members published lengthy reports on the remarkable Eusapia, and each of them came away from the exhaustive series of séances quite convinced that the medium had the ability to release an extremely potent paranormal force. They also noted that Mrs. Palladino would cheat if she were allowed to do so, but because of their strict controls, she was forced to abandon the easier path of trickery and produce genuine phenomena.

Working under the strictest control that the investigators could exert upon her, Eusapia allowed the committee to examine her as as thoroughly as they might wish. She utilized a spirit cabinet that was formed by stretching two black curtains across one of the corners of the room. Inside this makeshift affair, the investigators placed musical instruments and a variety of other small, movable objects. The medium sat directly in front of the closet with at least a foot of space between her chair and the curtains.

After warming up with simple displays of table levitation, Eusapia would call for a dimming of the lights. Almost instantly, the medium would summon her spirit control, John King, who would subsequently cause the objects behind the curtain to come floating out. Musical instruments would be played by unseen hands, and the sound would be easily heard by all sitters in the room. The highlight of every séance was the materialization of spirit hands and bodies. These materializations always came last in any séance, as if the woman's inborn sense of the dramatic knew how best to leave an audience wanting more.

In 1909, at a later sitting in New York, where Eusapia Palladino had been brought by great demand on the part of American psychical researchers, the medium capped her usual repertoire of paranormal feats by materializing a small hand in the air. Carrington later reported that the hand appeared white in the dim light of the laboratory and that its arm was visible up to a ghostly elbow. The wrist was encased in a lacy cuff. The hand and forearm were clearly seen by all the researchers in the room, and her own limbs were tied to two men, one on either side of her. While the investigators watched as if mesmerized, the ghostly hand moved to the medium's bonds and deftly untied the knots. When the spirit had undone the ropes, it threw one of the bonds at an observer and struck him in the chest. The other rope was thrown against the far wall of the sitting room.

The mystery of Eusapia Palladino's mediumship is a many-faceted one. Carrington wrote, for example, that she was often caught attempting the most crude kind of trickery—pranks that even the most inexperienced psychical researcher would be certain to catch. Her nature was permeated with mischief and guile, and she would try to cheat at card games or even croquet. Carrington felt that she did these things to those who would test her to see how far she might go in taunting them. When she found that she could not deceive the knowledgeable investigators from the various research committees—most of whom were accomplished amateur magicians—Eusapia Palladino would settle down to producing some of the most remarkable psychic phenomena ever recorded and witnessed by an investigating body of skeptics.

Leonora E. Piper (1857–1950)

Hereward Carrington considered Mrs. Leonora E. Piper to be the greatest psychical medium of her time. Mrs. Piper was a direct-voice medium, who, while entranced, would allow her body to be taken over by spirits who would use her voice to speak and, on occasion, to write messages to those persons assembled for her séances.

Eight-year-old Leonora (often spelled Leonore) had been playing in the family garden when she suddenly heard a kind of hissing sound that gradually became a voice repeating the letter "S." Once this had been resolved, Leonora clearly heard the same voice tell her that her Aunt Sara had died, but her spirit remained near. Leonora's mother made note of the day and the hour in which she had received the spirit communication, and a few days later the family learned that Sara had died at the very hour on the very day that Leonora had received the message.

One of the most famous American mediums, Leonora E. Piper was able to have spirits speak through her.

Although this event signaled the advent of Leonora's mediumship, her mother wisely insisted on the young girl enjoying a normal childhood and the dramatic impact of any subsequent paranormal phenomena was underplayed. When Leonora was twenty-two, she married William Piper of Boston, and shortly thereafter she developed a friendship with a blind clairvoyant named Dr. J. R. Cocke, who had been attracting a substantial following as a result of his accurate medical diagnoses and cures. At their very first meeting, Mrs. Piper had fallen into a trance, walked in such a state across the room, where she sat at a table, picked up pencil and paper, and began to write messages from spirit entities. Since there were often some very prominent Bostonians seated in the séance circle at Dr. Cocke's home, the remarkable accuracy of Mrs. Piper's trance communications quickly spread throughout the city, and she was soon being pursued by men and women who wished to sit with her in her own séances.

At the beginning of her mediumship, Mrs. Piper's spirit control claimed to be a young Native American girl, but within a very short time, Dr. Cocke's guide, Phinuit, a French doctor, had switched his allegiance to Leonora. Phinuit remained the medium's principal spirit control from 1884 to 1892, but there were other entities who spoke or wrote through her, notably the spirit of George Pelham, a friend of the well-known psychical researcher Dr. Richard Hodgson. Pelham communicated through automatic writing until sometime in 1897, when both he and Phinuit essentially retreated back into the spirit world upon the arrival of a powerful control known simply as the Imperator.

Harvard University psychologist William James, author of *The Varieties of Religious Experience,* was brought to Leonora Piper's séance room by some rather astonishing reports that he had heard from his mother-in-law and his sister-in-law. The elder woman had heard the medium give the names, both first and last, of distant relatives. Later, James's sister-in-law had approached Mrs. Piper with a letter written in Italian that had been sent to her by a writer who was known only to two people in the entire United States. The medium placed the letter to her forehead and gave details of its contents and described the physical appearance of the writer.

As he entered Mrs. Piper's séance room, Professor James identified himself with a false name in order not to provide the medium with even the slightest clue on which to work. In spite of his precautions, the psychologist came away from the sitting completely baffled as to how Mrs. Piper had been able to give accurate information on all of the subjects about which he had queried.

Mrs. Piper became William James's "one white raven." In a well-known passage from his works, James writes that the phenomena that he witnessed through the mediumship of Mrs. Piper had weakened his orthodox beliefs. "To use the language of logic," he states, "I will say that a universal supposition may become false because of one particular example. If you are taught that all crows are black, and you wish to destroy this belief, it is sufficient to you to present to your teacher one white raven. My only white raven is Mrs. Piper."

Sir Oliver Lodge, after a series of experiments with Mrs. Piper, told how the medium from Boston had completely convinced him "not only of human survival but also of the faculty possessed by disembodied spirits to communicate with people on earth."

Mrs. Piper died on July 3, 1950, at the age of ninety-one. The majority of researchers who sat with Leonora Piper were more than willing to agree with William James when he said of her: "I wish to certify here and now the presence of a supernatural knowledge; a knowledge the origin of which cannot be attributed to ordinary sources of information, that is, to our physical senses."

Carlos Mirabelli (1889–1951)

Cesar (Carlos) Augusto Mirabelli was born in 1889 in Botucatu in the state of São Paulo, Brazil. From his earliest childhood, he demonstrated a strong interest in religion. He hoped to enter into the service of the Roman Catholic Church, but these aspirations were never realized, and he took employment with a commercial firm in Rio de Janeiro.

Things did not go smoothly for Mirabelli on the job, and the strange happenings that had begun to occur around the place of business were soon attributed to the peculiar young man. While some of his fellow employees were drawn to the short man with the light blue eyes, others found him arrogant and conceited and complained that his eyes seemed to look right through them. And then there were the eerie manifestations that seemed always to take place around him.

Mirabelli was examined by medical doctors and sent to the Juqueri Asylum where the director, Dr. E. Costa, recognized the young man's peculiarities to be due to psychism rather than insanity. Dr. Costa conducted a number of tests with his patient and became the first doctor to verify the reality of Mirabelli's mediumship. Dr. Costa returned Mirabelli to Rio de Janeiro, where he arranged for the young medium to demonstrate his abilities. Under the strictest

The Brazilian medium Carlos Mirabelli was able to speak in foreign tongues on a variety of topics unfamiliar to him personally.

of controls, Mirabelli confounded an assembly of doctors by utilizing apparent teleportation to send a painting over a distance of several miles from one house to another. This experiment was reported in sensational detail in the Brazilian newspapers, and the career of the medium Mirabelli had been launched.

By 1926 Mirabelli had produced phenomena before a total of nearly six hundred witnesses, most of whom had been recruited from the ranks of Brazil's leading scientists, medical doctors, administrators, and writers, with an occasional learned visitor from abroad. As a trance-speaking medium, Mirabelli particularly excelled in xenoglossy, the ability to speak in languages unknown to him in his normal state. Not only did he speak in foreign tongues, but he gave spontaneous lectures on philosophy, astronomy, sociology, politics, medicine, history, and the natural sciences. These speeches were delivered alternately in German, French, Dutch, English, Greek, Polish, Syrian, Albanian, Czech, four Italian dialects, Arabic, Turkish, Hebrew, Chinese, Japanese, and several African dialects, in addition to Latin, Ancient Greek, and his native tongue, Portuguese.

As an automatic writing medium, he produced lengthy and erudite written dissertations in twenty-eight languages at a speed impossible to achieve under normal writing conditions. While entranced, it is said that Mirabelli wrote treatises in the style of Lombroso, Kepler, Voltaire, and Galileo. These works included an essay on evil written in Hebrew and signed by Moses, a tract on the instability of empires by Alexander the Great, and an essay on the mysterious things between Heaven and Earth by Shakespeare. Although unable to verify such prestigious authorship, linguists were said to be amazed at the masterful control that the medium exercised over each of the languages employed in these treatises. Such accomplishments are made the more impressive by noting that Mirabelli's formal education ended with primary school.

As a physical medium, Mirabelli once materialized the spirit bodies of a marshal and a bishop, both long deceased, both of whom were instantly recognizable to many who had assembled for the séance. Levitation seemed almost to be a specialty of the medium, and witnesses once observed him levitate an automobile to a height of six feet, where it was suspended for a period of three minutes. Once, when Mirabelli visited a pharmacy, a skull rose from the back of the laboratory and came to rest on the cash register. Before a gathering of doctors, who lent their names to a deposition, Mirabelli caused a violin to be played by spirit hands. To exhibit spirit control, Mirabelli caused billiard balls to roll and stop at his command.

While he was undergoing examination by the members of the Lombroso Academy, Mirabelli was bound to a chair in which he raised himself to a height of more than six feet and hung suspended for over two minutes. Several members of the academy walked beneath the levitated medium and satisfied themselves that they were witnessing an authentic phenomenon and not a magician's trick.

During one séance held for the academy at the unlikely hour of 9:00 A.M., the dead daughter of Dr. de Souza materialized. The doctor recognized his daughter and the dress in which she had been buried. He was allowed to embrace the spirit form and numerous photographs were taken of the remarkable scene. The spirit being remained in material form for a period of thirty-six minutes. This séance was witnessed by a large assembly, including twenty medical doctors and seven professors. Investigated by scientists and psychic researchers from all over the world, the mediumship of Mirabelli offered yet another question mark to the skeptical mind and another source of reassurance to the believer.

Eileen Garrett (1893–1970)

Eileen Garrett, who became one of the most respected mediums of the twentieth century, continued to study the phenomena of her mediumship throughout her long career, and she consistently questioned the source of the power that guided her for so many years.

Both of her parents committed suicide shortly after her birth in 1893 in Beauparc, County Meath, Ireland, and she was adopted by an aunt and uncle. Ms. Garrett had what many researchers recognize as a typical medium's childhood: She was ill a great deal, suffered many family tragedies, and began to experience visions and to see "people" who weren't there when very young. Little Eileen had imaginary playmates, saw various forms of light and energy around people and animals, and became aware at an early age that life did not end with physical death when she saw a kind of grayish smoke rising up from the bodies of pets after they died.

Ms. Garrett was plagued by tuberculosis and other respiratory illnesses throughout her childhood, and when she was fifteen she left Ireland for the milder climate of England. She lived there with relatives for only a very short time when an older gentleman named Clive began to call on her. After a courtship of a few months, she married him and during the course of their brief

Eileen Garrett was not only a medium but she conducted scientific research on this ability, writing books on the subject and founding the Parapsychology Foundation, Inc., in New York City.

marriage, she bore him three sons, all of whom died at very young ages. She eventually gave birth to a daughter, Eileen, and succumbed once again to ill health. By the time she had recovered, the marriage had ended in divorce.

During World War I, Eileen opened a hostel for convalescent soldiers. While she was caring for the wounded men, she attracted the attention of a young officer who asked her to marry him. Although she had a premonition that their life together would be very short, she agreed to a marriage just before he left for the front. Within a very brief period of time apart, she had a vision of his dying, and two days later she received word that he was missing in action. Shortly thereafter, she was notified that he had been killed in Ypres. She was recuperating from yet another illness when she met a young man whom she married one month before the Armistice in 1918—in spite of the fact that her intuitive abilities informed her that this union would not become any more permanent that her previous states of matrimony.

Eileen Garrett did not learn that she was a trance medium until shortly after the Armistice in November, when she accidentally fell asleep at a public meeting in London and the spirits of deceased relatives of the men and women seated around her began to speak through her. One gentleman present was familiar with the phenomenon of mediumship, and he explained to the young woman what had happened to her. He went on to say that he had communicated with an Asian spirit named Uvani that had manifested through her while she was entranced, and the entity had informed him that henceforth he would serve as Eileen Garrett's guide and spirit control. Uvani had declared that together they would do serious work to prove the validity of the survival of the human spirit after physical death.

Although she had another of her premonitions concerning the transient nature of her role as wife in the state of marriage, she had fallen in love and planned to be married for a fourth time. As strange as it might seem, both Eileen and her fiancé became ill on the same day. She barely survived a mastoid operation, and he died of pneumonia.

Confused about the course in life she was to follow, Eileen Garrett decided to come to the United States and devote herself to the process of understanding mediumship and survival after death by submitting to an intense barrage of tests at the hands of academic parapsychologists and psychical researchers

Hereward Carrington, one of the leading researchers during that period, had devoted decades to psychical investigations with a special emphasis on the various phenomena of mediumship. After years of scrupulous tests and experiments, he had concluded that 98 percent of all such phenomena are fraudulent. But when he began a series of tests with Garrett, he declared her to be a "medium's medium."

During the years in which she perfected her ability to communicate with the spirits of the deceased through her spirit guide, Garrett often expressed doubts about Uvani's spiritual independence and frequently voiced her suspicions that he might only be a segment of her own subconscious mind. Eventually, she had four trance communicators. Uvani, a fourteenth-century Arab soldier, remained always at the control, but there was also Abdul Latif, a seventeenth-century Persian physician, who dealt primarily with healing, and Tahotah and Ramah, who claimed no prior earthly incarnations and who spoke only seldomly and then only on philosophical and spiritual matters. Such indecisiveness about the source of her abilities dismayed the Spiritualists who in her developmental years in London had tutored her with the utmost seriousness of purpose.

Eileen Garrett became a persistent and highly qualified researcher in her own right. In 1951, she founded the Parapsychology Foundation, Inc., in New York City, and in 1952 reestablished her magazine, *Tomorrow*, as a quarterly journal of psychic science. In 1959, the foundation began publishing the *International Journal of Parapsychology* and, in 1970, the *Parapsychology Review*. She also authored such books as *Adventures in the Supernormal*, *The Sense and Nonsense of Prophecy*, and *Many Voices*.

To Eileen Garrett, mediumship was not a "breaking-down of the personality" but a state of wholeness. She wisely concluded that "communication with the 'other world' may well become a substitute for living in this world. Understanding that this world in which we live has priority in this existence is the core of mediumship ethics."

Garrett died on September 15, 1970, in Nice, France, following a period of declining health.

Arthur Augustus Ford (1897–1971)

Born into a Southern Baptist family on January 8, 1897, in Titusville, Florida, young Arthur had no real psychic experiences as a child, other than the occasional

Arthur Ford was a medium and clairaudient (he could hear voices from the spiritual world) who founded the Spiritual Frontiers Fellowship.

instances when he seemed to know what people were about to say. He was drawn to religion, but he annoyed the local clergy with his persistence in asking questions about church doctrines, especially those concerning life after death. Although he was excommunicated from the Baptist church at the age of sixteen, in 1917 Ford entered Transylvania College in Lexington, Kentucky, on a scholarship with the intention of becoming a minister. His education was interrupted when the United States entered the First World War that same year, and Ford joined the army in 1918.

Ford advanced to the rank of second lieutenant, but he never saw action in Europe for the war was over soon after he had enlisted. Ford did, however, observe firsthand the ravages of the terrible influenza epidemic as it struck the army camps. He began to have visions concerning those who would die of influenza, and at the same time, he heard the names of the soldiers who would be killed in action in Europe. For several frightening months, Ford thought that he was going insane. It was not until he had returned to his studies at Transylvania College that Dr. Elmer Snoddy, a psychology professor, suggested that Ford might be experiencing some kind of extrasensory phenomenon, rather than insanity.

In 1922, Ford married Sallie Stewart and was ordained a minister of the Disciples of Christ Church in Barbourville, Kentucky. He began to gain immediate attention as a powerful presence in the pulpit, but his developing mediumistic abilities were creating an increasing amount of friction with his conventional ministry and his personal relationships. After five years of marriage, he divorced his wife and left the church to begin lecturing about life after death. Soon, his lecture appearances included his entering self-induced states of trance and relaying messages from the spirit world to members of his audiences.

Ford's spiritistic talents were rather spontaneous and undisciplined, however, until he made the acquaintance of the great Hindu yogi Paramahansa Yogananda, who taught him how to achieve a yogic trance state and establish control of his burgeoning psychic abilities. In 1924, Ford encountered another very important influence in his life, the entity Fletcher.

In this particular instance, it was more a matter of reacquaintance, for Fletcher was a boyhood friend of Ford's who had been killed in action in Europe during World War I. With the advent of Fletcher as his spirit guide, Ford began a lifepath that would soon lead to world fame.

In the late 1920s, Ford established the First Spiritualist Church of New York, the first of numerous churches and spiritual organizations that he would found or lead. Such luminaries as Sir Arthur Conan Doyle called him one of the most amazing mental mediums of all times.

In 1929, Rev. Ford received a message that he believed to have originated from the spirit of the late master magician Houdini and conveyed it to Mrs. Houdini's attention. Immediately, a storm of fierce arguments pro and con erupted in the media. It was well known that before his death Houdini had left a coded message with his wife that he would attempt to send her from beyond the grave to prove life after death. Some feature writers championed the authenticity of Ford's relayed after-death communication from Houdini, while others quoted his widow as saying that the message was not correct.

> Such luminaries as Sir Arthur Conan Doyle called him one of the most amazing mental mediums of all times.

On February 9, 1929, however, according to Ford's supporters, Beatrice (Bess) Houdini wrote the medium to state with finality: "Regardless of any statement made to the contrary: I wish to declare that the message, in its entirety, and in the agreed upon sequence, given to me by Arthur Ford, is the correct message prearranged between Mr. Houdini and myself."

Eventually it came to be widely known that the various words in the Houdini code spelled out the secret message: "Rosabelle, believe."

Ford was at the center of another great after-life controversy when Fletcher brought forth Bishop James A. Pike's son James A. Pike Jr., who had committed suicide in February 1966 at the age of twenty-two, as well as other communicating entities during a séance on September 3, 1967.

This particular séance, which took place in Toronto, Ontario, was not limited to a drape-darkened room, but was taped and televised on CTV, the private Canadian television network. Allen Spraggett, the religion editor of the *Toronto Star* and a former pastor of the United Church of Canada, arranged the séance and later told the Associated Press that he believed that during the séance there had been strong evidence for communication with the dead or of extrasensory perception at the least.

Once he had attained the trance state, Fletcher soon made an appearance and said that he had two people eager to speak. The first communicating entity was that of a young man who had been mentally disturbed and confused before he departed. He revealed himself as James A. Pike Jr. He said how happy he was to speak with his father. Next Fletcher brought forward George Zobrisky, a lawyer who had taught history at Virginia Theological Seminary. Zobrisky said that he had more or less shaped Bishop Pike's thinking, a point that the clergyman readily conceded. Louis Pitt then sent greetings to the bishop, who recognized Pitt as having been acting chaplain at Columbia University before Pike had become chairman of the Department of Religion.

In many ways, the life of Arthur Ford was quite tragic. In 1930, a truck went out of control and struck the car in which he was driving with his sister and another woman as passengers. The two women were killed outright, and he suffered serious internal injuries, a broken jaw, and crushed ribs. During his long hospitalization, he became addicted to morphine and attempted to free himself of the resultant insomnia by drinking heavily. While at the height of his popularity, he was also an alcoholic, suffering blackouts and failing to appear for scheduled demonstrations.

In 1938, Ford married an English widow, Valerie McKeown, whom he had met while on tour, but in spite of their initial happiness together, his bouts with alcoholism doomed the marriage from the outset. His public displays of drunkenness had become so humiliating that his faithful spirit control, Fletcher, threatened to leave Ford unless he began to exercise some degree of self-control. Seemingly helpless to stop drinking, Fletcher left the medium, and soon thereafter, Ford entered a deep depression and suffered a complete physical breakdown.

In the 1950s, Fletcher returned as his spirit control, and Ford began once again to provide demonstrations of afterlife communications that many individuals found provided proof of survival of the spirit after death. Among Ford's many positive accomplishments during this period of revival was his participation in the founding of Spiritual Frontiers Fellowship in 1956. Arthur Ford spent the final years of his life in Miami, Florida, where he died of cardiac arrest on January 4, 1971.

Classic Hauntings and Ghost Encounters

"Marianne, Please Get Help!"

When I was just a boy, I developed a near obsession with the Borley Rectory haunting in England. Psychic investigator Harry Price became one of my early heroes, and later in life, I became friends and collaborators with the awesome clairvoyant John Pendragon, who also investigated the haunting at Borley Rectory. I was astonished when Pendragon made me his heir and left me with priceless artifacts from his investigation, including actual script messages left by the spirits and a lovely painting of the Phantom Nun.

The haunting phenomena usually began each night in Borley Rectory shortly after Reverend and Mrs. Smith had retired for the evening. They would be lying in bed, and they would hear the sound of heavy footsteps walking past their door. Reverend G. E. Smith soon took to crouching in the darkness outside of their room with a hockey stick gripped firmly in his hands. Several nights he lunged at "something" that passed their door—always without result.

Bells began to ring at all hours and became an intolerable nuisance. Hoarse, inaudible whispers sounded over their heads. Small pebbles appeared from nowhere to pelt them. A woman's voice began to moan from the center of an arch leading to the chapel. Keys popped from their locks and were found several feet from their doors. The Smiths found themselves living in what Dr. Harry Price would soon come to call "the most haunted house in England."

In the summer of 1929, Dr. Price answered the plea of the haunted rector and his wife. Leaving London, Dr. Price and an assistant drove to the small

This 1892 photo shows the Borley Rectory in Essex, which some consider the most haunted building in England.

village of Borley, reviewing what they already knew about the eerie rectory. The building, though constructed in modern times, stood on the site of a medieval monastery whose gloomy old vaults still lay beneath it. Close at hand had been a nunnery, whose ruins were much in evidence. About a quarter of a mile away stood a castle where many tragic events had occurred, ending with a siege by Oliver Cromwell. There was a persistent legend about a nun who had been walled up alive in the nunnery for eloping with a lay brother who had been employed at the monastery. The lay brother, who received the punishment meted out for such sins, was hanged. Inhabitants of the rectory, and several villagers, had reported seeing the veiled nun walking through the grounds. A headless nobleman and a black coach pursued by armed men had also been listed as a frequent phenomenon.

The rectory had been built in 1863 by the Rev. Henry Bull (sometimes called Martin in the literature). He had fathered fourteen children and had wanted a large rectory. He died in the Blue Room in 1892 and was succeeded in occupancy by his son, Harry, who died at the rectory in 1927. The building was vacant for a few months—while a dozen clergymen refused to take up residence there because of the eerie tales that they had heard—until Reverend G. E. Smith and his family accepted the call in 1928.

Price did not have to wait long for the phenomena to put on a show for him. He and his assistant had just shared a lunch with Rev. and Mrs. Smith when a glass candlestick struck an iron stove near the investigator's head and splashed him with splinters. A mothball came tumbling down the stairwell, followed by a number of pebbles.

Price busied himself for the next several days with interviewing the surviving daughters of Henry Bull, the builder of the rectory, and as many former servants as had remained in the village. The eldest of the three surviving daughters told of seeing the nun appear at a lawn party on a sunny July afternoon. She had approached the phantom and tried to engage it in conversation, but it had disappeared as she had drawn near to it. The sisters swore that the entire family had often seen the nun and the phantom coach and that their brother had said that, when dead, he would attempt to manifest himself in the same way. It was their father, Henry Bull, who had bricked up the dining room window so that the family might eat in peace and not be disturbed by the spectral nun peeping in at them.

A man who had served as gardener for the Bull family told Price that every night for eight months he and his wife heard footsteps in their rooms over the stables. Several former maids or grooms testified that they had remained in the employ of the Bulls for only one or two days before they were driven away by the strange occurrences that manifested themselves on the premises.

Mrs. Smith was not at all reluctant to admit that she, too, had seen the shadowy figure of a nun walking about the grounds of the rectory. On several occasions, she had hurried to confront the phantom, but it had always disappeared at the sound of her approach. The Smiths left the rectory shortly after Dr. Price's visit. They had both begun to suffer the ill effects of the lack of sleep and the enormous mental strain that had been placed on each of them.

Borley Rectory presents an interesting combination of a "haunting" and the phenomenon of poltergeistic activity. Harry Price maintained that approximately one-half of all hauntings include some type of poltergeistic disturbance. Henry Bull had fourteen children who lived in the rectory. Phenomena began to become active about ten years after he had moved into the rectory with his family. It is also interesting to record that the phenomena reached new heights of activity when the Rev. Lionel Algernon Foyster, a cousin of the Bull family, took up residence in the rectory on October 16, 1930. The reverend brought with him his wife, Marianne, and his four-year-old daughter, Adelaide. (Many accounts of Borley Rectory refer to the Foysters as Rev. B. and Marianne Morrison.)

The Foysters had lived there only a few days when Mrs. Foyster heard a voice softly calling, "Marianne, dear." The words were repeated many times, and, thinking her husband was summoning her, she ran upstairs. Foyster had not spoken a word, he told her, but he, too, had heard the calling voice.

Once, Mrs. Foyster laid her wristwatch by her side as she prepared to wash herself in the bathroom. When she completed her washing, she reached for the watch and discovered that the band had been removed. It was never returned.

Reverend Foyster was quick to realize that the weird tales that he had heard about Borley Rectory had all been true. He could hardly deny them in view of such dramatic evidence. He was not frightened, however, as he felt protected by his Christian faith. He used a holy relic to quiet the disturbances when they became particularly violent and remained calm enough to keep a detailed journal of the phenomena that he and his family witnessed.

Marianne Foyster received the full fury of the haunting's attack from the very beginning of their occupancy. One night, while carrying a candle on the way to their bedroom, she received such a violent blow to the eye that it produced a cut and a black bruise that was visible for several days. A hammerhead was thrown at her one night as she prepared for bed. She received a blow from a piece of metal that was hurled down a flight of stairs. Another time, she narrowly missed being struck by a flat iron, which smashed the chimney of the lamp that she was carrying.

In addition to persecuting Mrs. Foyster, paradoxically the entity seemed determined to establish contact with her. Messages were found scrawled on the walls: 'Marianne ... please ... get help."

The entity may or may not have been suggesting that the Foysters once again bring Dr. Harry Price upon the scene. At any rate, that is exactly what they did. Advised by the Bull sisters of the famed investigator's interest in the Borley phenomena, Reverend Foyster wrote to London to inform Dr. Price of renewed activity in the rectory.

> **The haunting wasted no time in welcoming the returning investigator. While he was examining an upstairs room, an empty wine bottle hurled itself through the air, narrowly missing him.**

Price gained permission to stay in the rectory with two friends, and upon arrival, the researcher and his party once again examined the house from attic to cellar. The haunting wasted no time in welcoming the returning investigator. While he was examining an upstairs room, an empty wine bottle hurled itself through the air, narrowly missing him. The party was brought back down to the kitchen by the screams of their chauffeur, who had remained behind to enjoy a leisurely smoke. The distraught man insisted that he had seen a large, black hand crawl across the kitchen floor.

During conversation, Mrs. Foyster disclosed that she had seen the "monster" that had been causing all the eerie disturbances. Reverend Foyster showed Dr. Price the entry that he had made in his journal on March 28, when his wife had confronted the entity while ascending a staircase. She had described it as a monstrosity—black, ugly, and ape-like. It had reached out and touched her on the shoulder. Price later learned that others had seen the creature on different occasions.

The Foysters also told Price and his team that the phenomena had begun to produce items that they had never seen before. A small tin trunk had appeared in the kitchen when the family was eating supper. A powder box and a wedding ring materialized in the bathroom, and, after they had been put away in a drawer, the ring disappeared overnight. Stone-throwing had become common, and Reverend Foyster complained of finding stones in their bed and under their pillows as well.

The Foysters endured the phenomena at the rectory for five years before leaving in October 1935. After the Morrisons left, the bishop decreed that the place was for sale.

In May 1937, Harry Price learned that the rectory was empty and offered to lease the place for a year as a kind of ghost laboratory. His sum was accepted,

Haunted: Malevolent Ghosts, Night Terrors, and Threatening Phantoms

and the investigator enlisted a crew of forty assistants, mostly men, who would take turns living in the rectory for a period of one year. Price outfitted the place and issued a booklet that told his army of researchers how to correctly observe and record any phenomena that might manifest themselves.

Shortly after the investigators began to arrive, strange pencillike writings began to appear on the walls. Each time a new marking was discovered, it would be carefully circled and dated. Two researchers reported seeing new writing form while they were busy ringing and dating another. It appeared that the entity missed Mrs. Foyster. "Marianne …Marianne…." it wrote over and over again. "Marianne … prayers … please help."

A photo taken on the grounds of the Borley Rectory appears to show a ghostly figure.

The organized investigators were quick to discover a phenomenon that had not been noted by any of the rectors who had lived in Borley. This was the location of a "cold spot" in one of the upstairs passages. Certain people began to shiver and feel faint whenever they passed through it. Another "cold spot" was discovered on the landing outside of the Blue Room. Thermometers indicated the temperature of these areas to be fixed at about forty-eight degrees, regardless of what the temperature of the rest of the house may have been.

The phantom nun was seen three times in one evening by one observer but was not noticed at all by any of the other investigators. A strange old cloak kept the researchers baffled by continually appearing and disappearing. Several of Price's crew reported being touched by unseen hands.

On the last day of Dr. Price's tenancy on May 19, 1938, Marianne Foyster's missing wedding ring once again materialized. The investigator snatched it up, lest it disappear, and brought it home to London with him.

In late 1938, the Borley Rectory was purchased by Captain W. H. Gregson, who renamed it "The Priory." He was not at all disturbed by warnings that the place was haunted, but he was upset when his faithful old dog went wild with terror on the day they moved in and ran away never to be seen again.

Captain Gregson did not have long to puzzle out the enigma of Borley. At midnight of February 27, 1939, the "most haunted house in England" was completely gutted by flames. Captain Gregson testified later that a number of books had flown from their places on the shelves and knocked over a lamp, which had immediately exploded into flame.

Borley Rectory has remained one of the most haunted houses in Britain, but in December 2000, Louis Mayerling, who claimed Borley was a second home to him until it burned in 1939, wrote a book entitled *We Faked the Ghosts of Borley Rectory* in which he claimed that Harry Price and the world had been taken in by hoaxsters. Mayerling states that he first arrived at Borley in 1918 to find Rev. Harry Bull and his family taking great delight in perpetuating local folklore about a phantom nun and other paranormal activity. According to the author, the Foysters were also in on the hoax, encouraging Mayerling, a teenager at the time, to walk around the gardens at dusk in a black cape.

> All at once, Mayerling recalls, all the kitchen bells clanged as one and a brilliant, silver-blue light seemed to implode around them from the walls and the ceilings.

Mayerling admits that there was one incident that he was unable to explain. On Easter in 1935, the acclaimed playwright George Bernard Shaw; T. E. Lawrence, the famous "Lawrence of Arabia"; Sir Montagu Norman, governor of the Bank of England; and Bernard Spilsbury, the Home Office criminal forensic scientist—all believers in the haunting phenomena at Borley—joined Mayerling and Marianne Foyster for a séance at the rectory. All at once, Mayerling recalls, all the kitchen bells clanged as one and a brilliant, silver-blue light seemed to implode around them from the walls and the ceilings. From his previous experience creating eerie sounds and noises in the rectory, Mayerling knew that it was impossible to make all the bells sound at once, and he had no idea what had caused the lightning-like flash around them. He was, in fact, blinded by the phenomenon and eventually recovered sight in only one eye. Shaw and Norman refused to stay the night after such a violent display of the paranormal, and Mayerling confesses in his book that memory of the experience still set his spine to tingling.

Mayerling's confession of pranks during the occupancy of the Bull and Foyster families does not explain the extensive phenomena reported by Price's team of researchers during its year-long observation of the rectory nor the manifestations noted by Gregson after he assumed ownership of Borley. Since the admitted pranksters were not present at the rectory during those years, the authenticity of the haunting of Borley will remain a controversial subject among psychical researchers.

America's First Super Star Haunting

In 1960 when I "discovered" the Bell Witch while doing research on early American cases of psychic phenomena, I thought that I had discovered supernatural pay dirt. At that time hardly anyone seemed to have heard of the classic case, and I even envisioned writing a novel based on the spooky events of the haunting. I had not yet written a book, and the Bell Witch seemed like an ideal project. [My first: Monsters, Maidens, and Mayhem: A Pictorial History of Hollywood Film Monsters. Chicago: Merit Books, 1965. See also: "Brad Steiger, Horror's First Historian" by Stephen Mosley, The Darkside, February 2016.]

And now the Bell Witch novel is chalked up on my "missed opportunities" blackboard. There have been several movies based, at least in part, on the Bell Witch legend, including The Blair Witch Project in 1999, The Bell Witch Haunting in 2004, An American Haunting in 2005, Bell Witch: The Movie in 2007, and The Bell Witch Haunting in 2013. The American television series Ghost Adventures filmed an episode at the Bell Witch Cave. The A&E television network based its October 2015 series Cursed: The Bell Witch, on the premise of the latest members of the Bell family trying to end the curse.

All right, but I am still fascinated by the story.

According to most accounts, the disturbances began one night in 1817 with mysterious rappings on the windows of the Bells' cabin near Clarksville, Tennessee. Twelve-year-old Elizabeth "Betsy" Bell began to complain of a rat gnawing on her bedpost at night, and the entire family, including the parents, John and Luce, experienced the midnight confusion of having their covers pulled off their beds.

When the Bell family arose one morning, stones littered the floor of their front room and the furniture had been overturned. The children, Betsy, John, Drewry, Joel, and Richard, were goggle-eyed and spoke of ghosts and goblins.

John Bell lectured his family severely. They would keep the problem to themselves. They didn't want their family to become the subject of common and unsavory gossip.

That night, Richard was awakened by something pulling his hair, raising his head right off the pillow. Joel began screaming at his brother's plight, and from her room, Betsy began howling that the gnawing rat had begun to pull her hair, too.

Most of the family awakened the next day with sore scalps, and John Bell reversed his decision. It was obvious that they needed help. That day he would confide in James Johnson, their nearest neighbor and closest friend.

The tale that Bell told was an incredible one, but Johnson knew that his neighbor was not given to flights of fancy. While he watched at Betsy's bedside that night, Johnson saw the young girl receive several blows on the cheeks from an invisible antagonist. He adjured the spirit to stop in the name of the Lord Jesus Christ, and there was no activity from the ghost for several minutes, then Betsy's hair received a yank that brought a cry of pain from her lips. Again Johnson adjured the evil spirit, and it released the girl's hair.

An 1894 artist's drawing of the tormented Betsy Bell.

Johnson concluded that the spirit understood the human language and that Betsy was the center of the haunting. He met with other neighbors, and they decided to help the Bell family as best they could. A committee kept watch at the Bell house all night to try to placate the spirit, but all this accomplished was to bring about an especially vicious attack on the unfortunate Betsy.

A number of neighbors volunteered their own daughters to sleep with Betsy, but this only managed to terrorize the other girls as well. Nor did it accomplish any useful purpose to take Betsy out of the cabin into the home of neighbors—the trouble simply followed her there and upset the entire house.

By now the haunting had achieved wide notoriety, and the disturbances were thought to be the work of a witch, who had set her evil spirits upon the Bell family. Each night the house was filled with those who sat up trying to get the "witch" to talk or to communicate with them by rapping on the walls. The disturbances soon became powerful enough to move outside the cabin and away from Betsy. Neighbors reported seeing lights "like candles or lamps" flitting through the fields, and farmers began to suffer stone-throwing attacks from the Bell Witch.

These particular peltings seemed to have been more in the nature of fun than some of the other manifestations of the spirit. Young boys in the area would often play catch with the Witch if she happened to throw something at them on their way home from school.

Once an observer witnessed several boys get suddenly pelted with sticks that flew from a nearby thicket. The sticks did not strike the boys with much force, and, with a great deal of laughter, the boys scooped the sticks up and hurled them back into the thicket. Once again, the sticks came flying back out. The observer cut notches in several of the sticks with his knife before the boys once again returned the Witch's volley. He was able to identify his markings when the playful entity once again flung the sticks from the thicket.

The Witch was not so gentle with the scoffers who came to the Bell home to expose the manifestations as trickery. Those who stayed the night invariably had their covers jerked from their beds. If they resisted the Witch's yanking, they were slapped soundly on the face.

Spiritists, clergymen, reporters, and curiosity seekers had waged a ceaseless campaign to urge the Witch to talk and declare herself and her intentions. At last, their efforts were rewarded. At first, the voice was only a whistling kind of indistinct babble, then it became bolder—a husky whisper speaking from darkened corners. Then it became a full-toned voice that spoke not only in darkness but also in lighted rooms and, finally, during the day as well as the night.

> Although the father, John Bell, was the butt of malicious pranks and cruel blows, Mrs. Bell was looked after solicitously by the Witch.

Immediately the charge of ventriloquism was heard from the skeptical. To put a halt to the accusations of trickery, John Jr. brought in a doctor, who placed his hand over Betsy's mouth and listened at her throat while the Witch's voice chatted amicably from a far corner of the room. The doctor decreed that the girl was in no way connected with the sounds.

From the very beginning of the Witch's visitation, it had minced no words in its dislike of John Bell, Betsy's father. The spirit often swore to visitors in the Bell home that she would keep after him until the end of his days.

To a visitor's question concerning her identity, the Witch once answered that she was a spirit who had once been very happy, but she had been disturbed by humans and made unhappy. Later, the Witch declared herself to be the spirit of an Indian. Finally, the Witch decided that she was the ghost of old Kate Batts, a woman who had been an eccentric recluse and who had earned the appellation of "witch" from the citizens of Clarksville. When the word spread that it was the ghost of old Kate who was haunting the Bells, the entire mystery became much more believable to several doubting neighbors—at least to those individuals who didn't know that old Kate was still alive.

The Bell home became more crowded when the Witch's "family" moved in with her. Four hell-raisers named Blackdog, Mathematics, Cypocryphy, and Jerusalem, each speaking in distinct voices of their own, made every night party time during their stay with their "mother."

When two local preachers arrived to investigate the disturbances, the Witch delivered each of their Sunday sermons word for word and in a perfect imitation of their own voices.

Although the father, John Bell, was the butt of malicious pranks and cruel blows, Mrs. Bell was looked after solicitously by the Witch. Once, when she was ill, the Witch was heard to tell her to hold out her hands. When Luce

Bell did so, a large quantity of hazelnuts dropped into her palms. When Mrs. Bell weakly complained that she could not crack them, family members and neighbors watched in wide-eyed fascination as the nuts cracked open and the meats were sorted from the shells.

John Jr., Betsy's favorite brother, was the only member of the family besides the mother who received decent treatment from the Witch. Joel and Richard were often whipped soundly by the invisible force, and Drewry was so frightened of the Witch that he never married, fearing that the entity might someday return and single out his own family for particular attention.

The cruelest act perpetrated on Betsy was the breaking of her engagement to Joshua Gardner (or Gardiner). The two young people were acclaimed by friends and family to be ideally suited for one another, but the Witch protested violently when the engagement was announced. The Witch screamed at Joshua whenever he entered the Bell home and embarrassed both young people by shouting obscenities about them in front of their friends.

A friend of the family, Frank Miles, learned of the Witch's objection to Betsy's engagement and resolved to stand up to the evil spirit on her behalf. He challenged the entity to take any form it wished, and he would soon send her packing. Suddenly, his head jerked backwards as if a solid slap had stung his cheeks. He put up his forearms to block a series of facial blows, then dropped his guard as he received a vicious punch in the stomach. Miles slumped against a wall, desperately shaking his head to recover his senses. Reluctantly, he picked up his hat and coat. A man couldn't fight an enemy he couldn't see.

General Andrew Jackson, Old Hickory himself, decided to have his try at defeating the Witch. An old friend of John Bell, Jackson set out from The Hermitage accompanied by a professional "witch layer" and several servants.

As his party approached the Bell place, Jackson was startled when the wheels of his coach suddenly froze, and the full strength of the horses could not make them budge an inch. A voice from the bushes cackled a greeting to Jackson and uttered a command that "unfroze" the wheels. The general and his men realized that the element of surprise was lost. The Witch knew they were coming.

That night the witch layer fled in terror when the Witch attacked him, and General Jackson's men followed him out the door. According to the old stories, Jackson told John Bell that fighting the Witch was worse than having faced the British at the Battle of New Orleans. Old Hickory wanted to stay a week and face down the spirit, but his committee of ghost chasers had had enough, so he left with his men.

With the decisive defeat of her champions, Miles and Jackson, Betsy had no choice but to give in to the Witch's demands and break her engagement with

Joshua Gardner. On the night in which Betsy returned the ring, the Witch's laughter could be heard ringing victoriously from every room in the house.

Shortly after the entity had accomplished the severing of Betsy's marriage agreement with her fiancé, it once more began to concentrate its energy on the destruction of John Bell. Richard was walking with his father on that day in December 1920, when John Bell collapsed into a spasmodically convulsing heap.

John Bell was brought home to his bed, where he lay for several days in a very weakened condition. Even during the man's illness, the Witch would not leave him in peace but continued to torment him by slapping his face and throwing his legs into the air.

The Bell home, where a farmer and his family were harassed by a witch from 1817 to 1821, is shown in this 1894 illustration.

On the morning of December 19, 1820, John Bell lapsed into a stupor from which he would never be aroused. The Witch sang bawdy songs all during John Bell's funeral and annoyed the assembled mourners with sounds of her crude celebration throughout the man's last rites.

After the death of John Bell, the Witch behaved much better toward Betsy. She never again inflicted pain upon her and actually addressed her in terms of endearment.

During the rest of the winter and on into the spring months, the manifestations decreased steadily. Then, one night after the evening meal, a large smoke ball seemed to roll down from the chimney of the fireplace out into the room. As it burst, a voice told the family: "I'm going now, and I will be gone for seven years."

True to its word, the Witch returned to the homestead in 1828. Betsy had entered into a successful marriage with another man; John Jr. had married and now farmed land of his own. Only Mrs. Bell, Joel, and Richard remained in the family home. The disturbances primarily consisted of the Witch's most elementary pranks—rappings, scratchings, pulling the covers off the bed—and the family agreed to ignore the unwanted guest.

Their plan worked, and the Witch left them after two weeks of pestering them for attention. The entity sought out John Jr. and told him in a fit of pique that it would return to one of his descendants in "one hundred years and seven."

Dr. Charles Bailey Bell should have been the recipient of the Bell Witch's unwelcome return visit, but Dr. Bell and his family survived the year

1935 without hearing the slightest unexplained scratch or undetermined rapping. Dr. Bell has written the official record of the mysterious disturbances endured by his ancestors in *The Bell Witch: A Mysterious Spirit.*

Today, the abandoned homestead of the Bell family is owned by a private trust, and no visitors are allowed to explore the property. The only site connected with the legends of the Bell Witch and open to the public is the Bell Witch Cave, which continues to produce accounts of unusual lights and eerie images on photographs.

THE WESLEYS' STRANGE GUEST IN EPWORTH RECTORY

Having been brought up Lutheran, I was told many stories when I was a child about that stalwart rebellious monk Martin Luther resisting not only the forces of Pope Leo X but also of Satan himself. What impressionable child could forget when Luther threw an ink pot at the Devil and commanded he leave his library so he could get some work done? No imp or demon would be invited as a guest or as a critic when Luther was in the process of creating such famous hymns as "A Mighty Fortress Is our God," "Shepherds as They Watched at Night," "Away in a Manger," or "From Heaven Above to Earth Below."

That is why I have always been puzzled that one of the most famous cases in the annals of hauntings is the one that visited the Reverend Samuel Wesley and his family at Epworth Rectory in 1716. I am particularly baffled because among the nineteen children of the Reverend Wesley were John and Charles, the founders of Methodism and the authors of some of Christendom's best loved hymns, such as "Christ the Lord Is Risen Today," "Hark! The Herald Angels Sing," and "Love Divine, All Love Excelling."

It was on the first of December 1716 that the children and the servants began to complain of eerie groans and mysterious knockings in their rooms. They also insisted that they could hear the sound of footsteps ascending and descending the stairs at all hours of the night.

Reverend Wesley heard no noises and severely lectured the child or servant who brought him any wild tale about a ghost walking about in the rectory. If there were any noises in the rectory, he told his family one night at dinner, they were undoubtedly caused by the silly young men who came around in the evenings.

The reverend had four grown daughters who had begun to entertain beaus and suitors, and their father's veiled sarcasm did not sit at all well with them. "I wish the ghost would come knocking at your door, Father," one of them told him.

The Epworth Rectory in Lincolnshire, England (shown here in an 1890 photograph), was plagued by one of the country's most famous cases of poltergeists in 1716.

The girls were so angry with their father that they fought down their fright and vowed to ignore the noises until they became so loud that their no-nonsense parent could not help acknowledging them. They didn't have long to wait. The very next night, nine loud knocks thudded on the walls of Reverend and Mrs. Wesley's bed chamber. The clergyman thought some mischief maker had managed to get into the rectory unnoticed and was trying to frighten them. He would buy a dog big enough to gobble up any intruder.

True to his word, the clergyman obtained a huge mastiff and brought it into the rectory. That night, however, as the knocks began to sound, Reverend Wesley was startled to see his canine bodyguard whimper and cower behind the frightened children.

The children had overcome their initial fear of the invisible being and had come to accept its antics as a welcome relief from the boredom of village life.

Two nights later, the sounds in the house seemed so violent that Wesley and his wife were forced out of bed to investigate. As they walked through the rectory, the noises seemed to move about them. Mysterious crashing sounds echoed in the darkness. Metallic clinks seemed to fall in front of them. Somehow managing to maintain their courage, the Wesleys searched every chamber but found nothing.

After he called a family meeting to pool their knowledge about the invisible guest, Reverend Wesley learned from one of the older girl's observations that the disturbances usually began at about ten o'clock in the evening and were always prefaced by a "signal" noise, a peculiar kind of winding sound.

The noises followed a pattern that seldom varied. They would begin in the kitchen, then suddenly fly up to visit a bed, knocking first at the foot, then the head. These seemed to be the ghost's warming-up exercises. After it had followed these preliminaries, it might indulge any spectral whim that appealed to it on that particular night.

"Why do you disturb innocent children?" Wesley roared in righteous indignation one night as the knockings in the nursery became especially violent. "If you have something to say, come to me in my study!"

As if in answer to Wesley's challenge, a knock sounded on the door of his study with such force that the cleric thought the boards must surely have been shattered.

Wesley decided to secure reinforcements in the fight against the "deaf and dumb devil" that had invaded his rectory. He sent for Mr. Hoole, the vicar of Hoxley, and told him the whole story. The vicar said that he would lead devotions that night and see if the thing would dare to manifest itself in his presence.

The "thing" was not the least bit awed by the vicar of Hoxley. In fact, it put on such a good show that night that the clergyman fled in terror, leaving Wesley alone to combat the demon as best he could.

The children had overcome their initial fear of the invisible being and had come to accept its antics as a welcome relief from the boredom of village life. "Old Jeffery," as they had begun to call their strange guest, had almost achieved the status of a pet, and it was soon observed that it was quite sensitive. If any visitor slighted Old Jeffery by claiming that the rappings were due to natural causes, such as rats, birds, or wind, the haunting phenomena were quickly intensified so that the doubter stood instantly corrected.

The disturbances maintained their scheduled arrival time of about ten o'clock in the evening until the day that Mrs. Wesley remembered the ancient remedy for ridding a house of evil spirits. They would get a large trumpet and blow it mightily throughout every room in the house. The sounds of a loud horn were said to be unpleasant to evil spirits.

The ear-splitting experiment in exorcism was not only a complete failure, but now the spirit began to manifest itself in the daylight as well. The children seemed almost to welcome the fact that Old Jeffery would be available during their playtime hours as well as being an amusing nighttime nuisance.

Several witnesses reported seeing a bed levitate itself to a considerable height while a number of the Wesley children squealed gaily from the floating mattress. The only thing that bothered the children was the creepy sound that Old Jeffery had begun to make, which was like that of a robe dragging along the floor.

One of the girls declared that she had seen the ghost of a man in a long, white robe that dragged on the floor. Other children claimed to have seen an animal similar in appearance to a badger, scurrying out from under their beds. The servants swore that they had seen the head of a rodent-like creature peering out at them from a crack near the kitchen fireplace.

Then, just as the Wesleys were getting accustomed to their weird visitor, the disturbances ended as abruptly as they had begun. Old Jeffery never returned to plague Epworth Rectory with its phenomena, but the memory of its occupancy has remained to bewilder scholars for more than two centuries.

MOTHMAN

On November 15, 1966, two young married couples, Steve and Mary Mallette and Roger and Linda Scarberry, were driving through the marshy area near the Ohio River outside of Point Pleasant, West Virginia, when a winged monster, at least seven feet tall and with glowing red eyes, loomed up in front of them. Later, they told Deputy Sheriff Millard Halstead that the creature followed them toward Point Pleasant on Route 62 even when their speed approached 100 mph (160 kph).

When news of the mysterious encounter achieved local celebrity status, Raymond and Cathy Wamsley, Marcella Bennett, and Ricky Thomas said that they

Author Nick Redfern standing by a Mothman statue.

had seen the giant, birdlike creature near an abandoned TNT plant a few miles north of Point Pleasant. A few days later, Thomas Ury said that an enormous flying creature with a wingspan of ten feet had chased his convertible into Point Pleasant at mph (113 kph).

More witnesses came forward with accounts of their sightings, and the legend of Mothman was born. Although the majority of witnesses described the tall, red-eyed monster as appearing birdlike, the media dubbed the creature "Mothman" because, as writer John A. Keel noted, the *Batman* television series was very popular at the time.

Intrigued by the stories, Keel visited Point Pleasant on numerous occasions and learned about the bizarre occurrences associated with Mothman's appearance, including the eerie forecast that the Silver Bridge in Point Pleasant would collapse and many people would be killed as a result. In1975, Keel wrote in *The Mothman Prophecies* that "there would be many changes in the lives of those touched by" Mothman, and a "few would even commit suicide." *The Mothman Prophecies* was made into a motion picture in 2002 with Richard Gere as investigator John Klein (John Keel) and Alan Bates as Alexander Leek (Keel spelled backwards) as the paranormalist with all the intriguing theories about Mothman and its mystical meaning.

Researchers of the phenomenon have various theories concerning the large, winged monster that haunts the marshy area near the McClintic Wildlife Management Area and the abandoned TNT plant north of Point Pleasant. Some say that excited, suggestible witnesses are simply sighting sandhill cranes, large birds indigenous to the area that can reach heights of six feet (two meters) and achieve wingspans of ten feet (three meters). UFO researchers make correlations between bright lights in the sky and the appearances of Mothman. Others suggest that toxic chemicals dumped at the TNT site during World War II may have caused bizarre mutations in wild birds. And then there are those who maintain that Mothman might be a multidimensional intelligence, angelic or demonic, that can warn witnesses of impending danger—or cause it to happen.

Loren Coleman, author of *Mothman and Other Curious Encounters* (2002), has been keeping tabs on the mysterious deaths that appear to be associated with the entity on his website, *The Cryptozoologist: Loren Coleman* (www.lorencoleman.com). Coleman lists the demises of nearly one hundred men and women who had some association with Mothman from the 1960s to the present day. Coleman's first list of victims were those unfortunates who became the Silver Bridge Victims, when at 5:04 P.M., on December 15, 1967, the bridge at Point Pleasant collapsed during rush hour. Forty-six lives were lost, and forty-four bodies were recovered.

THE JERSEY DEVIL

Some witnesses have said that the Jersey Devil that haunts the Pine Barrens in southeastern New Jersey is a cross between a goat and a dog with cloven hoofs and the head of a collie. Others swear that it has a horse's head with the body of a kangaroo. Most of the people who have sighted the creature also mention a long tail, and nearly all of the witnesses agree that the thing has wings. But it doesn't really fly as much as it hops and glides.

People have been sighting the Jersey Devil in the rural area around South Jersey since 1735, which, according to local legend, is the year that it was born. Reports say that there was a prominent family in South Jersey named Leeds whose patriarch demanded a large number of heirs to carry on his name to future generations. When Mrs. Leeds learned that she was about to bear her thirteenth child, she decided that she had grown tired of being continually pregnant in order to satisfy her husband's ego. In a fit of rage, she cursed the unborn child within her and cried out that she would rather bear the Devil's child than give birth to another Leeds for posterity.

Artist Dan Wolfman's take on what the Jersey Devil looks like.

Visualizing the image of Satan popular in the 1700s, Mrs. Leeds decreed that she wished the child to be born with claws and fangs, fierce and wild as some vicious beast. The old legend has it that Mrs. Leeds was granted her angry cry of revenge for having served as a brood mare for her selfish husband. The baby was born a monster with devilish fangs, claws, tail, and cloven hoofs, but the extremes of its viciousness soon eclipsed the borders of Mrs. Leeds's curse. The little monster ate every one of the other Leeds children and escaped out of the chimney to begin its reign of terror among the farmers and villagers of the region.

For well over two hundred years, generations of terrified witnesses have claimed to encounter the Jersey Devil. Although encounters with the monster are reported every year, the most famous series of sightings occurred in January 1909, when hundreds of men and women claimed to have seen or heard the frightening creature. So many people refused to leave the safety of their homes that local mills were forced to shut down for lack of workers.

Descriptions of Spring-heeled Jack have ranged from demonic to gentlemanly in appearance. Wearing a cape and helmet, the nineteenth-century figure resembled an eerie superhero. (Cover of an 1886 penny dreadful publication.)

SPRING-HEELED JACK

About the middle of November 1837, the lanes and commons of Middlesex, England, suddenly became places of dread. An eerie figure said to possess supernatural powers was stalking the frightened villagers by night and effortlessly avoiding capture by the police. Because of this creature's ability to leap over tall hedges and walls from a standing jump, he was given the name of Spring-heeled Jack.

Close witnesses who encountered Jack face-to-face described him as being tall, thin, and powerful. A prominent nose stuck out of his pinched physiognomy, and his ears were pointed like those of an animal. His long, bony fingers resembled claws.

The remarkably agile Spring-heeled Jack wore a long, flowing cape over his slender shoulders and a tall, metallic helmet on his head. Numerous witnesses testified that the mysterious intruder had what appeared to be metal mesh under his cloak and that he had a strange kind of lamp strapped to his chest.

It proved impossible to capture Spring-heeled Jack. Townspeople saw him leap eight-foot walls as he worked his way to the west, passing from village to village. Later, it was determined that Spring-heeled Jack stayed primarily in private parks during the day, coming out at night to knock at certain doors, as if he were seeking some particularly hospitable host. As far as it is known, the mysterious stranger never found anyone who invited him in for a visit. Most people reacted in the same manner as Jane Alsop, who went to answer the door assuming that a top-hatted, cloaked member of the horse patrol stood on the doorstep. Instead, the "most hideous appearance" of Spring-heeled Jack caused her to scream for help.

The monster's eyes, she later testified, were glowing red balls of fire. Before she could flee, he seized her in the powerful grip of his clawlike fingers and projected balls of fire that rendered both Jane and her sister unconscious. When the report of the Alsop sisters' encounter reached the press, it came to light that a Miss Scales had survived a similar encounter with Jack as she walked through Green Dragon Alley. Before she could scream for help, he spurted a blue flame into her face, thereby dropping her to the ground in a swoon.

According to old records, Spring-heeled Jack knocked on his last door on February 27, 1838, when he visited the house of one Mr. Ashworth. The servant who opened the door took one look at the bizarre inquirer, then set Spring-heeled Jack to running with his screams for help.

Inspector Hemer of the Liverpool police may have had the last mortal glimpse of the strange visitor when he was patrolling the long boundary of Toxteth Park one night in July. A sudden and vivid flash of what the inspector assumed to be lightning seized his attention and caused him to notice a large, fiery globe hovering motionless over a nearby field. The object remained stationary for about two more minutes, then, amid showers of sparks, lowered itself closer to the ground to receive the same strangely costumed character that all of England had been seeking. Inspector Hemer decided not to become the hero who captured Spring-heeled Jack, and he wheeled his horse away from the scene. When he looked back over his shoulder, the great ball of fire had disappeared.

FLATWOODS MONSTER

Among the first of the monstrous ghosts that became transmogrified into aliens from outer space during a description of an encounter was the frightening Flatwoods Monster.

Kathleen May described the alien being that she and seven other Flatwoods, West Virginia, residents saw on September 12, 1952, as looking more scary than the Frankenstein monster. A group of excited boys, including her sons, Eddie, thirteen, and Fred, twelve, had been at a nearby playground when they sighted a flying saucer emitting an exhaust that looked like red balls of fire. According to the boys, the UFO had landed on a hilltop in back of the May house.

Gene Lemon, a husky seventeen-year-old, found a flashlight and said that he was going to investigate. At the urging of her son, Mrs. May agreed to accompany him, and the other boys fell in behind them. About halfway up the hill, Lemon directed the beam of his flashlight on what he believed to be the green, glowing eyes of an animal. Instead, the beam spotlighted an immense, humanlike figure with a blood-red face and greenish eyes that blinked out from under a pointed hood. Behind the monster was a "glowing ball of fire as big as a house" that grew dimmer and brighter at intervals. Gene's courage left him in a long scream of terror, and the intrepid band of flying saucer hunters fled in panic from the sight that Lemon's flashlight had illuminated.

> Gene's courage left him in a long scream of terror, and the intrepid band of flying saucer hunters fled in panic from the sight that Lemon's flashlight had illuminated.

Later, Mrs. May described the monster as having "terrible claws." Some of the boys, however, had not noticed any arms at all, and some said that when it had moved toward them, it had not really walked on legs but "just moved." Most of the witnesses agreed that the being had worn dark clothing—probably dark green. dark green. Estimates of the monster's height ranged from seven to ten feet, but everyone agreed on one characteristic of the alien—it had emitted a sickening odor "like sulfur," Mrs. May said, yet unlike anything she had ever encountered.

A. Lee Stewart Jr. of the *Braxton Democrat* arrived on the scene only moments ahead of Sheriff Robert Carr, but the reporter found most of the witnesses too frightened to speak coherently, and some were receiving first aid for cuts and bruises suffered during their flight down the hill. A while later, he persuaded Lemon to accompany him to the spot where they had seen the monster.

Stewart saw no sign of the giant alien or of the pulsating red globe of light that ostensibly served as its spacecraft, but he did inhale enough of the unusual odor to declare it "sickening and irritating." In his report of his investigation, he stated that he had developed a familiarity with a wide variety of gases while serving in the Air Force, but he had never been confronted by any gas with a similar odor.

An illustration by Dan Wolfman of what the Dover Demon looks like.

Each of the witnesses later swore that the monster had definitely been moving toward them, but they also agreed that this apparent aggressive movement could have been due to the fact that they were between the alien and the large, glowing, globular object that was quite likely his spacecraft.

THE DOVER DEMON

William Bartlett stands by his story that the creature, the entity, the being, whatever it was that he and two other teenagers sighted April 21–23, 1977, in Dover, Massachusetts, was real. The "thing" that has become known as the Dover Demon was seen by Bartlett as it crept along a low stone wall on the side of the road. It stood about four feet tall and carried its hairless, rough-textured body on two spindly legs. Its arms were also thin and peach-colored. The creature's huge, watermelon-shaped head was disproportionate in size to its relatively small torso, and it bore two large, glowing, red-orange eyes.

Bartlett, who has made his career as a painter, told the *Boston Globe* on October 29, 2006, that he definitely saw something weird that night. "I didn't make it up," he said. "It's a thing that's been following me for years. Not the creature—the story."

Bartlett had his glimpse of the Demon atop the broken stone wall along Farm Street at around 10:30 P.M. About two hours later, fifteen-year-old John Baxter was walking home from his girlfriend's house when he claimed to have gotten within fifteen feet of the monster along a creek in a heavily wooded area along Miller Hill Road. At midnight the next night, another fifteen-year-old, Abby Brabham, was driving home with her boyfriend when she saw what appeared to be the same weird creature sitting upright on Springdale Avenue.

Loren Coleman, who began an investigation within days of the sightings in 1977, believes Bartlett and considers the case credible. Coleman was able to interview all four teens within a week of the reported sightings and is convinced that they had not concocted a hoax. Coleman, who also coined the name "Dover Demon," has commented that the same area in which the strange being was sighted has a tradition of unexplained activity dating from the 1700s, including an apparition of Satan on horseback and tales of buried treasure. "It's almost as if there are certain areas that 'collect' sightings, almost in a magnetic way," the investigator told Mark Sullivan, a *Boston Globe* correspondent.

No sightings of the Dover Demon have been reported since those strange nights in April 1977. Coleman observed that the Dover creature does not match the descriptions of chupacabras, Roswell aliens, or the bat-eared goblins said to have attacked a family in Hopkinsville, Kentucky, in 1955. "It doesn't really fit any place," Coleman said. "It's extremely unique. It has no real connections to any other inexplicable phenomena."

Tulpas and Out-Of-Body Projections

While in the ecstasy of meditation and enlightenment, an induced hypnotic state, or the semiconscious grip of physical pain, people down through the ages have testified to having left their physical bodies to travel briefly on other dimensions of reality in their spirit forms before they returned to the material plane.

Based on our research of over fifty years—and our personal experiences—we have found that such spontaneous out-of-body projections seem to fit into one of seven general categories:

1. Projections while the subjects sleep
2. Projections while the subjects undergo surgery, childbirth, tooth extraction, etc.
3. Projections at the time of an accident, during which the subjects receive a terrible physical jolt and seem to have their spirits literally thrown from their physical body
4. Projections during intense physical pain
5. Projections during the high fever of a severe illness
6. Projections during pseudo-death (the near-death experience) wherein the subjects "die" for several minutes and appear to a living percipient with whom they have an emotional link before being subsequently revived and restored to life
7. Conscious out-of-body projections in which the subjects deliberately seek to free their spirits from their material bodies

The pioneer psychical researcher Frederic W. H. Myers wrote that cases of astral projection present "the most extraordinary achievement of the human will. What can lie further outside any known capacity than the power to cause a semblance of oneself to appear at a distance? What can be more a central action—more manifestly the outcome of whatsoever is deepest and most unitary in man's whole being? Of all vital phenomena, I say, this is the most significant; this self-projection is the one definite act which it seems as though a man might perform equally well before and after bodily death."

Our Successful Experiments in Projecting Our Subject's Ghost

In the late 1960s and early 1970s, a small research group and I conducted tests in traveling clairvoyance with our hypnotized subject located in my office in Iowa and the target subjects in London, England; Long Island, New York; and Baltimore, Ohio. In one instance, our subject was able to move a mirror in a target's home, and in another she was able to read correctly the manufacturers' names on various appliances.

When we were invited on a national television program to provide a demonstration of time and space travel, we found awaiting us a panel of historians who challenged our subject to traverse the decades to November 19, 1863, the date of Abraham Lincoln's Gettysburg Address, and to describe any particular gestures the president might have used during the course of the speech.

At first it seemed as though we had been ambushed by skeptical scholars wishing to oppose the very thought of psychic time travel.

Even we were amazed when our subject was given an "A+" for providing the audience both in the studio and in their homes a history lesson. It happened that these were honest and brave scholars.

This is an actual photograph of Lincoln (circled) at Gettysburg. One of Brad and Sherry's hypnotized subjects was able to project themselves back in time and accurately describe the scene to a panel of historians.

According to the experts and all available contemporary newspaper and other documents that described Lincoln's gestures, our subject had recreated the historic occasion as if she were watching a motion picture of the event—as if she were beholding a gathering of ghosts caught forever in a slice of time and space.

Where had I discovered such a talented medium who could traverse the dimensions of time and space?

In the print shop next to my office, that's where.

It all started with my barber, Bob, who casually mentioned one afternoon as he was cutting my hair that his wife, Reva, was really interested in the mysteries and weirdness that I wrote about. Then he said that Reva was a twin and that she and her sister had experimented with hypnosis and ESP since they were children.

After a few more minutes of discussion and identification, I pieced together that Reva was the quiet and pretty blonde who worked next door in the print shop that produced the catalogs and brochures for our Other Dimensions company.

I invited Bob and his wife to my office one evening, and after a few test experiments, I realized that Reva was a natural mind traveler of many other dimensions.

I telephoned Loring G. Williams, the hypnotist with whom I had written *Other Lives* (1969), told him that I had found our medium, and he arranged at once to load up his mobile home in New Hampshire and head for Iowa. The rest of the story is two weeks of truly remarkable experiments of freeing the ghost within Reva to travel to some astonishing destinations.

The Sweet Little Old Lady Became a Ghost in Someone Else's Home

Mrs. Boulton sat down across the breakfast table from her husband, who was already deeply engrossed in the morning newspaper. "I dreamt of my house again last night," she said.

"That's nice, dear," her husband said mechanically. Mrs. Boulton had had a recurring dream of a house for the past several years.

"It seemed so real this time," Mrs. Boulton continued. "It seemed as if I were so much nearer to it than ever before."

Mrs. Boulton was soon to find out just how near she was. For many years she had been frequently dreaming of an elegant old mansion, and each time that her dreams took her there, she would meticulously walk through the house, inspecting each item of furniture, the windows, and the curtains, to make certain that each was in its place and that everything was in good condition. Over the years, Mrs. Boulton had come to know her "dream house" as well as she did her own.

Mrs. Boulton's husband was a man of many interests, but he was particularly fond of history, and he loved and studied the mysteries and folklore of the Scottish Highlands. When he learned that Lady Beresford, owner of Ballachulish House in the Appin district, was planning to go south to spend the summer, Boulton immediately wrote her in hopes of renting the famous old house during her absence. Although neither Boulton nor any member of his family had ever been in the house, he was well aware of its romantic and violent position in Scottish history. Lady Beresford answered Boulton's query with a letter approving his proposal to rent Ballachulish, and they worked out the details of the arrangement through correspondence.

Toward the end of the negotiations, Boulton visited Lady Beresford at Ballachulish. Thinking of the many stories and legends he had heard about the famous old place, he asked her if the ghosts in Ballachulish were as plentiful as ever.

"As a matter of fact," Lady Beresford answered, "there is only one at the present time. I hope that you won't be too disappointed."

"Not at all," Boulton chuckled, wondering which famous ghost walked the halls. "And who might this spirit be?"

"I really couldn't say," Lady Beresford said. "She's really much too docile to be of the Glencoe Massacre or any of the Highland wars. It seems to be the ghost of a sweet little lady, who makes her rounds like a night watchman."

Boulton returned to his wife completely exhilarated by the prospect of spending a summer in such a historic location. Mrs. Boulton was pleased to see her husband so excited, and she, too, was eager to obtain her first tour of Ballachulish. Lady Beresford had agreed to wait until the Boultons had taken up residence before she left for the continent. She would show them about the place and allow them to become accustomed to the mansion before she would leave them on their own.

As it turned out, Mrs. Boulton did not require the services of Lady Beresford to make an adjustment to life at Ballachulish. "This is my house," she told her husband as they approached the historic mansion. "This is my house!"

Warning his wife not to be silly, Boulton rang the doorbell. When Lady Beresford arrived to welcome them, her eyes widened in strange disbelief as she saw Mrs. Boulton.

"It was kind of you to wait," Mrs. Boulton smiled at the astonished Lady Beresford, "but a tour won't be necessary. I've walked through these halls for many years now, and I know where to find everything. This has been the house of my dreams!"

Lady Beresford nodded her head slowly in agreement. "And now I know who the little lady is who has been keeping such a close watch on the house. I recognized you as the 'ghost' of Ballachulish the moment I set eyes on you."

It was all a bit too much for Boulton, who stood by in amazement, as the two women traded stories about Mrs. Boulton's nocturnal projection.

"But it is true," Mrs. Boulton told her husband. "Come, I'll take you on a tour of Ballachulish."

Before Mrs. Boulton entered a room, she would describe its floor plan and give an exact description of the furniture to be found within. In each case, she was absolutely correct. It seemed that she made one mistake when she told of a staircase that had seemingly never been where she described it. But Lady Beresford quietly removed Mrs. Boulton's doubts when she told her that the staircase had been walled up to block the draft it caused in the upstairs corridors.

The Boultons spent a most pleasant summer at Ballachulish. Upon returning to their own home, Mrs. Boulton never again dreamt of touring the historic mansion, and Lady Beresford never again saw the ghost of the sweet little lady that she had come to know so well over the years.

Mrs. Boulton had produced her own "ghost," a phenomenon that is known as astral projection or out-of-body experience.

Sylvan Muldoon Believed Astral Projection Could be Learned

The late Sylvan J. Muldoon was one of those who claimed that astral projection could be learned, developed, and mastered by the serious-minded. In his two books, *The Projection of the Astral Body* (1929) and *The Case for Astral Projection* (1936), Muldoon offers a detailed record of many experiments he personally conducted and provides a systematic method of inducing the conditions necessary for astral projection. According to Muldoon, it is possible to leave the body at will and retain full consciousness in the "astral self." Muldoon is also cognizant of the "silver cord" as connecting connecting the phantom body and the physical body. This cord, says Muldoon, is extremely elastic and permits a journey of considerable distance. Muldoon claims to have been able to move objects while in his astral self and to have gained information that he could not have acquired via any of the normal sensory channels.

Muldoon is generous in providing the reader with copious descriptions of the mechanism of astral projection in order that the truly interested student can follow the procedures and attempt his or her own experimentation.

Sylvan Muldoon's (pictured) ideas about astral projection were also an influence behind the beliefs of Scientology founder, L. Ron Hubbard.

And I recall how generous he was when he sent me copies of his books. He had his near-death/out-of-body experience at the age of twelve in the Clinton, Iowa, Spiritualist Camp. The mediums at the camp were also generous and helpful individuals allowing me numerous times to interview them when I taught high school in Clinton.

The fundamental law of projection, according to Muldoon, is expressed in these words: "When the subconscious will becomes possessed of the idea to move the body, and the physical body is incapacitated, the subconscious will moves the astral body out of the physical."

AH, THAT BRITISH SENSE OF HUMOR— TURN YOURSELF INTO A GHOST, EH?

The American novelist Theodore Dreiser often told of the night during which he entertained the English writer John Cowper Powys. The Englishman had had to leave rather early, and both men expressed regret that their evening had been so short.

Seeing that Dreiser's concern was genuine, Powys told him: "I'll appear before you, right here, later this evening. You'll see me."

"Will you turn yourself into a ghost?" Dreiser asked, chuckling at the Englishman's peculiar sense of humor.

"I'm not certain yet," Powys told him. "I may return as a spirit or in some other astral form."

Philosopher and author John Cowper Powys appeared before his friend Theodore Dreiser in spirit form just as he had promised.

Several hours later, as Dreiser sat reading in his easy chair, he glanced up and was startled to see Powys standing before him, looking exactly as he had appeared earlier that evening. When the writer moved toward the apparition and spoke to it, the astral projection of Powys disappeared.

CONSCIOUS PROJECTIONS OF THE GHOST WITHIN

My friend and collaborator John Pendragon, the British seer, had the ability to exercise a peculiar function of the transcendent self to the extent that he could project his inner "phantom" at will.

One night a friend called at the home of Pendragon, and the two men began to reminisce about their school days.

Haunted: Malevolent Ghosts, Night Terrors, and Threatening Phantoms

"I wonder what became of Old Franklin?" Pendragon's friend wondered. "He wanted so very much to become an actor."

Pendragon allowed that he was also curious as to the fate of their friend. He wrote Franklin's name on a note pad and placed his finger upon the name. There were a few seconds of blurred motion before Pendragon found himself on the top deck of a bus. Seated in front of him was a man of his own age whom he recognized as "Old Franklin." Franklin's ginger hair was almost gray, but Pendragon knew that the man was his old school chum. Furthermore, he was terribly upset to see that Franklin was enveloped in gloom.

Pendragon wondered precisely where he was, and by effort of will, he "floated" out of the bus. He could not recognize any of the street names, but he had the distinct impression that he was in a suburb of Birmingham. He willed himself back onto the bus again, and presently Franklin got off, and he followed.

Franklin entered an empty theater. All was dreary. Franklin felt miserable. Some important project had failed. He went into an office and began to pack some items, quite oblivious to Pendragon's etheric presence.

Franklin snapped the case closed, left the theater, and boarded another bus. It was quite obvious to Pendragon that something very big had "gone bust" for Old Franklin.

Pendragon willed himself back to his apartment and his waiting friend. After the psychic felt himself "returned," he told his friend what he had seen. They both hoped that "Old Franklin" would come out of his doldrums and achieve the success that he had for so long been seeking.

GOLEMS ARE NOT TULPAS

The Golem is the Frankenstein monster of Jewish tradition—it is, in fact, in the eyes of many literary scholars, one of the principal inspirations for Mary Shelly's *Frankenstein, or The Modern Prometheus*. The Golem, however, is not patched together from the body parts of cadavers robbed from their graves but is rather created from virgin soil and pure spring water. It is also summoned, more than created, by those who purify themselves spiritually and physically, rather than by heretical scientists in foreboding castle laboratories who bring down electricity from the sky to animate their patchwork human.

The word "golem" appears only once in the Bible (Psalms 139:16). In Hebrew the word means "shapeless mass." The Talmudic teachings define the Golem as an entity "unformed" or "imperfect." The Talmud states that for the first twelve hours after his creation, Adam himself was a Golem, a body without a soul.

According to certain traditions, the creation of a Golem may only be accomplished when one has attained one of the advanced stages of development for serious practitioners of Kabbalah and alchemy. The *Sefer Yezirah*

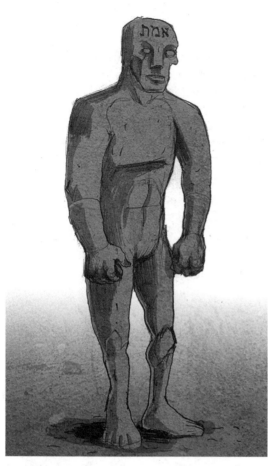

An illustration of a golem with the Hebrew word *emet* ("truth") on its forhead. Erase the first letter to get *met* ("death") and the creature will die.

(Book of Creation or Formation), a guide book of magic attributed to Rabbi Eleazar Rokeach in the tenth century, instructs those who would fashion a Golem to shape the collected soil into a figure resembling a man. Once the sculpting has been completed, the magicians were to use God's name, He who is the ultimate creator, to bring the Golem to life.

Other instructions in the ancient text advise the magician to dance around the creature fashioned of soil, reciting a combination of letters from the Hebrew alphabet and singing the secret name of God. Once the Golem has completed its assigned tasks or mission, it may be destroyed by walking or dancing around it in the opposite direction and reciting the letters and the words backwards.

The Kabbalah gives instruction that once the Golem had been formed, it was given life by the Kabbalist by placing under its tongue a piece of paper with the Tetragrammaton (the four-letter name of God) written on it. Other traditions state that one must write the Hebrew letters *aleph, mem* and *tav* on the forehead of the Golem. The letters represent *emet* (truth), and once the characters have been inscribed on the Golem's forehead, it comes alive. When it has completed the work assigned to him, the magician erases the *aleph*, leaving *mem* and *tav*, which is *met* (death).

In his modern adaptation of the ancient text, Rabbi Aryeh Kaplan stresses that the initiate should never attempt to make a Golem alone but rather should always be accompanied by one or two learned colleagues. Extreme care must be taken by its creators, for the Golem can become a monster and wreak havoc. When such a mistake occurs, the divine name must somehow be removed from the creature's tongue so that it will revert to dust.

"PHILIP," A KIND OF TULPA

In 1972, in Toronto, Ontario, Canada, a group of parapsychologists, led by Dr. A. R. G. Owen, proposed a theory that the paranormal phenomenon of ghosts was actually the physical manifestation of the human mind. They would conduct an experiment using the scientific method to replicate the events and experience of a ghost. The group included eight ordinary individuals with no acclaimed abilities, powers, fame, or knowledge of the paranormal. Among those participating were Dr. Owen's wife, Iris; psychiatrist Joel Whitten; and Margaret Spanous, former chairperson of Mensa in Canada.

The group's overall objective was to create a ghost through expectation, imagination, and visualization. The method to achieve this goal was to create a fictional character whom they could communicate with through séances. The group created Philip Aylesford, a seventeenth-century aristocratic Englishman who had a tragic love affair that led him to take his own life. All members of the group spent time in developing, discussing, and imagining Philip in preparation for the experiment.

For about a year, the group participated in séances to communicate with the fictional ghost. One night, Philip was able to communicate with them by tapping or rapping to yes/no answers. Soon, the group experienced increase paranormal activity as Philip would shake or move the table around, heard ghostly voices, saw lights dimming, and felt cold spots. Dr. Owen repeated the experiment with other groups, using the same effect, and concluded it to be successful. Even though the paranormal experience was believed to have resulted from the human mind, no scientific explanation was offered.

The Philip experiment was believed to be successful as it was able to be recorded and filmed. Despite all the documented results, the Philip experiment has been in an endless debate over whether it was created by forces of the human mind or a summonsed entity.

CHERISHED SECRET LORE OF TIBETAN ADEPTS

Among the secret lore of the Tibetan adepts is the claim that phantoms or tulpas may be created by those who have attained high mental and spiritual ability and been sent to accomplish tasks or missions assigned to them by their creators. Once the adept has endowed the tulpa with enough vitality to assume the form of an actual physical being, it frees itself from its creator's psychic "womb" and leaves to complete its assignment.

According to certain Eastern metaphysicians, thoughts, emotions, and mental emanations add to the strength of the tulpa, enabling it to accumulate power and grow. The tulpa may manifest apparent solidarity and vigor, and Yogis claim that they may even carry on intelligent conversations with these creatures born of their own minds. The duration of a tulpa's life and its vitality are in direct proportion to the tension and energy expended in its creation.

Sometimes, however, even the most accomplished of adepts and magicians confess that the phantom—the tulpa—becomes rebellious and may conduct itself independently of its creator. On occasions, the tulpa may become something of a zombie-like monster. And in certain instances, the highly developed Tibetan magicians have been forced to admit that they have unconsciously set loose a phantom zombie to wreak havoc on unsuspecting victims.

I have often theorized that the Yoga concept of the tulpa, the thought form that can appear to assume life independent of the human psyche that "feeds" it with emotions and mental emanations, might be responsible for many of the mysterious sightings reported of everything from zombies to werewolves.

Could it be plausible that many of the strange monsters that have been sighted around the world have been *created* by those who spotted them? Each individual's essential self may have the ability to influence and to shape a reality separate from that of the ordinary and the commonly accepted. It may require little effort at all for the transcendent self to skip blithely over, around, or through space and time and to manifest their own brand of tulpa.

> Could it be plausible that many of the strange monsters that have been sighted around the world have been *created* by those who spotted them?

And speaking of space and time, it is clear that we really have absolutely no final definition of the true nature of time or of how many dimensions of time and space truly exist.

On some occasions, a tulpa—whether consciously or unconsciously manifested—may appear so lifelike that its creator is amazed to learn that the phantom has traveled to other countries and interacted with people who were completely unaware that they were conversing with a spirit being and not the real person whom it mimicked.

The principle behind tulpas is that the mind creates the world of appearances; quantum physics substantiates this spiritual concept as it tells us we not only perceive our reality, but we participate in making it. Essentially, we create our perceived reality.

Tulpas seem to be created out of quantum stem cells that reside in the universe; these stem cells are commonly known as quantum particles by theoretical physicists. The belief is that tulpas can become anything or anyone in appearance by controlling these quantum particles; for them it is like taking a wad of shapeless clay in one's hand and not only forming it but endowing it with a kind of intelligence. The truly astounding incidents are the ones in which the tulpas manage to free themselves from their creators, having gained enough life-force to do so. Tibetan occultists say that this happens logically, just as a child is born when his or her body is completed and he or she is able to live on his or her own. Indeed, the quantum stem cells have then successfully formed a living being. A tulpa can be like a rebellious son; uncanny power struggles have been reported between the priests and their tulpas, creator and created.

The subject of tulpas is a huge one, steeped in ancient spiritual beliefs and abilities. Tibetan holy men devote a lifetime living in isolation and trying again and again to create thought-forms through the formidable powers of their minds. Buddhists believe that each individual can eventually achieve the god-status of creator and near perfection. Who is to say what we Westerners could accomplish if our lives were devoted to spiritual evolution?

What Is a Ghost—Really?

In his eighty-four years of life, Thomas Alva Edison became the fourth most prolific inventor in history, holding 1,093 patents in the United States alone. A brief listing of his best-known inventions includes the phonograph, the motion picture camera, the stock ticker, the power station, and the mimeograph.

Because you are reading a book about ghosts, I think it is quite likely that you knew that Edison was working on a machine that would allow the living to communicate with those who had gone on before them. The October 1920 issue of *American Magazine* contained an article written by Bertie Charles Forbes (founder of *Forbes Magazine*) in which the Genius of Menlo Park said:

> If our personality survives, then it is strictly logical and scientific to assume that it retains memory, intellect, and other faculties and knowledge that we acquire on Earth.... I am inclined to believe that our personality hereafter will be able to affect matter. If this reasoning be correct, then, if we can evolve an instrument so delicate as to be affected, moved, or manipulated ... by our personality as it survives in the next life, such an instrument, when made available, ought to record something.

In a private journal entry, Edison wrote: "I have been at work for some time building an apparatus to see if it is possible for personalities which have left this earth to communicate with us. ... I am engaged in the construction of one such apparatus now, and I hope to be able to finish it before very many months pass."

In a *Scientific American* piece in 1921, Edison was quoted as saying:

I don't claim anything, because I don't know anything … for that matter, no human being knows … but I do claim that it is possible to construct an apparatus which will be so delicate that if there are personalities in another existence who wish to get in touch with us … this apparatus will at least give them a better opportunity.

When I asked Brian Allan, editor of Great Britain's superb *Phenomena* magazine, the question "What is a ghost—really?" the author of such books as *Revenants: Haunted People and Haunted Places, I Cast Thee Out: Poltergeists, Possession, and Exorcism*, and *Strange Skies, Strange Eyes*, replied that asking him to answer that enigma was akin to asking him to hold steam in his hands. But, after some thought, Brian provided me with the excellent piece below.

What Is a Ghost—Really?

By Brian Allan

I should indicate from the outset that I have absolutely no doubt we are in contact with entities (souls, or ghosts if you like, although these terms may be too loose) that may or may not be the remnants of the departed. I say this because I have encountered them, but like many others operating in this area, although I have theories based on what I have seen, that is what they are, theories. In addition, because the subject of ghost phenomena is so varied and diverse, I have no fixed ideas regarding what ghosts are, or by which mechanism they function. I don't even know if they are truly sentient as we would understand the term, but nevertheless I am sure they exist.

What is a ghost … really?

Apparitions, wraiths, specters, shades, haunts, spirits, spooks, poltergeists, and, of course, ghosts—all are names describing the same phenomenon, but all have slightly different shades of meaning. Trying to describe the nature of a ghost is a bit like trying to hold steam in your hands—it's that difficult and it all depends on whom you ask because opinions vary and come from a range of special interest groups with different agendas. It is also difficult to know how to approach this subject because there are two ways: either subjective or objective. The subjective route is probably the easiest because one can draw on personal experience, but this has the inherent problem of bias because it is based on a personal (i.e., subjective) opinion, so the fairest way is to go the objective route, where various ideas can be factored in.

One thing that all definitions of ghosts have in common is the simple fact that they did not just suddenly appear as a result of the proliferation of reality TV shows purporting to demonstrate conclusive proof that they exist because they have been reported since the human race first appeared on the face of the planet; in fact, ghostly encounters even appear in the Bible. What these reality TV shows have done tends to be largely negative, alarming (let's face it, who wants a ghost story that is not terrifying because this is not what an audience wants and all these shows are ratings driven), and in many case wholly inaccurate. Self-styled investigators aside, the content of these shows is based on so-called "evidence" gathered from frightened people who, because of the trauma, may not be entirely sure what happened to them. Other than their testimony, there is no effective way of evaluating it. These shows also attempt to validate what they do by using various kinds of test equipment, and in many cases the people using it fail to understand what they are measuring. However, we'll get back to that.

One of the main problems with defining the nature of a ghost is that there is absolutely no general consensus of what creates the phenomenon in the first place. But let's consider a few examples. As far as mediums are concerned, ghosts are the spirits of the living that have left the physical body after death and inhabit some kind of nonphysical afterlife, where they can be contacted and communicated with. This may be accurate, but does that only apply to one type of ghost? If so, it does not explain why some ghosts appear to be confined to one particular location as if recorded into the fabric and only appear or

Everyone seems to know what a ghost is, yet when you ask people to define them there is no general consensus.

replay under specific conditions. This phenomenon has been called the Stone Tape Theory; by and large these ghosts (or recordings) are apparently nothing more than echoes of an event or person trapped in the fabric of reality. What mediums appear to communicate with is apparently sentient and (most of the time) willing to communicate. At least the mediums all appear to exhibit a measure of sympathy and respect for what they are communicating with.

At the other end of the scale are the scientists who are so tied into a material reductionist paradigm that they will not even consider the possibility that a form of consciousness (or mind, if you prefer) can continue after the body has ceased to function. In other words, consciousness (mind) exists only as a function of the brain, and once that shuts down, that's it—game over; it all stops. This is in spite of a school of thought that suggests that the brain does not create the mind; it limits it. Despite this theory, science continues to cling to its remarkably blinkered and defensive viewpoint because there are elements in the subjects studied by science that appear to contradict this narrow paradigm, a prime example being the twin slit experiment.

It is known that during this experiment, which has been repeated in controlled laboratory conditions hundreds of times, photons appear to be influenced when being observed by a detector and react in one way, but when they are not observed they behave in another. They can't be fooled either because if the detectors are left in place but are not switched on—that is, they are not "observing,"—somehow the photons know this and react accordingly. There is no known logical reason why this should be, and it irritates physicists who study this subject.

Another example of the anomaly appears to have been proved during an experiment conducted in 1989 by the U.S. Department of Mines in Boulder, Colorado. In this experiment, highly charged particles were sealed inside a "magnetic bottle" with the intention of testing their response when a laser beam was fired through the electromagnetic field. The particles altered their quantum state in greater numbers when the experiment was actually physically observed while the laser beam fired than when it was not. A similar result occurred in a slightly different setting; there is no easy or obvious reason for why that happened.

Noted scientist Brian Cox, the former keyboard player with the band D:Ream and a physics professor, is on record as saying that there are no ghosts because ghosts should be composed of energy of some kind and the experiments conducted at the Large Hadron Collider located on the Swiss/French border at the European Organization for Nuclear Research (Conseil Européen pour la Recherche Nucléaire, or CERN), have not revealed any possible way this could work. However, this assumes that scientists are looking in the right place to start with. While the professor is undoubtedly an extremely able man who regular presents cutting-edge TV shows, like many of his ilk he is a debunker and a sceptic, but for all his qualifications he cannot explain why photons behave the way that they do during the twin slit expedient.

He might mention one of the many odd theories that have emerged from the bizarre discipline of quantum physics, like the "observer effect," in which the very act of observing an experiment appears to affect the outcome. Professor Cox, who cheerfully refers to paranormal phenomena as "woo-woo" and those who study it as "nobbers," is happy (albeit uncomfortably) to accept this astonishing anomaly, yet he cannot accept that ghosts, or the essence and echoes of a departed consciousness, might also exist after physical death. Why he takes this view is open to question, but it hardly seems fair. Indeed, he does have a vested interest in the status quo, so any hint of deviating from the accepted model of reality might not do him much good with his similarly minded colleagues.

Another special interest group regarding ghosts is the thousands of self-styled ghost hunting organizations (a.k.a. ghostbusters) that have sprung up worldwide as a direct result of the influence of reality TV shows that have reduced a serious subject to the level of a sensationalist pastime. These amateur groups, for the most part, have no idea what a ghost actually is, but they assume they can measure or detect one by means of various kinds of test equipment that they barely know how to use, never mind interpret the readings they get back. There is a general assumption that ghosts generate electromagnetic fields, and if such a field is detected this is a sure sign that ghosts are present. Possibly, but they do not know if the ghost is generating the field or if the field is generating the ghost. One other point they seem to miss is that, assuming ghosts are sentient, how do the aspiring ghostbusters know that the ghosts want to be disturbed or investigated?

> These amateur groups, for the most part, have no idea what a ghost actually is, but they assume they can measure or detect one by means of various kinds of test equipment that they barely know how to use....

From my own point of view, I have seen this curious "field effect" occur during an investigation at the Covenanters Prison, which is at Greyfriars Kirkyard cemetery in Edinburgh, Scotland. In this case I was with a medium who stated that a ghost was passing right behind us. As she said this, the needle on the test meter I was using (a TriField) went full scale then dropped back to just above zero, which was the ambient reading. A few moments later in the same spot, she again said that "something" was passing us, and once again the needle on the meter went full scale. I can only report what I saw, but I have no rational explanation for it, and over the years I have had several encounters of a similar kind, fortunately with other witnesses present who saw and/or felt the same things. This is where the lack of consensus appears, simply because we don't know for sure and can only give a best guess. The only argument that can be put forward for this approach is that maybe, just maybe, ghosts sometimes manifest within the electromagnetic spectrum, or at least the part that we can measure. If so, that approach might be valid, but if not, then who knows?

Another group with an interest in ghosts, and indeed a whole range of associated phenomena, are psychologists and psychiatrists, who tend to see the subject as manifestations of the human condition. This includes such known psychiatric conditions as schizophrenia, sleep paralysis, hysteria, paranoia, and other manifestations of mental instability. Yet even this group of specialists admit that there are still many phenomena where scientific laws are currently unsupportable.

PRICE'S PSYCHIC ETHER THEORY OF HAUNTINGS

In his presidential address to the Society for Psychic Research in 1939, H. H. Price, a distinguished professor of logic at Oxford University, put forth his "psychic ether" theory of hauntings. Price hypothesized that a certain level of mind may be capable of creating a mental image that has a degree of persistence in the psychic ether. This mental image may also contain a degree of telepathic ability by which it can affect others. Price's theory holds that the collective emotions or thought images of a person who has lived in a house in the past may have intensely "charged" the psychic ether of the place—especially if there had been such powerful emotions as fear, hatred, or sorrow, supercharged by an act of violence. The original agent, Price theorized, has no direct part in the haunting. It is the charged psychic ether that, when presented with a percipient of suitable telepathic affinity, collaborates in the production of the idea-pattern of a ghost.

Ghosts, according to Price, may be manifestations of past events that have been brought to the minds of persons sensitive enough to receive a kind of "echo" from the past. These sensitive individuals receive impressions from those emotion-charted events that have left some trace of some energy in the inanimate objects at the place where they occurred. This information, or memory, may be transmitted as telepathic messages that can be received at some deep level of the human subconscious. These impressions then express themselves in the conscious mind in such a form as an uneasy feeling or a ghost.

Perhaps any edifice that has been much used as a setting for human activity almost certainly has been saturated with memory traces of the entire gamut of emotions. But it may be this very multiplicity of mental images that works against the chances of a ghost popping up in every hotel room and depot lobby. An oversaturation of idea-patterns in the majority of homes and public places may have left only a kaleidoscopic mass of impressions that combine to produce the peculiar atmosphere one senses in so many places. It is only when an idea-pattern that has been supercharged with enormous psychic intensity finds the mental level of a percipient with the necessary degree of telepathic affinity that a real ghost can appear.

A ghost, then, in Price's theory, has nothing to do with the "supernatural." The appearance of a specter is an out-of-the-ordinary occurrence—a paranormal happening—but there is a "natural" cause for the manifestation of the ghost.

THE SOUL TRAVELS BACK TO THE UNIVERSE AFTER DEATH

According to the quantum theory of consciousness of Dr. Stuart Hameroff, an American physicist and professor emeritus in the Department of Anesthesiology and Psychology at the University of Arizona, and Sir Roger Penrose, a mathematical physicist at Oxford University, the soul is maintained in microtubules of the brain cells. Human souls, they maintain, are more than just "interactions" of neurons in our brain and could have been present since the beginning of time.

According to their theory, the human brain is in fact a "biological computer," and the consciousness of humans is a program run by the quantum computer located inside the brain that even continues to exist after we die. As they explain it, "After people die, their soul comes back to the universe, and it does not die."

Both scientists argue that what humans perceive as "consciousness" is in fact the result of quantum gravity effects located within the so-called microtubules. Since 1996, their provocative theory has stated that the human soul is to be contained by the brain cells in structures inside them called microtubules

The debate about the existence of the soul and whether it is immortal or dies with the person is an endless story that for centuries has occupied the study of the great thinkers of universal history. Its mysterious nature continues to fascinate different areas of science, but now a group of researchers has discovered a new truth about it: the "soul" does not die; it returns to the universe.

This process, named by the two scientists "orchestrated objective reduction" (Orch-OR), states that when people enter a phase known as clinical death, the microtubules located in the brain lose their quantum state but maintain the information contained within them. Their soul returns to the universe, and it does not die.

A professor of anesthesiology, Dr. Stuart Hameroff also studies the nature of consciousness.

In a speech on the Science Channel's *Through the Wormhole* documentary, Dr. Hameroff said: "Let's say the heart stops beating, the blood stops flowing; the microtubules lose their quantum state. The quantum information within the microtubules is not destroyed—it can't be destroyed—and it just distributes and dissipates to the universe at large. If the patient is resuscitated, revived, this quantum information can go back into the microtubules and the patient says, 'I had a near-death experience.' If they're not revived, and the patient dies, it's possible that this quantum information can exist outside the body, perhaps indefinitely, as a soul."

JIM HAROLD PONDERS, "WHAT IS A GHOST?"

Jim Harold is America's most popular paranormal podcaster. His programs have been downloaded over twenty-seven million times. You can find his programs at jimharold.com, on Apple Podcasts, Google Play, and via many other online outlets.

I was honored tremendously when Brad and Sherry Steiger asked me to contribute a written piece on the question of ghosts and their true nature. After puffing out my chest a bit, the next emotion was that of terror! After all, in my dozen years of asking people, who are much smarter than I, about these subjects on my programs, I'm not sure I've ever heard a definitive answer on the subject. Nothing has struck me as the ultimate solution.

After a bit of reflection, I realized that the real answers didn't come when interviewing the "experts." My greatest enlightenment about the supernatural has come at the hands of normal people who have had strange experiences that, for the most part, they weren't seeking out. Just as Hawthorne said that happiness is like a butterfly that will light on your shoulder when you don't seek it out, I've found that truth has a way of showing itself to my callers when they weren't looking for it.

On my Campfire podcast, listeners phone in with their stories of the supernatural. After fielding hundreds and hundreds of calls over the years, here are some of my opinions on the topics of ghosts. These are my best guesses from thousands of hours of discussing the paranormal and hopefully intelligent ones. I make no claims that these are absolute truths, just my opinions.

Ghosts are real! I don't know what they are, but I believe that ghosts are objectively real ... not in a "they are real if they are real for you" way but as real as the book you are reading now. Ghosts exist, and they occasionally pay us a friendly or sometimes not-so-friendly visit. I do not believe all apparitions are sentient. I believe some ghosts are simply a type of replay.

The great parapsychologist Loyd Auerbach tells a story of a murder that was reported to be seen by witnesses multiple times after the fact. The catch? The killer seen during these "replays" was still alive and incarcerated at the time

Haunted: Malevolent Ghosts, Night Terrors, and Threatening Phantoms

There are many things about the nature of human existence that we do not comprehend. The true nature of reality is beyond most people's ability to grasp. (Art by Bill Oliver.)

of the sightings! To me, when a very emotional event happens, there is some environmental charge that results in these cosmic instant replays, and these types of ghosts are no more self-aware than an old VHS tape of *The X-Files*.

Some ghosts are sentient and may be here to comfort us. I have heard too many stories about "Aunt Millie" or "Uncle John" making their presence known to loved ones. Sometimes this can be quite dramatic, but very often these experiences can be very subtle yet strikingly real to those experiencing them. These happen, I believe, to help us through grief and the loss of a loved one.

I do wonder, although I am not sure of it—are some ghosts trapped? Do they not know they are dead or in some state of perpetual torment? I find these cases to be the most disturbing. The thought that someone may wander aimlessly throughout eternity is troubling. I hope it is not true, but some reports do bear this possibility out.

In rarer cases, my listeners tell me that a ghost can be malevolent. This does not seem nearly as common as the above cases, but it occurs, and I feel that conjuring spirits in various ways is serious business and can have very real-life consequences. Shadow people and other disturbing apparitions are often reported, and I have no cause to doubt their reality. Sometimes, there seems to be no rhyme or reason to these reports. Could some be "leftovers" from past tenants of a home or other structure? In other cases, there seems to be some event that leads up to the upset. Suffice it to say, if you play with the spirit world in a disrespectful way, I think it can make its presence known. It can hit back. The supernatural is not a plaything. Just my two cents.

I believe that paranormal investigators should be respectful of people and property. The "people" part of that statement should extend to those who happen to be traveling without a physical body. Although I am not an investigator, I cringe every time I hear of "ghost hunters" destroying property, hoaxing, or otherwise giving the field a black eye. There are some great researchers out there who are trying to follow their passion in the right way. Plus, there is a lot of good work going on in the investigative community to assist in the preservation of historical sites via fundraising efforts and the like. It is a shame a few bad apples can give all of us interested in these topics a bad name.

> I cringe every time I hear of "ghost hunters" destroying property, hoaxing, or otherwise giving the field a black eye.

Another thing I find troubling is the idea of "provoking." If we accept the premise that at least some of the spirits encountered during investigations are people who have passed and who are sentient, would we treat them this way in life? Would we yell at them and otherwise boss them around? My rule is if you wouldn't talk to someone living that way, why treat them as such when they are on the other side? If you can't say something nice....

Finally, my "proof" for the existence of ghosts is something the skeptics would say is not proof at all. It is the oral tradition. For millennia, people from various and sundry cultures have spoken of the spirits. Yes, Virginia, I should mention that this was way before *Ghost Hunters*! Where did these stories come from as far back as primitive man if there wasn't some inherent truth to the existence of ghosts?

The question of the afterlife and, by extension, that of ghosts is my favorite Fortean topic. We might not all see Bigfoot, a UFO, or any other bogeyman in our days. However, as much as I hate to be the one to break it to you, we are all going to die. The question of ghosts is universal and one that I believe we will get the answer to when we each cross that Lonesome Valley.

Oh, if a certain Grim Reaper is reading this, I'll be OK waiting a bit longer. Another fifty or sixty years sounds like a good round number. I have a lot more podcasts to produce before I make my exit!

Joshua P. Warren's Definition of What a Ghost Really Is

Joshua P. Warren has appeared on the National Geographic Channel, History, Discovery Channel, SyFy, TLC, Animal Planet, and many other networks. He is the author of more than a dozen books, including Simon & Schuster's How to Hunt Ghosts, Pet Ghosts, Haunted Asheville and The Secret Wisdom of Kukulkan. He and his team made

Haunted: Malevolent Ghosts, Night Terrors, and Threatening Phantoms

the cover of the scientific Electric Spacecraft Journal, in 2004 for groundbreaking work on ghostly plasmas. He hosts the Speaking of Strange radio program, frequently appears on Coast to Coast AM, and owns and directs the L.E.M.U.R. Lab and Free Museum in Asheville, North Carolina.

When I began writing my book *How to Hunt Ghosts*, my first struggle was answering the question: "How do I define a ghost?"

A lot of people simply think of a ghost as the spirit of a dead person. However, the subject is much more vast and complex.

There are, for example, many ghosts of inanimate objects, like ghost ships, or ghost stagecoaches (and ghost horses pulling the coaches). And, of course, there are very few nude ghosts, so how do we account for clothes if this is solely the product of a biological source?

After thinking deeply about all options, I finally hammered out this most general definition: "A ghost is some paranormal aspect of the physical form and/or mental presence that appears to exist apart from the original, physical form."

I still feel this is the best clinical definition of a ghost. But it is filled with fudge factors due to necessity.

From there, we must break the ghost down into profoundly different types.

Generally speaking, we have ghosts that appear to be noninteractive, redundant, and predictable, like some recording burned into the environment that replays itself, over and over, under certain circumstances and/or for certain people. It is simplest to call these "imprints."

Next we have the opposite: ghosts that appear to be very interactive, aware, conscious, and unpredictable. It is simplest to call those "entities."

Though we can talk about imprints and entities as loose, and easily understood, terms, each of those categories can also be divided in a myriad of ways.

For example, an entity might be the essence of someone who once lived as a

Author, radio host, and paranormal researcher Joshua P. Warren is the director of the L.E.M.U.R. Lab.

Haunted: Malevolent Ghosts, Night Terrors, and Threatening Phantoms

human as we do, or it could be a spirit that has never inhabited a human form, though it may or may not resemble a human.

And imprints might literally be some holographic recording captured by some unknown property of the environment, or it could be the manifestation of someone's "psychic" glimpse of a fixed event from the past.

It is absolutely fascinating to dig deep into all the implications, especially since the world's smartest physicists and cosmologists tell us all events in time—past, present, and future—are actually occurring simultaneously, and we are simply observing them from various, relative points of view, simulating the experience of this flexible thing we call time.

Thus, I think we must ultimately accept the one solid bedrock of undeniable fact: No matter what scientific instruments we use to measure these phantasmal things, those very instruments were conceived by humans, designed by humans, built by humans, calibrated by humans, used by humans, and interpreted by humans. Everything originates and ends within the human nervous system. So, are ghosts real? They are absolutely real in terms of the human experience. People see ghosts. But what someone sees depends on the person.

So enjoy my technical definition that ought to sate the need for definitions. But in practice, defining a ghost may be as difficult as defining your image when one peers into a mirror.

Paul (left) and Ben Eno host the radio show Beyond the Paranormal.

It's Only the First Day of School for Humankind

By Paul and Ben Eno

Paul and Ben Eno are a world-famous father–son team of paranormal adventurers, broadcasters, authors, and lecturers, who have a combined experience of nearly sixty years in the field of the unexplained.

Paul's early mentors included parapsychology pioneer Dr. Louisa Rhine, Fr. John J. Nicola S.J. (technical advisor for the film *The Exorcist*), and legendary, first-generation "grandparents of ghost hunting" Ed and Lorraine Warren. Paul graduated from two seminaries but was expelled from a third because of his paranormal work with about a year to go before ordination. He turned to journalism, ending up in a distinguished career as a newspaper and magazine reporter and editor. Today, he is an award-winning New England journalist, a former news editor at the *Providence Journal,* and the author of seven books.

Ben is Paul's twenty-five-year-old son and understudy in the paranormal. Starting in radio at the age of sixteen, he became the youngest syndicated talk-show host in America and is the winner of the 2011 Bob Fish Memorial Scholarship from the Rhode Island Broadcasters Association.

Together, the father-and-son duo have authored such books as *Behind the Paranormal 2: Bigfoot, Mothman and Monsters You Never Heard Of* (Barking Cat Books, June 2017) and *Behind the Paranormal: Everything You Know Is Wrong* (Schiffer Books, November 2016). Paul Eno alone has written *Turning Home: God, Ghosts and Human Destiny* (New River Press, 2006), *Footsteps in the Attic: More First-Hand Accounts of the Paranormal in New England* (New River Press, 2002), and *Faces at the Window: First-Hand Accounts of the Paranormal in Southern New England* (New River Press, 1998).

It didn't take more than one day of his first case for Paul Eno to become suspicious. He was a seminary student who had no problem believing in spirits, which are, by definition, nonphysical. But in the woods of Pomfret, Connecticut, in 1971, he and six other witnesses encountered the very physical sounds of invisible cows, dogs, people, farm implements, and even oxcarts, right down to a team driver wielding a whip.

That's when Paul began suspecting that the old ideas about ghosts being spirits of the dead just weren't good enough. If they're "dead," why are they doing, let alone saying, anything? How can they speak without the physical means to do so (vocal cords)? Without our bodies, would we still be "us"? Do the laws of physics even permit the existence of disembodied spirits? Why do we sometimes see them wearing clothes and driving cars? Are we dealing more with time than we are with death? But does time even exist in any objective, linear form? Albert Einstein didn't think so. If time doesn't exist, then how can death exist?

These questions only multiplied over the years. By the late 1970s, Paul was running into ghosts of people who weren't dead, people who saw ghosts of themselves, appearing and disappearing buildings—shockers suggesting that not even reality, let alone the big, mean local ghost, is what we think it is.

By the mid-1980s, Paul had settled on several tentative conclusions:

1. Nothing in the paranormal is what it appears to be, especially from our narrow paradigm.

2. The "multiple worlds interpretation" of quantum mechanics, in some form, is the most likely explanation for all paranormal phenomena.

3. Everything we know is wrong.

By the time we became a father–son team in 2005, our theories and methods bore little resemblance to what most other paranormal investigators were doing.

Our working hypothesis today is that we daily move through, perhaps, millions of parallel worlds that have the same or very similar laws of physics. We call this a "world family." The mass consciousness of the biosphere probably guides our flow through our world family, and we experience the illusion of moving from past to future.

So where do ghosts come in?

Across the multiverse, everything and everyone seems to live multiple lives. If we're properly interpreting what we run into in our paranormal adventures, there are many versions of ourselves and everyone else out there. Everything from geotechnics to our own consciousness can draw us close enough to other world families, where things may be quite different, so that we can experience an intersect, overlap, or overwash. To us, this is the paranormal.

So, when you walk into your kitchen and see yourself sitting at the table, you're probably experiencing a parallel-world intersect where another version of yourself (but still a part of the greater "you") is already seated.

Lorraine Warren and friend Paul Bartholomew

When you amble down the street, and Uncle Boris, who died ten years before, passes you, then disappears, you've just walked through a parallel-world overlap with a world in which dear old Boris never died.

When Paul Eno stood in a Bridgeport, Connecticut, kitchen with six first responders in 1974, and they all watched a refrigerator float, they were most likely experiencing the overwash of a parallel world with very different laws of physics.

And the poltergeist that was tormenting the family in that house, which Paul, Ed and Lorraine Warren, and Fr. Bill Charbonneau at the time thought was a demon?

Parasites. Life forms that can access different parallel worlds in order to feed on various forms of energy. We see them do it.

As any shaman will tell you, our remote ancestors knew all about the multiverse. But our more recent ancestors had long forgotten this, adopting instead a

Ghosts are many things to many people, but what they are, most importantly, is a reminder that there is something more to our existence than the day-to-day material world. (Art by Bill Oliver.)

materialist, dualist, and rather two-dimensional view of reality. So, from that point of view, Uncle Boris must be the spirit or remnant or psychic residuum of Uncle Boris. What else could it be? And so forth.

Perhaps we're naïve or self-satisfied, but we find that by returning to the multiverse view, we end up with a far deeper interpretation of cases, far fewer unanswered questions, permanent results, and contacts with some very interesting and misunderstood life forms.

We truly believe it's the first day of school.

WHAT ARE GHOSTS FOR ME?

Ghosts are the men and women walking through the childhood home that was built on the old stagecoach stop. Seldom did they pay any attention to our parents or my sister—just often enough to make the siblings life-long insomniacs.

A ghost is the lady who materialized some nights to speak to our mother and to provide guidance regarding planting, harvest, and safety.

A ghostlike entity is the nisse or elf that has accompanied me throughout my life, as if it were a kind of bodyguard with a nasty sense of humor.

A ghost is the invisible being that would tip over furniture, pound on walls, and run up and down stairs when I was a teenager at home alone.

A ghost is a wicked entity that could cry like a little girl in pain, then slam me into a wall when I came to investigate.

A ghost is a beast that tried to lock me into a closet, then got tricked by my friends and ended up being locked in itself. But only briefly. It tore off the door of the closet, thudded up the stairs, and lifted all eight investigators present into the air.

A ghost is an entity that so loves its material possessions and home that it frightens the children of the new owner who seeks to modernize the dwelling.

I recently read a fascinating article by Simon Worrall that included an interview with Daniel C. Taylor regarding his new book *Yeti: The Ecology of a Mystery*. Taylor, it seems, has been hunting for an answer to the mystery of the Yeti for sixty years, just as I have been searching for some acceptable answers to the mystery of ghosts for even longer. Worrall asks Taylor how such a lengthy odyssey has affected his life.

Taylor answers that such a mission changed his life, because now he understood "life in a different way. In a world that is increasingly urban, it is important that we understand that we are a part of life, connected to life. There are Yeti legends all over the world. There is a Russian legend about the Jungle Man, and there's a Chinese legend. This leads us to the question, what is this human hunger for these humanoid experiences?"

Taylor then summarizes the search that has always driven the world: "The deep mystery at our core is that we want to be connected to the great beyond. And we need symbols to help us understand the connection. That's why we believe in God or angels or the Loch Ness Monster. Throughout human history and across cultures, we have developed messengers from the great beyond. Ultimately, that's what the Yeti is."

And certainly, in varying degrees of individual reality, that is what a ghost is—our individual messenger from the great beyond sent to prove that our struggle for hope and immortality is not in vain.

FURTHER READING

Alper, Matthew. *The "God" Part of the Brain*. New Hartford, NY: Rogue Press, 2001.

Anderson, Joan Wester. *In the Arms of Angels: True Stories of Heavenly Guardians*. Chicago: Loyola Press, 2004.

———. *Where Angels Walk*. New York: Ballantine Books, 1993.

Asala, Joanne, editor. *Scandinavian Ghost Stories*. Iowa City, IA: Penfield Press, 1995.

Atwater, P. M. H. *Beyond the Light*. New York: Avon, 1997.

Auerbach, Lloyd, and Annette Martin. *The Ghost Detective's Guide to Haunted San Francisco*. Fresno, CA: Linden, 2011.

Baird, A.T, editor. *One Hundred Cases for Survival after Death*. New York: Bernard Ackerman, 1944.

Bach, Marcus. *The Inner Ecstasy*. New York and Cleveland: World Publishing, 1969.

Bayless, Raymond. *The Other Side of Death*. New Hyde Park, NY: University Books, 1971.

Bennett, Hal Zina. *Spirit Animals and the Wheel of Life*. Charlottesville, VA: Hampton Roads Publishing Company, 2000.

Booss, Claire, editor. *Scandinavian Folk & Fairy Tales*. New York: Gramercy Books, 1984.

Burnham, Sophy. *A Book of Angels*. New York: Fawcett Columbine, 1995.

Carrington, Hereward. *The Case for Psychic Survival*. New York: The Citadel Press, 1957.

———, and Nandor Fodor. *Haunted People*. New York: New American Library, 1968.

Clark, Jerome. *Unexplained! Strange Sightings, Incredible Occurrences, and Puzzling Physical Phenomena*, third edition, Detroit: Visible Ink Press, 2012.

Copper, Arnold, and Coralee Leon. *Psychic Summer*. New York: The Dial Press, 1976.

Crawford, W.J. *The Psychic Structures of the Goligher Circle*. New York: E.P. Dutton & Company, 1921.

Crookall, Robert. *Intimations of Immortality*. London: James Clarke, 1968.

———. *More Astral Projections*. London: Aquarian Press, 1964.

DuBois, Pierre. *The Great Encyclopedia of Fairies*. Illustrated by Roland Sabatier and Claudine Sabatier. New York: Simon & Schuster, 2000.

Ebon, Martin, editor. *True Experiences in Communicating with the Dead*. New York: New American Library, 1968.

Ensley, Eddie. *Visions: The Soul's Path to the Sacred*. New Orleans: Loyola Press, 2001.

Estep, Sarah Wilson. *Voices of Eternity*. New York: Ballantine Books, 1988.

Evans, Hilary. *Gods, Spirits, Cosmic Guardians: A Comparative Study of the Encounter Experience*. Wellingborough, Northamptonshire, UK: The Aquarian Press, 1987.

Fiore, Dr. Edith. *The Unquiet Dead*. New York: Doubleday, 1987.

Flammarion, Camille. *Death and Its Mystery after Death: Manifestations and Apparitions of the Dead; The Soul after Death*. Translation by Latrobe Carroll. New York and London: The Century Co., 1923.

————. *Haunted Houses*. London: T. Fisher Unwin, 1924.

Fodor, Nador. *Between Two Worlds*. New York: Paperback Library, 1967

————. *The Haunted Mind: A Psychoanalyst Looks at the Supernatural*. New York: New American Library, 1968.

————. *Mind Over Space and Time*. New York: The Citadel Press, 1962.

————. *These Mysterious People*. London: Rider & Co, 1935.

Froud, Brian. *Good Faeries, Bad Faeries*. New York: Simon & Schuster, 1998

Garrett, Eileen. *Many Voices: The Autobiography of a Medium*. New York: G. P. Putnam's Sons, 1968.

Goldman, Karen. *Angel Encounters: Real Stories of Angelic Intervention*. New York: Simon & Schuster, 1995.

Goode, Caron B. *Kids Who See Ghosts: How to Guide Them through Fear*. San Francisco, CA/Newburyport, MA: Weiser Books, 2010.

Gordon, Stuart. *The Encyclopedia of Myths and Legends*. London: Headline Books, 1994.

Harner, Michael. *The Way of the Shaman*. New York: Bantam Books, 1982.

Hastings, Arthur. *With the Tongues of Men and Angels: A Study of Channeling*. New York: Holt, Rinehart, & Winston, 1991.

Hauk, Dennis William. *Haunted Places*. Reprint edition. New York: Penguin USA, 1996.

————. *International Directory of Haunted Places*. New York: Penguin, 2000.

Hirschfelder, Arlene, and Paulette Molin. *The Encyclopedia of Native American Religions*. New York: MJF Books, 1992.

Holzer, Hans. *Yankee Ghosts*. New York: Ace Books, 1966.

Jacobson, Laurie, and Mark Wanamaker. *Hollywood Haunted*. Los Angeles: Angel City Press, 1999.

Keightley, Thomas. *The World Guide to Gnomes, Fairies, Elves, and Other Little People*. New York: Random House, 2000.

Kerman, Frances. *Ghostly Encounters: True Stories of America's Haunted Inns and Hotels*. New York: Warner Books, 2002.

Kinnaman, Gary. *Angels Dark and Light*. Ann Arbor, MI: Servant Publications, 1994.

Kolb, Janice Gray. *Compassion for All Creatures*. Nevada City, CA: Blue Dolphin Publishing, 1997.

Haunted: Malevolent Ghosts, Night Terrors, and Threatening Phantoms

Krippner, Stanley, with Etzel Cardena and Steven J. Lynn. *Varieties of Anomalous Experience: Examining the Scientific Evidence*. Washington, DC: American Psychological Association, 2000.

Larousse Dictionary of World Folklore. New York: Larousse, 1995.

LeShan, Lawrence. *The Medium, the Mystic, and the Physicist*. New York: Viking Press, 1974.

Lissner, Ivar. *Man, God and Magic*. New York: G. P. Putnam's Sons, 1961.

Mack, Carol K., and Dinah Mack. *A Field Guide to Demons, Fairies, Fallen Angels, and Other Subversive Spirits*. New York: Henry Holt and Company, 1999

May, Antoinette. *Haunted Houses and Wandering Ghosts of California*. San Francisco: San Francisco Examiner Division, 1977.

McComas, Henry C. *Ghosts I Have Talked With*. Baltimore, MD: The Williams & Wilkins Company, 1937.

Monroe, Robert A. *Far Journeys*. Garden City, NY: Doubleday, 1987.

Moolenburg, H. C. *Meetings with Angels*. New York: Barnes & Noble, 1995.

Morse, Melvin. *Parting Visions: Uses and Meaning of Pre-Death*. New York: Villard Books, 1994.

Murphy, Gardner. *The Challenge of Psychical Research*. New York: Harper & Row, 1970.

Norman, Michael, and Beth Scott. *Haunted Heritage*. New York: A Forge Book, Tom Doherty Associates, 2002.

———. *Historic Haunted America*. New York: Tor Books, 1996.

Oesterreich, T.K. *Possession: Demonical & Other among Primitive Races, in Antiquity, the Middle Ages, and Modern Times*. New Hyde Park, NY: University Books, 1966.

Pitkin, David J. *New England Ghosts*. Chestertown, NY: Aurora Publications, 2010.

Price, Harry. *Poltergeist Over England*. London: Country Life, Ltd., 1945.

———. *The Most Haunted House in England*. London: Longmans, Green & Co, 1940.

Ramsland, Katherine. *Ghost: A Firsthand Account into the World of Paranormal Activity*. New York: St. Martin's Press, 2001.

Rider, Fremont. *Are the Dead Alive?* New York: B. W. Dodge & Company, 1909.

Ring, Kenneth. *Life at Death*. New York: Coward, McCann & Geoghegan, 1980.

Rose, Carol. *Spirits, Fairies, Leprechauns, and Goblins: An Encyclopedia*. New York: W.W. Norton & Company, 1998.

Simek, Rudolf, *Dictionary of Northern Mythology*. Translated by Angela Hall. Rochester, NY: D. S. Brewer, 1993.

Sitwell, Sacheverell. *Poltergeists*. New York: University Books, 1959.

Smith, Alson J. *Immortality: The Scientific Evidence*. New York: Prentice Hall, 1954.

Smith, Susy. *Haunted Houses for the Millions*. Los Angeles: Sherbourne Press, Inc., 1967.

———. *Prominent American Ghosts*. New York: Dell, 1969.

Spence, Lewis. *An Encyclopedia of Occultism*. New Hyde Park, NY: University Books, 1960.

———. *The Fairy Tradition in Britain*. London: Rider and Company, 1948.

Stallings, Nancy L. *Show Me One Soul: A True Haunting*. Baltimore, MD: Noble House, 1996.

Steiger, Brad. *Angels Around the World*. New York: Random House, 1996.

———. *Guardian Angels and Spirit Guides*. New York: Plume Books, 1995.

————. *Montezuma's Serpent and Other True Supernatural Tales of the Southwest*. New York, 1992.

————. *Totems: The Transformative Power of Your Personal Animal Totem*. San Francisco: HarperSanFrancisco, 1997.

————, and Sherry Hansen Steiger. *Angels Over Their Shoulders: Children's Encounters with Angels*. New York: Fawcett-Columbine, 1995.

————. *Hollywood and the Supernatural*. New York: St. Martin's Press, 1990.

Steinour, Harold. *Exploring the Unseen World*. New York: The Citadel Press, 1959.

Stevens, William Oliver. *Unbidden Guests*. New York: Dodd, Mead & Company, 1957.

Stonehouse, Frederick. *Haunted Lakes: Great Lakes Ghost Stories, Superstitions, and Sea Serpents*. Duluth, MN: Lake Superior Port Cities, Inc., 1997.

Sullivan, Lawrence E, editor. *Death, Afterlife, and the Soul*. New York: Macmillan Publishing Company, 1989.

Tucker, George Holbert. *Virginia Supernatural Tales*. Norfolk, VA: Donning Company, 1977.

Turnage, Sheila. *Haunted Inns of the Southwest*. Winston-Salem, MA: John F. Blair, 2001.

Tyrrell, G. N. M. *Apparitions*. New York: Collier Books, 1963.

Uphoff, Walter, and Mary Jo Uphoff. *New Psychic Frontiers*. Gerrards Cross, Bucks, UK: Colin Smythe, Ltd., 1975.

Van Dusen, Wilson. *The Presence of Other Worlds: The Findings of Emanuel Swedenborg*. New York: Harper & Row, 1974.

Watson, Lyall. *The Romeo Error*. New York: Dell Books, 1976.

White, Steward Edward. *The Road I Know*. New York: E. P. Dutton, 1942.

Willis-Brandon, Carla. *One Last Hug before I Go: The Mystery and Meaning of Deathbed Visions*. Deerfield Beach, FL: Health Communications, 2000.

Haunted: Malevolent Ghosts, Night Terrors, and Threatening Phantoms

INDEX

Note: (ill.) indicates photos and illustrations.

Haunted: Malevolent Ghosts, Night Terrors, and Threatening Phantoms

Haunted: Malevolent Ghosts, Night Terrors, and Threatening Phantoms

Haunted: Malevolent Ghosts, Night Terrors, and Threatening Phantoms

Haunted: Malevolent Ghosts, Night Terrors, and Threatening Phantoms

Haunted: Malevolent Ghosts, Night Terrors, and Threatening Phantoms